Introduction to Business Software

DEVELOPED BY QUE® CORPORATION

Text and graphics pages developed by

Marianne B. Fox, Lawrence C. Metzelaar, David F. Noble, David P. Ewing, Charles O. Stewart III, and Kathie-Jo Arnoff

Que® Corporation

Carmel, Indiana

Introduction to Business Software

Library of Congress Catalog No.: 89-62438

ISBN No.: 0-88022-496-7

92 91 90   8 7 6 5 4

Interpretation of the printing code: the rightmost double-digit number is the year of the book's printing; the rightmost single-digit number, the number of the book's printing. For example, a printing code of 89-1 shows that the first printing of the book occurred in 1989.

Introduction to Business Software is based on DOS versions 3.0 and later, version 5.0 of WordPerfect, 1-2-3 Release 2.01, and dBASE III Plus.

About the Authors

Marianne B. Fox, CPA, holds a full-time faculty position with Butler University where she teaches a variety of accounting and computer-related courses. She is co-owner of A & M Services, Inc., a firm specializing in microcomputer systems design, requirement analysis, and training. She is coauthor of *1-2-3 Release 3 Workbook and Disk, 1-2-3 Release 2.2 Workbook and Disk, dBASE IV QuickStart*, and *WordPerfect 5 Workbook and Disk*. She is a contributing author to *Using 1-2-3*, Special Edition, and *Using 1-2-3 Release 2.2*.

Lawrence C. Metzelaar lectures at Vincennes University and Ohio State University. He is co-owner of A & M Services, Inc., a firm specializing in microcomputer systems design, requirement analysis, and training. He is coauthor of *1-2-3 Release 3 Workbook and Disk, 1-2-3 Release 2.2 Workbook and Disk, dBASE IV QuickStart*, and *WordPerfect 5 Workbook and Disk*. He is a contributing author to *Using 1-2-3*, Special Edition, and *Using 1-2-3 Release 2.2*.

David F. Noble, Ph.D., a publishing consultant, was an associate professor of English at the University of Indianapolis and was Que's editorial director from 1982 to 1989. He is coauthor of *Improve Your Writing with Word Processing* (Que Corporation, 1984). While at Que, he helped to develop and edit a wide variety of Que's publications, including a number of Que's books on DOS, 1-2-3, WordPerfect, and dBASE. Currently, he is a visiting associate professor of technical communication at Purdue University, School of Engineering and Technology, Department of Supervision, at Indianapolis/IUPUI.

David P. Ewing is publishing director for Que Corporation. He is the author of Que's *1-2-3 Macro Library, Using 1-2-3 Workbook and Disk,* and *Using 1-2-3 Workbook Instructor's Guide*; coauthor of Que's *Using Symphony, Using Q&A, Using Javelin,* and *1-2-3 Macro Workbook*; and contributing author to *Using 1-2-3,* Special Edition, *1-2-3 QuickStart,* and *Upgrading to 1-2-3 Release 3.* Over the past five years, in addition to authoring and coauthoring a number of Que titles, Mr. Ewing has served as product development director for many of Que's application software and DOS titles. He has directed the development of such Que series as the Que workbooks and instructor's guides, QueCards, and QuickStart books.

Charles O. Stewart III is a product line director and staff writer at Que Corporation. He assisted Thomas W. Carlton with the writing of Que's *dBASE III Plus Application Library,* coauthored *WordPerfect Tips, Tricks, and Traps,* 2nd Edition, and contributed to *Using WordPerfect 5.* Early in his tenure at Que, Mr. Stewart was a production editor for a wide range of Que titles. In his current capacity as a product line director, Mr. Stewart continues to play a central role in developing and maintaining Que's line of WordPerfect books.

Kathie-Jo Arnoff is a developmental editor at Que Corporation. Over the past four years, she has helped to develop and edit popular titles including *WordPerfect QuickStart* and *Using 1-2-3 Release 3,* as well as numerous other titles on WordPerfect, 1-2-3, dBASE, DOS, and Excel. Her editorial influence is particularly evident throughout Que's line of QuickStart books, workbooks, and instructor's guides. For 10 years prior to coming to Que, she worked as a writer, editor, and public relations director for several national associations.

Acknowledgments

Introduction to Business Software represents the collaborative efforts of many talented people. Que Corporation thanks the following individuals for their contributions to the development of this book.

David P. Ewing, for his work on the 1-2-3 graphics and data management chapters, and for his product direction and invaluable advice during all stages of the project.

David Noble, for his skillful and meticulous work on Chapter 1 and the MS-DOS and 1-2-3 sections of the book.

Marianne Fox and Lawrence Metzelaar, for their timely and well-focused development of the dBASE section, and their "can-do" attitude throughout—despite a busy schedule filled with many other responsibilities.

Kathie-Jo Arnoff, for joining the project in midstream and applying her excellent editorial skills and good judgment to the WordPerfect and dBASE sections.

Bill Hartman, of Hartman Publishing, for his design contributions, for his willingness to make numerous modifications and additions to the text, and for his constant support and assistance throughout all stages of the book's production.

David Solomon, for his unfailingly sound advice on the MS-DOS and dBASE sections, for a preliminary draft of Chapter 27, and—unofficially—for his droll wit and priceless analogies.

David Longstreet, for his prompt and thorough review of the technical content of the book.

Bill McGirr, for his preliminary work on the dBASE section.

Tim Stanley, for his contribution to Chapter 10 and for providing technical support to the editors.

Terrie Lynn Solomon, for her remarkable organizational skills and for managing the flow of materials between authors and editors.

Stacey Beheler, for her administrative assistance to the editors and authors working on this book.

Lori A. Lyons and David Kline, for their excellent proofing on all chapters and for keeping chaos at bay.

Sharon Hilgenberg and Kathy Murray, for their excellent index.

Doug Dunn, Jennifer Mathews, and Corinne Harmon, for coordinating and managing the final production stages of this book.

The Que Production department, for their skillful paste-up and photographic work and their efforts during this book's production.

Publishing Director
David P. Ewing

Product Director
Charles O. Stewart III

Acquisitions Editor
Terrie Lynn Solomon

Developmental Editor
Kathie-Jo Arnoff

Technical Editor
David Longstreet

Technical Support
Tim Stanley
Rajinder Heir

Acquisitions Aide
Stacey Beheler

Book Production
William Hartman
Corinne Harmon
Jennifer Matthews
Dennis Sheehan
Brad Chinn
Cindy Phipps
Joe Ramon

Proofreaders
Lori A. Lyons
David Kline

Indexed by
Sharon Hilgenberg
and reVisions Plus, Inc.

Composed in Garamond by
William Hartman, Hartman Publishing

Trademark Acknowledgements

Contents at a Glance

Contents

Part I: MS-DOS

Contents

Part III: WordPerfect

Contents

Part IV: dBASE

Introduction

Many students entering the work force today are expected to be able to use microcomputers for basic business applications such as word processing, financial analysis, and record keeping. To meet the expectations of employers, schools are increasing their efforts to provide students from a range of disciplines with the basic computer skills they need to compete in today's job market. To be prepared for these tasks, students should be familiar with basic system hardware for personal computers, the fundamentals of disk operating systems, and the features and applications of the most popular software used in business. *Introduction to Business Software* was conceived to meet those needs.

Distinctive Features of This Book

Few textbooks provide any coverage at all of the most popular software for personal computers used in business. Fewer still provide anything more than a superficial treatment of the software's features and its business applications. After beginning with an introduction to personal computer systems, *Introduction to Business Software* furnishes the student with a solid conceptual overview of the four most popular software programs for personal computers: MS-DOS, Lotus 1-2-3, WordPerfect, and dBASE.

This book was designed to serve as either a primary or supplemental text in a course in microcomputing applications. The distinctive features of this book include the following:

- An introductory chapter in each of the four major sections of the book provides a comprehensive overview of the particular software package and its applications.
- Program features are explored in enough detail to give students a clear idea of how these particular software packages are used in business.
- Numerous graphics throughout highlight program features and real-world examples and help students visualize key concepts.

1

- Step-by-step information is included at critical junctures to give students a feel for each program's operation.
- Learning objectives, lists of key terms, summaries, and review questions help students assimilate the material.
- A unique page design allows students to locate their place in the text immediately by major section, chapter, and major topic.

After completing this book, the student should have a good working knowledge of MS-DOS, Lotus 1-2-3, WordPerfect, and dBASE.

Introduction to Business Software provides practical preparation for a business environment. By focusing on the most popular applications and showing how they are used in real-world situations, this book teaches students the computer skills they will need in the workplace.

Who Should Read This Book

This book was designed for students, first-time users, instructors, or corporate trainers—anyone who needs a comprehensive introduction to the most popular operating system and applications software for personal computers in business.

If you're a student or first-time user, this text gives you a basic understanding of operating systems, spreadsheets, word processing, and database management. You can use this material as a springboard for further individual study or as a prerequisite for intermediate-to-advanced courses in MS-DOS, 1-2-3, WordPerfect, or dBASE.

If you're an instructor or corporate trainer, this book is the ideal text for beginning courses in microcomputing. You can use this as a primary or secondary text to give students or employees a quick introduction to personal computers and the use of the major software packages.

Why These Programs Were Chosen

The programs chosen for this book—MS-DOS, 1-2-3, WordPerfect, and dBASE— represent the most commonly used "types" of software in business today. Students who have a good conceptual grasp of these representative programs (operating

Distinctive Features of This Book	Who Should Read This Book	Why These Programs Were Chosen	How This Book Is Organized	How To Use This Book	A Note to the Instructor

Introduction

system, spreadsheet, word processor, and database manager) will be better prepared to use microcomputers in the workplace.

Many large corporations have installed these basic programs throughout their organizations. Of the four programs discussed in this book, DOS (either MS-DOS or PC DOS) has the widest distribution because IBM or IBM-compatible personal computers cannot function or run applications software without an operating system. And it's not at all uncommon to find 1-2-3, WordPerfect, and dBASE adopted as corporate standards throughout an organization. Nor is it unusual to find data exchanged among these application programs. For example, a business report created with WordPerfect 5 may incorporate data from a 1-2-3 worksheet or a dBASE database. With WordPerfect's capability to integrate text and graphics, you can create a graph in 1-2-3 and import it into a WordPerfect document.

MS-DOS

MS-DOS (or, to most personal computer users, DOS) is the most widely used disk operating system for personal computers. Current estimates suggest that there are anywhere from 10 to 14 million copies of MS-DOS in use today. DOS is a set of programs that gives the user control over the computer's resources. Not only is DOS the link between user and computer, but DOS also makes it possible for applications programs, such as spreadsheets, word processors, and databases, to be used on personal computers.

This book covers all versions of DOS up through version 4.0.

1-2-3

For more than five years, 1-2-3 has been the dominant spreadsheet software product used in businesses worldwide. Today, 1-2-3 is used by 5 million people and continues to be the industry standard. When first introduced in 1983, 1-2-3 revolutionized microcomputing by replacing the dominant spreadsheet product at the time, VisiCalc, and soon became the program identified with the IBM PC and the established tool for financial analysis.

Why is 1-2-3 so popular? 1-2-3 provides users with three fundamental applications integrated into one program. Without having to learn three separate kinds of software, users can perform financial analysis with the 1-2-3 worksheet, create database applications, and create graphs. Commands for all three applications are combined in one main menu and are accessed easily.

Although 1-2-3 Releases 2.2 and 3 were released in 1989, this book focuses on Release 2.01, which to date remains the most popular version of 1-2-3.

WordPerfect

WordPerfect has become the standard word processor in the corporate world. Recent estimates suggest that more than 60% of all businesses use WordPerfect for their document needs.

WordPerfect has become deeply entrenched in corporate America because it has all the "basic" features users expect in a word processor, plus a full complement of advanced features. The program is suited to the typical business user's needs, whether they entail short memos or complex documents. An editing screen uncluttered by menus or cryptic codes, an abundance of features, support for a wide range of printers, and unparalleled customer assistance are just a few of the reasons why WordPerfect is so popular.

This book is based on the latest release of WordPerfect, version 5.0, because of its tremendous popularity in business, government, education, and industry.

dBASE

dBASE is the most popular database manager used in business. Just a few years ago, only users of small, expensive computer systems could enjoy the power of database management. The introduction of dBASE changed the way data was organized and manipulated on small, yet powerful, microcomputers. Ashton-Tate, the developer and marketer of both dBASE III Plus and dBASE IV, indicates that more than 4 million people use this software for their business needs.

The emphasis in this book is on dBASE III Plus, which remains the most popular version of the software to date. This book includes information about dBASE IV where appropriate to give students a sense of the latter's enhancements.

How This Book Is Organized

Introduction to Business Software is divided into four main sections devoted to MS-DOS, 1-2-3, WordPerfect, and dBASE. Chapter 1 precedes the MS-DOS section to provide an orientation to personal computers. Each of the four main sections begins with a solid conceptual overview of the software and its business applications. Each chapter begins with a set of learning objectives and a list of key terms, and concludes with review questions.

Chapter 1, "Understanding Personal Computer Systems," covers the hardware components of computer systems, helps students understand how computers handle data, and prepares them for the discussion of operating systems in Part I.

Part I introduces the topic of disk operating systems for microcomputers. Eight chapters explore in detail the purposes and features of MS-DOS. Students learn how to boot the computer, issue DOS commands, format floppy disks, establish hierarchical directories on a hard disk, work with files, back up files, use special commands, and create batch files.

Part II begins the first consideration of an application program, 1-2-3 Release 2.01. An overview chapter introduces the topic of electronic spreadsheets and highlights the distinctive features and capabilities of 1-2-3. Subsequent chapters cover getting started with 1-2-3, understanding 1-2-3 basics, creating worksheets, printing reports, creating and printing graphs, and using 1-2-3 as a database manager.

Part III moves to a comprehensive look at WordPerfect 5.0 and word processing in the office. An overview chapter introduces word processing, describes WordPerfect's distinctive features, and explains how to start using the software. Subsequent chapters cover editing and working with blocks of text; formatting lines, paragraphs, and pages; using the speller and thesaurus; printing; managing files; creating macros; merging, sorting, and selecting data; creating text columns; using WordPerfect's referencing tools; and integrating text and graphics.

Part IV looks at dBASE and database management in the office. The first chapter in this part introduces database management, characterizes the types of database models and interfaces available, and describes the salient features of dBASE. Additional chapters cover getting started with the software; designing, creating, and editing a database; organizing, searching, and viewing data; designing reports and labels; and programming in dBASE. Although the focus is on dBASE III Plus, the major differences between dBASE III Plus and dBASE IV are noted where appropriate.

How To Use This Book

This text provides a primarily *conceptual* introduction to business software, but some step-by-step information was included to give you a feel for each program's operation. Illustrations have been provided to help you visualize key concepts. If you have access to a personal computer and the appropriate software, you can use the examples as stepping-off points to increase your level of mastery. Your instructor may want to provide in-class demonstrations, if possible, as well as hands-on exercises and additional supplemental materials.

Access to a personal computer is not a prerequisite for this book, however. Even if you don't have a computer, this book will give you a solid grounding in business software for personal computers.

Chapter overviews and summaries, clear learning objectives, lists of key terms, and review questions help you assimilate the material quickly. A unique page design helps you locate precisely your position in the text. The major sections of the book are listed across the top of each left page, with the current topic selected. Within each major section of the book, you'll find chapter titles listed down the side of the right page, with a red rectangle marking the title of the chapter you're reading. The major topics of the chapter appear across the top of the right page with the current topic highlighted in red.

A Note to the Instructor

To provide ideas about how to use this book in class, a separate *Instructor's Guide* is available. The guide covers such topics as course design and classroom activities, provides additional review questions and exercises, and includes numerous transparency masters.

1 *Understanding Personal Computer Systems*

Until a few years ago, computers were large and expensive electronic devices not available to individual users. During the 1970s, however, advances in computer technology produced smaller computer parts called *microprocessors*, or chips. Most of the essential information a computer needed could be contained on one of these chips. Computers that used microprocessors were called *microcomputers*. By the end of the 1970s, several companies had begun to sell microcomputers.

In the early 1980s, International Business Machines (IBM) introduced the Personal Computer, which was an immediate success. Before long, the IBM PC captured the infant microcomputer industry and shaped its formative years.

Today, many manufacturers sell computers that are functionally almost equivalent to the IBM Personal Computer. These computers have been dubbed *compatibles*. In this chapter, you learn about the elements of IBM PC and compatible computer systems.

After completing this chapter, you should

- Understand the basic components of personal computer systems
- Comprehend how monitors display text and graphics
- Know about personal computer keyboards and their special keys
- Know about disk drives and disks
- Know some peripherals computers commonly use
- Understand the differences among printers and how they work
- Comprehend how computer systems work with data

Key Terms in This Chapter

Display	A screen or monitor.
Peripheral	Other than the main components, any device connected to the computer to help it do tasks.
Disk	A plastic or metal platter coated with magnetic material for storing files. A disk drive records and plays back information on disks.
Input	Any data a computer reads.
Output	Any data a computer puts out.
Bit	A *bi*nary digi*t*. The smallest discrete representation of a value a computer can manipulate.
Byte	A collection of eight bits that a computer usually stores and manipulates as a unit.
K (kilobyte)	1,024 bytes; a measure of size or capacity in computer systems.
M (megabyte)	1,000 kilobytes; a measure of values or capacities greater than 999K.
Data	A catch-all term meaning words, numbers, symbols, graphics, photos, sounds—any information stored in bytes in computer form.
File	A named group of data in electronic form.

Understanding the Components of Computer Systems

Personal computer systems based on the IBM PC are functionally the same, even though they come in all sizes and shapes, from traditional desktop computers to portable laptop models and compact computers. The many kinds of PC software operate equally well in any of these hardware configurations. As long as computers have the main components, the computers' shape and size matter little. The following illustration shows a typical desktop computer system..

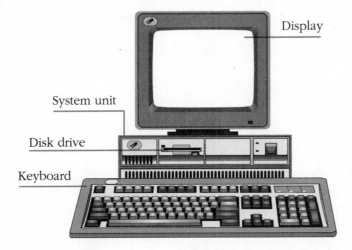

Desktop Computer

Hardware and *software* are the two main elements of a computer system. Both must be present for a computer to do useful tasks. Computer hardware and software can be compared to a VCR and a taped movie. The VCR is like computer hardware because both are electromechanical. The taped movie is like software because the videotape contains the information and control signals necessary for the VCR to display images on the TV screen.

Computer Hardware

In general, the term *hardware* refers to the system unit, keyboard, screen display, disk drives, and printer of a computer system. Hardware includes all electronic and mechanical devices used by the computer.

The hardware of a computer system can be classified as *system hardware* and *peripheral hardware*. System hardware is directly associated with processing or computing activity. Peripheral hardware is technically any device used by a computer for the input or output of data. Peripherals are discussed later in this chapter.

9

Computer Software

You can program (instruct) a computer to perform a wide variety of operations. Almost anything you can reduce to calculations can be made into a program and then entered into the computer. With the proper software, your computer can serve as a word processor, a spreadsheet, a project manager, a mailing list generator, or even a wily chess opponent!

Software provides information in electronic form to instruct the hardware how to act. Software can be stored in various ways. The two most frequently used media are silicon chips and magnetic disks. Instructions on silicon chips are called *electronic memory*, or just *memory*. Disks provide *magnetic storage*.

The operating system is the most important type of software for the PC. Operating systems provide a foundation of services for other programs. These services supply a uniform means for programs to gain access to the full resources of the hardware. Operating systems that help programs to access disk resources are called *disk operating systems*, or just *DOS*.

Part of this book is about the most common operating system for the IBM PC and compatibles. The IBM versions of DOS and the various versions of Microsoft Corporation's MS-DOS are highly compatible. For this reason, DOS will be used as a generic term to refer to both.

Understanding the Display

The display, also called the *monitor* or the screen, is the part of the computer's hardware that produces visual output. The display is the *default*, or normal, location for the PC's output. This device takes electrical signals and translate   them into patterns that you can recognize as characters or figures on the screen.   An image on a computer screen is made up of pixels, a word coined from the phrase "picture (*pix*) *el*ement." The more pixels a display has, the sharper the visual image is.

The *resolution*, or sharpness, of the visual image is a function of both the display and the *display adapter*, which controls the computer display. In some PCs the display circuitry is part of the motherboard (see the later section "Understanding the System Unit"). Display circuitry also can be on a separate board that fits into a slot in the

Understanding the
Components of
Computer Systems

**Understanding
the Display**

Understanding
the Keyboard

Understanding
the System Unit
and Disk Drives

Understanding
Peripherals

Understanding
How Computers
Handle Data

Summary

computer. The display adapter can be a monochrome display adapter (MDA), color graphics adapter (CGA), enhanced graphics adapter (EGA), video graphics array adapter (VGA), or some special type of display adapter.

Displaying Text

When you see letters, numbers, or punctuation on your display, you recognize these images as text. This text comes from your computer's memory, where the information has been stored according to a standard most computers recognize: the American Standard Code for Information Interchange (ASCII).

Each ASCII code represents a letter or a symbol. Each character is sent to the display adapter so that you can see the character on the screen. Because ASCII is the standard, the display adapter can use an electronic table to pull the correct pixel pattern for any letter, number, or punctuation symbol.

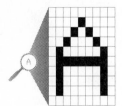

The arrangement of pixels for the letter A. More pixels in a given area produce a sharper image. The sharpness of an image is called its *resolution*.

Displaying Graphics

Graphics displays can show any pixel or pattern of pixels. Thus, graphics displays can produce complex figures with curves and fine details. The computer, however, must work harder to create a graphics image instead of a text image. To light a particular point on the screen, the display adapter must find the correct horizontal and vertical coordinates for each pixel. No table of predetermined pixels exists as in text mode.

Graphics adapters offer varying combinations of pixel density (pixel resolution), color, and intensity. As the number of pixels increases, the detail of the display becomes finer, as shown in the following illustration. In addition, each pixel has characteristics that tell the graphics adapter what the color or intensity of the pixel should be. As the number of colors and intensities increases, the amount of necessary memory space becomes larger.

11

A low-resolution image.   A higher-resolution image (with four
                                           times as many pixels).

Understanding the Keyboard

The keyboard is the main component for entering information into the computer. Each character you type is converted into a code the computer can process. The keyboard is thus an *input* device.

Just like a typewriter, the keyboard of a computer contains all the letters of the alphabet. The numbers, symbols, and punctuation characters are virtually the same. The computer keyboard has the familiar QWERTY layout. The name QWERTY comes from the first six letters of the top row of letters on a standard typewriter.

A computer keyboard, however, is different from a typewriter keyboard in several important ways. The most notable difference is the use of *special* keys—those not on a typewriter. These keys are described in table 1.2. Depending on the type of computer you use, you will also find 10 or 12 *function* keys, which can be used different ways by different programs.

The Special Keys

A number of the keys on the keyboard are special keys for particular functions, such as arrow keys for moving the cursor, an Enter key for entering data, and an Escape key for leaving an operation before it is completed. Table 1.2 lists these special keys and describes their function(s). Note that if the keyboard has a special key that can be found on a typewriter, such as a Shift key or Backspace key, that key can do things on a computer that can't be done on a typewriter.

**Understanding
Personal
Computer
Systems**

Table 1.2
Special Keys on the Computer Keyboard

	Key	*Function*
Enter	Enter	Signals the computer to respond to the commands you type. Also functions as a carriage return in programs that simulate the operations of a typewriter.
↑ ← ↓ →	Cursor keys	Change your location on the screen. Included are the arrow, PgUp, PgDn, Home, and End keys.
←	Backspace	Moves the cursor backward one space at a time, deleting any character in that space.
Del	Del	Deletes, or erases, any character at the location of the cursor.
Insert	Ins	Inserts any character at the location of the cursor.
Shift	Shift	Enables you to capitalize letters when Shift is held down while the letter is typed. When pressed in combination with another key, can change the standard function of that key.
Caps Lock	Caps Lock	When pressed to the lock position, all characters typed are uppercase, or capitalized. Caps Lock does not shift the keys, however. To release, press the key again.
Ctrl	Ctrl	The Control key. When pressed in combination with another key, changes the standard function of that key.

cont.

13

Table 1.2—*continued*
Special Keys on the Computer Keyboard

Key		*Function*
Alt	Alt	The Alternate key. When pressed in combination with another key, changes the standard function of that key.
Esc	Esc	In some situations, pressing it allows you to "escape" from a current operation to a previous one. Sometimes Esc has no effect on current operation.
Num Lock	Num Lock	Changes the numeric keypad from cursor-movement mode to numeric-function mode.
PrtSc	PrtSc	Used with the Shift key to send the characters on the display to the printer.
Print Screen	Print Screen	Found on enhanced keyboards. Same as Shift-PrtSc.
Scroll Lock	Scroll Lock	Locks the scrolling function to the cursor control keys. Instead of the cursor moving, the screen scrolls.
Pause	Pause	Suspends display output until another key is pressed. (Not provided with standard keyboards.)
Scroll Lock	Break	Stops a program in progress from running.
Numeric keypad		A cluster of keys to the right of the standard alphanumeric keyboard. The numeric keypad includes numbered keys from 0 to 9, as well as cursor-movement keys and other special keys.

Many of the special keys are designed for use with other special keys. For example, pressing the Shift key in combination with the PrtSc key causes DOS to print the

Understanding the
Components of
Computer Systems

Understanding
the Display

**Understanding
the Keyboard**

Understanding
the System Unit
and Disk Drives

Understanding
Peripherals

Understanding
How Computers
Handle Data

Summary

contents of the current screen. Pressing Ctrl-C or Ctrl-Break stops execution of a program. And pressing Ctrl-Alt-Del, also known as a "warm boot", restarts MS-DOS (this is called a system reset).

The Function Keys

The function keys are shortcuts. Not all programs use these keys, and some use only a few of them. When used, however, they carry out useful operations for you. For example, many programs make the F1 key a Help key. Pressing such a key displays instructions from the computer's memory to help you understand a particular operation. The DOS V4.0 Shell uses the F3 key to back out of one operation and move into another automatically. The F10 key moves the cursor to various parts of the screen.

The PC, AT, and Enhanced Keyboards

Many early PC-compatible computers use a standard keyboard like that of the IBM PC. Other machines use Personal Computer AT keyboards. IBM's new PS/2 computers use the 101-key Enhanced Keyboard. Some users prefer the keyboard arrangement of the standard keyboard, and others prefer the Enhanced Keyboard.

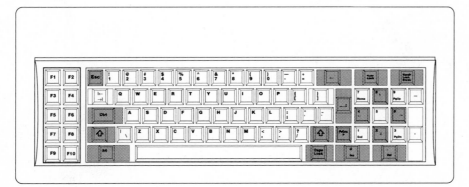

The IBM PC keyboard

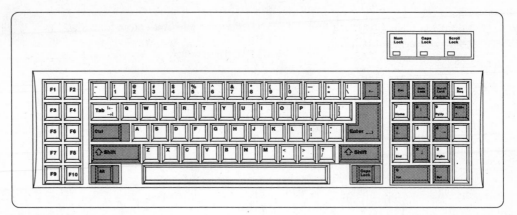

The Personal Computer AT keyboard

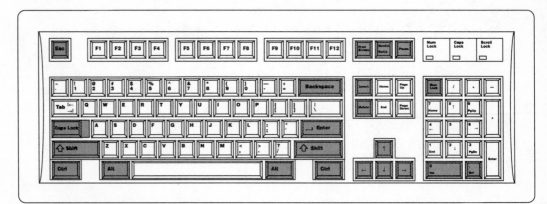

The Enhanced Keyboard

Understanding the System Unit and Disk Drives

If you look at a standard desktop PC, you will find a box-shaped cabinet to which all other parts of the PC are connected. This box is called the system unit. The devices connected to it are peripherals. The system unit and the peripherals make up the complete computer system.

The System Unit

The system unit houses all but a few parts of a PC. Included are various circuit boards, a power supply, and even a small speaker. System units vary in appearance, but a horizontal box shape is the most common. A vertical "tower" shape is becoming popular because it frees desk or table space.

The system unit houses the main circuit board of the computer. This circuit board, called the motherboard, holds the main electronic components of the computer. The central processing unit (CPU), or microprocessor, and the various circuits and chips that support it are the primary components on the motherboard. Normally there are electrical sockets where users can plug in various adapter circuit boards. These electrical sockets are often referred to as expansion slots.

Chips that provide the computer with its memory are located on the motherboard. In some cases, an additional memory adapter can be plugged into an available expansion slot to increase the system's memory. The number of available expansion slots varies with the PC's manufacturer. Most motherboards have a socket for a math coprocessor. Math coprocessors help number-intensive programs do calculations more quickly and accurately.

The following illustration of a hypothetical system unit shows the placement of the diskette and hard disk drives and the motherboard.

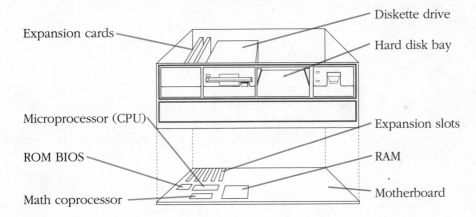

Disk Drives and Disks

Disk drives are complex mechanisms, but they carry out a basically simple function. They spin disks. *Disks* are circular platters or pieces of plastic that have magnetized surfaces. As the disk spins, the drive converts electrical signals that represent data into magnetic fields on the disk. This process is called *writing* data to the disk. Disk drives also *read*, or recover, the magnetically stored data and present it to the computer as electrical signals.

When computers write to the disk, they store data as collections the operating system knows as *files*. Magnetically stored data is not lost when the computer's power is turned off.

You know that a drive is writing to or reading from a disk when a small light on the front of the disk drive comes on. Generally, you should not open a disk drive door or eject a disk until the light goes out.

The components of a disk drive are similar to those of a phonograph. The disk, like a record, spins. A positioner arm, like a tone arm, moves across the radius of the disk. A head, like a pickup cartridge, translates the encoded information to electrical signals. But, unlike phonographs, disk drives do not have spiral grooves on the disk's surface. The disk's surface is recorded in concentric *tracks*, or rings. The tighter these tracks are packed on the disk, the greater is the storage capacity of the disk.

Both sides of a disk are used for encoding information. Such a disk is called a *double-sided* disk, and the drive that uses it is known as a double-sided disk drive.

Two types of disks are available: diskettes and hard disks. *Diskettes* are removable and of lower capacity than hard disks. *Hard disks*, also called *fixed disks*, are usually nonremovable, high-capacity rigid platters.

Diskettes

Diskettes store from 360K to 1.44M bytes of data and come in two common sizes: 5 1/4 inches and 3 1/2-inches. The measurement refers to the size of the disk's jacket. The 5 1/4 diskettes are flexible and are sometimes called "minifloppies," "floppy disks," or just "floppies." The 3 1/2-inch diskettes are inside a rigid case. Even though the case does not bend, these diskettes are sometimes called "microfloppies" to distinguish them from "minifloppies." In this book the word "diskette" refers to both 5 1/4-inch and 3 1/2-inch diskettes. The word "disk" refers to a hard disk or is used when the reference is valid for diskettes and hard disks.

Make sure that you know the specifications of your drive(s) before you buy or interchange diskettes. They can be of the same size but can have different capacities, making some or all incompatible with a particular drive.

Fixed Disks

Hard disks often consist of multiple, rigid-disk platters. The platters spin at approximately 3,600 RPM, which is much faster than a floppy disk drive spins. As the

Understanding the
Components of
Computer Systems

Understanding
the Display

Understanding
the Keyboard

Understanding
the System Unit
and Disk Drives

Understanding
Peripherals

Understanding
How Computers
Handle Data

Summary

platters spin within the drive, the head positioners make small, precise movements above the tracks of the disk. Because of this precision, hard disks can store enormous quantities of data—from 10 megabytes to more than 100 megabytes of information.

Despite their precision, hard disks are reasonably rugged devices. Factory sealing prevents contamination of the housing. With proper care, hard disks should give years of service.

Hard disks range from 3 1/2 to 8 inches in diameter. The most common size, 5 1/4 inches, holds between 2 1/2 and 10 megabytes of information per side.

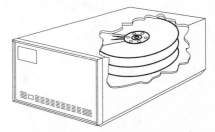

Flexible 5 1/4-inch
diskette

Rigid 3 1/2-inch
diskette

Hard disk drive with
sealed platters

Understanding Peripherals

Besides the display and the keyboard, a variety of peripherals is useful to a user. Many state-of-the-art computer programs require that you use a mouse to take best advantage of the program's features. Other peripherals, such as printers and modems, let you use the output of your computer as you want.

The Mouse

A small, hand-held device that you move on the surface of your work space to move a pointer in a corresponding manner on the display is called a *mouse*. It is contoured so that your hand fits over the mouse comfortably. Positioned beneath your fingers are one, two, or sometimes three switch buttons. The contoured shape, the eye-like switch buttons, and a cable together make the unit look like a mouse sitting on the table.

19

Not all software supports mouse input, but many popular programs do. Generally, mouse-based programs expect the user to point to options on the display and click one of the buttons on the mouse to select a task.

Printers

Printers accept signals (*input*) from the CPU and convert them to characters (*output*), which are usually imprinted on paper. You can classify printers in the following two ways: by the way the printers receive input from the computer, and by the manner in which they produce output.

The terms *parallel* and *serial* describe the two ways printers receive input from personal computers. And the terms *dot matrix, daisywheel,* and *laser* are the generic names of printers that produce their output in three different ways. Printers are usually rated by their printing speed and the quality of the finished print.

Parallel and Serial Printers

You connect printers to the system unit through a port. A *port* is an electrical doorway through which data can flow between the system unit and an outside peripheral. A port can have its own expansion adapter or can share an expansion adapter with other ports or circuits, such as a CGA.

The terms "serial" and "parallel" refer to the way electrical data is delivered from the port to the printer. A *serial* port delivers the bits of a data byte in single file one after another. Sending one complete byte (one character) serially takes longer but requires fewer cable wires. Furthermore, the distance between the port and a serial printer can be much longer than with parallel communications.

In *parallel* communications, each bit of a data byte is sent through a separate wire synchronously with the other bits one complete byte (character) at a time. Cables for parallel communications therefore contain parallel wires. This method of transmission is more common than serial transmission.

Dot-Matrix, Daisywheel, and Laser Printers

The most common printer uses a dot matrix to produce characters. Dot-matrix printers have a print head that contains a row of pins or wires to form the characters. As the print head advances, the wires press corresponding small dots of the ribbon against the paper, leaving inked dot impressions.

A daisywheel printer also steps the print head across the page but strikes the page with a complete character for each step. All the characters of the alphabet, numbers, punctuation marks, and certain symbols are arranged at the ends of holders that resemble spokes on a wheel. Because the characters are fully formed rather than made of dots, the quality of daisywheel printing is high.

Laser printers use a technology that closely resembles that of photocopying. Instead of a light-sensitive drum picking up the image of an original, the drum is painted with the light of a laser diode. The image from the drum becomes transferred as high-dot-density output to the paper. With high density, the output characters look fully formed. Laser printers can also produce graphics images on paper. The combination of high-quality text and graphics is very useful for desktop publishing.

Modems

Modems are peripheral devices that allow your PC to communicate over standard telephone lines. As serial communications peripherals, modems send or receive characters or data one bit at a time. Modems can communicate with other modems at speeds from 30 to 960 bytes per second. Modems require communications software to coordinate their communications with other modems.

Understanding How Computers Handle Data

Computers perform many useful tasks by accepting data as input, processing it, and releasing it as output. Data is any information. It can be a set of numbers, a memo, an arrow key to move a game symbol, or just about anything else you can conceive. Input comes from you and is translated into electrical signals that move through a set of electronic controls. Output can be thought of in three ways:

- As characters the computer displays on the screen
- As signals the computer holds in its memory
- As signals stored magnetically on disk

Computers receive and send output in the form of electrical signals. These signals are stable in two states: on and off. Think of these states as you would the power in the wire from a light switch you can turn on and off. Computers contain millions of electronic switches that can be either on or off. All input and output follows this two-state principle.

The computer name for the two-state principle is *binary*, which means something made of two things or two parts. Computers represent data with two *binary* digi*ts*, or *bits*—1 and 0 for on and off, respectively. For convenience, computers group eight bits together. This 8-bit grouping is called a *byte*. Bytes are sometimes packaged in 2-, 4-, or 8-byte packages when the computer moves information internally.

Computers move bits and bytes across electrical highways called *buses*. Normally, a computer has three buses: a control bus, a data bus, and an address bus. The *control bus* manages the devices attached to the PC and determines *how* the electrical operations proceed. The *data bus* is the highway for information transfer and determines *what* the data should be. The *address bus* determines *where* data or instructions are located in random-access memory (RAM).

The microprocessor (CPU) is connected to all three buses and supervises their activity. Program instructions held in RAM are fetched and executed by the CPU. Resulting computations are stored in RAM.

Because the microprocessor can access the memory at any address and in any order, the memory is called *random-access memory*, or *RAM*. Some RAM information is permanent. This permanent memory is called *read-only memory*, or *ROM*. It is useful for holding unalterable instructions in the computer system.

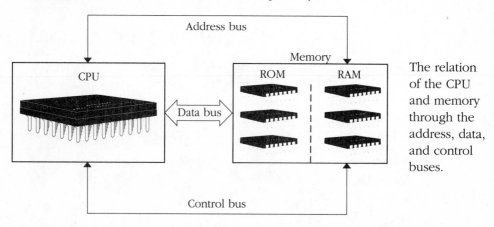

The relation of the CPU and memory through the address, data, and control buses.

The microprocessor depends on you to give it instructions in the form of a *program*. A program is a set of binary-coded instructions that produces a desired result. The microprocessor decodes the binary information and carries out the instruction from the program.

You could begin from scratch and type programs or data into the computer each time you turn on the power. But, of course, you wouldn't want to start from the beginning each time if you didn't have to. Luckily, the computer can store both information and start-up data, usually on a disk. Disks store data in binary form in *files*.

Understanding the
Components of
Computer Systems

Understanding
the Display

Understanding
the Keyboard

Understanding
the System Unit
and Disk Drives

Understanding
Peripherals

Understanding
How Computers
Handle Data

Summary

To the computer, a file is just a collection of bytes identified by a unique name. These bytes can be a memo, a word processing program, or some other program. The file's task is to hold binary data or programs safely until the microprocessor calls for that data or program. When the call comes, the drive reads the file and writes the contents into RAM.

Summary

This chapter introduced you to microcomputer systems. You learned that the hardware of a microcomputer system usually consists of a system unit, a screen, a keyboard, disk drives, and a printer. The system unit has a microprocessor, or central processing unit (CPU), which controls the system.

Computer software provides instructions that make the hardware perform a variety of applications. With the appropriate software, a microcomputer can be a spreadsheet, a word processor, or a database for example. The most important software for a microcomputer is the disk operating systems (DOS), which enables applications programs to make use of the computer's resources.

You learned about different types of displays that have different levels of resolution, depending on the number of pixels in the display. Lower-resolution displays are adequate for monochrome text characters, but only higher-resolution displays are suitable for sharp graphics images in many colors.

Microcomputer keyboards differ from typewriter keyboards by having special keys for computer operations and a set of 10 to 12 function keys to which different software programs can assign their own program features. Several keyboard layouts are available. Enhanced keyboards have more keys for additional flexibility.

In a closer look at the system unit and peripheral hardware, you learned about disk drives for diskettes and hard, or fixed, disk drives. You became acquainted with two more hardware devices—the mouse and the modem—and found out more about printers. Dot-matrix printers use tiny pins to produce characters made up of tiny dots within a matrix. Daisywheel printers use a wheel of separate characters to make high-quality impressions on paper. Laser printers use a laser diode to transfer an image of the highest quality onto paper.

Finally, the chapter introduced you to how binary data travels within a computer. Data, as tiny bits in on or off states, travels over buses between the CPU and memory.

23

The gateway to the use of software applications in a microcomputer system is a working knowledge of the computer's operating system. The next chapter gives you an overview of MS-DOS, which is the subject of the first part of this introduction to business software.

Review Questions

1. Explain the distinction between hardware and software.

2. Name the main components of a personal computer system and indicate the purpose of each.

3. Name some of the special keys on the computer keyboard and indicate the purpose of each.

4. What does the system unit of a personal computer contain?

5. How does a hard disk differ from a diskette?

6. What is the meaning of the terms RAM and ROM, and what is their essential difference?

7. What is the difference between dot-matrix, daisywheel, and laser printers?

Part I
MS-DOS

IBM DOS

An Overview of DOS
Booting the Computer
Issuing DOS Commands
Preparing Disks
Hierarchical Directories
Copying, Renaming, and Deleting Files
Protecting Data
Special Commands and Files

2 *An Overview of DOS*

Chapter 1 introduced personal computer systems and their component parts, described software, and showed how data moves in the computer. This part of the book acquaints you with an important link between the hardware, the software, and you. This link is the *disk operating system*, or *DOS*.

Anyone intending to use a personal computer will benefit from some knowledge of DOS. Consider the fact that you can't use your computer at all unless you start it with DOS. You can rely on someone to do DOS-related work for you, but you will be less proficient at computing. Learn about DOS, and the results will greatly exceed your efforts.

After completing this chapter, you should

- Understand the fundamentals of disk operating systems (DOS)
- Be able to describe the structure of DOS
- Comprehend the purpose of DOS and be able to explain its principal functions
- Be familiar with the versions of DOS

Key Terms in This Chapter

Disk operating system A set of programs that lets a user and other programs use the hardware of a computer system.

Command interpreter A command file (COMMAND.COM in DOS) that translates your keyboard instructions into actions by the computer.

BIOS Basic Input/Output System. The software that performs basic communications between the computer and the peripherals.

Utility program	A program that performs a housekeeping task.
Interface	A connection between parts of the computer, especially between hardware devices; also the interaction between a user and an applications program.
The DOS Shell	A graphical interface available with DOS 4.0 that provides an easy-to-use alternative for selecting commands.
Redirection	A change in the source or destination normally used for input and output.
Applications program	A set of instructions that tells the computer to perform a specific task, such as word processing.
Formatting	Preparing a disk so that it can be used by the computer.
Batch file	A series of DOS commands placed in a disk file. DOS executes batch-file commands one at a time.
Extension	One to three characters that follow the dot (.) in a file name. The extension often indicates the file's function. For example, a COM extension is used for a command file.

What Is a Disk Operating System?

A disk *operating system* is a collection of computer programs that provides recurring services to other programs or to the user of a computer. If the computer's operating system did not provide these services, the user would have to deal directly with the details of the hardware. Without a disk operating system, for example, every computer program would have to contain instructions telling the hardware each step it should take to do its job. But because an operating system already contains instructions, any program can call on it. Disk operating systems get their name from the attention they give to the disks in the computer system.

Companies that develop commercial programs rely on this standard method for gaining access to the computer's resources. Personal computer operators rely on this standard to be able to operate computers as word processors, database managers, electronic spreadsheets, and even diversionary game opponents. Because the core of DOS remains constant in its many versions, manufacturers of personal computer

An Overview of DOS

Booting the Computer

Issuing DOS Commands

Preparing Disks

Hierarchical Directories

Copying, Renaming, and Deleting Files

Protecting Data

Special Commands and Files

products as well as end users of personal computers have a stable operating basis for their work.

From your point of view, DOS is likely to be a set of commands typed on your keyboard. This is the practical, user's point of view. Learning these DOS commands takes you from seeing a personal computer as a mysterious box of complicated equipment to using a personal computer as a system for independence and productivity.

IBM-compatible personal computers use versions of DOS called MS-DOS, the world's most popular disk operating system, developed by Microsoft Corporation. Manufacturers of personal computers, such as Zenith, IBM, and COMPAQ, tailor MS-DOS for use on their computers. The manufacturers may put their own names on the diskettes and package a different manual for the supplied version of DOS. But all of these versions of DOS are similar when they operate on a PC. When you read about DOS in this book, you can assume that the material is relevant for your manufacturer's version of DOS.

The Three Parts of DOS

DOS has three main components:

- COMMAND.COM, the command interpreter
- The Input/Output System
- The Utility Files

These components are contained in files that come with your DOS package. The following sections introduce you to the components and their functions.

The Command Interpreter

The *command interpreter* is DOS's "friendly host." It interacts with you through the keyboard and screen when you operate your computer. The command interpreter is also known as the command processor and often is referred to simply as COMMAND.COM ("command dot com"). All of your communications with DOS are actually instructions to COMMAND.COM.

Because you instruct COMMAND.COM rather than the hardware, you never need to know the details of how the hardware operates. COMMAND.COM prints DOS's requests on your display. When you enter a command, COMMAND.COM interprets what you have typed and processes your input so that DOS can take appropriate action. COMMAND.COM handles the technical details of such common tasks as displaying a list of the contents of a disk; copying files; and, of course, starting your programs.

The *DOS Shell* is a user-friendly program *interface* between your need for DOS services and the details of DOS commands. The Shell, available with version 4.0, is an additional layer that insulates you from having to know how to control details of the computer's hardware electronically. For more information about the Shell, see Chapter 3.

The Input/Output System

System files, known simply as the *input/output system,* are another part of the operating system. These files are two or three special "hidden" files (the number depends on your computer) that define the hardware to the software. When you start a computer, these DOS system files are loaded into RAM. Combined, the files provide a unified set of routines for controlling the computer's operations.

The hidden files interact with special read-only memory (ROM) on the motherboard. The special ROM is called the ROM Basic Input Output System, or *BIOS* (pronounced BYE-ose). Responding to a program's request for service, the system files translate the request and pass it to the ROM BIOS. The BIOS provides a further translation of the request that links the request to the hardware.

The DOS input/output system, through the special BIOS, largely determines the degree to which a non-IBM PC is "IBM compatible."

The Utility Files

DOS has certain *utility programs* that carry out useful housekeeping tasks, such as preparing disks, comparing files, finding free space on a disk, and background printing. Some of the utilities provide statistics on disk size and available memory. The utility programs are files that reside on disk and are loaded into memory by COMMAND.COM when you type their command names. Because the programs are not built into DOS, they are often called *external commands.*

Disk operating systems eliminate the need for you and your programs to know exactly how to make the hardware work. For example, to list the contents of a disk in a disk drive, you don't need to know the capacity or recording format of the disk or how to get the computer to direct the output to the screen. Another example: An

What Is a Disk   The Three   DOS Files   The   The   What
Operating   Parts of   and   Functions   Versions   Hardware
System?   DOS   Extensions   of DOS   of DOS   You Need   Summary

An
Overview of
DOS

Booting the
Computer

Issuing DOS
Commands

Preparing
Disks

Hierarchical
Directories

Copying,
Renaming,
and
Deleting
Files

Protecting
Data

Special
Commands
and Files

applications program that needs to store data on the disk does not have to reserve space on the disk, keep track of where on the disk the data is stored, or know how the data was encoded. DOS takes care of all these tasks.

DOS provides a uniform service to the hardware by getting assistance from the permanent ROM BIOS in the computer. ROM BIOS can vary among computer makers, but the computers will be highly compatible if the design of the ROM BIOS is integrated with DOS.

DOS Files and Extensions

Disk operating systems are collections of programs that carry out specific tasks. The kinds of files that hold these programs can be identified by the last three letters of the file name. These letters are called the *extension*. This list shows the names of the DOS files.

```
ASSIGN    COM
BACKUP    COM
BASIC     COM
BASICA    COM
CHKDSK    COM
COMMAND   COM
COMP      COM
DEBUG     COM
DISKCOMP  COM
DISKCOPY  COM
EDLIN     COM
FDISK     COM
FORMAT    COM
GRAFTABL  COM
GRAPHICS  COM
KEYB      COM
LABEL     COM
MODE      COM
MORE      COM
PRINT     COM
RECOVER   COM
RESTORE   COM
SELECT    COM
SHELLB    COM
SYS       COM
TREE      COM

5202      CPI
4208      CPI
4201      CPI
EGA       CPI
LCD       CPI
```

The COM file extension identifies a *com*mand file. Command files are derived from the earliest operating system for personal computers, CP/M. As you learn DOS, you will recognize that these file names are the names of external DOS commands.

Files with CPI extensions operate the display screen.

31

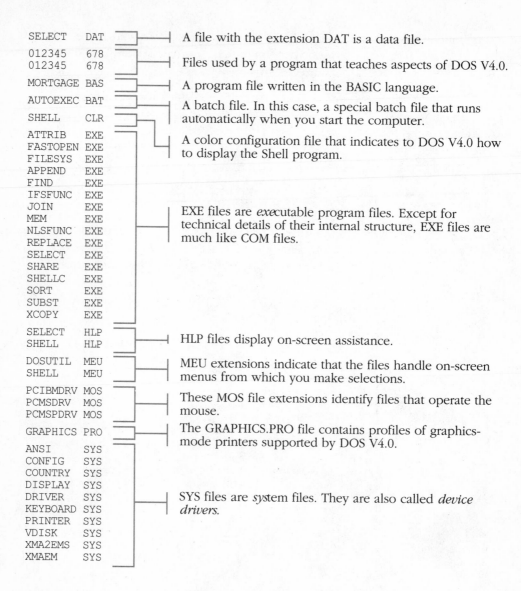

SELECT   DAT — A file with the extension DAT is a data file.

012345   678
012345   678 — Files used by a program that teaches aspects of DOS V4.0.

MORTGAGE BAS — A program file written in the BASIC language.

AUTOEXEC BAT
SHELL   CLR — A batch file. In this case, a special batch file that runs automatically when you start the computer.

ATTRIB   EXE
FASTOPEN EXE — A color configuration file that indicates to DOS V4.0 how to display the Shell program.
FILESYS   EXE
APPEND   EXE
FIND   EXE
IFSFUNC   EXE
JOIN   EXE
MEM   EXE — EXE files are *executable* program files. Except for technical details of their internal structure, EXE files are much like COM files.
NLSFUNC   EXE
REPLACE   EXE
SELECT   EXE
SHARE   EXE
SHELLC   EXE
SORT   EXE
SUBST   EXE
XCOPY   EXE

SELECT   HLP
SHELL   HLP — HLP files display on-screen assistance.

DOSUTIL   MEU
SHELL   MEU — MEU extensions indicate that the files handle on-screen menus from which you make selections.

PCIBMDRV MOS
PCMSDRV   MOS — These MOS file extensions identify files that operate the mouse.
PCMSPDRV MOS

GRAPHICS PRO — The GRAPHICS.PRO file contains profiles of graphics-mode printers supported by DOS V4.0.

ANSI   SYS
CONFIG   SYS
COUNTRY   SYS
DISPLAY   SYS
DRIVER   SYS — SYS files are *sys*tem files. They are also called *device drivers*.
KEYBOARD SYS
PRINTER   SYS
VDISK   SYS
XMA2EMS   SYS
XMAEM   SYS

The Functions of DOS

DOS provides standard routines or functions that you and your programs can use to access the services of your PC's components. Although DOS has some miscellaneous functions, like setting the computer's calendar and clock, DOS's most important functions include managing disks and files, redirecting input and output, and running batch files and applications programs.

Managing Files

One of DOS's primary functions is to help you organize the files that you store on your disks. Organized files are a sign of good computer housekeeping. Good housekeeping becomes crucial once you begin to take advantage of the storage capacity available on today's disks.

Think, for example, about the fact that the smallest-capacity diskette can hold the equivalent of 100 letter-sized pages of information. Now, imagine that each sheet of information makes up one file: you have 100 files to keep track of. If you use disks (such as a hard disk) that can hold more information than a standard diskette, file organization becomes even more crucial.

Fortunately, DOS gives you the tools to be a good computer housekeeper. DOS lists files for you, tells you their names and sizes, and gives you the dates when they were created. And you can use this information for many organizational purposes. In addition to organizing files, DOS can duplicate files, discard files no longer useful, and replace files with matching file names.

Managing Disks

Certain DOS functions are essential to all computer users. For example, all disks must be prepared before they can be used in your computer. This preparation is called *formatting* and includes checking disks for available space. Here is a list of other DOS disk-management functions:

- Labeling disks electronically
- Making restorable backup copies of files for security purposes
- Restoring damaged files on a disk
- Copying disks
- Viewing the contents of files on a disk

Redirecting Input and Output

DOS "expects" its input to come from a standard place, such as the keyboard. DOS sends its output to a standard place, such as the display screen. Designers of DOS

Booting the Computer

Issuing DOS Commands

Preparing Disks

Hierarchical Directories

Copying, Renaming, and Deleting Files

Protecting Data

Special Commands and Files

recognized that it would sometimes be convenient to send output to another device, such as a printer. These designers provided DOS with the ability to redirect, or send in another direction, the output that normally goes to the standard output. Through *redirection*, a list of files that usually appears on the screen can be sent to the printer.

Running Applications Programs

Computers require complex and exact instructions, or programs, to provide useful output. Computing would be altogether impractical if you had to write a program each time you had a job to do. Happily, that is not the case. Programmers spend months doing the specialized work that allows a computer to function as many different things, such as a spreadsheet, a word processor, or a database manipulator. Through a program, the computer's capabilities are applied to a task—thus, the term *applications programs*. The programs covered later in this book—1-2-3, WordPerfect, and dBASE—are some of the most popular applications programs.

Applications programs are distributed on diskettes. DOS is the go-between that allows you access to these programs through the computer. By simply inserting a diskette into a computer's drive and pressing a few keys on the keyboard, you can instantly have an astonishingly wide variety of easy-to-use applications at your disposal.

Applications constantly need to read data from disk files, to see what you have typed, and to send information to the screen or printer. These input and output tasks are common, repetitive computer tasks. DOS provides applications with an easy-to-use connection or program interface that sees to the details of these repetitive activities. As the user of the computer, you want easy-to-understand information about disk files, memory size, and computer configuration. DOS provides this information.

Running Batch Files

Most of your interaction with DOS will take place through the keyboard. You type commands for COMMAND.COM to carry out. However, commands also can be placed in a disk file called a *batch file* and "played back" to COMMAND.COM. COMMAND.COM responds to these batches of commands from the file just as it would respond to commands typed from the keyboard. Batch files can automate often-used command sequences, making keyboard operation simpler. Difficult-to-remember command sequences are ideal candidates for batch-file treatment.

The Versions of DOS

The first version of MS-DOS appeared in 1981. Each new version or version upgrade (signified by the version number and a decimal) contained changes to accommodate developments in computer hardware. The following brief list indicates the new features of the various versions and upgrades.

Booting the Computer

Issuing DOS Commands

Preparing Disks

Hierarchical Directories

Copying, Renaming, and Deleting Files

Protecting Data

Special Commands and Files

Quick Reference to Versions of DOS	
MS-DOS Version	*Significant Change(s)*
1.0	Original version of DOS.
1.25	Accommodates double-sided diskettes.
2.0	Includes multiple directories needed to organize hard disks.
3.0	Uses high-capacity diskettes, the RAM disk, volume names, and the ATTRIB command. The ATTRIB command allows you to mark and unmark files, making them "read-only." This means that they can't be accidentally changed or erased while being used.
3.1	Includes networking.
3.2	Accommodates 3 1/2-inch drives.
3.3	Accommodates high-capacity 3 1/2-inch drives; includes new commands.
4.0	Introduces the DOS Shell and the MEM command; accommodates larger files and disk capacities.

What Hardware You Need

The type of personal computer most likely to use MS-DOS is one that is compatible to a great extent with the IBM PC. COMPAQ, Zenith Data Systems, Tandy, AT&T, AST, EPSON, Wang, NEC, Toshiba, Sharp, Leading Edge, Hewlett Packard, and many other companies manufacture or market MS-DOS based personal computers.

The computer should have at least 256 kilobytes (256K) of system RAM, at least one floppy disk drive, a display (screen), and a keyboard. These suggestions are minimal; most MS-DOS PCs sold today exceed these requirements. For convenience and processing power, you may want to include a second floppy disk drive, a hard disk with at least 10 megabytes of storage capacity, a printer, and a color graphics display.

35

Summary

This chapter introduced the fundamentals of disk operating systems, which allow users to access computer hardware and run specific applications programs, such as spreadsheets, word processors, and databases. MS-DOS, the world's most popular disk operating system, was first released in 1981 and has continued to evolve since then.

MS-DOS consists of a command processor, an input/output system, and utility files. Perhaps the most important component is the command processor, which interacts with you through the keyboard and screen when you operate the computer. The input/output system consists of several hidden files that interact with the computer's ROM and control the computer's use of hardware components in the system. The utility files are external commands that COMMAND.COM loads to carry out housekeeping tasks like formatting disks; determining disk size; listing, copying, comparing, backing up, and deleting files; and checking available memory.

Knowing how to use MS-DOS is important because it performs tasks essential for computing. It manages disks and preserves their information. DOS redirects output to different devices. Batch files can automate some of these tasks by replacing instructions normally typed on the keyboard.

As you read the following chapters, you will find that DOS can be useful in a variety of ways. More than 50 DOS commands and functions are available. This book emphasizes those commands that are essential to running off-the-shelf programs on a personal computer.

An Overview of DOS

Booting the Computer

Issuing DOS Commands

Preparing Disks

Hierarchical Directories

Copying, Renaming, and Deleting Files

Protecting Data

Special Commands and Files

Review Questions

1. Name the three main parts of DOS and indicate the purpose of each.

2. What does BIOS stand for, and what is its chief function?

3. What is an interface in a computer system?

4. What is an extension? Name three common DOS extensions and specify the meaning of each.

5. What disk-management services does DOS provide?

6. Define redirection and give an example of how it may be used.

7. What are applications programs? Indicate three kinds.

8. What is a batch file, and why would you want to use one?

3 *Booting the Computer*

An
Overview of
DOS

Booting the
Computer

Issuing DOS
Commands

Preparing
Disks

Hierarchical
Directories

Copying,
Renaming,
and
Deleting
Files

Protecting
Data

Special
Commands
and Files

Operators of early computers started them by entering a binary program and then instructing the computer to run the program. The binary program was called a "bootstrap loader" because the computer figuratively pulled itself up by the bootstraps to perform tasks. The term *booting* stuck, and "booting the computer" still means starting the computer.

The first time you start your computer, you may not know what to expect. Fortunately, the process of booting is simple. Once you learn a few computer terms and perform the basic start-up procedure, you begin to feel at ease. Then you are ready to learn other simple procedures, such as setting the date and time of the computer's clock, specifying the current drive, and stopping the computer if necessary.

After completing this chapter, you should

- Be able to explain what happens when DOS is "booted"
- Understand the difference between a "cold" and "warm" boot, and be able to do both
- Be able to call up the DOS Shell (if you have DOS V4.0)
- Know how to set the computer's internal clock
- Know how to specify the logged drive

▼

Key Terms in This Chapter

Booting	The process of starting a PC.
Cold boot	The process of starting a PC from a power-off condition.
Warm boot	The process of restarting a PC while the power is on.
Cursor	The blinking line or solid block that marks where the next keyboard entry will appear.
Default	A condition or value that the computer, the program, or DOS uses if you choose not to supply your own.

39

DOS prompt   The characters that COMMAND.COM displays to let you know that you can enter a DOS command. An example is C>.

Logged drive   The current default disk drive that DOS uses to carry out commands which involve disk services. Unless you change the prompt with a command, the default drive letter will be that of the DOS prompt.

▲

Booting DOS the First Time

A *cold boot* occurs when the computer's power is off, the unit is not yet warm, and you turn on the computer. To simplify booting, keep handy the diskette you use to boot your computer. For easy recognition, you can give the boot diskette a name like "Startup," "System," "Main," or "DOS." Check your manual if you are not sure which diskette is bootable, or ask your computer specialist to provide a bootable DOS system diskette. From this point on, the bootable DOS diskette will be called the DOS Master Disk.

Cold Booting

Learning how to boot from a diskette is the best way to understand the process of booting. To perform a cold boot, insert the DOS Master Disk in drive A. The cold boot consist of two steps: inserting a diskette in drive A and turning the computer switch on. Check your PC's system manual for the location of drive A and for diskette insertion instructions. Usually, the label should face up on horizontal drives and to the left on vertical drives. Do not force the diskette into the drive. If you use reasonably firm pressure and the diskette does not go into the slot, make sure that the drive doesn't contain another diskette. Never jam or bend a diskette during insertion, because you could cause permanent damage both to the diskette and to the drive.

You insert diskettes into horizontal and vertical drives in the same way. To complete the insertion of a 5 1/4-inch diskette, close the drive door or turn the latch clockwise.

**Booting DOS
the First Time**   The Two Faces   Completing   Specifying the
of DOS V4.0   the Boot   Logged Drive   Summary

An
Overview of
DOS

**Booting the
Computer**

Issuing DOS
Commands

Preparing
Disks

Hierarchical
Directories

Copying,
Renaming,
and
Deleting
Files

Protecting
Data

Special
Commands
and Files

Insert 3 1/2-inch diskettes gently, pushing until you hear a click. The drive closes by itself.

If you have a lock on the front of the system unit, make certain that the unit is unlocked. Next, turn on the display switch if necessary. Some displays are powered from the system unit and do not have a switch. Locate the computer's power switch. It is usually on the right side toward the rear of the system unit. Snap on the switch, and the cold boot begins.

If your computer has a hard disk, and your supplier installed DOS on the hard disk, you can boot automatically from the hard disk just by turning on the computer.

Watching the Boot

The instant you turn on the switch, the computer's electronics do a power-on reset (POR). The RAM, the microprocessor, and other electronics are "zeroed," which is like cleaning the slate. The system then begins a power-on self-test (POST) to check whether the computer is working properly. The POST, which ensures that your PC can handle your valuable data responsibly, can take from a few seconds to a couple of minutes. During the POST, you may see on the display a description of the test or a cursor. The *cursor* is a blinking line or solid box that indicates where the next character you type will be positioned. When the POST concludes, you will hear one beep, and activity will start on drive A. The bootstrap loader then loads DOS from the DOS Master Disk into RAM.

The following sequence of screens illustrates the cold boot from power on to the display of the system prompt. These examples assume that your computer does not have a built-in automatic clock. If your system does have an automatic clock, you will not see the prompts for date and time.

```
ABC Computer Co.
Turbo
RAM check
640K
OK
```

Memory check

Some computers let you watch the action of the power-on self-test (POST).

41

Date prompt

Unless you have an automatic system clock, you will need to enter the current date at the prompt.

```
Current date is Mon 01-16-1989
Enter new date (mm-dd-yy):
```

Time prompt

When prompted, enter the current time. You can include a figure for seconds, but it isn't required.

```
Current time is 11:17:00.75a
Enter new time:
```

You can enter DOS commands when the system prompt appears. The cold boot is complete.

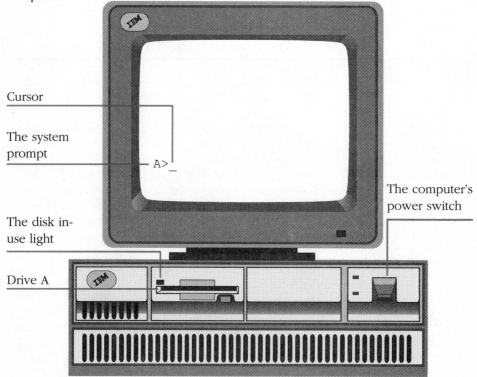

Cursor

The system prompt

A>_

The computer's power switch

The disk in-use light

Drive A

An
Overview of
DOS

Booting the
Computer

Issuing DOS
Commands

Preparing
Disks

Hierarchical
Directories

Copying,
Renaming,
and
Deleting
Files

Protecting
Data

Special
Commands
and Files

The Two Faces of DOS V4.0

With DOS V4.0, you have two view options:

- The prompt view
- The DOS Shell view

The *prompt* view is the traditional look of DOS for any version earlier that DOS V4.0.

```
A>
```

The DOS prompt appears on a plain screen with one letter of the alphabet representing the current, or active, drive. The letter is followed by a "greater than" symbol. The most common DOS prompts are A> for diskette systems and C> for hard disk systems.

The *Shell* view is an optional view new with DOS version 4.0. The Shell view provides a full screen with various menus, pop-up help windows, and graphic representations of directories and files. If your computer system has a "mouse," you can use it to select some standard DOS commands from the Shell screen and pop-up windows.

On this opening screen for the Shell view in DOS V4.0, the command prompt is highlighted. Pressing F1 brings up information about the command prompt.

The Shell view is the friendliest way to use DOS, but you should learn the basic commands from the prompt view. The reason becomes clear as you gain experience. With the Shell, you must learn not only the Shell commands, but the DOS commands for which they stand. And there is another complicating factor. It is unlikely that the Shell commands will be the same on the various compatible computers. The prompt view remains essentially the same.

Just remember that even though using the Shell is easy, you still need to know something about DOS commands and terminology. They remain substantially unchanged from previous versions of DOS. The Shell is simply a shortcut for someone who already understands the basics of DOS!

Completing the Boot

For the following discussion, assume that you are working from the command prompt, either because you do not use the DOS Shell or because you have used the Shell to reach the command prompt. The tasks covered here are miscellaneous items: learning to do a warm boot, setting the date and time directly from the command prompt, and learning about the logged disk drive. After reading this section, you'll be ready to take control of your computer with DOS.

Warm Booting

The warm boot differs little from the cold boot. For the cold boot, you inserted the DOS Master Disk and then switched on the computer. For the *warm boot*, your PC is already switched on. Make sure you have the DOS Master Disk in the A drive. If you are booting from a hard drive, make sure that there is no disk in drive A. You then press three keys.

Look at the keyboard and locate the Ctrl, Alt, and Del keys. The warm boot takes no more effort than pressing and holding Ctrl and Alt while you then press Del. The PC skips the preliminary tests and immediately loads DOS.

Setting the Date and Time

Most contemporary computers come with a built-in, battery-powered calendar and clock. This means that the correct date and time are the default values. A *default* value is a suggested response or recommended choice or action. If you make no

An
Overview of
DOS

**Booting the
Computer**

Issuing DOS
Commands

Preparing
Disks

Hierarchical
Directories

Copying,
Renaming,
and
Deleting
Files

Protecting
Data

Special
Commands
and Files

specific choice when the computer prompts you, DOS accepts the built-in suggestion by default. You usually press Enter to accept the default.

You press Enter to activate the command you type. Enter is like a "Go" key that instructs DOS to execute a command. When a computer boots, it automatically enters the time and date from the system, offers default values, or requires you to enter each manually.

If your computer is set up to record automatically the date and time, you do nothing during the boot process. Otherwise, DOS prompts you to enter the correct date and time.

Specifying the Logged Drive

Once the boot is complete, the system prompt indicates the logged drive. The *logged drive* is the active drive—the drive that responds to commands. For example, an A> and a blinking cursor tell you that DOS is logged onto drive A, which is usually a diskette drive. A C> and a blinking cursor mean that DOS is logged onto drive C, which is usually a hard disk drive. You can change the logged drive from A to C by typing **C:** at the prompt and pressing Enter. DOS reads the drive letter and colon as the disk drive's name.

DOS remembers the logged drive as the current drive. Many commands use the current drive and other current information without your having to specify them in the command. You'll learn about this phenomenon as the "rule of currents" in Chapter 6.

Remember that you need not specify the drive if you are requesting information from the logged drive. (Note: If you are using two floppy drives, substitute B: for C: in the examples and exercises.) You'll learn later how to include the drive name when you request information from a noncurrent drive.

Summary

In this chapter, you learned how to start a computer by cold booting it if it has been turned off, or warm booting it if it is on and running and you want to restart it. You learned also what to look for during booting and what steps to take to make sure that booting is successful.

The chapter introduced you to a feature new with DOS V4.0: the DOS Shell, which is a user interface that simplifies the selection of DOS commands and operations. You were given ideas of what to do after booting, such as setting the date and time, and specifying the logged drive.

After a successful boot, you are ready to do the next step: issue a DOS command at the system prompt. The following chapter tells you how to issue a DOS command.

Review Questions

1. What does it mean to "boot" a computer? What is the difference between a "cold" and "warm" boot?

2. What is the difference between the "prompt" view and the "Shell" view? What is the purpose of the DOS Shell? Which version of DOS introduced this new feature?

3. What is the logged drive? How do you change it?

4 *Issuing DOS Commands*

An
Overview of
DOS

Booting the
Computer

**Issuing DOS
Commands**

Preparing
Disks

Hierarchical
Directories

Copying,
Renaming,
and
Deleting
Files

Protecting
Data

Special
Commands
and Files

To communicate your need for service to DOS, you enter DOS commands. A *command* is an instruction made up of groups of characters that are separated or delimited by certain other characters. A command you give to DOS is similar to a written instruction you might give to a work associate. Both the DOS command and the written instruction must communicate your intentions. Both must communicate in proper form what action you want carried out and what the objects of that action are.

DOS recognizes and responds to well over 50 commands. The most useful of these are built into the command processor and are immediately available at the system prompt. Because these commands are built-in, they are called *internal commands.*

Other commands are stored as programs on your DOS diskette or in a hard disk directory. Because these commands are on disk, they are called *external commands.* They are loaded when you want to use them. Like internal commands, external commands are executed when you enter them at the system prompt.

Learning the "ins and outs" of issuing DOS commands takes some practice. Fortunately, the structure of what you type to use DOS commands is somewhat uniform, and you will soon branch out from examples to your own forms of the DOS commands. This chapter focuses on DIR, or the *Dir*ectory command, to help you become familiar with this uniform structure.

After completing this chapter, you should

- Understand DOS syntax and how parameters are used in a command line to vary the action of commands
- Be able to type and correct commands
- Know how to use the DIR command to list files
- Be familiar with the directory listing
- Be able to use wild cards with DIR

Key Terms in This Chapter

Command	A group of characters that may be thought of as a word that tells the computer what to do.
Syntax	The proper formation of commands and parameters at the prompt so that COMMAND.COM can interpret them.
Parameter	An additional instruction that defines specifically what you want a DOS command to do.
Directory	An area of the DOS file system that holds information about files. A directory appears as a list of files.
Switch	A part of the command syntax that turns on an optional function of a command.
Delimiter	A character that separates the "words" in a command. Common delimiters are the space and the slash.
Wild card	A character in a command that represents one or more other characters. In DOS the **?** represents any single character. The ***** represents the remaining characters in a "word" in the command.

Understanding DOS Commands

DOS is easier to use when you understand the concepts behind the commands. To begin to understand those concepts, you need to know two fundamental facts:

- DOS requires that you use a specific set of rules or syntax when you issue commands.
- Parameters, which are a part of a command's syntax, can change the way a command is executed.

Syntax is the order in which you type the elements of the DOS command. Using proper syntax when you enter a DOS command is like using proper English when you speak. DOS must clearly understand what you are typing in order to carry out the command.

**Understanding
DOS Commands**
Typing and
Correcting
Commands
Using DIR To
List Files in a
Directory
Summary

DOS is programmed to accept a limited number of instructions. These instructions must be issued in a specific form—that is, you must use the proper syntax. DOS's all-purpose response to an improperly formed command is Bad command or file name.

You can think of the command name as the action part of a DOS command. In addition to the name, many commands require or allow further directions. Any such additions are called *parameters*. Parameters tell DOS what to apply the action to or how to apply the action. Using DOS commands is really quite easy as long as you follow the rules of order and use the correct parameters.

Understanding Syntax

This chapter uses a symbolic form to describe command syntax. When you enter the command, you substitute real values for the symbolic name. Examples show you commands that you can enter exactly as shown.

DOS commands can have various correct forms—from simple versions to complete versions. Even though the simple versions of DOS syntax work effectively, most DOS manuals show the complete syntax for a command, making the command look complex. For example, the syntax for the DIR command looks like this if we use symbolic names for the parameters (switches are explained in the next section):

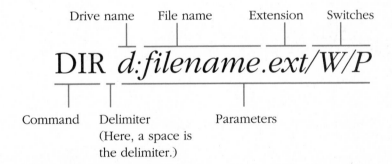

You use the DIR command to display a list of the files stored in a disk directory. A *directory* is an area of the DOS file system that holds information about files and directories. The DIR command may look formidable, but its command syntax is easy to understand if you look at the command-line elements one at a time.

Some parts of a DOS command are mandatory—that is, required information needed by MS-DOS. When you enter only the mandatory command elements, DOS in many cases uses default parameters. The command can therefore be simple to issue.

Other command parts are optional. When you enter all syntax elements, DOS uses the exact instructions in place of default values. For the DIR command example, the **DIR** is mandatory. The rest of the command, *d:filename.ext /W/P*, is optional. Remember that *d:filename.ext* is a symbolic example of parameters. A real command would have actual parameters instead of symbols.

You can type upper- or lowercase letters in commands. DOS reads both as uppercase letters. You must type the syntax samples shown in this book letter for letter, but you can ignore case. Items shown in lowercase letters are variables. You type in the appropriate information for the items shown in lowercase.

In the example, the lowercase *d:* identifies the disk drive the command will use for its action. Replace the *d:* with A:, B:, or C:, depending on the drive names in your computer system. The *filename.ext* stands for the name of a file, including its extension. In DOS, file names can have up to eight letters. You can also have an extension, which consists of a dot, or period, and up to three more characters. In this case, you might type in the file name MYFILE.123.

Note that spaces or the slash (/) separate, or delimit, the command name and parameters. *Delimiters* are important to DOS because they separate individual command elements and keep them distinct. For example, DIR A: is correct, but DIRA: is incorrect because no space keeps A: apart from DIR. Typing DIRA: causes DOS to display the error message `Bad command or file name`. You will see this error message whenever you fail to use proper syntax and the right parameters.

Using Switches

A *switch* is a parameter that turns on an optional function of a command. In the DIR example, /W and /P are switches. Note that each switch is a character preceded by a slash. Not all DOS commands have switches. In addition, switches may have different meanings for different commands.

Normally, the DIR command displays a directory with one file listing per line, with information about the size of the file and when it was created or last altered. Sometimes, however, a disk may contain too many files to display on one screen. As

Understanding
DOS Commands

Typing and
Correcting
Commands

Using DIR To
List Files in a
Directory

Summary

An
Overview of
DOS

Booting the
Computer

**Issuing DOS
Commands**

Preparing
Disks

Hierarchical
Directories

Copying,
Renaming,
and
Deleting
Files

Protecting
Data

Special
Commands
and Files

the screen fills, the first files scroll beyond the top of the display. To overcome this problem, you can use the /W or /P switches.

You can use the /W switch with the DIR command to display a *wide* directory of files. This wide directory contains only file names and extensions. Therefore, for an average size directory, usually all of the directory's files are listed on the screen.

```
Volume in drive A has no label
Volume Serial Number is 0FDA-3762
Directory of  A:\

COMMAND  COM   ANSI     SYS   APPEND   EXE   COUNTRY  SYS   DISPLAY  SYS
DRIVER   SYS   CONFIG   SYS   GRAFTABL COM   GRAPHICS COM   GRAPHICS PRO
KEYB     COM   KEYBOARD SYS   MODE     COM   NLSFUNC  EXE   PRINTER  SYS
VDISK    SYS   4201     CPI   4208     CPI   5202     CPI
        19 File(s)        57856 bytes free
```

The command DIR/W displays the directory listing in a wide arrangement, but you lose information about the individual files.

You use the /P switch with the DIR command to *pause* the scrolling after 23 lines of files, or approximately one screen, are displayed. At the bottom of a paused directory, DOS prompts you to Press any key to continue to move to the next screenful of files. The /P switch thus allows you to see all the files in the directory, one screen at a time.

```
Volume in drive A has no label
Volume Serial Number is 0FDA-3762
Directory of  A:\

COMMAND   COM     37637  06-17-88    12:00p
ANSI      SYS      9148  06-17-88    12:00p
APPEND    EXE     11170  06-17-88    12:00p
COUNTRY   SYS     12838  06-17-88    12:00p
DISPLAY   SYS     15741  06-17-88    12:00p
DRIVER    SYS      5274  06-17-88    12:00p
CONFIG    SYS        99  10-14-88     8:23a
GRAFTABL  COM     10271  06-17-88    12:00p
GRAPHICS  COM     16733  06-17-88    12:00p
GRAPHICS  PRO      9413  06-17-88    12:00p
KEYB      COM     14759  06-17-88    12:00p
KEYBOARD  SYS     23360  06-17-88    12:00p
MODE      COM     23040  06-17-88    12:00p
NLSFUNC   EXE      6910  06-17-88    12:00p
PRINTER   SYS     18946  06-17-88    12:00p
```

The command DIR/P displays the directory listing screen-by-screen.

When DOS says Press any key to continue, it really means to press *almost* any key. If you press the Shift, Alt, Caps Lock, Num Lock, or Scroll Lock keys, DOS ignores you. The easiest keys to press are the space bar and the Enter key.

Note that you can use /P with /W to pause a wide listing of files from a very large directory. In addition, you can use commands other than the /P switch to pause the scrolling of a long list of files. Pressing Ctrl-S (or the Pause key on an Enhanced keyboard) stops the scrolling until you press any key to continue scrolling.

Typing and Correcting Commands

To use DOS, you must know how to type the command correctly. You should know also how to correct a command if you make a mistake. The following sections cover entering command names, adding parameters to commands, correcting mistakes in a command line, and recalling a command from DOS's keyboard input buffer.

Typing the Command Name

You enter a command when the screen displays the DOS prompt. As you learned in Chapter 2, this prompt usually consists of the drive letter followed by the > character. Notice that immediately following the > is the blinking cursor.

The command name is like a key to the DOS operating system. You will recall that COMMAND.COM is the DOS command processor that reads the command you type. COMMAND.COM can carry out several "built-in" commands. It also knows how to load and run the external utility programs that you enter at the DOS prompt. Because you enter the built-in commands and the external commands at the DOS prompt, both are referred to as *command names*.

When you type a command, do not leave a space after the > of the DOS prompt. Enter all DOS command names directly after the prompt. If the command has no parameters or switches, then press the Enter key after the last letter of the command name. For example, you would type the directory command as C>**DIR** and then press Enter. Note that in this book, the characters you type are in boldface.

```
A>DIR
```

Typing the command name. Do not leave a space between the > symbol and the command name.

Understanding
DOS Commands

**Typing and
Correcting
Commands**

Using DIR To
List Files in a
Directory

Summary

An
Overview of
DOS

Booting the
Computer

**Issuing DOS
Commands**

Preparing
Disks

Hierarchical
Directories

Copying,
Renaming,
and
Deleting
Files

Protecting
Data

Special
Commands
and Files

Adding Parameters

When you are to enter parameters that are not switches, this book will show them in one of two ways: lowercase or uppercase. You are to supply the value for the lowercase text. The lowercase letters are shorthand for the full names of the parts of a command. As in the command name, uppercase means that you enter letter-for-letter what you see.

Remember that you delimit parameters from the rest of the command. Most of the time the delimiter is a space, but other delimiters such as **.**, ****, and **:** exist. Just look at the examples in this book to see the correct delimiter.

If the example text has switches, you will recognize them by the preceding slash (/). Always enter the switch letter as shown. Do not forget to type the slash. The slash tells DOS that a switch is about to follow.

```
A>DIR C:MYFILE.TXT
```

Adding a filename parameter. In symbolic notation, MYFILE.TXT would be shown as *filename.ext.*

```
A>DIR/W
```

Adding a switch parameter to display a directory in five columns.

Correcting Mistakes in a Command Line

If you make a mistake when you are entering a command, DOS does not act on the command until you press the Enter key. You can therefore correct any mistake if you have not pressed Enter. To correct an error, use the left-arrow key or Backspace key to move the cursor backward to the point where you want to make the correction. (If you use Backspace, characters are erased as the cursor moves backward.) After you correct the error, press Enter to activate the command.

If you don't want to correct the error but type an entirely new command, you can press Esc or Ctrl-C. Pressing Esc plants a backslash (\) in the command line to mark the interruption and moves the cursor to the next line so that you can start over, as shown in the following screen.

Pressing Esc to redo a command line without erasing it. The backslash marks the interruption.

New position of cursor. ————

```
A>DIR C:MYFILE\
```

Ctrl-C also withdraws the command entry altogether but gives you a new prompt on a new line. Keep in mind that these line-editing and canceling tips work only before you press the Enter key.

Remember that the Enter key is the action key for DOS commands. Make it a habit to stop and read what you typed before you press the Enter key. After you press Enter, the computer gets busy and carries out your command.

Reusing a Command

During the processing of the command, DOS does not display your keystrokes. DOS, however, does remember your keystrokes. When you type a command line and press the Enter key, DOS copies the line into an input *buffer*, which is a storage area for commands. You can use the command in the buffer if you want to repeat the command. For example, if you want to pull the last command line from the buffer and use it again, press F3 at the DOS prompt. The full command appears. If, after you start typing a command, you realize that it is the same as the preceding command, you can still use F3. Press F3, and the command's remaining letters that you haven't typed will appear on the command line. You will find this feature helpful.

Using DIR To List Files in a Directory

Knowing what files are on your disks and when you created or altered the files is important. You could keep a list of files manually, but that would be quite a task. Why not let DOS do this job for you? You can use the DOS DIR command to get a list of directory files on your diskettes or hard disk. With the DIR command, you get a volume label, five columns of information about the files, and the amount of unused space on the disk.

To use the DIR command, type **DIR** and press press Enter so that DOS can execute the command. DOS displays a list of files from the logged drive. You can instead type **DIR A:** to specify drive A or **DIR C:** to list the files on drive C. The A or C is the optional drive parameter. If you specify no drive, DOS uses the logged drive by default.

You can change the logged drive by typing in the drive letter, a colon, and pressing Enter. For example, typing **A:** at the DOS prompt changes the logged drive to drive A. A disk must be in a drive before DOS can make it the logged drive. Remember that you can log only to a drive your system contains. By changing the logged drive, you can switch between a hard disk and a diskette.

Understanding the Directory Listing

The first line you see in the directory listing is the volume label. A volume label is an identification that you specify when you prepare the disk. The volume label is optional, but it can ease your organization of disks.

The Volume serial number on the second line is assigned arbitrarily by DOS V4.0 for its own internal reference. The third line identifies the disk drive and directory you are viewing.

The next lines in the directory listing contain file information. Each line in the directory describes one file. You see the file name, extension, and size of file in bytes. You see also the date and time when you created or last changed the file (if you entered the time and date when you booted your computer). The following illustration points out the information supplied by the directory listing.

An Overview of DOS

Booting the Computer

Issuing DOS Commands

Preparing Disks

Hierarchical Directories

Copying, Renaming, and Deleting Files

Protecting Data

Special Commands and Files

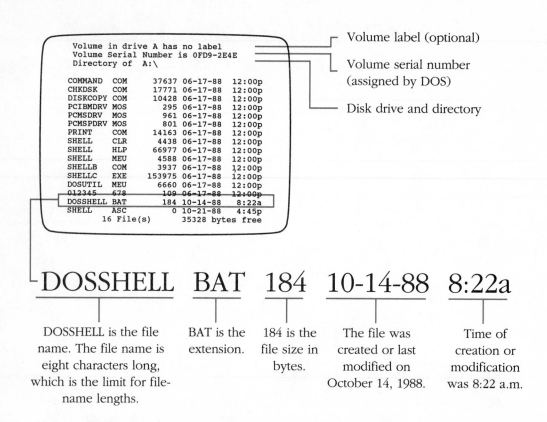

```
     Volume in drive A has no label
     Volume Serial Number is 0FD9-2E4E
     Directory of  A:\

     COMMAND   COM     37637 06-17-88   12:00p
     CHKDSK    COM     17771 06-17-88   12:00p
     DISKCOPY  COM     10428 06-17-88   12:00p
     PCIBMDRV  MOS       295 06-17-88   12:00p
     PCMSDRV   MOS       961 06-17-88   12:00p
     PCMSPDRV  MOS       801 06-17-88   12:00p
     PRINT     COM     14163 06-17-88   12:00p
     SHELL     CLR      4438 06-17-88   12:00p
     SHELL     HLP     66977 06-17-88   12:00p
     SHELL     MEU      4588 06-17-88   12:00p
     SHELLB    COM      3937 06-17-88   12:00p
     SHELLC    EXE    153975 06-17-88   12:00p
     DOSUTIL   MEU      6660 06-17-88   12:00p
     012345    678       109 06-17-88   12:00p
     DOSSHELL  BAT       184 10-14-88    8:22a
     SHELL     ASC         0 10-21-88    4:45p
          16 File(s)     35328 bytes free
```

Volume label (optional)

Volume serial number (assigned by DOS)

Disk drive and directory

DOSSHELL BAT 184 10-14-88 8:22a

DOSSHELL is the file name. The file name is eight characters long, which is the limit for file-name lengths.

BAT is the extension.

184 is the file size in bytes.

The file was created or last modified on October 14, 1988.

Time of creation or modification was 8:22 a.m.

Using Wild Cards in the DIR Command

Just about everyone has seen Western movies where a poker-playing cowboy says, "Deuces are wild!" Of course, this means that the number two cards can take on a meaning other than their own. Computer linguistics borrowed this wild-card concept and applied it to file-name operations on computers. You can use wild-card characters in file names to copy, rename, delete, list, or otherwise manipulate file names.

Wild Cards in the DIR Command

[?]　　　　　With wild cards, you can tailor DOS commands. The ? replaces
　　　　　　any single character in a file specification.

[*]　　　　　The * replaces every character from the asterisk to the end of
　　　　　　the part of the command where the asterisk is located.

[*].[*]　　The wild-card filename replaces every character in the root file
　　　　　　name and every character in the extension; therefore, *.* selects
　　　　　　all files in a directory.

Examples:

DIR MYFILE.123	Presents directory information for the file MYFILE.123
DIR *.123	Lists each file that has the extension 123.
DIR M*.*	Lists each file whose file name begins with the letter M.
DIR *.*	Lists all files in the directory.
DIR *.	Lists all files that have no extension.
DIR ???.BAT	Lists all three-letter file names that have a BAT extension.
DIR MYFILE.???	Lists all files named MYFILE that have three-letter extensions.

Summary

This chapter introduced you to DOS commands, to the rules for issuing them with
delimiters at the system prompt, and to optional switches for affecting the way the
commands perform. Certain switches like /P and /W give you control over the use
of the DIR command to list files in a directory. You learned how to correct a
command if you make a mistake in typing it, and how to reissue a command.

Special attention was given to directory listings so that you would understand file
names and extensions, information about file size, and the date-time stamp. You
learned how to use wild cards with the DIR command to list only certain kinds of
files in a directory.

Before a disk can hold files, it has to be prepared through a process called
formatting. That process, initiated with the FORMAT command, is the topic of the
next chapter.

Review Questions

1. What two fundamental facts do you need to remember about DOS commands?

2. What is the DIR command and how is it used?

3. Name two command delimiters and describe how they work.

4. How are switches used in a DOS command? What two switches would you use with the DIR command, for example, and why?

5. What are some of the methods for correcting mistakes in a command line?

6. What happens when you press F3 at the DOS prompt?

7. What information is supplied in a directory listing?

8. Provide some examples of how to use wild cards properly with the DIR command.

5 *Preparing Disks*

An
Overview of
DOS

Booting the
Computer

Issuing DOS
Commands

**Preparing
Disks**

Hierarchical
Directories

Copying,
Renaming,
and
Deleting
Files

Protecting
Data

Special
Commands
and Files

When you purchase a new diskette, it is just a round piece of Mylar in a plastic jacket. Before you can store information on the diskette, you must prepare it electronically. This preparation is called *formatting*.

DOS's FORMAT command prepares diskettes for use by the computer. You do nothing more than enter the command. FORMAT analyzes a diskette for defects, generates a root directory, sets up a special storage table that will help DOS locate files on the diskette, and makes other technical modifications.

Before you learn how to issue the FORMAT command, however, you must understand logged, or current, drives and how they relate to the relative locations of FORMAT.COM and the diskette to be formatted. Therefore, this chapter begins with a consideration of disk drives before moving to a discussion of disk preparation.

After completing this chapter, you should

- Understand the logged, or current, drive and how it relates to the FORMAT command
- Know more about the difference between internal and external DOS commands
- Be able to format diskettes on floppy as well as hard drive systems
- Understand the various switches for modifying the FORMAT command
- Know how to interpret FORMAT's error messages

Key Terms in This Chapter

Format   Initial preparation of a disk for data storage.

Volume   A disk-level name that identifies a particular disk.

Track   A circular section of a disk's surface that holds data.

Sector	A section of a track that acts as the disk's smallest storage unit.
Internal command	A DOS command that is built into COMMAND.COM.
External command	A DOS command that must be located from a file and loaded by COMMAND.COM before it can execute.

▲

Understanding FORMAT and the Logged Drive

Earlier in the book, you learned that a single letter, followed by a colon, designates a disk drive. When the letter and colon are used in a command, DOS understands them as the drive specifier. You also used the DIR command, for which you leave the drive specifier out of the command line. In this case, DOS "assumes" that the previously logged drive is the default for the directory.

Understanding Default Values

DOS uses certain prepackaged, or default, values to carry out its services. You can override many of these values through commands or switches. Some values, such as a /S switch for FORMAT, remain in effect only for one instance. (You learn about FORMAT's switches later in this chapter.) Changing other values, like the name of the logged drive, causes the default to change to the new value.

When you boot your computer, DOS automatically logs to the drive that holds the bootable disk. This drive is the default drive. DOS normally displays the default drive name in the DOS prompt and uses this drive to execute commands. If the drive specifier is the same as the default drive, you do not have to designate the drive letter. If, however, you want to issue a command to another disk drive, you must enter the drive specifier for that disk in the command line.

Whenever possible, make a command shorter and cleaner by leaving out the defaults. Many examples of commands in this book are based on default values, and they are omitted. A default that is frequently omitted is the logged drive.

Understanding
FORMAT and the   Formatting   Using Switches
Logged Drive   Diskettes   with FORMAT

Understanding   Formatting a
FORMAT'S Error   Hard Disk:
Messages   Some Cautions   Summary

An
Overview of
DOS

Booting the
Computer

Issuing DOS
Commands

**Preparing
Disks**

Hierarchical
Directories

Copying,
Renaming,
and
Deleting
Files

Protecting
Data

Special
Commands
and Files

Using FORMAT on Another Drive

You will recall that COMMAND.COM contains built-in, internal DOS commands, and that external DOS commands reside on disk. You can issue internal commands regardless of which drive is the logged (current) drive. COMMAND.COM must find and load external commands, such as FORMAT, before executing them.

Internal DOS Commands

BREAK	DATE	PROMPT
CHCP	VER	DIR
RENAME	VERIFY	COPY
DEL	RMDIR	VOL
CHDIR	ERASE	SET
CKS	MKDIR	TIME
CTTY	PATH	TYPE

Common External DOS Commands

BACKUP	DISKCOPY	RESTORE
CHDIR (CD)	ECHO	RMDIR (RD)
CHKDSK	ERASE	SORT
CLS	FIND	SYS
COPY	FORMAT	TIME
DATE	MKDIR (MD)	TREE
DELETE	MORE	TYPE
DEVICE	PATH	VER
DIR	PROMPT	VERIFY
DISKCOMP	RENAME	VOL

If the external commands are not on the logged disk, then you must enter a drive specifier before the command name. The drive specifier is the name of the drive that contains the command's program file. You will learn in the next chapter how to give DOS the correct path to the external commands.

Suppose that you want to format a diskette in drive B. You have DOS loaded in drive A and a blank diskette in drive B. Type **A:** and press Enter to make the drive holding the DOS Working diskette the default drive. Then type **FORMAT B:** to format the blank diskette in drive B.

If you changed to drive B and issued the FORMAT B: command, DOS would produce an error message. The reason is that drive B has become the current drive, and DOS cannot find on drive B the program FORMAT.COM to format a diskette on drive B.

One solution to this problem is to issue the command **A:FORMAT B:**. DOS finds the format command on the DOS diskette in drive A as specified in the command. The formatting is done on the blank diskette in drive B as specified in the command.

The FORMAT command in DOS versions 3.0 and later requires that you specify the drive for the disk to be formatted even if the drive is the default. Prior DOS versions don't require you to name the drive in the command. Be careful not to format the wrong disk by default!

With external commands like FORMAT, DOS prompts you to place the proper diskette into the drive before the command is carried out. If you have a floppy-disk system wth one diskette drive, you can remove the DOS Working copy that contains the FORMAT program, insert the diskette to be formatted, and press any key.

Formatting Diskettes

As noted at the beginning of the chapter, the FORMAT command prepares diskettes for use by the computer. You can format new, blank diskettes or previously used diskettes.

Think of unformatted and formatted diskettes as comparable to blank and lined sheets of paper. The lines on the sheet of paper provide you with an orderly way to record written information. The lines also act as a guide for the reader of your information. New diskettes (blank diskettes) are like blank sheets of paper to DOS.

Understanding
FORMAT and the
Logged Drive

Formatting
Diskettes

Using Switches
with FORMAT

Understanding
FORMAT'S Error
Messages

Formatting a
Hard Disk:
Some Cautions

Summary

An
Overview of
DOS

Booting the
Computer

Issuing DOS
Commands

**Preparing
Disks**

Hierarchical
Directories

Copying,
Renaming,
and
Deleting
Files

Protecting
Data

Special
Commands
and Files

When you format a blank diskette, DOS *encodes*, or programs, data storage divisions on the diskette's surface. The divisions are concentric circles called *tracks*. DOS decides what type of drive you have and then positions the tracks accordingly. Each track is further divided into segments called *sectors*. DOS stores data in the sectors and uses the track number and sector number to retrieve the data. Just as the lines on the paper are guides for the reader, so are the tracks and sectors on the disk guides for the computer.

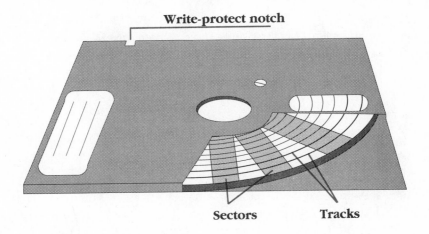

Write-protect notch

Sectors   **Tracks**

Anatomy of a 5 1/4-inch diskette

A standard 5 1/4-inch diskette (one that holds 360K of data) has 40 tracks per side. A standard 3 1/2-inch diskette (720K) has 80 tracks per side. Disks with larger capacities have more tracks and more sectors.

To format a diskette, write "Formatted" on the label and follow the directions for your system. For formatting, you need to have a Working diskette that contains the external FORMAT command. The DOS V4.0 installation process creates a working diskette. If you have an earlier version of DOS, you will need a working copy of the system diskette.

The following sections cover formatting diskettes on floppy disk drive and hard drive systems, respectively.

Diskette Drive Systems

For floppy disk drive systems, make certain that the DOS Working diskette is inserted into drive A before you begin the formatting procedure.

For a system with only one diskette drive, you follow these steps:

1. Close the drive door if necessary.
2. At the A> prompt, you type **FORMAT B:/V** and press Enter. (You will learn about /V, the volume switch, in the next section.)

    Your computer treats your single drive as both drive A and drive B.
3. Following the prompts, replace the DOS Working diskette in drive A with the diskette labeled "Formatted."
4. Press Enter.

After the diskette is formatted, DOS displays information about the diskette's capacity. DOS V4.0 expresses this capacity in bytes and allocation units; versions of DOS prior to V4.0 display bytes only.

When you see the message FORMAT Another? (Y/N), you can format another diskette by answering **Y**es to the prompt and pressing Enter. You can keep formatting diskettes as long as the FORMAT program is loaded in the system's RAM. If you don't want to format another diskette, answer **N**o and press Enter. You then return to "system level."

Caution: Versions of DOS prior to 3.0 do not require that you specify the drive that holds the diskette you want to format.

DOS V4.0 indicates what percentage of the diskette's surface is formatted. When formatting is complete, you may give the diskette a volume name, using up to 11 characters, or you may press Enter to omit the volume name. The volume switch on DOS V4.0 is automatic.

For a system with two diskette drives, you follow these steps:

1. Close the drive door if necessary.
2. Insert the diskette labeled "Formatted" in drive B.
3. At the A> prompt, you type **FORMAT B:/V** and press Enter.

DOS formats the disk in drive B and then displays the information about the diskette's storage capacity.

Understanding
FORMAT and the   Formatting   Using Switches   FORMAT'S Error   Hard Disk:
Logged Drive   Diskettes   with FORMAT   Messages   Some Cautions   Summary

Understanding   Formatting a

An
Overview of
DOS

Booting the
Computer

Issuing DOS
Commands

**Preparing
Disks**

Hierarchical
Directories

Copying,
Renaming,
and
Deleting
Files

Protecting
Data

Special
Commands
and Files

When you see the message Format Another? (Y/N), you can format another diskette by answering **Y**es to the prompt and pressing Enter. If you don't want to format another diskette, answer **N**o and press Enter. You then return to "system level."

Hard Disk Drive Systems

If you have a hard disk system with DOS and its external commands already installed on the hard disk, the procedure is slightly different:

1. Check to see that drive C is your logged disk drive and that the C> prompt is displayed.
2. Insert the disk labeled "Formatted" in drive A.
3. Type the **FORMAT A:/V** command and press Enter.

After the diskette is formatted, information about the diskette's memory capacity appears on the screen.

When you see the message Format Another? (Y/N), you can format another diskette by answering **Y**es to the prompt and pressing Enter. If you don't want to format another diskette, answer **N**o and press Enter. You then return to "system level."

Using Switches with FORMAT

As with many DOS commands, you can add switches to modify the FORMAT command. You separate the switch from the command with a slash (/). You can add more than one switch to a command. For example, **FORMAT B:/V/S** is a valid command.

/V (Volume Label)

DOS reserves a few bytes of data space on disks so that you can place an electronic identification, called a volume label, on each disk. Think of a volume label for a disk in the same context as the volume number of a book. DOS V4.0 automatically builds this switch into the FORMAT command. After formatting a disk, DOS prompts you for an 11-character volume name.

/S (System)

The /S switch places the DOS system files on a formatted disk. Use this switch if you want to be able to boot your PC with the disk you are formatting. You cannot see these hidden files in the directory of the disk, but the files are there, along with COMMAND.COM, which you can see. The /S switch reduces the available storage capacity of the disk by about 80K.

/4

The /4 switch allows you to format a diskette in a high-capacity drive for double-density use. Use this switch to prepare a diskette in your 1.2M drive for use in a 360K drive. Note: Despite this provision for downward compatibility, diskettes prepared in this way often are not readable on a 360K drive.

/1, /8, /B, /N, and /T

Primarily, these FORMAT switches allow current versions of DOS to format diskettes for very early computers or computers that use the first version of DOS. Although you never may need to use these switches, brief descriptions may be helpful.

The /1 switch tells DOS to prepare a single-sided diskette for use in a single-sided drive, and /8 prepares a diskette with 8 sectors per track. The /B switch allows room for system files on an 8 sectors-per-track diskette. Both /N and /T allow you to vary the number of tracks and sectors on high-capacity diskettes.

Understanding FORMAT'S Error Messages

Errors that can occur during formatting usually are not serious. For example, if you insert a blank diskette in the drive where DOS expects to find the FORMAT command *and then* issue the FORMAT command, DOS displays the message:

```
General failure reading drive A
Abort, Retry, Fail?
```

Since DOS cannot find the internal file tables on the blank disk when it attempts to load FORMAT, DOS assumes that the disk or the drive has failed. The solution is to place the DOS diskette in the drive and enter **R** to retry.

An
Overview of
DOS

Booting the
Computer

Issuing DOS
Commands

**Preparing
Disks**

Hierarchical
Directories

Copying,
Renaming,
and
Deleting
Files

Protecting
Data

Special
Commands
and Files

You get the `General failure` message also when the disk is not correctly formatted or the disk's formatting is wrong for the computer you are using. Try formatting the disk again, making sure that the disk is formatted for your system.

Some disks do not format properly the first time. If, after the second format attempt, the error message is still present, the diskette is probably damaged, so replace it.

When you insert and remove disks during formatting sessions, you can give DOS the "go ahead" too soon when you are prompted to `Press any key when ready`. When you make this error, DOS displays the message:

```
Not ready
Format terminated
Format another (Y/N)?
```

This message usually means that the drive door is still open or that you forgot to insert a diskette into the drive. An open drive door isn't uncommon when you are swapping diskettes in and out of drives. To recover, remove the diskette and reinsert it, close the drive door carefully, enter **R** at the prompt, and issue the FORMAT command again. You can usually run FORMAT a second time by answering Y to the question `Format another (Y/N)?` and pressing Enter. If formatting still does not occur, type **A** to abort.

These first two error conditions happen during formatting activity, but they could happen as you use other DOS commands as well. Because FORMAT is an external command and works on blank disks, these errors are likely to occur with FORMAT.

If the FORMAT command detects errors on a disk, you will see a line describing the problem in the report. For example, the line might state

```
2048 bytes in bad sectors
```

The `bytes in bad sectors` message means that DOS found bad sectors on the disk. These sectors cannot hold information, so the total amount of free space on the disk is reduced by the number of bytes in bad sectors. Try reformatting the disk. If, after the second format attempt, the bad sectors message is still present, you can ask your dealer to replace the disk, or you can use the disk as is. If you choose to do the latter, keep in mind that bad sectors can cause trouble with the diskette.

Occasionally, you may see the message

```
Write protect error
Format terminated
Format another (Y/N)?
```

This error occurred because DOS attempted to format a write-protected disk. Write protection saved the disk from accidental erasure.

The worst disk error message is

```
Invalid media or Track 0 bad - disk unusable
Format terminated
Format another (Y/N)?
```

The `Invalid media` part of the message may stem from your use of a diskette whose capacity is wrong for your computer system. The magnetic oxides on disk surfaces differ among particular capacities. Using a diskette with a capacity higher than necessary will cause disk errors. The `Track 0 bad` part of the message may mean that the disk has a scratched surface and that DOS is unable to read disk-level information on the first track.

Formatting a Hard Disk: Some Cautions

Hard disks are a desirable part of a computer system because of their speed and storage capacity. And, just like diskettes, hard disks must be formatted before you use them. Unless you are very familiar with the procedure, however, **DO NOT ATTEMPT TO FORMAT YOUR HARD DISK!**

If you purchased your hard disk separately from your computer, consult the guide that came with your drive for installation instructions. The space in this book does not allow for a discussion of the many variations of hard disk installation. If you bought the drive from a full-service dealer, ask for assistance.

Before you attempt to format your hard disk, do a complete backup. Make sure that you are familiar with the RESTORE command (see Chapter 8). You also should have a bootable diskette with a copy of the RESTORE program on it.

Remember that FORMAT erases all data that a disk contains. Always check the directory of the disk you want to format. It may contain data you need. Make a

Understanding
FORMAT and the
Logged Drive   Formatting
Diskettes   Using Switches
with FORMAT   Understanding
FORMAT'S Error
Messages   Formatting a
Hard Disk:
Some Cautions   **Summary**

mental note to check the command line thoroughly when you use the FORMAT command. For example, if you are used to typing **C:** as a drive specifier, habit might send you into a disastrous format mistake.

It is a good policy to format your hard disk at least once a year. Why? Because accumulating and erasing files fragments individual files across the disk. Backing up the disk, formatting the disk, and restoring the backed up files "restores" the disk's speed performance. However, using a software program designed to improve your hard disk's performance is a better and safer alternative than formatting. Disk Optimizer is one such program, but other programs exist. Ask your computer dealer or instructor for the best program for your system.

Summary

This chapter showed you how to format disks so that they can store information for use by a computer. You learned about the logged, or current, drive and how it relates to the FORMAT command. You learned also the meaning of default values and of the difference between internal and external DOS commands.

The chapter included instructions for formatting diskettes on diskette drive systems and on hard disk systems. You were told that DOS provides optional switches, such as /V to supply a volume label, /S to transfer system files and make a bootable diskette, and /4 to use a high-density drive to create a double-density diskette. You were introduced to some error messages that DOS displays during error conditions in formatting. Finally, you were cautioned about formatting a hard disk because of the tremendous loss of information that could occur if it has not been carefully preserved on backup diskettes.

After you have one or more formatted diskettes or begin to work on a computer with a formatted hard disk, you are ready to store files in directories. The next chapter explains DOS's hierarchical directory system and how to organize files in a meaningful way.

Review Questions

1. What is the difference between "internal" and "external" DOS commands? Which kind is FORMAT?

2. What do you need to remember about FORMAT and the logged (current) drive?

3. What does the FORMAT command do? Why do you need to be careful when using this command?

4. Describe the purpose of the /V, /S, and /4 switches when these are used with FORMAT.

5. What are "bad sectors"?

6. How often should a hard disk be reformatted? What do you need to do beforehand?

An
Overview of
DOS

Booting the
Computer

Issuing DOS
Commands

Preparing
Disks

**Hierarchical
Directories**

Copying,
Renaming,
and
Deleting
Files

Protecting
Data

Special
Commands
and Files

6 *Hierarchical Directories*

In Chapter 4, you learned how to issue the DIR command to see a list of the contents of a disk directory. A disk directory is not only a file list that you see on-screen, but also an internal software list. The directory is the disk's "letter of introduction" to your computer. In this chapter, you will learn more about important directory commands.

This chapter explains DOS's hierarchical directory structure, which is especially useful for hard disk users. You will learn how to use the PATH command to move around your disk in a logical way. You will learn how to use also the hierarchical structure to group and organize files. This chapter introduces DOS commands that deal directly with directory organization.

After completing this chapter, you should

- Understand how DOS organizes files into hierarchical levels of directories
- Understand how path names enable DOS to find a file or carry out a command
- Be able to organize a hierarchical directory
- Know how to use the DOS commands for creating, navigating, removing, and displaying hierarchical directories

Key Terms in This Chapter

Hierarchical directory   An organizational structure used by DOS to segregate files into levels of subdirectories.

Tree structure   A term applied to hierarchical directories to describe the conceptual scheme in which directories "belong" to higher directories and "own" lower directories. Viewed graphically, the ownership relationships resemble an inverted tree.

Root directory	The highest directory of the tree structure of DOS. All DOS disks have a root directory, which is automatically created by DOS (versions 2.0 and later).
Subdirectory	A directory created in another directory and subordinate to that directory. Also referred to simply as a directory.
Directory specifier	A DOS command parameter that tells DOS where to find a file or where to carry out a command.
Path name	Another name for the directory specifier. The path name gives DOS the directions it needs to trace the directory tree to the directory containing desired commands or files.
PATH command	The command that instructs DOS to search through a specified set of directories for files with .BAT, .COM, and .EXE extensions. DOS searches this path if the selected batch, command, or executable file can't be found in the current directory.

▲

Understanding Hierarchical Directories

DOS uses the directory to find files on a disk. The directory is held in computer format on the disk itself and contains information about the name, size, and creation or revision date of each file. Computer operators use the directory of a disk to find specific files. DOS also uses some or all of this directory information to service efficiently requests for data stored in the files on your disks.

All MS-DOS-based disks have at least one directory. One directory is usually adequate for a diskette. Because diskettes have relatively limited capacities, the number of files you can store on a diskette is limited. Fixed disks, or hard disks, on the other hand, have relatively large capacities. A fixed disk can contain hundreds or even thousands of files. Without an organizational method, both DOS and you would have to sift and sort through all directory entries to find a specific file.

Starting with version 2, MS-DOS incorporated a *hierarchical directory* system. This multilevel file structure lets you create a filing system for your many programs and files. Hierarchical directories are beneficial. You can store your disk files in smaller, more logically grouped directories so that you (and DOS) can locate those files.

The term *tree structure* refers to the organization of files into hierarchical levels of directories. Try picturing the tree structure as an inverted tree. You can visualize the file system with the first-level directory as the root, or trunk, of the tree. The trunk branches into major limbs to the next level of directories below the root. These directories branch into other directories. The directories have files, like leaves, attached to them. Directories below the root directory are called *subdirectories*. The terms *directory* and *subdirectory* frequently are used interchangeably, however.

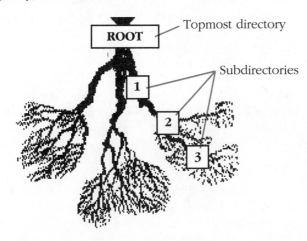

The tree-structure analogy loses some of its neatness when it is expanded to cover the capabilities of the hierarchical directory structure. The reason is that any directory, except the root, can have as many subdirectories as disk space allows, as the following illustration shows.

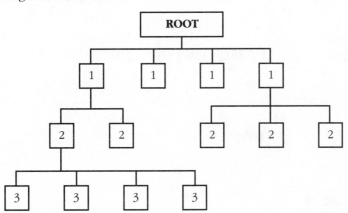

Sometimes disk directories are referred to as "parent" and "child" directories. Each "child" of the parent can have "children" of its own. In the directory hierarchy, each directory's "parent" is the directory just above it.

At any time, you can work within a directory that is at any branch of the tree. By naming the branches, you can describe where you are working in the tree structure. You simply start at the root and name each branch that leads to your current branch.

When you prepare a disk for your computer, DOS creates one directory for that disk. This main directory is called the root directory. The root directory is the default directory until you change to another directory. DOS designates the root directory with the backslash (\) character. You cannot delete the root directory.

A subdirectory is any directory other than the root directory. Like the root directory, however, a subdirectory can contain data files as well as other, lower subdirectories. Subdirectory names must conform to the rules for naming DOS files, but subdirectory names normally do not have extensions. It is a good idea to name subdirectories for the type of files they contain. In this way, you can remember what type of files each subdirectory contains.

Directories do not share information about their contents with other directories. In this way, each subdirectory is segregated and private. Privacy extends to the DOS commands you issue. The directory structure allows DOS commands to act on the contents of the current directory but leave other directories undisturbed.

The directory in which you are working is the *default*, or current, directory. When you issue a command that specifies a file but not a directory, DOS uses your current directory. You can remain in the current directory and access any point in the tree structure.

Understanding Paths in Hierarchical Directories

To find a file or to carry out a command on a file, DOS must know where the file is located in a hierarchical directory. That is, DOS must know the path to the file's location. A simple *path name* consists of the drive name, the directory name, and the file name. Combined, these pieces of information are called a *directory specifier*.

Using Path Names

To specify a directory and file, you type the disk drive name (followed by a colon); a backslash (\) to tell DOS to begin from the root directory; the directory (or subdirectory) name; a backslash to delimit, or separate, the file name from the directory name; and then the file name. In symbolic notation, the directory specifier looks like this:

> *c:\directory\filename.ext*

DOS then uses this information to find the file.

For example, suppose that MYFILE.123 is a data file in a LOTUS subdirectory. The complete path name for this file is the chain of directories that tells DOS how to find MYFILE.123. In this case, the chain consists of just two directories: the root (\) and \LOTUS. The path name is

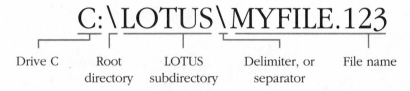

| Drive C | Root directory | LOTUS subdirectory | Delimiter, or separator | File name |

A path name can be also a chain of directory names that tells DOS how to find the file you want. You type the drive name, a subdirectory name or sequence of subdirectory names, and the file name. You use a backslash to separate subdirectory names from each other. In symbolic notation, the path name chain looks like this:

> *d:\directory\directory. . .\filename.ext*

If you omit the drive specifier (*d:*) in this notation, DOS uses the logged drive as the default drive. After the drive specifier, *directory\directory. . .* names the directories you want to search. The ellipsis (. . .) means that you can include more backslashes and directory names if the path is longer. If you omit the directory specifier from the path name, DOS assumes that the directory you want to use is the current directory. The last part of the path name—*filename.ext*—is the file name. Again, you use a backslash to separate the file name from the preceding directory name. The full path name thus describes to DOS where to direct its search for the file.

Understanding Where the Search Starts

When you type a path name, DOS searches in the first specified directory and passes through any other specified directory branches until DOS reaches the file. All directories grow from the root directory, which has no name but is represented

An
Overview of
DOS

Booting the
Computer

Issuing DOS
Commands

Preparing
Disks

**Hierarchical
Directories**

Copying,
Renaming,
and
Deleting
Files

Protecting
Data

Special
Commands
and Files

by a backslash. If you want the search path to start at the root directory, begin the directory specification with a backslash. (That is why a backslash followed the drive name in the two preceding symbolic notations.) DOS will begin its search in the root directory and follow the specified subdirectory chain until the file is found.

Organizing Hierarchical Directories

Although you may not know what kind of directory organization you need, now is a good time to give some thought to establishing your directory tree. If your computer is part of a network, check with the network administrator before you make any changes.

The Root Directory

DOS creates the root directory for you, but you control which files to include in the root. The root is the top directory in the inverted tree, and therefore, you should avoid cluttering the root directory with files. Because the root is the default directory for DOS when you boot your system, you should include COMMAND.COM. in the root directory. DOS expects to find COMMAND.COM in the current directory when you boot. If DOS cannot load COMMAND.COM, DOS cannot communicate with you. DOS only manages to warn you that it cannot find the command interpreter.

In addition to COMMAND.COM, the root directory will likely contain the AUTOEXEC.BAT and CONFIG.SYS files. You will learn about these files in Chapter 9. The AUTOEXEC.BAT file usually contains the PATH command that sets the search paths automatically. The root also contains the primary subdirectories for your computer. If your disk has no subdirectories, you will add the first one to the root directory.

The following diagram shows the structure of a simple directory system. The structure consists of six subdirectories, each a subdirectory of the root directory. Note that subdirectories have been created for DOS as well as several applications programs. The text that follows explains this directory structure.

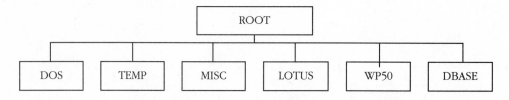

An Overview of DOS

Booting the Computer

Issuing DOS Commands

Preparing Disks

Hierarchical Directories

Copying, Renaming, and Deleting Files

Protecting Data

Special Commands and Files

The \DOS Directory

You should create a \DOS directory and include it in your PATH command. All the utility files from your original DOS disks should be copied into this directory. You will then have all of your DOS functions grouped into one directory.

A \TEMP Directory

Many users find they need a directory to store temporary files. You might find a directory named \TEMP useful. You can copy files to \TEMP as a temporary storage place until you copy the files to a more appropriate directory. A \TEMP directory is also useful for making copies of diskettes in a single diskette, low-memory system.

A \MISC or \KEEP Directory

You may have files in different directories that are no longer active, but that you feel you may still need. Inactive files in a directory tend to increase clutter and make sorting through the directory confusing. With a \MISC or a \KEEP directory, you can have an easy-to-remember home for those inactive files. Of course, you should delete only those files that are obviously of no more use to you.

Applications Software Directories

Many applications programs create directories when you install them on your hard disk. For example, Lotus 1-2-3 Release 3 creates the default main directory "123R3"; WordPerfect 5.0 supplies "WP50" as the default directory; and dBASE IV uses "DBASE." Many of these let you supply your own subdirectory names during installation.

Using Hierarchical Directory Commands

So far, this chapter has provided information on the structure of hierarchical directories and the use of path names. Now you will learn DOS commands for making, changing, and removing directories within a hierarchical structure. These directory commands consist of the command name and parameters. You can use these commands to customize your file system and navigate through it.

Making a Directory (MKDIR or MD)

To add a directory to your disk, use the MKDIR command. MKDIR means MaKe DIRectory. This command name has an abbreviated form, which is MD. You can use either the full command name or the short form: the two are interchangeable. Decide on a name for your proposed new directory and use the MKDIR command with the following symbolic notation at the DOS prompt:

MKDIR *directory specifier*

Directory specifier is the directory path name, with subdirectories separated by a backslash. The new directory is to be created on the logged drive by default. If you omit the leading backslash in your path, the new directory will be added below your current directory. For example, assume that drive C is the logged drive. You want to add a directory called TEMP to hold files temporarily. At the DOS prompt, enter

MKDIR \TEMP

Press the Enter key. (Although you do not need to press the space bar after typing **MKDIR**, putting a space between the command and its parameters makes it easier to identify all the elements in the command line.) DOS then creates the TEMP directory directly under the root directory (\). You can use the DIR command to verify that the TEMP directory exists.

Changing to a Different Directory (CHDIR or CD)

Use the CHDIR, or CD, command to change to another directory or to display the path name of the current directory. Like MD, CD is an optional alternative to the full command name. The CHDIR command changes your position in the tree structure of directories. Decide which subdirectory you want as a working directory. Issue at the DOS prompt the command in the abbreviated form

CD *directory specifier*

Directory specifier is the path name of the directory to which you want to change. Notice that the CD command has the same form as the MKDIR command. To change to the TEMP directory of the preceding example, enter the command

CD \TEMP

To confirm that DOS has changed your working directory to \TEMP, just issue the CD command with no parameters. DOS will display the current directory's path name.

Understanding   Understanding Paths   Organizing   **Using Hierarchical**
Hierarchical   in Hierarchical   Hierarchical   **Directory**
Directories   Directories   Directories   **Commands**   Summary

An
Overview of
DOS

Booting the
Computer

Issuing DOS
Commands

Preparing
Disks

**Hierarchical
Directories**

Copying,
Renaming,
and
Deleting
Files

Protecting
Data

Special
Commands
and Files

CD is thus an important command for DOS beginners. You can use CD to change to a directory from which you want information. Remember that when you are positioned in the directory which holds the commands or data you need to use, you can omit the directory name from the command line. When you issue the CD command, the directory to which you change becomes the default directory.

The following screen shows the process of making and changing a directory and viewing its contents. The last line of the directory listing indicates the number of files in the directory. Note that TEMP is empty except for two files created by DOS. The period (.) is DOS's shorthand for the current directory. The double period (..) represents the parent of the current directory.

```
C>CD              Shows the current directory

C>C:\             Current directory is the root directory ( \ )

C>MKDIR \TEMP     Makes a new directory called TEMP

C>CD \TEMP        Changes the current directory to TEMP

C>DIR             Displays contents of the TEMP directory


Volume in drive C has no label
Volume Serial Number is 146E-3CA4
Directory of C:\TEMP
.         <DIR> 12-20-88   3:45p
..        <DIR> 12-20-88   3:45p
2 File(s)   3956736 bytes free
```

Making a Subdirectory of a Subdirectory

To create a subdirectory of a subdirectory from anywhere in the file system, you must use the MD command with the full path name of the new directory. For example, to create the MISC subdirectory below \TEMP you would use the command **MD \TEMP\MISC**.

If you make the \TEMP subdirectory the current directory, only the new directory name needs to be specified to create the MISC subdirectory below \TEMP, as indicated in the following screen. When you display a directory listing, MISC appears as a subdirectory of \TEMP.

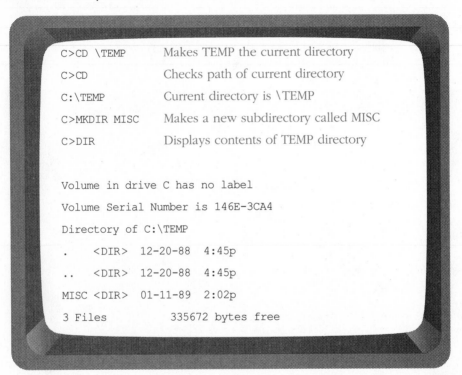

```
C>CD \TEMP          Makes TEMP the current directory

C>CD                Checks path of current directory

C:\TEMP             Current directory is \TEMP

C>MKDIR MISC        Makes a new subdirectory called MISC

C>DIR               Displays contents of TEMP directory


Volume in drive C has no label

Volume Serial Number is 146E-3CA4

Directory of C:\TEMP

.       <DIR>  12-20-88   4:45p

..      <DIR>  12-20-88   4:45p

MISC <DIR>  01-11-89   2:02p

3 Files           335672 bytes free
```

Removing (Deleting) a Directory (RMDIR or RD)

You use the RMDIR, or RD, command to remove a directory when you no longer need it. The RMDIR command and its abbreviated form, RD, work exactly alike. Before you remove a directory, the directory must be empty of all files and subdirectories. You cannot delete your current working directory. If you want to delete it, you must first change to another directory and delete all the files from the unwanted directory. For RMDIR to work, the directory to which you change must not contain as part of its path name the directory you want to delete.

An
Overview of
DOS

Booting the
Computer

Issuing DOS
Commands

Preparing
Disks

Hierarchical
Directories

Copying,
Renaming,
and
Deleting
Files

Protecting
Data

Special
Commands
and Files

To remove a directory from the logged drive, you issue at the DOS prompt the RMDIR command in the form

RMDIR *directory pathname*

To delete the TEMP directory used in the examples, you issue the command as

RMDIR \TEMP

The reason for the backslash is that the TEMP directory was created as a subdirectory of the root directory.

The usual reason you get error messages when you use hierarchical directory commands such as RMDIR is that you are not where you think you are in the hierarchical directory structure. Get into the habit of using the CD command to verify your location in the directory structure.

Specifying a Path (PATH)

If the file for the command you want DOS to execute is not in the current directory, you must give DOS the correct *path*. The PATH command instructs DOS to search through a specified set of directories for files with .BAT, .COM, and .EXE extensions. DOS searches this path if the selected batch, command, or executable file can't be found in the current directory. Most often, you will use the PATH command to find an external DOS command. COMMAND.COM also uses the PATH command to find and start programs that are not in the current directory.

DOS retains the PATH until you change the command or reboot the computer. If you include more than one directory path in the command, you must separate the paths with a semicolon (;). To issue the PATH command for the logged drive, at the DOS prompt type

PATH *d:path specifier;d:path specifier;. . .*

The drive specifier *d:* names the drive on which DOS is to search. The first *path specifier* is the first alternative search path. The semicolon (;) separates the first search path from the optional second path. The ellipsis (. . .) simply means that you can have other path specifiers in your command line.

If you have created a \DOS directory to store the DOS utility files, you can issue the following PATH command:

PATH C:\DOS

Once this command is issued, whenever you use an external DOS command in a directory other than \DOS, the PATH specification leads COMMAND.COM to the appropriate program or batch file in the \DOS directory.

Displaying the Hierarchical Directory and Files (TREE)

When you add many directories to your disk, you may lose track of the directory names and what files they contain. You can keep track of the organization of the directory with the TREE command.

You can use TREE to display all directory paths on the logged disk, and as an option, each directory's files. TREE works a bit differently depending on your version of DOS. In DOS V4.0, to list all directories and their files, starting with the root directory, you issue the TREE command at the DOS prompt in this form:

TREE \/F

Note that a space is necessary before the backslash, which specifies that the listing should begin with the root directory. The optional **/F** switch, before which no space is necessary, tells DOS to list the file names in the listing of directories.

For versions of DOS prior to V4.0, to list all directories and their files, starting with the root directory, you issue the TREE command at the DOS prompt in this form:

TREE /F

If the output information is too much for one screen, you can stop the scrolling with the Ctrl-S key sequence. You restart the scrolling by pressing any key. If you want to interrupt the listing of directories and their files, press Ctrl-C. If you want a printout of the results of the TREE command, see Chapter 9, which shows you how to redirect a command's output to your printer or to a file.

Summary

In this chapter, you were introduced to DOS's system of hierarchical directories. You saw how this system is like an inverted tree, with the root directory at the top and subdirectories, like branches, fanning out below the root directory. You learned about paths and path names and how both are important for searching for files in other locations of the tree.

An
Overview of
DOS

Booting the
Computer

Issuing DOS
Commands

Preparing
Disks

**Hierarchical
Directories**

Copying,
Renaming,
and
Deleting
Files

Protecting
Data

Special
Commands
and Files

The chapter showed you how to organize a hierarchical directory so that DOS files would be in one directory and files for an applications program would be in a separate directory. You became acquainted with the various directory commands: MKDIR (or MD) for making a directory, CHDIR (or CD) for changing to a different directory, and RMDIR (or RD) for removing a directory when it contains no files. The chapter also told you about the PATH command for specifying a path to files with .BAT, .COM, and .EXE extensions, and about the TREE command for viewing the organization of your hierarchical directory.

Now that you familiar with hierarchical directories, you are ready to learn about copying, renaming, and deleting files within a directory tree. File handling is the subject of Chapter 7.

Review Questions

1. What is the root directory? What are subdirectories?

2. What is the purpose of a hierarchical directory system? Why does it resemble an inverted tree structure?

3. What is the default directory?

4. Suppose that NOTES.TXT is a text file in the SCHOOL subdirectory under the WP50 subdirectory off the root. Write the complete path name that would enable DOS to find this file.

5. What is the directory specifier? What happens when you omit the directory specifier from the path name?

6. What special files are likely to be found in the root directory? Which ones *must* be located there?

7. What does the MKDIR command do?

8. What does the CHDIR command do? Describe various situations in which you would want to use CHDIR.

9. What does the RMDIR command do? Under what circumstances will RMDIR not work?

10. What doe the PATH command do? When does COMMAND.COM use the PATH command?

11. What does the TREE command do?

An
Overview of
DOS

Booting the
Computer

Issuing DOS
Commands

Preparing
Disks

Hierarchical
Directories

**Copying,
Renaming,
and
Deleting
Files**

Protecting
Data

Special
Commands
and Files

7 *Copying, Renaming, and Deleting Files*

Disk files are the primary storage place for data and programs. A knowledge of how to manage these files is essential. If you want to be in control of your work, you must be in control of your files. This chapter tells you how to use the DOS commands for copying diskettes and files, renaming existing files, and erasing unneeded files.

After completing this chapter, you should

- Be able to copy the contents of one diskette to another and compare the two
- Be able to copy a single file or groups of files from one diskette to another
- Know how to use COPY to optimize disk organization
- Be able to copy a file, giving the same or a different file name
- Know how to rename a file or erase files and groups of files

Key Terms in This Chapter

Source	The disk or file from which you are copying.
Destination	The disk or file to which you are copying.
Target	The same as destination.
Rule of currents	The condition that DOS will use the current drive, directory, or file name if a different drive, directory, or destination file name is not specified in the command line.
Fragmentation	The condition that results when a disk file is contained in sectors that are not contiguous because of adding and deleting files.
Current directory	The directory that DOS uses as the default directory. The root directory is the current directory on the logged drive until you use CHDIR (CD) to change to another directory.
Overwrite	Writing new information over old in a disk file.

Copying and Comparing Diskettes

The DISKCOPY command makes an exact copy of a diskette. DISKCOPY reads the input, or *source*, diskette and then writes the data to another diskette—the *destination* diskette. DISKCOPY is good to use when you want to make a working copy of a master diskette. You then can store the master diskette in a safe place. DISKCOPY also copies the system files from a bootable source diskette to make a bootable copy.

In this chapter, you learn a simple form of the DISKCOPY command. For basic use of the DISKCOPY command, your source and destination diskettes should be of the same size and capacity.

Using DISKCOPY To Copy Diskettes

DISKCOPY is an external command that you load from disk. You must have the disk that contains DISKCOPY in your default drive, or set the correct path with the PATH command (see Chapter 6). Use the DISKCOPY command to copy diskettes only. The correct syntax for DISKCOPY is

> **DISKCOPY** *source d: destination d:*

The *source d:* is the name of the drive that holds the diskette you want to copy. The *destination d:* is the name of the drive that holds the diskette to receive the copy. As always, type a colon after the drive name. Insert a space between the source and destination drive names. If you use a blank diskette as the destination diskette, DOS first formats it. An example of the command is

> **DISKCOPY A: B:**

After you issue the DISKCOPY command, DOS prompts you to put the diskettes into the proper drives. Make sure that you insert them into the correct drives. If drives or diskettes are not compatible, you will get an error message, and copying will not take place. If you write-protect the source diskette, you safeguard its contents in case of a mix-up. Press any key and copying begins. When copying is finished, DOS asks whether you want to make another copy. Answer **Y** or **N**. You can make another copy at this time. If you answer Y, you do not have to access DISKCOPY again, because DOS has the program in memory.

An Overview of DOS

Booting the Computer

Issuing DOS Commands

Preparing Disks

Hierarchical Directories

Copying, Renaming, and Deleting Files

Protecting Data

Special Commands and Files

```
A>DISKCOPY A: B:

Insert SOURCE diskette in drive A:

Insert TARGET diskette in drive B:

Press any key to continue . . .

Copying 40 tracks
9 Sectors/Track, 2 Side(s)

Copy another diskette (Y/N)? N

A>
```

The common syntax for DISKCOPY is DISKCOPY A: B:. DOS prompts you to insert the diskettes before copying begins.

If you leave out the drive names in the DISKCOPY command line, DOS uses the default drive as the specifier. To avoid confusion, always give both the source and destination drive names.

If the DISKCOPY command is issued with no drive parameters, DOS will copy using just one drive. DOS will prompt you to switch alternately between inserting the source and destination diskettes. Depending on your system's memory, you will swap diskettes once or several times. Make sure you don't get the diskettes confused during swapping.

Using DISKCOMP To Compare Diskettes

By using the external DISKCOMP command, you can confirm that two diskettes are identical. Normally, you use DISKCOMP to test diskettes that were made from originals by the DISKCOPY command. DISKCOMP compares diskettes sector by sector. Remember that the diskettes and their capacities must be the same for both diskettes in the comparison. Any difference in diskettes made with DISKCOPY is a sign of a problem diskette. Issue the command in the form

> **DISKCOMP** *source d: destination d:*

Notice that the syntax for DISKCOMP is like the syntax for DISKCOPY. Load the two diskettes at the prompt, and DOS will confirm the comparison or point out the differences. If the diskettes compare, DOS gives the message Compare OK. As with DISKCOPY, you can repeat the DISKCOMP command. An example of the DISKCOMP command is

> **DISKCOMP A: B:**

Again, if you omit a drive designator, DOS uses the default drive.

If the DISKCOMP command is issued with no drive parameters, DOS will carry out the comparison using just one drive. DOS will alternately prompt you to switch between inserting the first and second diskettes. Depending on your system's memory, you will swap diskettes once or several times. Make sure that you don't get the diskettes confused during swapping.

Copying Files with COPY

The internal COPY command is a DOS workhorse. DISKCOPY works with diskettes; COPY works with files. Because COPY is an internal command, you can issue the command anytime at the DOS prompt. You can use COPY to move files between disks of different sizes and capacities and to give new names to the destination files.

Understanding the COPY Command

COPY is a versatile command that allows wild cards in the syntax. To learn every use of the COPY command would be a large task. In this book, you learn just those features of the COPY command you are likely to use in daily computing.

The symbolic syntax of the copy command is

> **COPY** *sd:\path\filename.ext dd:\path\filename.ext/V*

The *sd:* is the source file's drive name, and *dd:* is the destination file's drive name. The *\path\filename.ext* is the full path name for the file in the directory tree structure. The */V* is an optional switch that tells DOS to verify that the copy is correct. A delimiting space separates the source and destination parts of the command. An example of the full COPY command is

> **COPY C:\MISC\MYFILE.MEM A:\KEEP\MYFILE.KEP/V**

MYFILE.MEM is a file located on drive C in the \MISC directory and is copied to a new file named MYFILE.KEP in the \KEEP directory on drive A. Because of defaults in this example, you might omit some of the items of syntax without disturbing the copying process.

In the following illustration, the full copy command gives DOS all the parameters needed to locate and copy a file from the directory tree of the source drive to the directory and file name of the destination. The /V at the end of the command is a

Copying and
Comparing
Disketts

**Copying Files
with COPY**

Renaming and
Erasing Files

Summary

An
Overview of
DOS

Booting the
Computer

ᴵssuing DOS
Commands

Preparing
Disks

Hierarchical
Directories

**Copying,
Renaming,
and
Deleting
Files**

Protecting
Data

Special
Commands
and Files

switch that tells DOS to verify the copied file after the copy is made. The full
version of COPY does not rely on DOS's current default drive or directory.

Command as issued:

```
COPY C:\MISC\MYFILE.MEM A:\KEEP\MYFILE.KEP/V
```

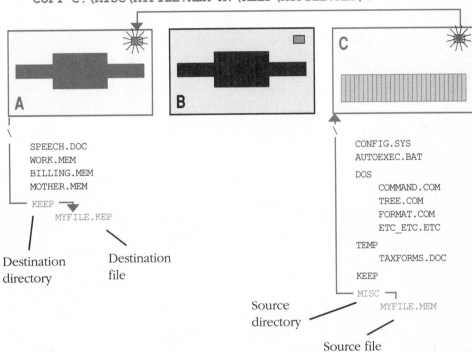

You learned about default values in earlier chapters, but you also need to
understand how DOS handles defaults with the COPY command. The *rule of
currents* states that if you do not specify one of the drives in the COPY command,
DOS will use the current (default or logged) drive. If you do not specify a path in
the command, DOS will use the current directory of the disk in question. If you do
not specify a destination file name, the copied file keeps the current file name of
the source file. You will see how the rule of currents applies to COPY in later
examples.

If you give a disk drive and path for the source file, but omit the file name, DOS
assumes that you want to copy *all* files in the directory. This assumption is
equivalent to using the wild card *.* as the file specifier for the source file.

COPY can be a dangerous command because it overwrites on the destination disk any file whose name is the same as that of a file on the source disk. If you are uncertain about COPY syntax, you can write-protect your source disk if it is a diskette. Keep the rule of currents in mind, and you can customize the examples to do almost any file-copying task.

Copying All Files in a Directory

As you add and delete files from a disk, the free space for new file information becomes physically spread around the surface of the disk. This phenomenon is called *fragmentation*. DOS allocates data storage space by finding the next available disk space. If the next available space is too small to hold an entire file, DOS uses all of that space and puts the rest of the file into the next available space(s). Fragmented files lower disk performance.

If you use DISKCOPY on a fragmented diskette, you get an exact image of the fragmented disk. To avoid copying fragmentation, or to make an efficient copy of a fragmented diskette, use the COPY command. First, format the destination diskette and make sure that the diskette contains enough room to hold all of the source files. Then copy the source files to the destination diskette with no fragmentation. To do so, place the source diskette in drive A and the destination diskette in drive B and type

> **COPY A:*.* B:**

In this example, you copied all of the files on the diskette in drive A to the diskette in drive B, keeping the same file names. (Remember the rule of currents.) By changing to a directory on your hard disk, you can copy all of the files of the last example to that directory by using C: in place of B:. If you want the destination diskette to be bootable, first format it with the /S switch. You cannot, however, use the COPY command to copy DOS's hidden system files.

Copying Files from Diskette to Diskette

You can copy one file or many files to another diskette for safe keeping, to move data to another computer, or for any other purpose. Simply use the COPY command with a file name or a wild card that matches the file(s) you want to move to the other diskette. Put the diskette with the source file(s) in drive A. Put the destination diskette in drive B. Type **DIR A:** to see and calculate the size of the file(s) you want to copy. Then type **DIR B:** to see if the destination diskette contains sufficient free space. If the space is adequate, enter the COPY command. An example is

> **COPY A:*.MEM B:/V**

Copying and
Comparing
Diskettes

**Copying Files
with COPY**

Renaming and
Erasing Files

Summary

An
Overview of
DOS

Booting the
Computer

Issuing DOS
Commands

Preparing
Disks

Hierarchical
Directories

**Copying,
Renaming,
and
Deleting
Files**

Protecting
Data

Special
Commands
and Files

In this command, DOS copies all files with the extension MEM to the diskette in drive B and verifies the copy. The destination file name was omitted. DOS accepts the original names by default unless you tell it otherwise. You can omit the name of your logged drive from this example, but to be on the safe side, you should include it.

In the following illustration, COPY is used to copy multiple files from diskette to diskette. In this case, the working current directory of both the diskette in drive A and that in drive B is \ (the root directory). Since both root directories are current on their respective diskettes, DOS knows the path specifier, and you may omit it in both the source and destination. The source filename *.MEM tells DOS to copy any file from the source directory that matches the MEM extension. Since the destination file name and extension are omitted, DOS uses the file names of the source files for the copy.

Command as issued:

```
COPY A:*.MEM B:
```

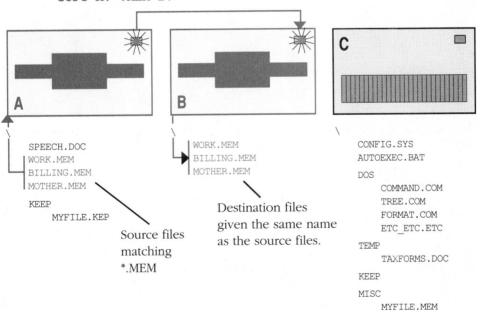

```
A                          B                          C

SPEECH.DOC                 WORK.MEM                   CONFIG.SYS
WORK.MEM                   BILLING.MEM                AUTOEXEC.BAT
BILLING.MEM                MOTHER.MEM
MOTHER.MEM                                            DOS
                                                         COMMAND.COM
KEEP                                                      TREE.COM
    MYFILE.KEP                                            FORMAT.COM
                           Destination files             ETC_ETC.ETC
          Source files     given the same name
          matching         as the source files.      TEMP
          *.MEM                                          TAXFORMS.DOC

                                                      KEEP

                                                      MISC
                                                         MYFILE.MEM
```

To copy one file from the source diskette to a different destination diskette, you might enter

COPY A:SPEECH.DOC B:/V

91

This command copies the SPEECH.DOC file from the diskette in drive A to another in drive B. Again, the name remains the same.

If you have a hard disk, you can use a command like this:

COPY A:SPEECH.DOC C:/V

This command line copies the SPEECH.DOC file from the diskette in drive A to the current directory of the hard disk. Similarly, you can copy from your current hard disk directory to a diskette:

COPY SPEECH.DOC A:

DOS finds the SPEECH.DOC file in the current directory of the logged C drive and copies it with the same name to the diskette in drive A.

Copying Files to the Same Directory

You often may want to place a duplicate copy of a file on the same disk. (For this example, you can assume that diskettes have only a root directory.) You cannot have duplicate file names and extensions in one directory. You also cannot copy a file onto itself. To copy the file into the same directory, you must give the file another name, another extension, or both. Most people give the file a different extension and keep the file name the same.

To duplicate a file and place it in the same directory, you must enter a source file name and a destination file name in the command line. Change to the drive and directory of the file you want to duplicate and type:

COPY SPEECH.DOC SPEECH.BAK

This example uses the rule of currents. Because a drive is not specified, DOS uses the default drive. You now have a duplicate copy of SPEECH.DOC, named SPEECH.BAK. By using the BAK extension, you can recognize the new file as a backup of the original file. You also might give the destination file a completely new name. In this example, you can list both files with the command

DIR SPEECH.*.

Copying Files across Directories

If you have a hard disk, you need a method of copying files from one directory to another. For this use of COPY, assume that you are in the directory that contains the

Copying and
Comparing
Diskettes

**Copying Files
with COPY**

Renaming and
Erasing Files

Summary

An
Overview of
DOS

Booting the
Computer

Issuing DOS
Commands

Preparing
Disks

Hierarchical
Directories

**Copying,
Renaming,
and
Deleting
Files**

Protecting
Data

Special
Commands
and Files

source file(s) and that you have created the destination directory. Although this discussion of COPY can apply to diskettes with subdirectories, users of hard disks are the ones most likely encounter this situation.

In the following illustration of COPY, a file is copied from one directory to another on the same disk. The current drive is C, and the current directory is \KEEP. Since C:\KEEP is the current drive and directory, it is omitted from the source parameters. Only the destination directory is given in the destination part of the COPY command, since C: is current and the destination file name and extension are to match the source. DOS allows duplicate file names on the same disk as long as they are in different directories.

Command as issued:

```
COPY SPEECH.DOC \MISC
```

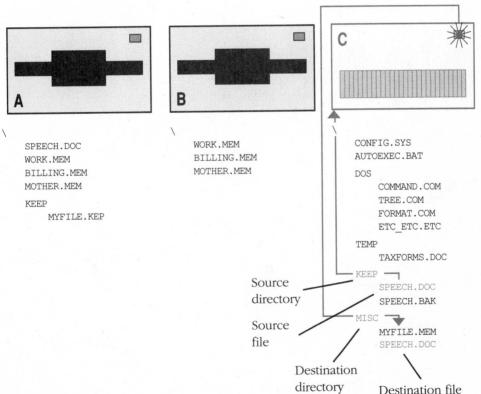

\
    SPEECH.DOC
    WORK.MEM
    BILLING.MEM
    MOTHER.MEM
    KEEP
        MYFILE.KEP

\
    WORK.MEM
    BILLING.MEM
    MOTHER.MEM

\
    CONFIG.SYS
    AUTOEXEC.BAT
    DOS
        COMMAND.COM
        TREE.COM
        FORMAT.COM
        ETC_ETC.ETC
    TEMP
        TAXFORMS.DOC
    KEEP
        SPEECH.DOC
        SPEECH.BAK
    MISC
        MYFILE.MEM
        SPEECH.DOC

Source
directory

Source
file

Destination
directory

Destination file

93

When you copy files between subdirectories, the DOS CD command is useful. Using CD with a directory name changes the default directory. Remember that you can verify your location by using the CD command with no parameters. Use CD to change the current directory to the source file's directory. You can then take advantage of the rule of currents by omitting the source file's drive and path names in the command.

Renaming and Erasing Files

Two additional procedures often used with copying are renaming and erasing files. You rename a file to improve the name or to make a backup file. You erase an old file you no longer want to keep. Renaming is a constructive procedure, for its main purpose is to conserve files. Although erasing may seem to be only a destructive task, it can increase the amount of valuable memory space on diskettes and hard disks.

Renaming Files (RENAME or REN)

You can use RENAME to choose a better name for a file or to make a backup file. If you use a program that overwrites a file each time the program runs, you can retain the last version of the file by renaming it before you run the program again. You can then have both the original file and a copy having a new name.

When you name a file, the name you choose is not permanent. You can use the RENAME (abbreviated REN) command to rename a file. The commands work exactly alike, but RENAME is probably easier to remember.

You can use RENAME to change the file name, the extension, or both. DOS assumes that a * wild card in the destination file name or extension means "use the original." Using wild cards in the source file name or extension can have unexpected results in the renaming process. Use the DIR command with the proposed wild card to see which files will be affected. Again, change to the disk and directory of the file(s) so that you can take advantage of DOS's defaults. You would issue a command like this:

RENAME SPEECH.BAK SPEECH.DOC

Copying and
Comparing
Diskettes

Copying Files
with COPY

**Renaming and
Erasing Files**

Summary

An
Overview of
DOS

Booting the
Computer

Issuing DOS
Commands

Preparing
Disks

Hierarchical
Directories

**Copying,
Renaming,
and
Deleting
Files**

Protecting
Data

Special
Commands
and Files

Remember that you cannot duplicate a file name in the directory. If a name conflict arises, rename or erase the file with the conflicting name and then issue the RENAME command.

Erasing Files (ERASE or DEL)

When you no longer need a file, you can use the ERASE or DEL command to remove the file from the disk. The internal commands ERASE or DEL work exactly alike. Both commands delete files. You may find ERASE easier to remember, but DEL is quicker to type. Erasing files can be hazardous if you don't make sure you issue the command correctly. Use extreme caution when you use wild cards with the ERASE command! DOS carries out the ERASE command when you press Enter. If you make a mistake, pressing Ctrl-C or Ctrl-Break may stop the ERASE command in time to minimize the damage to your files.

The safest way to use the ERASE command is to change to the drive and directory that holds the file(s) you want to delete. You can use wild cards in the file name, but first check the file directory for other file names that match the wild card. You may not want to delete all files that match the wild card. With the current drive and directory as default type

     ERASE SPEECH.DOC

or

     DEL SPEECH.DOC

If you use wild cards in the command, you can erase several files at one time. DOS issues an `Are you sure?` confirmation prompt if you use the wild card `*.*`. In all other cases, DOS is silent while deleting files. Caution: if you omit the file name specifier, but include a path specifier, DOS assumes that you want to use the `*.*` wild card.

Use extreme caution when you erase files. Be even more cautious when you use wild cards to erase files. The following illustration demonstrates the correct use of wild cards to erase three files with the same extension.

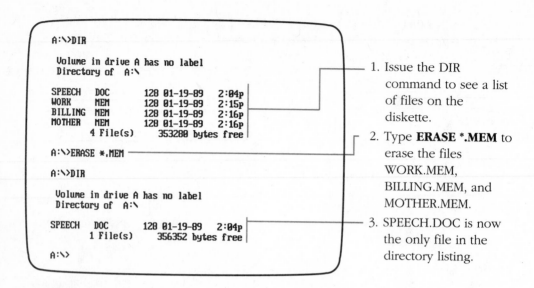

```
A:\>DIR

Volume in drive A has no label
Directory of  A:\

SPEECH   DOC      128 01-19-89   2:04p
WORK     MEM      128 01-19-89   2:15p
BILLING  MEM      128 01-19-89   2:16p
MOTHER   MEM      128 01-19-89   2:16p
     4 File(s)        353280 bytes free

A:\>ERASE *.MEM

A:\>DIR

Volume in drive A has no label
Directory of  A:\

SPEECH   DOC      128 01-19-89   2:04p
     1 File(s)        356352 bytes free

A:\>
```

1. Issue the DIR command to see a list of files on the diskette.

2. Type **ERASE *.MEM** to erase the files WORK.MEM, BILLING.MEM, and MOTHER.MEM.

3. SPEECH.DOC is now the only file in the directory listing.

Summary

This chapter has shown you how to copy, rename, and delete files. The DISKCOPY command copies the entire contents of a source diskette to a destination diskette, formatting the destination disk if it is unformatted. The DISKCOMP command compares two diskettes of equal size and capacity in order to show whether they are identical.

Whereas the DISKCOPY command is for copying diskettes, the COPY command is for copying files. You can copy just one file or as many as all the files in a directory. You copy one file by simply naming it. By using different combinations of matching characters and wild cards, you can use COPY to copy files having different root names but the same extension, the same root name but different extensions, or similar root names and extensions.

You also have considerable control over *where* files are copied. You can copy a file from from one diskette to another, from a diskette to a hard disk, from a hard disk to a diskette, within the same directory by assigning a new name to the destination file, or from one subdirectory to another on the same or different drives.

Copying and
Comparing
Diskettes

Copying Files
with COPY

Renaming and
Erasing Files

Summary

An
Overview of
DOS

Booting the
Computer

Issuing DOS
Commands

Preparing
Disks

Hierarchical
Directories

**Copying,
Renaming,
and
Deleting
Files**

Protecting
Data

Special
Commands
and Files

You learned about two other useful commands: RENAME (or REN) and ERASE (or DEL) for renaming and deleting files, respectively. RENAME is useful for protecting a file so that it won't be overwritten by a COPY command. ERASE is for deleting obsolete files and increasing disk space.

There are ways to protect your information from inadvertent loss. The protection of data is the subject of the next chapter.

Review Questions

1. What does the DISKCOPY command do?

2. What does the DISKCOMP command do?

3. What does the COPY command do? Is COPY an internal or external DOS command?

4. What is the *rule of currents* and how does it apply to the COPY command?

5. Suppose that you have a number of files with a TXT extension on a floppy in drive A. You want to copy all of them to a floppy in drive B, and you want to have DOS verify the copy. Assuming that the logged drive is C:, describe the correct command for this operation.

6. What is file fragmentation and how does it affect disk performance?

7. Suppose that the logged (current) directory is drive A. You want to copy NOTES.TXT in subdirectory \WP50 on drive C to a floppy disk in drive B. What command line would you enter to do this?

8. What does the RENAME command do? When would you want to use this command?

9. What do the ERASE and DEL commands do? What cautions should you observe when using these commands?

8 *Protecting Data*

As you use your computer, you will create a multitude of files. Many of these will contain information you find very important. The best protection you can have is a full backup of your disk files. Although DISKCOPY and COPY are adequate for making "safety" copies of diskettes, hard disk files are often too big to fit on a diskette. And yet, just one errant wild-card ERASE command can delete dozens of files from a hard disk in seconds. What can you do for insurance against the loss of hours of work? You can use the DOS BACKUP command to make regular backup diskettes of your files. Of course, you also should know how to use the complement to BACKUP: the RESTORE command. It takes your backup diskettes and places their files back onto your hard disk.

In this chapter, you learn the basics of the BACKUP and RESTORE commands for backing up and restoring an entire hard disk. You learn also about the various switches of these two commands. Together, BACKUP and RESTORE are effective insurance against the loss of important files.

After reading this chapter, you should be able to

- Explain how to prevent hardware and software failure
- Back up files for protection
- Restore backed-up files for further use

Key Terms in This Chapter

Surge protector   A protective device inserted between a power outlet and a computer's power plug. Surge protectors block power surges that could damage the computer's circuits.

Static electricity   An electrical charge that builds on an object and discharges when another object is touched. With high voltages, static electricity can damage sensitive electronic components.

| Ground | The center receptacle of an outlet for three-pronged plugs leads to an AC (electrical) ground in house wiring. Grounds can safely dissipate static electricity discharges. |
| *Voltage regulator* | An electrical device that stabilizes fluctuations in voltage before it reaches an electrical device. Regulators usually don't stop power surges. |

Avoiding Data Loss

Today's personal computers are reliable and economical data processing machines. The PCs of today do the work of computers of a decade ago. Like any machine, however, computers are subject to failures and operator errors. Nevertheless, you can take certain measures to avoid the loss of data. The sections that follow explore various precautions for avoiding hardware and software problems and mistakes in general.

Preventing Hardware Failures

Always be cautious about your computer's environment. If your power flutters and lights flicker, you might need to purchase a line voltage regulator from your computer dealer. Make sure that any electrical appliances you have near your computer do not pollute your power source.

Is the fan on the back of your computer choked with dust? Clean the air vents and make certain that your computer has room to breathe. Your computer can do unexpected things when it is too hot. Because circuits are not reliable when they overheat, you may get jumbled data.

You generate *static electricity* on your body when you wear synthetic fabrics or walk on carpet—especially when the humidity is low. Just by touching a keyboard while you carry a static charge, you can give your computer a damaging jolt. This can jumble the data or cause circuit failure. Fortunately, you can avoid static problems by touching your grounded system cabinet before touching the keyboard. If static electricity is a serious problem for you, ask your dealer about antistatic liquid for rugs or carpets, or antistatic floor mats.

Preventing Software Failures

Each software program you buy is a set of instructions for the microprocessor. A small number of software packages sometimes have flawed instructions called *bugs*.

They usually are minor and rarely cause more than locked keyboards or chaotic displays. A software bug, however, can cause a disk drive to operate in an erratic way and thus damage or lose files. Fortunately, most companies test and debug their software before marketing their packages. To protect your files against any uncorrected or undetected bugs, back up your files regularly.

Handle your 5 1/4- or 3 1/2-inch diskettes with care. Don't expose them to extremes of temperature, moisture, or magnetic fields. Because a 5 1/4-inch diskette is more vulnerable to abuse than a 3 1/2-inch diskette, be careful not to touch the diskette's magnetic surface, don't bend the diskette, and keep it in its protective sleeve when not in use.

Preparing for a Backup

The BACKUP command selectively copies files from your hard disk to the destination diskette. The internal format of the backed up file on the diskette is different from the format of normal files. Therefore, you cannot use COPY to retrieve files stored on a backup disk. The RESTORE command takes the files from your backup disks and copies them on your hard disk.

Your computer may have a tape backup unit as part of its peripheral hardware. The methods used for backing up files to tape vary. You should know how to do disk-based backups, however, in case you need to restore files to a computer that is not equipped with a tape backup.

You can use the BACKUP command to back up an entire fixed disk with one command. You also can use switches and parameters to make partial backups of the disk, backing up selected files only. You can select files by time, date, directory, activity, and file name.

A full backup makes backup copies of all files on the hard disk. BACKUP even copies hidden files. When you perform a full backup, you have the complete contents of your fixed disk on backup diskettes.

Preparing Backup Diskettes

Before you do a complete backup, make sure that you have enough diskettes to hold all the files. You don't want to run out to the computer store in the middle of a backup to buy more diskettes!

DOS versions 3.3 and 4.0 are more efficient than older versions in using backup space. You can rely on some rules of thumb when you calculate the space you need for an entire backup.

To get an idea of how full your hard disk is, change to drive C. Type **C:CD ** and press Enter. You then can issue the DIR command. Take the number of free bytes the directory displays and divide the number by 1,000,000. The remainder gives you a ballpark figure of the number of megabytes left on the disk. Subtract the number of megabytes from the disk's total capacity. You now have the approximate number of megabytes that you need to perform the backup. When you know the approximate number of megabytes, you can use table 8.1 to estimate the number of diskettes you will need. If you run out of diskettes, you can stop the backup by pressing Ctrl-C. The worst consequence is your lost time.

Table 8.1
Determining the Number of Diskettes Needed for a Backup

Megabytes Used	Diskette Capacity			
	360K	720K	1.2M	1.44M
10M	29	15	9	8
20M	59	29	18	15
30M	83	44	27	22
40M	116	58	35	29
70M	200	100	60	50

Format the diskettes and number them consecutively. BACKUP copies diskettes in sequence so that the RESTORE command can replace the files on your hard disk in the same sequence. When you finish the backup, arrange the diskettes numerically. Place them in a convenient part of your work space where they will stay in sequence.

If you have DOS V3.3, you can skip the formatting step. Simply include a /F (format) switch when you issue the BACKUP command. DOS V4.0 detects unformatted diskettes and formats them. Note that the BACKUP command itself will take longer to execute when BACKUP takes care of the formatting for you.

Using BACKUP and RESTORE

Your computer can use the files produced by BACKUP only after you run them through the RESTORE program. BACKUP is an external command; therefore you should include in the command line the path to the BACKUP command. Or the current directory should be the directory where the BACKUP command resides.

Understanding BACKUP Syntax

The symbolic syntax for BACKUP is

> **BACKUP** *sd:spath\sfilename.ext dd: /switches*

The *sd:* is the letter of the drive that contains the source disk. This drive is usually the C drive. The *spath* symbolizes the path to the files you want to make backups of. The *sfilename.ext* notation is the full file name of the file(s) you want to back up. Full file names may contain wild cards for selective backup of matching files. The *dd:* is the drive that receives the backup files. The */switches* are optional switches that modify the basic BACKUP command. Not all switches are available on all versions of DOS. The DOS defaults also may vary from version to version. You can use the examples in this chapter as a model for your commands. Besides the /S switch, you can use a number of other switches with BACKUP, as shown in table 8.2

Table 8.2
BACKUP Switches

/M	Selects files whose contents have changed since the last backup with the BACKUP command.
/D	Selects files based on the date.
/T	Selects files based on the time (V3.3 and 4.0).
/A	Adds files to an existing backup diskette series and leaves the existing backup files intact.
/F	Formats the destination diskette as part of the BACKUP procedure in V3.3. V4.0 automatically formats the diskette if needed.

An
Overview of
DOS

Booting the
Computer

Issuing DOS
Commands

Preparing
Disks

Hierarchical
Directories

Copying,
Renaming,
and
Deleting
Files

**Protecting
Data**

Special
Commands
and Files

Backing Up All Files

The full backup puts all files on your backup diskettes. The full backup requires about one minute for each diskette to be used in the backup.

Change to the root directory and enter the command

BACKUP C:*.* A:/S

This command tells DOS to back up all files from the root directory and to include all subdirectories (/S switch) in the directory tree to drive A. DOS prompts you when to insert and change diskettes. Always put the backup date on the diskettes for future reference. Put the backup diskettes in the proper sequence and store them in a safe place.

Backing Up Selected Files

By specifying source directory paths, wild-card file names or extensions, and switches, you can back up selected files. Selective backups are useful when you have changed only some of your data between full backups, or when you want to move specific files from one computer system to another.

Specifying Directory and File Names

BACKUP always starts in the directory you place in the path. If you place a directory name in the path that is at some point in the tree other than root, you can use /S to back up files in that directory and in its subdirectories. You can add further selectivity by using wild cards in the file name. For example, placing *.DOC in the file name would give you a backup of files with the extension DOC.

Understanding RESTORE Syntax

The companion command to BACKUP is the external command RESTORE. It is the only command that copies backed-up files to the hard disk. RESTORE's syntax is very similar to BACKUP's syntax. Seen symbolically, the syntax is

RESTORE *sd: dd:\dpath\dfilename.ext /switches*

In this command line, *sd:* is the source drive letter that holds the diskettes you want to restore, and *dd:* is the hard disk drive (usually C drive) to which you want to restore the diskettes. In the command, *dpath* is the hard disk directory that will receive the restored files. If a backup diskette has any files that did not come from the *dpath*, they will not be restored. The next part of the command line, *dfilename.ext*, is the file name for the file(s) to be restored. You can use wild cards in the file name to select specific files. Finally, */switches* stands for the optional switches you can add for even more selectivity in using the RESTORE command (see table 8.3).

Table 8.3
RESTORE Switches

/S	Includes files from subdirectories below the specified directory.
/P	Prompts the user if the file should be restored if it has been marked as read only or has been changed since the last backup.
/N	Only files that are no longer on the hard disk. This switch is useful if hard disk files were deleted accidentally and need restoring from backups (new in DOS 3.3).
/M	Does the same as /N but also restores files that have changed since the backup (new in DOS 3.3).
/B:date	Restores all files created or modified on or before the date.
/A:date	Restores all files created or modified on or after the specified date. This switch uses the DATE command format (DOS 3.3).
/E:time	Restores all files modified at or earlier than the specified time. This switch uses the TIME command format (DOS 3.3).
/L:time	Restores all files modified at or later than the specified time.

Restoring One File

You can choose to restore a single file by using a complete path and file name in the command. As in all selective restoring, DOS prompts you to insert sequential diskettes until it locates the specified file. Suppose that you want to restore the file \KEEP\SPEECH.DOC from a backup disk. The proper syntax is

    RESTORE A: C:\KEEP\SPEECH.DOC

An
Overview of
DOS

Booting the
Computer

Issuing DOS
Commands

Preparing
Disks

Hierarchical
Directories

Copying,
Renaming,
and
Deleting
Files

**Protecting
Data**

Special
Commands
and Files

Restoring More Than One File

You can choose to restore more than one file. For example, suppose that you want to restore all files with a TXT extension to the \KEEP directory. The command to type is

RESTORE A: C:\KEEP*.TXT

The wild card *.TXT selects all files with the TXT extension from the KEEP directory.

If you want to restore all files in a directory *and* all subdirectories below the directory, use the **/S** switch. The command **RESTORE A: C:\KEEP*.*/S** would restore all files in directories subordinate to the \KEEP directory. For example, MOMS.LET in the subdirectory LETTERS would be restored to the KEEP directory.

Avoiding DOS Version Conflicts

Starting with version 3.3, DOS uses a different method to produce the contents of a backup disk. DOS versions 3.3 and greater can restore files that you backed up with previous versions of DOS. Versions earlier than 3.3, however, cannot restore backups made with versions 3.3 or 4.0. Also realize that if you restore all files from a full backup to a computer with a different version of DOS, the hidden system files and utility command programs will be those taken from the backup files. Finally, the RESTORE program from another MS-DOS vendor may simply not work.

Summary

In this chapter, you learned how to avoid the loss of data by preventing hardware and software failures. Care about the computer's physical environment, static electricity, and correct responses to important prompts can minimize unnecessary loss of important information.

You learned also how to use the BACKUP command and diskettes to back up information on a hard disk. You can perform a complete backup of all the files in all the directories, or you can back up selected files. You became acquainted with the companion RESTORE command, which copies one or more backed-up files from diskettes to the hard disk.

An
Overview of
DOS

Booting the
Computer

Issuing DOS
Commands

Preparing
Disks

Hierarchical
Directories

Copying,
Renaming,
and
Deleting
Files

**Protecting
Data**

Special
Commands
and Files

Finally, you were alerted to possible conflicts between versions of DOS. You cannot use an early version of DOS to restore files backed up with version 3.3 or later. If you restore hidden system files of one version of DOS to a computer using another version, you may find other incompatibilities.

DOS has a number of special commands and files that can make your use of DOS simpler. These are the subject of the next chapter.

Review Questions

1. What are the steps you can take to prevent power surges, voltage fluctuations, or static electricity from damaging your computer or causing the loss of important data?

2. What are the basic guidelines for caring properly for your diskettes?

3. Name some of the reasons why routinely backing up your files is important.

4. What does the BACKUP command do? What should you do before using this command?

5. Describe the command line that would back up all the files on your hard disk to diskettes in drive A.

6. What does the RESTORE command do?

An
Overview of
DOS

Booting the
Computer

Issuing DOS
Commands

Preparing
Disks

Hierarchical
Directories

Copying,
Renaming,
and
Deleting
Files

Protecting
Data

**Special
Commands
and Files**

9 *Special Commands and Files*

Although DOS has dozens of commands, some are not as useful as others. Some long-time DOS users have not used half of the available DOS commands. This chapter, however, looks at some of the more common DOS commands that you will find useful in your computing. You can think of these as DOS "survival" commands.

This chapter also covers the topics of DOS devices and redirection. In DOS, the keyboard and display are the standard, or default, *devices* for messages, prompts, and input. The term *redirection* means to change the source or destination used normally for input and output.

After a consideration of DOS devices and redirection, this chapter treats the use of *batch files*, which are text files that contain DOS commands. DOS executes the commands in batch files one line at a time, treating them as though you had issued each one individually. Batch files are useful for automatically issuing commands that are hard to remember or that are easy to mistype at the command line. In their advanced form, batch files can resemble computer programs. In this chapter, you learn about simpler, yet useful, forms of batch files.

After reading this chapter, you should be able to

- Check on available memory
- Use the CON device to create text files
- Redirect the input and output of DOS commands
- Create text for a batch file
- Make AUTOEXEC.BAT and CONFIG.SYS files

Key Terms in This Chapter

Redirection	Taking input from some place other than the keyboard or sending output to some place other than the screen.
Device	A hardware component or peripheral that DOS can use in some commands as though the component were a file.

109

Console	The device DOS uses for keyboard input and screen output. DOS recognizes the console as CON.
ASCII file	A file whose contents are alphanumeric and control characters, which can be text or other information readable by humans.
Batch file	A text file that contains DOS commands, which DOS executes as though the commands were entered at the DOS prompt. Batch files always have a BAT extension.
AUTOEXEC.BAT file	An optional, but often included, batch file in the root directory of a boot disk.
CONFIG.SYS file	A file whose contents are used by DOS to tailor hardware devices and allocate the computer's resources.
Buffer	An area of RAM allocated by DOS as a temporary storage area for data moving between disks and an executing program.
Directive	A command-like DOS element that establishes the status or value of a system setting which can be modified.

Using Special Commands

The commands presented so far should enable you to get control over your computer. The first section of this chapter presents a group of commands that perform simple, practical tasks such as clearing the screen, reporting available memory, indicating your version of DOS, displaying the volume name, and checking disk space.

Clearing the Screen (CLS)

This internal CLS command erases or clears the display and positions the cursor at the top left corner of the blank screen. Use CLS when the screen becomes too "busy" with the effects of previous commands. CLS has no parameters. You simply enter CLS at the DOS prompt, and the screen clears.

An Overview of DOS

Booting the Computer

Issuing DOS Commands

Preparing Disks

Hierarchical Directories

Copying, Renaming, and Deleting Files

Protecting Data

Special Commands and Files

Reporting Available Memory (MEM)

The MEM command is new in DOS V4.0. MEM causes DOS to report the amount of system memory available for programs to load and run. In its simple form, you can issue MEM from the DOS prompt with no parameters. You can redirect MEM's output to the PRN device.

Indicating the DOS Version (VER)

The VER command indicates the DOS version your computer is using. VER is useful if you must work on another person's computer. Before you start work, you can issue this command to see which version of DOS is installed on the computer. In this way, you know which commands or switches are acceptable. VER is also useful when you boot your system from a diskette you did not prepare. The diskette may contain system files from a version of DOS you normally do not use. The VER command has no parameters and is issued at the DOS prompt.

Displaying the Volume Name (VOL)

You will recall that the /V switch used with the **FORMAT** command enables you to enter a disk volume name for a disk you are formatting. When you type **VOL** at the DOS prompt, DOS displays the volume name of the current disk. Viewing volume names is much easier than wading through directory listings when you sort through diskettes.

Checking Disk Space (CHKDSK)

CHKDSK is an external command that checks disk space and reports disk and memory status. CHKDSK can also repair certain errors on the disk. Because CHKDSK is an external command, you must specify a path to its directory with the PATH command or give the path on the command line. The symbolic syntax for CHKDSK is

> **CHKDSK** *d:path\filename.ext/F/V*

In this command, *d:* is the name of the drive that contains the disk you want to check, *path* is the directory, and *filename.ext* is the file name. The /F switch tells DOS to fix problems on the disk if errors are found. The /V switch is the "verbose" switch. It causes DOS to display detailed information about any errors detected.

```
C>CHKDSK

Volume Serial Number is 146E-3CA4
30203904 bytes total disk space
71680 bytes in 2 hidden files
114688 bytes in 48 directories
26601472 bytes in 1334 user files
30720 bytes in bad sectors
3385344 bytes available on disk

2048 bytes in each allocation unit
14748 total allocation units on disk
1653 available allocation units on disk

655360 total bytes memory
234144 bytes free
```

CHKDSK provides a detailed report of disk and memory status.

Using DOS Devices and Redirection

As you learned at the beginning of the chapter, the keyboard and display are the standard *devices* in DOS for messages, prompts, and input. When you use the keyboard to type a command, COMMAND.COM carries the text or messages and displays them on-screen. You can also send the output to another device, such as a printer. You can do this because DOS lets you change or *redirect* the source or destination used normally for input and output.

The sections that follow introduce DOS devices and explain how to use redirection to change both the standard source and standard destination of input and output.

Controlling DOS Devices

DOS views devices as extensions of the main unit of the computer. As noted previously, examples of devices are the keyboard, the video display, and the printer. DOS controls devices through its system files and the ROM BIOS. Fortunately, the details of how DOS handles the devices are not important. Devices can be classified as input, output, or input and output.

As a useful example of using a DOS device, you can create a file that contains characters you input directly from the keyboard. You'll use the familiar COPY command. This time, however, you will copy data from the CON or *console device*. CON is DOS's device name for the keyboard. You can send the characters to a file named TEST.TXT. At the DOS prompt type

COPY CON TEST.TXT

You have just told DOS: "Copy data from the console and send the output to the file TEST.TXT."

When you press Enter, the cursor drops to the next line, and no DOS prompt appears. You can begin typing characters as the input to the file. Each time you press Enter, DOS holds the line you typed in RAM. You can type several lines, and when you finish, press F6 or Ctrl-Z. DOS recognizes F6 or Ctrl-Z as the end-of-file character. After you press F6 or Ctrl-Z, the information you typed is entered into the new file and DOS displays on-screen the 1 file(s) copied message. To verify that the new file exists, you can use the DIR command and look for the file name TEST.TXT. You have just entered a text file into your computer, using a DOS device!

Using Redirection Symbols

You must use special redirection symbols to tell DOS to use nondefault devices in a command. The redirection symbols are <, >, and >>. The < symbol points away from the device or file and says, "Take input from here." The > symbol points toward the device or file and says, "Put output there." The >> symbol redirects a program's output, but adds the text to an established file. When you issue a redirection command, place the redirection symbol after the DOS command but before the device name.

Using TYPE To Display a Text File

To display the contents of the new text file, use the DOS TYPE command. TYPE tells DOS to send the contents of a file to the display. At the DOS prompt, type

TYPE TEST.TXT

DOS takes input from the TEST.TXT file up to the end-of-file marker and displays it on your screen. The TYPE command works on text files, which are called ASCII files. *ASCII* is an acronym for American Standard Code for Information Interchange, and ASCII files are in a standard format that many programs can use without conversion of the files to some other format. Don't bother trying to use the TYPE command to display files with the extensions COM and EXE. Both of these extensions are for *binary* (program) files. The extensions MOS and OVL also indicate binary files.

An Overview of DOS

Booting the Computer

Issuing DOS Commands

Preparing Disks

Hierarchical Directories

Copying, Renaming, and Deleting Files

Protecting Data

Special Commands and Files

Redirecting to a Printer

The output of a DIR or TREE command can be directed to a printer (PRN) through redirection. Make certain that the printer is turned on and connected to the computer. Then type

DIR/W >PRN

When you press Enter, the output of the DIR command goes to the printer. The /W (wide display) switch puts the files in five columns.

Using Batch Files

As you learned earlier, a batch file is a text file that contains DOS commands which are executed one line at a time. Batch files always have the extension BAT in their full file names. When you type a batch file's name at the DOS prompt, COMMAND.COM looks in the current directory for that file name with the BAT extension, reads the file, and executes the DOS commands the file contains. The whole process is automatic. You enter the batch file name, and DOS does the work.

Batch files contain ASCII text characters. You can create a text file with many word processing programs in nondocument mode. *Nondocument mode* is a setting that omits special formatting and control characters which word processing programs use for internal purposes. Composing batch files in nondocument mode eliminates errors in syntax that the special characters might cause.

You also may use the DOS line editor, EDLIN, to create a batch file. The easiest way to create a batch file, however, is to use the COPY CON device.

Caution: Never pick a name for your batch file that is the same as a DOS external command. If you do, DOS will run the batch file instead of the command.

When you create batch files, you must follow certain rules. The following list is a summary of those rules.

1. Batch files must be ASCII text files. If you use a word processor, be sure that it is in programming, or nondocument, mode.
2. The name of the batch file can be from one to eight characters long. The name must conform to the rules for naming files. It is best to use alphabetical characters in batch file names.
3. The file name must end with a BAT extension.

An Overview of DOS

Booting the Computer

Issuing DOS Commands

Preparing Disks

Hierarchical Directories

Copying, Renaming, and Deleting Files

Protecting Data

Special Commands and Files

4. The batch file name should not be the same as a program file name (a file with an EXE or COM extension).

5. The batch file name should not be the same as an internal DOS command (such as COPY or DATE).

6. The batch file can contain any valid DOS commands that you might enter at the DOS prompt.

7. You can include in the batch file program names that you usually type at the DOS prompt.

8. Use only one command or program name per line in the batch file.

Understanding the AUTOEXEC.BAT File

The AUTOEXEC.BAT batch file has special significance to DOS. This file is the place to put commands you would want to enter every time you start your system. DOS automatically searches for this file in the root directory when you boot your computer. If an AUTOEXEC.BAT file is present in the root directory, DOS executes the commands in the file.

Because the AUTOEXEC.BAT file is optional, not every PC has this file. However, most users or their system managers include an AUTOEXEC.BAT file of their own design on their boot disk because the file allows them to benefit from commands that establish operating parameters automatically.

Some software programs come with installation programs that create or modify AUTOEXEC.BAT as one of the installation steps for the package's main program. If you have doubts about what commands you should include in your AUTOEXEC.BAT file, the following sections will give you some ideas.

Consider the contents of the following AUTOEXEC.BAT file:

```
DATE
TIME
PATH=C:\DOS;C:KEEP;C\;
PROMPT $P$G
DIR
CD\DOS
ECHO Good Day, Mate
```

In this example, the DATE and TIME commands establish the correct date and time, respectively. The PATH command line instructs DOS to search the named subdirectories to find files that have EXE, COM, or BAT extensions. PROMPT customizes the prompt to show the current drive and the greater than (>) character. The DIR command shows a listing of the root directory as soon as the computer boots. CD\DOS makes \DOS the current directory. Finally, ECHO displays the on-screen message "Good Day, Mate" as part of your start-up procedure.

Setting a Search Path (PATH)

You know how to issue the PATH command to tell DOS where to search for .COM, .EXE, and .BAT files. In this section, you learn how to put the PATH command that contains the search paths into the AUTOEXEC.BAT file. With this information, DOS will know the search path as soon as you boot the computer. For example, suppose that you create on your hard disk a directory called \DOS. To tell DOS to search the \DOS directory, you would type

PATH C:\DOS

If you want DOS to search in the root directory first, the \DOS directory next, and another directory—such as \TEMP—last, type

PATH C:\;C:\DOS;C:\TEMP

Notice that semicolons separate the three directory names. The path you include in the AUTOEXEC.BAT file becomes DOS's default search path. Of course, you can change this default path. Simply issue the PATH command with a new path or set of paths at the DOS prompt.

Changing the Prompt (PROMPT)

You know what your DOS prompt looks like, but did you know that you can change it? With the PROMPT command, you can change the DOS prompt to a wide variety of looks. The symbolic syntax for the PROMPT command is

PROMPT text

The text is any combination of words or special characters.

If you want your prompt to tell you the current DOS path, type the command

PROMPT THE CURRENT PATH IS $P

If your current location is on drive C in the DOS directory, the PROMPT command will produce the this prompt:

```
THE CURRENT PATH IS C:\DOS
```

To add the > sign, use the following command:

PROMPT THE CURRENT PATH IS PG

Now your DOS prompt will be this:

```
THE CURRENT PATH IS C:\DOS>
```

Making an AUTOEXEC.BAT File

The AUTOEXEC.BAT file is a privileged batch file because DOS executes its batch of commands each time you boot your computer. In every other sense, however, AUTOEXEC.BAT is like any other batch file. The following sections cover checking your system for a preexisting AUTOEXEC.BAT file, backing up an existing file (if found), and creating a new AUTOEXEC.BAT file.

Viewing the AUTOEXEC.BAT File

You can easily see if AUTOEXEC.BAT exists in your root directory or on your logged diskette. If your hard disk is the logged drive, change to the root directory by typing **CD**. You can look at the directory listing of all the files with .BAT extensions by typing **DIR *.BAT**. You can view the contents of AUTOEXEC.BAT on-screen by typing **TYPE AUTOEXEC.BAT**. You also can get a printed copy of the AUTOEXEC.BAT file by redirecting output to the printer with the command **TYPE AUTOEXEC.BAT >PRN**.

Backing Up the Existing File

Always make a backup copy of your existing AUTOEXEC.BAT file before you make any changes in the file. Save the current version by renaming it with a different extension. Type the command

RENAME AUTOEXEC.BAT AUTOEXEC.OLD

and press Enter. RENAME transfers the name AUTOEXEC.BAT to the AUTOEXEC.OLD file. In effect, the name AUTOEXEC.BAT is available for use with a new file. If you find that the new AUTOEXEC.BAT file does not work or does not

An Overview of DOS

Booting the Computer

Issuing DOS Commands

Preparing Disks

Hierarchical Directories

Copying, Renaming, and Deleting Files

Protecting Data

Special Commands and Files

117

do what you want, you can always erase the new file. Then, using the RENAME command, you can rename the AUTOEXEC.OLD file AUTOEXEC.BAT and be back where you started.

Entering a New File

Now you are ready to use COPY CON to enter your new or revised AUTOEXEC.BAT file. Type the command **COPY CON AUTOEXEC.BAT**. Enter the commands you want to include. Type one command per line and correct any mistakes before you press Enter. When you finish, press F6 or Ctrl-Z to write the new file to disk. Now when you boot your computer, DOS executes your new AUTOEXEC.BAT file.

Understanding the CONFIG.SYS File

AUTOEXEC.BAT is not the only file that DOS looks for when you boot your computer. DOS also looks for a *CONFIG.SYS* file. This file is DOS's additional configuration file. DOS not only provides built-in services for disks and other hardware but also extends its services for add-on hardware. The additional instructions that DOS needs to incorporate outside services, such as some devices, are included in the CONFIG.SYS file.

CONFIG.SYS is also the location for naming the values of DOS configuration items that can be "tuned." Files and buffers, which are discussed in the next section, are two "tunable" DOS items. CONFIG.SYS is a text file like AUTOEXEC.BAT, so you can display it on-screen or print it. You also can change the contents of CONFIG.SYS with the COPY CON command or with a text editor.

Although CONFIG.SYS is not a batch file, it is very similar to one. DOS does not execute CONFIG.SYS as it does AUTOEXEC.BAT. Instead, DOS reads the values in the file and configures your computer in accordance with those values. Many software packages modify or add a CONFIG.SYS file to the root directory. The range of possible values in the file is wide, but there are some common values that you can include.

Specifying Files and Buffers

When DOS moves data to and from disks, it does so in the most efficient manner possible. For each file that DOS works with during an operation, there is a built-in area in system RAM that helps DOS keep track of the operating system details of that

An Overview of DOS

Booting the Computer

Issuing DOS Commands

Preparing Disks

Hierarchical Directories

Copying, Renaming, and Deleting Files

Protecting Data

Special Commands and Files

file. The number of built-in RAM areas for this tracking operation is controlled by the FILES directive in CONFIG.SYS. A *directive* establishes in the CONFIG.SYS file the value of a system setting that can be modified. If a program attempts to open more files than the FILES directive indicates, DOS will tell you that too many files are open. As a rule of thumb, the best compromise is to set the FILES directive to 20 open files. The line you type in CONFIG.SYS to set the number of open files to 20 is:

FILES = 20

Similar to the FILES directive is the BUFFERS directive. *Buffers* are holding areas in RAM that store information coming from or going to disk files. To make the disk operation more efficient, DOS stores disk information in file buffers in RAM. It then uses RAM, instead of the disk drives, for input and output whenever possible. If the file information needed is not already in the buffer, new information is read into the buffer from the disk file. The information that DOS reads includes the needed information and as much additional file information as the buffer will hold. With this buffer of needed information, there is a good chance that DOS can avoid constant disk access.

Like the FILES directive, however, the BUFFERS directive should not be too high, for an unnecessarily high number takes needed RAM away from programs and dedicates it to the buffers. As a rule, 20 buffers should work effectively for most programs.

To include the FILES and BUFFERS directives in the CONFIG.SYS file during the COPY CON command, type **FILES=20** and press Enter. Then type **BUFFERS=20** on the next line. Keep in mind that some programs make their own changes to FILES and BUFFERS in the CONFIG.SYS file. Most applications software tells you what the values of FILES and BUFFERS should be. Check your program manual for details.

Designating Device Drivers

You'll recall that DOS works with peripherals, such as disk drives, printers, and displays. These peripherals also are called devices. DOS has built-in instructions, called *drivers*, to handle these devices. But some devices, like a mouse, are foreign to DOS. DOS does not have any built-in capability to handle them. To issue directions to devices DOS has no built-in instructions for, use the DEVICE directive. The syntax for the directive is

DEVICE=device driver file name

For example, the device driver for a mouse can be in a file called MOUSE.SYS. So that DOS can know how to use the mouse, you would enter a command like this:

DEVICE=MOUSE.SYS

The DEVICE directive tells DOS to find and load the driver program for the new device. Then, DOS can control the device.

Most peripherals come with a disk that contains a device-driver file. This file contains the necessary instructions to control or drive the device.

Making a CONFIG.SYS File

You should back up your disk before you add to or change a CONFIG.SYS file. Make sure that the CONFIG.SYS file is in your root directory, or on your boot diskette. If your directory contains CONFIG.SYS, use the TYPE command to see the contents of the file on the screen. If you have a printer, you can redirect the TYPE command's output to the printer.

If you need to change your CONFIG.SYS file, rename it CONFIG.OLD. Now you can use the command COPY CON CONFIG.SYS to make a new version. Type your directives and pay close attention to syntax. When you finish, press F6 or Ctrl-Z. Reboot your computer. The new configuration will take effect. If you get DOS error messages, TYPE your new CONFIG.SYS and check for mistakes. If you find errors, erase the file and use COPY CON to type the lines again. A sample CONFIG.SYS file might contain these lines:

FILES=20
BUFFERS=20
DEVICE=\DOS\DRIVERS\ANSI.SYS
DEVICE=\DOS\DRIVERS\MOUSE.SYS

Summary

This chapter began by focusing on a number of special and sometimes overlooked DOS commands that give you greater control over your system.

Next, you learned how DOS uses the keyboard, video display, printer, and other devices for input, output, or both, in some cases. With DOS you can "redirect" keyboard entry to a file, for example, or send the results of a command such as DIR

An Overview of DOS

Booting the Computer

Issuing DOS Commands

Preparing Disks

Hierarchical Directories

Copying, Renaming, and Deleting Files

Protecting Data

Special Commands and Files

to a printer. The TYPE command lets you display the contents of a text file on the screen.

You became familiar with the usefulness of batch files, which are text files that contain a sequence of DOS commands executed one line at a time. You learned the general rules for creating batch files. You saw how to create the most important batch file in your system—AUTOEXEC.BAT—into which you place commands that you would want to enter every time you start your system.

Finally, you learned how to create a CONFIG.SYS file for your system. DOS needs this file for additional configuration information, such as the number of files and buffers that are needed to run applications programs, or the types of device drivers that may be attached to your system.

Review Questions

1. Describe the operation of the CLS, MEM, VER, and VOL commands.

2. What does the CHKDSK command do? What is the effect of the /F and /V switches when used with CHKDSK?

3. What are the standard "devices" used by DOS? What is the purpose of redirection?

4. What does the TYPE command do?

5. What extension does a batch file have? Name some of the general rules for creating batch files.

6. What is the special significance of the AUTOEXEC.BAT file? What are some of the methods for creating this file? Describe the commands that are typically included in this file.

7. What does the PROMPT command do?

8. What is the purpose of the CONFIG.SYS file? What information is typically included in this file?

Part II

1-2-3

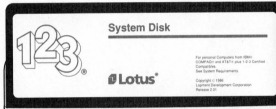

System Disk

For personal Computers from IBM®
COMPAQ® and AT&T® plus 1-2-3 Certified
Compatibles.
See System Requirements.

⦿Lotus®

Copyright © 1986
Lopment Development Corporation
Release 2.01

An Overview of 1-2-3
Getting Started
Understanding 1-2-3 Basics
Creating a Worksheet
Printing Reports
Creating and Printing Graphs
Managing Data

10 *An Overview of 1-2-3*

An Overview of 1-2-3

Getting Started

1-2-3 Basics

Creating a Worksheet

Printing Reports

Creating and Printing Graphs

Managing Data

1-2-3 is designed as an "electronic" replacement for the traditional tools of accounting. The columnar pad, pencil, and calculator have been replaced with a screen, cursor, and coprocessor that together give users more power, speed, and accuracy for all their financial calculations. When you start 1-2-3, your computer screen displays a column/row area into which you can enter text, numbers, or formulas as an accountant would on one sheet of a columnar pad (and with the help of a calculator).

Although there are several popular spreadsheet programs on the market, 1-2-3 has been the dominant spreadsheet software product used in businesses worldwide since 1983. 1-2-3 has been popular because it provides users with three fundamental applications integrated into one program. Without having to learn three separate kinds of software, you can perform financial analysis with the 1-2-3 worksheet, create database applications, and create graphs.

But, before you put your fingers to a keyboard and start using 1-2-3, you need to know what a spreadsheet is and how it is used. This chapter begins with contrasting examples of "manual" and "electronic" spreadsheets, shows you the wide range of capabilities offered by 1-2-3, and helps you understand how 1-2-3 is useful for many business applications.

After completing this chapter, you should be able to describe the following:

- 1-2-3's integrated spreadsheet
- 1-2-3's commands and functions
- 1-2-3's graphics capabilities
- 1-2-3's data manager
- 1-2-3's macros and the Command Language
- 1-2-3 Release 2.01's hardware requirements
- The major enhancements with 1-2-3 Release 2.2 and 3

What Is a Spreadsheet?

Sometimes known as a "ledger sheet" or accountant's pad, a *spreadsheet* is a specialized piece of paper on which information is recorded in columns and rows. Spreadsheets usually contain a mix of descriptive text with accompanying numbers and calculations. Typical business applications include balance sheets, income statements, inventory sheets, and sales reports.

Athough you may be unfamiliar with business applications for spreadsheets, if you keep a checkbook, you're already using a rudimentary spreadsheet. Similar to an accountant's pad, a checkbook register is a paper grid divided by lines into rows and columns. Within this grid you record the number of the check, the date, a description of the transaction, the amount of the check, a record of any deposits, and a running balance, as shown in the following example:

An Overview of 1-2-3

Getting Started

1-2-3 Basics

Creating a Worksheet

Printing Reports

Creating and Printing Graphs

Managing Data

NUMBER	DATE	DESCRIPTION OF TRANSACTION	PAYMENT/DEBT (−)	FEE (FANY) (−)	DEPOSIT/CREDIT (+)	BALANCE $1000 00	
1001	9/3/89	Department Store Credit	51 03			948	97
1002	9/13/89	Electric	95 12			853	85
1003	9/14/89	Grocery	74 25			779	60
1004	9/15/89	Class Supplies	354 57			425	03
	9/16/89	Deposit			250 00	675	03
1005	9/21/89	Telephone	49 43			625	60

A manual checkbook register.

What happens when you make an invalid entry in your checkbook register, or have to void an entry? Such procedures can be quite messy because you have to erase or cross out entries, rewrite them, and perform all of your calculations once again. The limitations of manual spreadsheets are apparent even with the simple example of a checkbook register.

For complex business applications, the dynamic quality of an "electronic" spreadsheet such as 1-2-3 is indispensable. You can change one number and recalculate the entire spreadsheet in an instant. Entering new values is nearly effortless. Calculating a column or row of numbers is done by formulas—the same type of formula that you would use on a calculator.

Compare the manual checkbook register to the following electronic one. Notice that the electronic checkbook register is set up with columns and rows. Columns are marked by letters; rows are numbered. Each transaction is recorded on a row just as you would record it in a manual checkbook.

```
F8: (,2) [W11] +F7-D8+E8                              READY
        A        B            C         D        E        F
        CHECK                         PAYMENT/  DEPOSIT/
  1
  2     NO.     DATE    DESCRIPTION     DEBIT    CREDIT   BALANCE
  3     01    01-Sep-89 Beginning Balance       $1,000.00 $1,000.00
  4     1001  03-Sep-89 Department store credit  51.03            948.97
  5     1002  13-Sep-89 Electric                 95.12            853.85
  6     1003  14-Sep-89 Grocery                  74.25            779.60
  7     1004  15-Sep-89 Class supplies          354.57            425.03
  8     02    16-Sep-89 Deposit                           250.00  675.03
  9     1005  21-Sep-89 Telephone                49.43            625.60
 10     1006  23-Sep-89 Clothing store           62.35            563.25
 11     ************SEPTEMBER AMOUNTS            686.75  1,250.00 ***********
 12     1007  02-Oct-89 Grocery                   65.83            497.42
 13     03    07-Oct-89 Deposit                           275.00  772.42
 14     1008  10-Oct-89 Department store credit   50.00            722.42
 15     1009  10-Oct-89 Electric                  75.34            647.08
 16     1010  15-Oct-89 Bookstore                 95.24            551.84
 17     1011  21-Oct-89 Hardware store            31.24            520.60
 18     1012  21-Oct-89 Deposit                           250.00  770.60
 19     04    22-Oct-89 Grocery                   85.21            685.39
 20     *************OCTOBER AMOUNTS             402.86   525.00 ***********
        31-Jul-89  04:43 PM        UNDO              NUM
```

An "electronic" checkbook register.

Assigning column letters and row numbers lends itself well to creating formulas. Note the following formula in the upper left corner of the electronic checkbook:

> +F7–D8+E8

These instructions to 1-2-3 translate as:

> Previous BALANCE minus PAYMENT/DEBIT plus DEPOSIT/CREDIT

As you can see from this simple example, formulas let you establish mathematical relationships between values stored in certain places on your spreadsheet. The principal calculation involved in your checkbook is to keep an accurate running balance. Formulas make it easy to make changes to a spreadsheet and see the results quickly. In the electronic checkbook, if you delete an entire transaction (row), the spreadsheet automatically recalculates itself. Or, you may change an amount and not have to worry about recalculating your balance. The electronic spreadsheet takes care of updating all balances.

If you find that you forgot to record a check or deposit, 1-2-3 lets you insert a new row at the point where the transaction was omitted and enter the transaction information. Subsequent entries are moved down one row. Inserting new columns is just as easy. You indicate where you want the new column to go, and 1-2-3 inserts a blank column at that point, moving information to the right over one column.

What if you wanted to calculate how much you have spent at the local department store since the beginning of the year? With a manual checkbook, you would have to look for each check written to the department store, and then total the amounts. Not only would this take considerable time, but you might overlook one of the checks. An electronic checkbook would let you sort your checks by description so that all like transactions are together. You could create a formula that totals all the checks written to the department store, for example.

This simple example of a checkbook suggests the tremendous value of an electronic spreadsheet for maintaining financial data. Although you might not want to use 1-2-3 to balance your checkbook, an electronic spreadsheet is an indispensible tool in today's modern office.

The 1-2-3 Integrated Spreadsheet

1-2-3 has a number of capabilities, but the electronic spreadsheet is the foundation of the 1-2-3 program. The framework of this spreadsheet contains the graphics and data-

What Is A
Spreadsheet?

**The 1-2-3
Integrated
Spreadsheet**

1-2-3
Graphics

1-2-3
Database

Macros and
the Command
Language

What
Hardware
You Need

1-2-3 Releases
2.2 and 3

Summary

management elements of the program. You produce graphics through the use of spreadsheet commands. Data management occurs in the standard row-column spreadsheet layout.

The importance of the spreadsheet as the basis for the whole product cannot be overemphasized. All the commands for the related features are initiated from the same main command menu as the spreadsheet commands and have the same style. All of 1-2-3's special features originate from the spreadsheet. All the commands for displaying graphs refer to entries in the spreadsheet and use these entries to draw graphs on the screen. In data management, the database is composed of records that are cell entries in a spreadsheet.

Getting
Started

1-2-3 Basics

Creating a
Worksheet

Printing
Reports

Creating
and
Printing
Graphs

Managing
Data

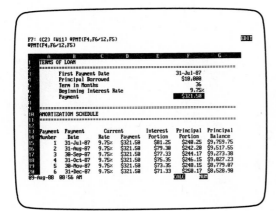

1-2-3 is an integrated electronic spreadsheet that replaces traditional financial modeling tools, reducing the time and effort needed to do sophisticated accounting tasks.

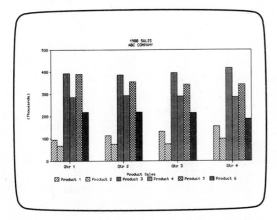

With 1-2-3's graphics capabilities, you can create five different types of graphs.

129

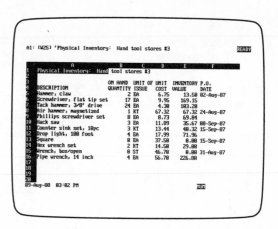

You can use 1-2-3's database commands and statistical functions to manage and manipulate data.

Understanding the Size of 1-2-3's Spreadsheet

With 256 columns and 8,192 rows, the 1-2-3 worksheet contains more than 2,000,000 cells. Each column is assigned a letter value ranging from A for the first column to IV for the last. A good way to visualize the worksheet is to picture it as one giant sheet of grid paper about 21 feet wide and 171 feet high.

Although the 1-2-3 spreadsheet contains that many columns and rows, there are some limitations to using the entire sheet. If you imagine storing just one character in each of the 2,097,152 available cells, you end up with a worksheet that is far larger than the 640K maximum RAM of an IBM PC.

Understanding the Worksheet Window

Because the 1-2-3 grid is large, you cannot view the entire spreadsheet on the screen at one time. The screen thus serves as a *window* onto the worksheet. To view other parts of the sheet, you scroll the cell pointer across and down (or up) the worksheet with the arrow keys. When the cell pointer reaches the edge of the current window, the window begins to shift to follow the cell pointer across and down (or up) the spreadsheet.

To illustrate the window concept, imagine cutting a one-inch square in a piece of cardboard. If you placed the cardboard on this page, you would be able to see only a one-inch square piece of text. Naturally, the rest of the text is still on the page; it is simply hidden from view. When you move the cardboard around the page (in much the same way that the window moves when the cursor-movement keys are used), different parts of the page become visible.

An Overview of 1-2-3

Getting Started

1-2-3 Basics

Creating a Worksheet

Printing Reports

Creating and Printing Graphs

Managing Data

The default 1-2-3 window displays 8 columns (each 9 characters wide) and 20 rows. The width of the columns is adjustable; therefore, the number of displayed columns is variable. If you reduce the width of one or more columns, the window displays more columns; if you the expand the width of one or more columns, the screen displays fewer columns.

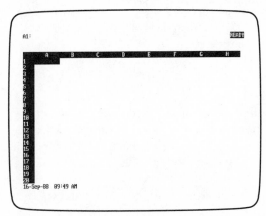

The default 1-2-3 window displays 8 columns (each 9 characters wide) and 20 rows.

Understanding Cells

Each row in 1-2-3 is assigned a number, and each column is assigned a letter. The intersections of the rows and columns are called *cells*. Cells are identified by their row-column coordinates. For example, the cell located at the intersection of column A and row 1 is called A1. Cells can be filled with three kinds of information: numbers; mathematical formulas, including special spreadsheet functions; and text (or labels).

A *cell pointer* allows you to write information into the cells much as a pencil lets you write on a piece of paper. In 1-2-3, as in most spreadsheets, the cell pointer looks like a bright rectangle on the computer's screen. The cell pointer typically is one column wide and one row high.

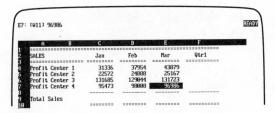

Cell pointer highlighting a numeric value in cell E7.

Electronic spreadsheets allow mathematical relationships to be created between cells. For example, if the cell named C1 contains the formula

   +A1+B1

then C1 will display the sum of the contents of cells A1 and B1. (The + sign before A1 tells 1-2-3 that what you have entered into this cell is a formula, not text.) The cell references serve as variables in the equation. No matter what numbers you enter into cells A1 and B1, cell C1 will always return their sum.

Playing "What If"

Because 1-2-3 remembers the relationships between cells and does not simply calculate values, you can change a value in a cell and see what happens when your formulas recalculate automatically. This "what if" capability makes 1-2-3 an incredibly powerful tool for many types of analysis. You can, for example, analyze the effect of an expected increase in the cost of goods and determine what kind of price increase may be needed to maintain your current profit margins. Creating formulas is discussed in Chapter 12.

Understanding 1-2-3's Functions

As you know, you can create simple formulas involving only a few cells if you refer to the cell addresses and use the appropriate operators (+, −, /, *). These formulas are stored in memory, and you see the values of the formulas in the cells.

If you want to create complex formulas, you can use 1-2-3 functions. Spreadsheet functions are shortcuts that help the user perform common mathematical computations with a minimum of typing. Functions are like abbreviations for otherwise long and cumbersome formulas. You use an @ symbol to signal 1-2-3 that an expression is a function. For instance, the @SUM function in 1-2-3 is written as @SUM(A1..C1).

Without the capabilities to calculate complex mathematical, statistical, logical, financial, and other types of formulas, building applications in 1-2-3 would be difficult. 1-2-3 comes with many functions that let you create complex formulas for a wide range of applications, including business, scientific, and engineering applications. You learn more about 1-2-3's functions in Chapter 12.

An Overview of 1-2-3

Getting Started

1-2-3 Basics

Creating a Worksheet

Printing Reports

Creating and Printing Graphs

Managing Data

Understanding 1-2-3's Commands

You use spreadsheet commands at every phase of building and using an application. You activate commands by pressing the slash (/) key. This action displays a menu of commands from which you can choose the command you want.

1-2-3 has many commands that allow you to perform a number of tasks in the spreadsheet. Commands are available to format the worksheet, name ranges, erase and copy data, perform calculations, store files, protect worksheet cells, protect files with passwords, and print your spreadsheets. You learn more about 1-2-3's many commands in Chapters 12 through 14.

1-2-3 Graphics

The spreadsheet alone makes 1-2-3 a powerful program with all the capabilities needed by many users. 1-2-3 has five basic graph types: bar, stacked bar, line, scatter, and pie. You can represent up to six ranges of data on a single graph (except for pie graphs and scatter diagrams). This capability means, for example, that you can create a line graph with six different lines.

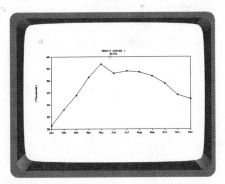

1-2-3 displays data as a line graph if you do not specify a particular graph type.

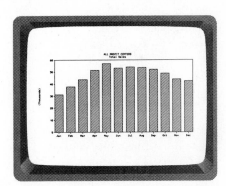

A bar graph often compares two or more data items and typically shows the trend of numeric data across time.

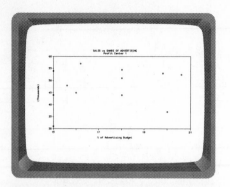

An XY graph compares two numeric data series across time and shows how one set of values appears to depend on the other.

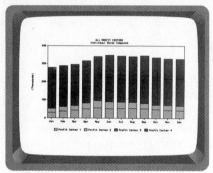

A stacked-bar graph compares two or more data series that total 100 percent of a specific category.

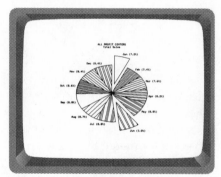

A pie graph illustrates only one data series, the components of which total 100 percent of a specific numeric category.

1-2-3 Database

The column-row structure for storing data in a spreadsheet program is similar to the structure of a relational database. 1-2-3 provides database management commands and functions so that you can sort, query, extract, and perform statistical analyses on data in up to 8,192 records.

A row in 1-2-3 is equal to a record in a conventional database. In that record, you might store a client's name, address, and phone number. With 1-2-3's sort and search operations, you can order the database on any number of items and by a number of criteria, and you can locate a particular record with a few simple keystrokes. The following screen shows a deductible expenses database created in 1-2-3.

An Overview of 1-2-3

Getting Started

1-2-3 Basics

Creating a Worksheet

Printing Reports

Creating and Printing Graphs

Managing Data

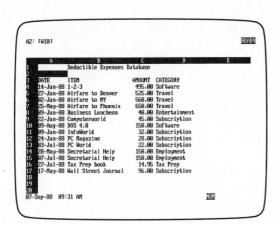

Building a database in 1-2-3.

Macros and the Command Language

In addition to all of the capabilities available from the commands in 1-2-3's main menu, two other features make 1-2-3 extremely versatile. Using 1-2-3's macros and the Command Language, you can automate and customize 1-2-3 for your particular applications.

With 1-2-3 macros, you can reduce multiple keystrokes to a two-keystroke operation. Simply press two keys, and 1-2-3 does the rest, whether you're formatting a range, creating a graph, or printing a spreadsheet.

You can create a macro, for example, to move the cell pointer to a specific part of the worksheet. Suppose that you have positioned a database section in the range R23..Z100. Because 1-2-3 is first displayed with the cell pointer at A1, you will have to use quite a few keystrokes to get to cell R23 when you want to work with the database. You can create a macro that will, in effect, "record" your actions as you specify the keystrokes necessary to get to cell R23. Then, after you assign a name and save the macro, you can access that part of the worksheet by simply typing the macro name.

You can best think of macros as the building blocks for Command Language programs. When you begin to add commands from the Command Language to simple keystroke macros, you can control and automate many of the actions required to build, modify, and update 1-2-3 models. At its most sophisticated level, 1-2-3's Command Language can be used as a full-fledged programming language for developing custom business applications.

135

What Hardware You Need

You can run 1-2-3 Release 2.01 on an IBM personal computer or compatible with 256K of RAM and at least one double-sided disk drive. For convenience and processing power, you may want to include a second floppy disk drive and a hard disk with at least 10 megabytes of storage capacity. If you want to view 1-2-3's color graphics, you'll need a color monitor.

1-2-3 Releases 2.2 and 3

Although the coverage of 1-2-3 in *Introduction to Business Software* is based on Release 2.01, you should know that Lotus introduced Releases 3 and 2.2, in that order, within two months of each other in 1989. Release 3 represents a total ground-up rewrite of the software, but Release 2.2 maintains much of the "look and feel" of Release 2.01 and previous releases.

The major enhancements to Release 2.2 over all previous releases include the capability to "link" the cells of one worksheet to another worksheet, improved report and graph printing, the capability to undo a worksheet change or command operation, a minimal recalculation capability that lets 1-2-3 Release 2.2 recalculate only those cells affected by a change in the worksheet, and new macro commands and capabilities.

Release 3 represents a dramatic change in the software. Unlike Releases 2.2 and 2.01, you cannot run Release 3 on an 8088- or 8086-based personal computer—you must have at least an AT-type 80286-based system. Among the major enhancements to Release 3 are the capability to have up to 256 worksheets in one file and multiple files in memory at one time, the capability to create graphs automatically, higher quality printed reports and on-screen and printed graphs, and the capability to access external databases.

Summary

In this overview chapter, you saw how one of the simplest examples of a spreadsheet—a checkbook register—could become easier to use in "electronic" form.

You were introduced to the features of 1-2-3's spreadsheet, such as its size, window, and cells. You learned how they are designated and can be recalculated for "what if"

An Overview of 1-2-3

Getting Started

1-2-3 Basics

Creating a Worksheet

Printing Reports

Creating and Printing Graphs

Managing Data

analyses. And you had your first look at 1-2-3's powerful commands and functions, with which you can build formulas for a wide variety of applications.

The chapter gave you a glimpse at 1-2-3's flexible graphics capabilities and the types of available. You had a quick view of 1-2-3's database and its power for managing and reporting on stored data. The chapter touched on macros and the Command Language, with which you can automate and customize your use of 1-2-3 and its integrated graphics and database. Finally, you got a quick glimpse of the enhancements provided by Releases 2.2 and 3 of 1-2-3.

The power of 1-2-3 is best realized in actually using the program. The next chapter shows you how to get started.

Review Questions

1. What three applications are provided by 1-2-3?

2. What is a spreadsheet?

3. Name some typical business applications of spreadsheets.

4. How many rows and how many columns are in the 1-2-3 worksheet?

5.   What is the cross section of a row and column where data can be entered?

6.   What makes 1-2-3 an "integrated spreadsheet program"?

7.   What are 1-2-3 functions?

8.   What key do you press to access the main 1-2-3 menu?

9.   What are the five types of graphs that 1-2-3 can create?

10.   What is a macro?

An
Overview of
1-2-3

**Getting
Started**

1-2-3 Basics

Creating a
Worksheet

Printing
Reports

Creating
and
Printing
Graphs

Managing
Data

11 *Getting Started*

The purpose of this chapter is to introduce you to the 1-2-3 environment. You are shown the ways to enter and leave 1-2-3. You are made aware of the importance of saving your work before exiting 1-2-3. Understanding how a program makes use of the keyboard is essential, so you become acquainted with the three areas of the keyboard—the alphanumeric keys, the numeric keypad, and the function keys—and how they relate to the program. 1-2-3 displays a number of indicators to keep the user informed of what the program is doing, so you learn about these indicators and their meaning. Finally, so that you can see that 1-2-3 is a "friendly" program, you are introduced to the ever-ready help system and the tutorial that comes with the program.

After completing this chapter, you should

- Be able to start and exit 1-2-3

- Know how to save a 1-2-3 worksheet file

- Know how to use the keyboard with 1-2-3

- Understand the 1-2-3 screen

- Be familiar with the 1-2-3 help system and tutorial

▼

Key Terms in This Chapter

1-2-3 Access System The 1-2-3 menu system that links all of 1-2-3's different functions, including the main 1-2-3 program and programs for printing graphs, translating non-1-2-3 files, installing 1-2-3, and accessing the 1-2-3 tutorial.

Alphanumeric keys The keys in the center section of the computer keyboard. Many of these keys function the same as those on a typewriter.

Numeric keypad The keys on the right side of the IBM PC, AT, and Enhanced keyboards. This keypad is used for entering and calculating numbers and can be used also for moving the cursor on the computer screen.

Function keys	The 10 keys on the left side of the PC and AT keyboards and the 12 keys at the top of the enhanced keyboard. These keys are used for special functions, such as accessing help, editing cells, and recalculating the worksheet.
Control panel	The area above the inverse-video border of the 1-2-3 worksheet, containing three lines that display important information about the contents of a cell, command options and explanations, or special prompts and messages.

Starting 1-2-3

Getting into 1-2-3 is quite easy, particularly if the program is installed on a hard disk. Starting from DOS, you can go directly to a fresh worksheet, or you can enter 1-2-3 by way of the 1-2-3 Access System, which provides a number of menu options. The following discussion shows you both ways to enter 1-2-3. Directions are given for hard disk systems and for systems having just diskette drives.

Starting 1-2-3 from DOS

Starting 1-2-3 from DOS requires several steps. Suppose that the 1-2-3 program is on a hard disk in a subdirectory named 123. To start 1-2-3 on a hard disk system, you do these steps:

1. With the C> system prompt displayed on the screen, change to the 123 directory by typing **cd\123** and pressing Enter.
2. Start 1-2-3 by typing **123** and pressing Enter.

If you have a two-diskette system, the startup procedure is slightly different. To start 1-2-3 on a diskette system, you do these steps:

1. After using your DOS diskette to boot your computer, remove the diskette and place the 1-2-3 System diskette into drive A.
2. If the A> prompt is not displayed, type **a:** and press Enter.
3. Start 1-2-3 by typing **123** at the A> system prompt and pressing Enter.

After a few seconds, the 1-2-3 logo appears. It remains on-screen for a few seconds; then the worksheet appears, and you are ready to use 1-2-3.

An
Overview of
1-2-3

**Getting
Started**

1-2-3 Basics

Creating a
Worksheet

Printing
Reports

Creating
and
Printing
Graphs

Managing
Data

Starting 1-2-3 from the 1-2-3 Access System

Lotus devised the 1-2-3 Access System as a way to link all of 1-2-3's different functions. This system is useful for moving quickly between the programs in the 1-2-3 package. Additionally, the Access System provides a series of menus that enable you to translate between 1-2-3 and other programs, such as dBASE, Symphony, and VisiCalc.

To start the 1-2-3 Access System on a hard disk system,

1. Type **cd\123** and press Enter.
2. Type **lotus** at the C> prompt and press Enter.

To start the 1-2-3 Access System on a diskette system,

1. Place the 1-2-3 System disk into drive A.
2. Type **a:** and press Enter.
3. Type **lotus** and press Enter.

The 1-2-3 Access System then appears. The following paragraphs explain each of the options in the Access System's menu bar.

123, logically enough, starts 1-2-3. Be sure that you have the System disk in drive A if you are using a two-drive system.

PrintGraph initiates the PrintGraph program for printing graphs. For more about this topic, see Chapter 15.

Translate accesses the Translate utility. It provides a link between Releases 1A and 2 of 1-2-3, and between 1-2-3 and outside programs like dBASE, Symphony, and VisiCalc.

Install accesses the Install program, which you use to change the options set during installation. For more information and complete installation instructions, see the software manual.

View takes you though the 1-2-3 tutorial, "A View of 1-2-3."

Exit quits the 1-2-3 program and takes you to DOS.

Exiting 1-2-3

After you have entered 1-2-3, there are two ways to leave the 1-2-3 program to return to DOS: the /System command and the /Quit command. Both commands are accessible from the 1-2-3 main command menu. To access the menu, press the slash (/) key. The two commands are among the options on this menu.

Using /System To Leave 1-2-3 Temporarily

The /System command returns you to the DOS system prompt but does not exit the 1-2-3 program. Your departure is only temporary. To select the /System option, type **s** or use the pointer to highlight the selection and then press Enter. While you are at the DOS level, you can perform system operations, including changing directories and drives. To return to the 1-2-3 spreadsheet, type **exit**.

You will find that /System is a useful command when you need to check the amount of memory you have on disk before you copy a file to it, or when you want to see how much memory a particular spreadsheet uses before you load it. /System saves you the trouble of having to quit the 1-2-3 program, issue the appropriate DOS commands, and then get back into the spreadsheet.

Using /Quit To Exit 1-2-3

If you select the /Quit command from the 1-2-3 main menu, you exit the worksheet and the 1-2-3 program. You are asked to verify this choice before you actually exit 1-2-3, because your data will be lost if you quit 1-2-3 without saving your file. To verify that you want to exit, type **y** or move the pointer to **Y**es and press Enter.

Note that if you started 1-2-3 from the 1-2-3 Access System, you will be returned to the Access System when you select /Quit. To leave the 1-2-3 Access System and return to the operating system, type **e** or use the arrow keys to move the cursor to **E**xit and press Enter.

Saving before You Quit 1-2-3

Computerized spreadsheeting has one danger that does not exist in the paper-and-pencil world: the potential loss of data. An unexpected power outage or a careless

Starting   **Exiting**   Learning the   Understanding   Accessing the 1-2-3
1-2-3   **1-2-3**   Keyboard   the 1-2-3   Help Feature and
                                           Screen   Tutorial   Summary

An
Overview of
1-2-3

**Getting
Started**

1-2-3 Basics

Creating a
Worksheet

Printing
Reports

Creating
and
Printing
Graphs

Managing
Data

human error can cause the loss of important data and time. For example, if you select /**Q**uit without having saved your file and then—not thinking—choose **Y**es at the verification prompt, you are out of luck as far as your data is concerned. Any work you have done since you last saved the file is lost. You can recover the data only by retyping it into the worksheet.

To use the /**F**ile **S**ave command,

1. Display the 1-2-3 main menu by typing a slash (/).
2. Select **F**ile by positioning the cursor on that item and pressing Enter, or by typing **f**.
3. Choose **S**ave and press Enter, or type **s**.
4. Enter a file name you haven't used before—one that in some way identifies the file so that you will be able to find it later. (See Chapter 12 for details on valid file names.)
5. Press Enter, and the file is saved to disk.

Learning the Keyboard

Before you begin learning 1-2-3, you need to know how your keyboard relates to 1-2-3. You will recall from Chapter 1 that the three most popular keyboards have three sections: the alphanumeric keys in the center, the numeric keypad on the right, and the function keys on the left or across the top. The IBM Enhanced keyboard, used on PS/2 computers, has a separate grouping of cursor-movement keys between the alphanumeric keys and the numeric keypad.

The Alphanumeric Keys

Although most alphanumeric keys are the same as those on a typewriter, several of the keys have special functions in 1-2-3. For example, the slash (/) key accesses the 1-2-3 menu, and the period (.) key separates addresses in the definition of a range of cells. The function of each of these important keys is explained in table 11.1.

The Numeric Keypad and Cursor-Movement Keys

The keys of the numeric keypad on the right side of the IBM PC and AT keyboards can be used for either cursor movement or data entry. When you want to use the numeric keypad to enter numbers rather than position the cursor (on the PC or AT keyboards), you can press either Num Lock before and after you enter the numbers, or press and hold down a Shift key while you press the number keys. While it is pressed down, the alternate function of the numeric keypad is operative. You would use the same method if you were using the keypad for data entry and wanted to use the keypad temporarily for cursor movement.

The Function Keys

The function keys F1 through F10 are for special tasks, such as accessing Help, editing cells, and recalculating the worksheet. A plastic function-key template that reminds you of each key's function is provided by Lotus. Table 11.2 explains the purpose of each function key.

Table 11.1
The Special Alphanumeric Keys

 Moves cursor one screen right. ⌐Shift⌐Tab⌐ moves cursor one screen left.

 When used with other keystrokes, invokes macros and Command Language programs.

 Changes lowercase letters and characters to uppercase. When not in Num Lock mode, allows you to type numbers on the numeric keypad.

 During cell definition, erases the previous character in a cell.

 Calls up the 1-2-3 main menu and can function as a division sign.

 Separates cell addresses and anchors cell addresses during pointing. Also used as a decimal point.

 Activates the numeric character of keys in the numeric keypad.

 Escapes from command menu and moves to previous menu, erases current entry during range of command specification, and returns from a help screen.

 Deletes character above cursor during editing process.

 In Scroll Lock position, scrolls entire screen one row or column when pointer is moved; in Break position, is used with Ctrl to return 1-2-3 to READY mode or to halt execution of macro.

An
Overview of
1-2-3

**Getting
Started**

1-2-3 Basics

Creating a
Worksheet

Printing
Reports

Creating
and
Printing
Graphs

Managing
Data

Table 11.2

The Function Keys

F1 **(Help)** Accesses 1-2-3's on-line help facility.	**F6** **(Window)** Moves cursor to the other side of a split screen.
F2 **(Edit)** Shifts 1-2-3 to EDIT mode.	**F7** **(Query)** Repeats the most recent Data Query operation.
F3 **(Name)** In POINT mode, displays a list of range names in the worksheet. Pressing F3 a second time switches to a full-screen display of range names.	**F8** **(Table)** Repeats the most recent Data Table operation.
F4 **(Abs)** During cell definition, changes a relative cell address into an absolute or mixed address.	**F9** **(Calc)** Recalculates the worksheet.
F5 **(GoTo)** Moves cursor to cell coordinates (or range name) provided.	**F10** **(Graph)** Redraws graph defined by the current graph settings.

Understanding the 1-2-3 Screen

The main 1-2-3 display is divided into two parts: the control panel at the top of the screen and the worksheet area. An inverse-video border separates the two areas. This border contains the letters and numbers that mark the columns and rows.

Other important areas of the screen are the mode indicators (upper right corner), the lock key indicators (lower right corner), and the message area (lower left corner). The message area normally shows the date and time, but will show an error message when certain kinds of errors are made.

The Control Panel

The control panel is the area above the inverse-video border. This area has three lines, each with a special purpose. In the following illustration, the first line, F7: (C2) [W11] @PMT(F4,F6/12,F5), contains information about the *current cell* (the cell where the pointer is located). This line shows the address of the cell, the display format chosen, the cell width in number of characters, and the content of the cell. This line may also show the protection status of the cell. The second line contains the characters that are being entered or edited. When a command is highlighted on a command menu, the third line explains the function of the command.

The control panel contains information about the current cell.

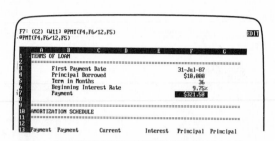

The main menu with the **W**orksheet menu option highlighted.

The Mode Indicators

One of 1-2-3's different modes is always in effect, depending on what you are doing. The mode indicator is shown in inverse video in the upper right corner of the screen. For example, READY is evident whenever the way is clear to add data or other information to the worksheet. VALUE is the indicator when you are entering numbers or formulas, and LABEL appears when you enter letters, as in a title or label. You see the EDIT indicator after you have pressed F2 and want to edit a formula or label in the control panel. A full list of the mode indicators and their meaning appears in table 11.3.

The Status Indicators

Other indicators report the status of the worksheet. They include general message indicators, such as CALC or OVR, and warnings, such as CIRC and MEM. These appear in inverse video in the lower right corner of the screen. Note that when an error occurs, 1-2-3 displays a message in the lower left corner. To clear the error and get back to READY mode, press Esc or Enter. See table 11.3 for more information about the status indicators.

An
Overview of
1-2-3

**Getting
Started**

1-2-3 Basics

Creating a
Worksheet

Printing
Reports

Creating
and
Printing
Graphs

Managing
Data

The Key Indicators

IBM PCs and compatibles have three indicators, NUM, CAPS, and SCROLL, for the Num Lock, Caps Lock, and Scroll Lock keys, respectively. These keys are "lock" keys because they lock the keyboard into a certain function. When a lock key is active, 1-2-3 displays the key's symbol in inverse video in the lower right corner of the screen. Each lock key is a *toggle*, which means that pressing the key repeatedly turns its function alternately on and off. Therefore, to turn off a lock key that is on, you simply press it again.

Two other key indicators are OVR for the Insert key and END for the End key. When OVR appears in inverse video in the lower left corner of the screen, you know that 1-2-3 is in typeover mode. That is, whatever you type replaces existing characters, numerals, or symbols. Table 11.3 contains information about the key indicators.

Table 11.3
The 1-2-3 Indicators

The Mode Indicators

READY	1-2-3 is waiting for a command or cell entry.
VALUE	A number or formula is being entered.
LABEL	A label is being entered.
EDIT	A cell entry is being edited.
POINT	A range is being pointed to.
FILES	1-2-3 is waiting for you to select a file name from the list of file names.
NAMES	1-2-3 is waiting for you to select a range from the list of range names.
MENU	A menu item is being selected.
HELP	1-2-3 is displaying a help screen.
ERROR	An error has occurred, and 1-2-3 is waiting for you to press Esc or ↵Enter to acknowledge the error.
WAIT	1-2-3 is in the middle of a command and cannot respond to commands. WAIT flashes on and off.
FIND	1-2-3 is in the middle of a Data Query operation and cannot respond to commands.

Table **11.3**—*continued*

The Status Indicators

STAT 1-2-3 is displaying the status of your worksheet.

CALC The worksheet has not been recalculated since the last change to cell contents.

CIRC A circular reference has been found.

MEM Random-access memory is almost exhausted. MEM flashes on and off.

SST A keyboard macro or Command Language program is in single- step execution.

HAL HAL, a Lotus add-in that provides a natural-language interface for 1-2-3, is active and can be accessed by pressing the backslash (\) key.

CMD A keyboard macro or Command Language program is executing.

STEP Alt 2 has been pressed, and you are currently stepping through a macro or Command Language program one cell at a time.

The Key Indicators

OVR The key has been pressed, and 1-2-3 is in typeover mode.

NUM Num Lock has been pressed.

CAPS Caps Lock Lock has been pressed.

SCROLL Scroll Lock has been pressed.

END The End key has been pressed.

Accessing the 1-2-3 Help Feature and Tutorial

1-2-3 provides on-line help at the touch of a key. You can be in the middle of any operation and press the Help (F1) key at any time to get one or more screens of explanations and advice on what to do next. If you press F1 while in READY mode, a Help Index appears from which you choose from 25 topics to get to the other help screens.

The most conspicuous user-friendly feature of 1-2-3 is the support Lotus provides for new users who are learning 1-2-3. Lotus provides "A View of 1-2-3," an on-line introduction to the features and business applications of 1-2-3.

An Overview of 1-2-3

Getting Started

1-2-3 Basics

Creating a Worksheet

Printing Reports

Creating and Printing Graphs

Managing Data

1-2-3 also has a tutorial, which consist of three sections: an introductory section that presents an overview of 1-2-3; a sample business-analysis session that shows how 1-2-3 can be used to evaluate alternative business strategies; and for the experienced Release 1 or 1A user, a section that describes the differences between Release 2 and Release 1A. You access the tutorial by selecting **V**iew from the 1-2-3 Access System menu.

Summary

In this chapter, you learned that you can enter 1-2-3 directly from the DOS prompt or through the 1-2-3 Access System. You can exit 1-2-3 temporarily to go to DOS or quit 1-2-3 after verifying your intention to leave the program. If entered 1-2-3 by way of the 1-2-3 Access System, you leave by that route and by selecting **E**xit from the Access System menu.

The chapter introduced you to the three sections of the keyboard: the alphanumeric keys, the numeric keypad, and the function keys. You were shown how various keys of these section are important to 1-2-3. The chapter also called attention to the features of 1-2-3's screen: the control panel, the mode indicators, the status indicators, and the key indicators. You were told the meaning of each indicator so that you would feel at home with the 1-2-3 display.

Finally, the chapter acquainted you with two features designed especially to make 1-2-3 friendly: the help system and the 1-2-3 tutorial. You can readily gain access to the context-sensitive help system by pressing the F1 function key. You enter the tutorial by way of the Access System menu.

Now that you have become familiar with the 1-2-3 environment, you are ready to begin using 1-2-3 by entering data and formulas.

Review Questions

1. Suppose that you are at system level—that is, at the DOS prompt—in the drive and directory that contain the 1-2-3 program files. What do you type to go directly to a fresh worksheet in 1-2-3? What do you type if you want to enter 1-2-3 by way of the 1-2-3 Access System?

2. How do you enter 1-2-3's Translate utility? What is its main purpose?

3. Suppose that you are working on a spreadsheet and want to leave 1-2-3 temporarily to go to DOS. What would you do to go to system level? How you get back to 1-2-3?

4. If you are working on a spreadsheet and want to leave 1-2-3, what would you do?

5. Suppose that you wanted to type a long list of numbers into a 1-2-3 database . What key would you use to change the cursor- movement keys on the numeric keypad to numeric keys? What key would you later use to change those numeric keys back to cursor-movement keys and why?

6. What key would you press to edit a formula in the control panel?

7. What key would you press to recalculate the worksheet?

8. You see OVR in inverse video in the lower right corner of the screen. What does that indicator mean?

9. You see VALUE in inverse video in the upper right corner of the screen. What does that indicator mean?

10. What key do you press to access 1-2-3's help system? How do you access 1-2-3's tutorial?

An
Overview of
1-2-3

Getting
Started

1-2-3 Basics

Creating a
Worksheet

Printing
Reports

Creating
and
Printing
Graphs

Managing
Data

12 *Understanding 1-2-3 Basics*

In a previous chapter, you learned that 1-2-3 is an integrated program that can do much more than crunch numbers. Depending on your business needs or assigned tasks, you can use 1-2-3 to create spreadsheets, develop databases, produce graphics that illustrate spreadsheet data, and generate reports. This chapter explores some of the most elementary operations in 1-2-3: moving around the spreadsheet, entering data, using formulas and functions, and managing files.

After completing this chapter, you will know how to do these basic 1-2-3 tasks:

- Move the cell pointer around the worksheet
- Enter numbers and formulas, using mathematical operators and functions
- Enter labels
- Edit worksheet data
- Name, Save, Retrieve, Delete, List, and Transfer Files

▼

Key Terms in This Chapter

Cursor-movement keys	The keys on the right side of the IBM PC and AT that function also as a numeric keypad when the Num Lock key is pressed. On the PS/2 Enhanced Keyboard, a separate cursor-movement keypad is positioned between the alphanumeric keys and the numeric keypad.
Function keys	The keys on the left side of the keyboard (or across the top of the alphanumeric keys on the Enhanced Keyboard) that are used for special functions.
Cell pointer	The highlighted block that allows you to enter data into a cell on the spreadsheet.
Values	Numbers or formulas. (Note: Formulas can include 1-2-3's built-in functions as well.)

Data	The term to describe any information entered in a cell on the spreadsheet.
Operators	Mathematical or logical operators that specify actions to be performed on data.
Order of precedence	The order in which an equation or formula is executed, determining which operators are acted on first.

▲

Moving Around the Spreadsheet

Soon after you start entering data in your worksheet, you will find you need some easy ways to move the cell pointer quickly and accurately. The sections that follow describe the keys you use to move the pointer to any location in a 1-2-3 worksheet.

Using the Arrow Keys

You use the cursor-movement keys to move the cell pointer when 1- 2-3 is in READY mode. These keys are the arrow keys on the numeric keypad, or also on a separate pad of the Enhanced Keyboard. The cell pointer moves in the direction of the arrow on the key as long as you hold down the key. When you reach the edge of the screen, the worksheet scrolls in the direction of the arrow.

When 1-2-3 is in POINT mode, you use these keys to point out a range. Note that you cannot use these keys, or they have a different action, when you are editing in EDIT mode, making a cell entry, or entering a 1-2-3 command.

Scrolling

If you press the Scroll Lock key to activate the scroll function, the worksheet scrolls in the direction of whatever arrow key you press, no matter where the cell pointer is positioned on the screen. Leaving the scroll function off is usually easier and less confusing.

You can scroll the worksheet one screenful at a time to the right or left by holding down the Ctrl key and pressing the right- or left-arrow key, respectively. You can also use the Tab key to scroll the worksheet to the right, or Shift-Tab to scroll the worksheet to the left. (For Shift-Tab, you hold down the Shift key while you press the

An
Overview of
1-2-3

Getting
Started

1-2-3 Basics

Creating a
Worksheet

Printing
Reports

Creating
and
Printing
Graphs

Managing
Data

Tab key.) These four key combinations provide quick ways of "paging through" the worksheet. To scroll up or down, you use the PgUp and PgDn keys, not the up- and down-arrow keys.

Using the Home and End Keys

The Home key provides a quick way to return to the beginning of the worksheet. Wherever you are in the worksheet, pressing Home causes the cell pointer to return to cell A1. (Note: As you will learn later in this chapter, some keys, such as Home and End, have different actions in EDIT mode.)

1-2-3 uses the End key in a unique way. If you press and release the End key and then press an arrow key, the cell pointer moves in the direction of the arrow key to the next boundary between a blank cell and a cell that contains data. Remember, however, that if there are gaps in the blocks of data, the End key procedure will probably be less useful because the cell pointer will go to the boundaries of each gap.

You can also use the End key, followed by the Home key, to move the cell pointer from any position on the spreadsheet to the lower right corner of the active worksheet. In a sense, the effect of using the Home key after the End key is the opposite of that of using the Home key alone. The Home key always moves the cell pointer to cell A1, the upper left corner of every spreadsheet.

Using the GoTo Key (F5)

The F5 (GoTo) function key gives you a way to jump directly to a cell location. To move the cell pointer to any cell on the spreadsheet, just press the F5 function key. When 1-2-3 asks you for the address to go to, type in the cell address you want.

Entering Data and Formulas

You enter data into a cell simply by highlighting the cell with the cell pointer and then typing the entry. To complete the entry, press Enter or any of the cursor-movement keys discussed in this chapter.

If you enter data into a cell that already contains information, the new data replaces that information. This is one way to change information in a cell. The other way, which involves the F2 (Edit) key, is explained later in the section "Editing Data in the Worksheet."

There are two types of cell entries: *values* and *labels*. Values can be either numbers or formulas (including functions, which 1-2-3 treats as built-in formulas). 1-2-3 determines from the first character you enter which type of cell entry you are making. If you start with one of the following characters,

    0 1 2 3 4 5 6 7 8 9 + - . (@ # $

1-2-3 treats your entry as a value (a number or a formula). If you begin by entering a character other than one of the above, 1-2-3 treats your entry as a label.

Entering Numbers

To enter a number, start typing with one of the following characters:

    0 1 2 3 4 5 6 7 8 9 + - . ($

You enter decimals normally. For percentages, you end a number with a percent sign (%), and the number will automatically be divided by 100 and entered as a decimal fraction.

If you do not follow these rules, 1-2-3 will beep when you press Enter, and 1-2-3 will automatically shift to EDIT mode as if you had pressed F2.

Entering Formulas

In addition to entering simple numbers, you can also enter formulas into cells. You enter formulas either by *typing* the formula into the cell or by *pointing*, which means moving the cell pointer so that 1-2-3 enters the cell addresses for you.

Suppose that you want to create a formula that adds a row of numbers. For example, suppose that you want to add amounts in cells C4, C5, C6, and C7, and place the result in cell C9. To do this by *typing*, you just type **+C4+C5+C6+C7** into cell C9. The + sign at the beginning of the formula causes 1-2-3 to recognize that the formula is a formula and not a label. 1-2-3 then switches to VALUE mode, which is the appropriate mode for entering numbers and formulas.

The following sequence of screens illustrates entering a formula by pointing.

An
Overview of
1-2-3

Getting
Started

1-2-3 Basics

Creating a
Worksheet

Printing
Reports

Creating
and
Printing
Graphs

Managing
Data

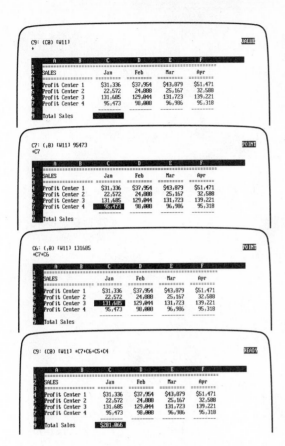

To create a formula by pointing, begin on the cell that will hold the formula. Then type +.

Move to the first cell address used in the formula and type +.

Move to the next cell address used in the formula and type +.

Repeat this procedure until all the necessary cell addresses are included. Then press ↵Enter to end the process.

Using Mathematical Operators in Formulas

Operators indicate arithmetic operations in formulas. Operators can be separated into two types: mathematical and logical. The mathematical operators are

Operator	Meaning
^	Exponentiation
+, -	Positive, negative
*, /	Multiplication, division
+, -	Addition, subtraction

This list indicates from the top of the list downward the *order of precedence*—that is, the order in which these operators are evaluated. For example, exponentiation takes place before multiplication, and division occurs before subtraction.

155

Operations inside a set of parentheses are always evaluated first. Operators at the same level of precedence are evaluated in turn in the formula from left to right.

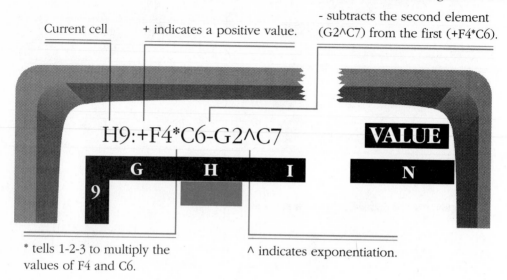

Current cell   + indicates a positive value.   - subtracts the second element (G2^C7) from the first (+F4*C6).

H9:+F4*C6-G2^C7   **VALUE**

* tells 1-2-3 to multiply the values of F4 and C6.   ^ indicates exponentiation.

Using Functions in Formulas

1-2-3's functions fall into seven categories: (1) mathematical and trigonometric, (2) statistical, (3) financial and accounting, (4) logical, (5) special, (6) date and time, and (7) string. The following paragraphs briefly describe some of 1-2-3's functions.

The mathematical and trigonometric functions provide you with tools for performing a variety of standard arithmetic operations such as computing absolute value (@ABS) or the square root (@SQRT); rounding numbers to a specified precision (@ROUND); and computing the sine (@SIN), cosine (@COS), and tangent @TAN.

The statistical functions allow you to perform all the standard statistical calculations such as calculating averages (@AVG), finding minimum and maximum values (@MIN and @MAX), computing standard deviations and variances (@STD and @VAR), and summing a list of values (@SUM).

The financial and accounting functions include those for calculating returns on investments (@IRR and @RATE), calculating loan investments (@PMT), calculating present values (@NPV and @PV), calculating future values (@FV), calculating compound growth (@TERM and @CTERM), and calculating asset depreciation (@SLN, @DDB, and @SYD).

The logical functions such as @IF, @TRUE, and @FALSE let you add standard Boolean logic to your worksheet.

The special functions are tools for dealing with the worksheet itself. @CELL and @CELLPOINTER, for example, can return up to 10 different characteristics of a cell, including the type of address and prefix, format, and width of a cell.

The date and time functions such as @DATE and @TIME allow you to convert dates and times to serial numbers and then use these serial numbers to perform date and time arithmetic, or to document your worksheets and reports.

The string functions help you manipulate text. You can use use string functions to repeat text characters, to convert letters to upper- or lowercase, and to change strings to numbers and numbers to strings.

How To Enter a 1-2-3 Function

1-2-3 functions consist of three parts: an @ sign, the function, and an argument or range of cells. So identified, functions can be distinguished easily from all other entries.

The @ symbol
The @ symbol tells 1-2-3 to read as a function the information that follows the symbol.

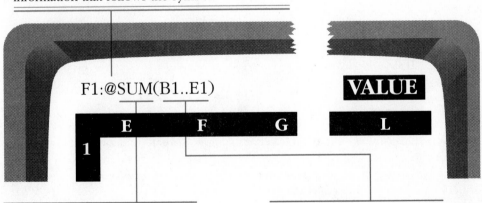

F1:@SUM(B1..E1)   VALUE

The function
In this instance, the function is SUM. 1-2-3 has a wide variety of functions capable of performing various tasks—from simple addition and division to complex statistical analysis and depreciation analysis.

The range
The range in this function is B1 to E1, meaning that all values in the cells in the rectangular area starting at and including B1 through E1 will be added by the SUM function.

When you enter a formula containing a function that requires a cell address, you can enter the cell address by typing or pointing. For example, to enter at cell C9 the formula @SUM(C7..C4) by pointing, follow this procedure:

Move the cell pointer to the cell where you want to locate the formula, and type @SUM(.

Move the cell point to C7 and press [.] to anchor the cell pointer.

Press the [↑] key three times to highlight the range of cells from C7 through C4.

Finally, type the closing [)] and press [↵Enter]. 1-2-3 will enter in C9 the sum of C7..C4.

Some functions can be quite complex. For example, several functions can be combined in a single cell by having one function use other functions as its arguments. The length of an argument, however, is limited; like formulas, functions can contain a maximum of 240 characters per cell.

Entering Labels

Labels play an important role in spreadsheet development. Without labels on a spreadsheet, *you* might know that column F is January data and row 11 is Accounts

158

An Overview of 1-2-3

Getting Started

1-2-3 Basics

Creating a Worksheet

Printing Reports

Creating and Printing Graphs

Managing Data

Receivable, but how would someone else who is not familiar with the spreadsheet know?

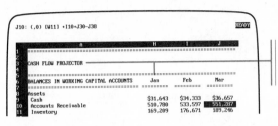

Labels make values more evident in a spreadsheet and help people find information quickly.

Labels may be up to 240 characters long and contain any string of characters and numbers. A label that is too long for the width of a cell continues (for display purposes) across the cells to the right, as long as the neighboring cells contain no other entries.

When you make an entry into a cell and the first character is not a number or an indicator for entering numbers and formulas, 1-2-3 assumes that you are entering a label. As you type the first character, 1-2-3 shifts to LABEL mode.

One of the advantages of 1-2-3 is that you can control how the labels are displayed in the cell. By entering a *label prefix* character, you can tell 1-2-3 to left-justify ('), center (^), right-justify ("), or repeat (\) labels when you display them.

Editing Data in the Worksheet

When you start using 1-2-3, one of the first things you will want to do is modify the contents of cells without retyping the complete entry. This modification is quite easy to do in 1-2-3. You begin by moving the cell pointer to the appropriate cell and pressing the F2 (Edit) key.

After you press F2, the mode indicator in the upper right corner of the screen changes to EDIT. The contents of the cell are duplicated in the second line of the control panel (the edit line), the cursor appears at the end of the entry, and you are ready for editing.

When 1-2-3 is in insert mode, any new character is inserted at the cursor, and any characters to the right of the cursor are pushed one character to the right. If you activate overtype mode by pressing the Insert key on the numeric keypad, any new character replaces the character directly above the cursor, and the cursor moves one character to the right.

To edit data in a cell, move the cell pointer to the cell whose contents you want to change, and press F2 (Edit). Notice that the mode indicator changes to EDIT mode.

With the contents of the cell displayed in the second line of the control panel, move the cursor to the part of the entry you want to edit.

Use one or more editing keys to modify the cell's contents. In this example, press the Del key to delete the character above the cursor.

Press ↵Enter to complete the edit and return the worksheet to READY mode.

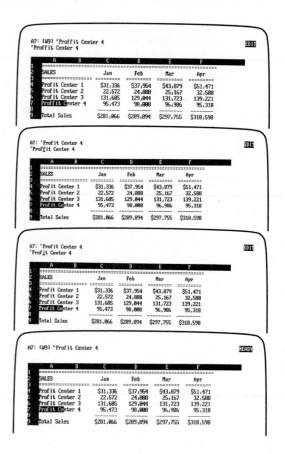

One thing to remember about EDIT mode is that you can use it also when you enter data into a cell for the first time. Then, if you make a mistake while you are entering data in EDIT mode, you do not have to retype the entire entry. You can just correct the error.

Managing 1-2-3 Files

Storing, retrieving, and deleting files to and from disks are capabilities common to all spreadsheet programs. What makes 1-2-3 unique is its scale in performing these functions. Lotus wrote 1-2-3 for users who intend to mix and match many large files that will be moved in and out of storage quite frequently.

An
Overview of
1-2-3

Getting
Started

1-2-3 Basics

Creating a
Worksheet

Printing
Reports

Creating
and
Printing
Graphs

Managing
Data

This section describes the file operations that beginning 1-2-3 users need most often: naming, saving, retrieving, deleting, and listing files. For more specialized file operations, such as combining and transferring files and using the Translate Utility, only general information is provided.

Naming Files

The conventions for naming files in 1-2-3 adhere closely to those for naming files in DOS. For example, 1-2-3 file names can be up to eight characters long with a three-character extension. In addition, you should use only letters of the alphabet and numbers, not spaces or a period.

Although you determine the eight-character name, 1-2-3 automatically creates an extension according to the type of file you are handling. The three possible file extensions are

WK1   For worksheet files (WKS for 1-2-3 files before Release 2)

PRN   For print files

PIC   For graph files

Besides creating files with WK1, PRN, and PIC extensions, 1-2-3 lets you supply your own extensions. Simply type a file name according to the rules listed in the preceding section, type a period, add an extension of one to three characters, and press Enter.

Saving Files

1-2-3's basic method of storing files is easy to use. The /**F**ile **S**ave command allows you to save an entire worksheet in a file on disk. The command makes an exact copy of the current worksheet, including all the formats, range names, and settings you have specified.

When you enter this command, 1-2-3 will try to help you by supplying a list of the current worksheet files on the disk. You can either point to one of the entries or enter a new file name. To enter a new file name, you must use the rules previously explained. 1-2-3 will automatically supply a WK1 extension.

Retrieving Files

To bring into the worksheet a file stored on disk, use the **/File Retrieve** command. 1-2-3 displays a list of all files with WK1 and WKS extensions in the current drive and directory.

To get a full screen of the names, press ⌊F3⌋ (Names) while 1-2-3 is showing the list of file names.

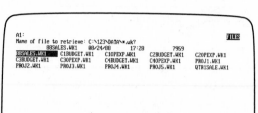

If the name of the file you want is in the list, you can select the name by moving the cursor to it and pressing Enter, or you can type the name.

Saving and Retrieving Partial Files

Sometimes you will want to store only part of a worksheet (a range of cells, for instance) in a separate file on disk. One of the best uses for a partial save is breaking up worksheet files that are too large to be stored on a single disk. With the **/File Xtract** command, you can save part of the worksheet file—either the formulas existing in a range of cells or the current values of the formulas in the range, depending on the option you select. The **Formulas** option saves a file with all of the formulas intact. The **Values** option saves only the current values, so the new worksheet file will contain numbers but no formulas. Either option creates a worksheet file that you can reload into 1-2-3 with the **/File Retrieve** command.

Another procedure you will want to use is that of making copies of certain ranges of cells from other worksheets and placing them into strategic spots in the current worksheet. For example, if you work for a large firm, you may want to combine the balance sheets and income statements of several divisions into one consolidated worksheet. To do this, you use the **/File Combine** command, which has three options: **Copy**, **Add**, and **Subtract**. The **Copy** option copies the incoming worksheet or range over the existing worksheet or range. The **Add** option adds the incoming values to the existing values. The **Subtract** option subtracts the incoming values from the existing values.

An
Overview of
1-2-3

Getting
Started

1-2-3 Basics

Creating a
Worksheet

Printing
Reports

Creating
and
Printing
Graphs

Managing
Data

Deleting Files

When you save files to a diskette, you may sometimes find that it is full. To alert you, 1-2-3 flashes the message Disk full in the screen's lower left corner. You can then either swap diskettes or delete one or more of the current files occupying space on the diskette.

You have two ways to delete stored files in 1-2-3: by using /File Erase or by accessing DOS with the /System command and erasing the file at DOS level.

To use the /File Erase command, you type /FE. A menu prompt asks whether you want to erase a Worksheet, Print, Graph, or Other file. After you make your selection, 1-2-3 lists the appropriate files. You can then point to the particular file you want erased, or type its name and press Enter.

Listing Different Types of Files

You can use the /File List command to list all the names of a certain type of file on the active drive and directory. The choices for file types are

> Worksheet Print Graph Other

After you choose one of these options and press Enter, the list of files is displayed. Worksheet, Print, and Graph list the three types of 1-2-3 data files. The fourth choice, Other, lists all files of all types on the current drive and directory.

You use the /Worksheet Global Default Directory or the /File Directory commands to change the drive and directory. /Worksheet Global Default Directory can change the default drive and directory. /File Directory, on the other hand, changes the drive and directory temporarily for only the current worksheet session.

Transferring Files

A powerful feature of 1-2-3 is its capability to interface with outside programs. For this, you use the /File Import, /Print File Options Other Unformatted commands, and the Translate Utility.

Use the /File Import command to copy standard ASCII files to specific locations in the current worksheet. PRN (print) files are one example of standard ASCII text files created to print after the current 1-2-3 session. Other standard ASCII files include those produced by different word processing, database, and BASIC programs.

The Translate Utility is used to import files from dBASE II, dBASE III, dBASE III Plus, and VisiCalc into 1-2-3, and to export 1-2-3 files in dBASE II, dBASE III, dBASE III Plus, and DIF formats. This feature provides good communication with dBASE, including dBASE III Plus (which is not listed on the menu but can be accessed by selecting dBASE III). The Translate Utility also provides translation capabilities among all of Lotus's products, allowing free interchange of worksheets among 1-2-3 Release 2.01, Symphony, and earlier releases of 1-2-3.

Summary

This chapter on 1-2-3 basics covered the keys you use to move the cell pointer around the spreadsheet; the entry and editing of data, formulas, and labels; and the handling of 1-2-3 files.

You learned that with just the arrow keys, you can move the cell pointer cell-by-cell in any direction horizontally or vertically. Used with the End key, however, the arrow keys can move the cell pointer quickly, even to remote borders of 1-2-3's large spreadsheet. The Home key can make the cell pointer leap to the upper left corner of a worksheet. If you specify a cell address for the GoTo (F5) function key, you can make the cell pointer jump almost instantly to any cell in the entire worksheet.

Part of 1-2-3's power resides in its capability of accepting and computing complex numerical data, formulas, and functions. As you enter this information into a spreadsheet, you can easily edit the information if you make a mistake in entry. You can also supply text labels as titles to make it easier for others to comprehend and use the spreadsheets you create.

Knowing how to manage files is essential for efficient use of 1- 2-3. You learned how to name, save, and retrieve files. You can save partial files if you want to extract or combine portions of a worksheet. You can list and delete files with ease if you know how to specify drives, subdirectories, and file names accurately. You can even import files from, or export them to, other leading software programs.

When you work with a 1-2-3 worksheet, you must know how to create cell ranges, and to move and copy them to other locations in the worksheet. These necessary maneuvers are the subject of the next chapter.

Review Questions

1. Where does the cell pointer move when you press the following keys:

   End (down)

   End (right)

   End Home

2. Besides the integers 0, 1, 2, 3 4, 5, 6, 7, 8, 9, what characters does 1-2-3 interpret as the beginning of a value (a number or formula)?

3. Which function key is the GoTo key?

4. What are the two methods of entering a formula in 1-2-3?

5. Number from 1-4 the order in which 1-2-3 evaluates the following operators?

   * Multiplication   _____

   \+ Addition   _____

   / Division   _____

   – Subtraction   _____

6. What function key enables you to edit the contents of a cell?

7. List the file extensions that 1-2-3 uses to identify the following types of files.

File	Extension
/**W**orksheet	_____
/**P**rint	_____
/**G**raph	_____

8. What sequence of commands enables you to retrieve a worksheet file?

9. What are the two methods available for erasing files?

10. What two command sequences enable you to change the default drive and directory? What are the differences between these two commands?

An
Overview of
1-2-3

Getting
Started

1-2-3 Basics

**Creating a
Worksheet**

Printing
Reports

Creating
and
Printing
Graphs

Managing
Data

13 *Creating a Worksheet*

This chapter tells you how to use 1-2-3's commands and shows you some that are necessary for building worksheets. To be expected, many of these commands are found in the /**W**orksheet menu. In general, the commands are not discussed in the order in which they appear in a menu but as you need them in creating a worksheet. (For information on the commands for saving a worksheet and accessing DOS from within 1-2-3, see Chapter 11, "Getting Started.")

Some 1-2-3 commands affect the entire worksheet; others affect only certain cells or rectangular blocks of cells called *ranges*. Many useful 1-2-3 actions involve ranges. To make good use of 1-2-3, you must know how to define and use ranges. To that end, this chapter includes commands that manipulate ranges.

▼

Key Terms in This Chapter

Range	A range is a rectangular group of cells that is used in a worksheet operation. For example, the rectangular area A10..D10 is a range.
/Range commands	These commands manipulate cells in specified ranges. The /**R**ange command is found on the 1-2-3 main menu.
/Worksheet commands	These commands affect the entire worksheet or predefined areas of the worksheet. The /**W**orksheet command is available on the main menu.
Relative cell addressing	When you copy or move a formula, the addresses of the cells in that formula are changed to fit the new location.
Absolute cell addressing	When you copy or move a formula and do not want a cell address to change, you can create an absolute address, meaning that the address will not change.

▲

167

After completing this chapter, you will know how to do the following:

- Use **/R**ange commands
- Name, list, and erase ranges
- Use **/W**orksheet commands
- Create windows and freeze titles
- Insert, delete, and hide columns and rows
- Format cell contents
- Copy and move cells and ranges
- Use relative, absolute, and mixed addressing

Selecting Commands from Command Menus

If commands are the tools for performing 1-2-3 tasks, command menus are the toolboxes. The menus display the commands available for use. If you select the wrong command, you can press Esc at any time to return to the preceding command menu. In 1-2-3, the command menus are especially helpful for several reasons.

First of all, you can access the main command menu easily. When you want to display the main command menu to select a command, make certain that 1-2-3 is in READY mode and then press the slash (/) key. The main command menu appears at the top of the screen, and each available command is evident as a full word, as shown in the following screen:

The main 1-2-3 menu appears on the second line of the control panel.

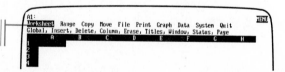

A second feature of the command menu is its informative third line. This line contains a brief explanation of the **W**orksheet menu item on which the command pointer is positioned. In fact, as you point to different commands by moving the pointer across the command menu, a new explanation appears as each command is highlighted. This action occurs with every command menu.

A third friendly aspect of command menus relates to how a command is initiated. You can either point to the option you want, or you can just type the first letter of the command name. To *point* to a command on a menu, use the left- and right-arrow keys on the right side of the keyboard. When the highlighted pointer is on the command you want, press Enter.

An Overview of 1-2-3

Getting Started

1-2-3 Basics

Creating a Worksheet

Printing Reports

Creating and Printing Graphs

Managing Data

Using Ranges in the Worksheet

1-2-3's commands and functions often require that you work with ranges. You learned earlier in this chapter that a 1-2-3 range is a rectangular block of cells. Actually, the smallest possible range is just one cell, and the largest, the entire worksheet.

You access the /**R**ange commands by selecting **R**ange from the main command menu. You then see the following submenu of commands:

Format **L**abel **E**rase **N**ame **J**ustify **P**rotect **U**nprotect **I**nput **V**alue **T**ranspose

Table 13.1 gives you a capsule description of the function of each of these subcommands.

Table 13.1
The Range Commands and Their Functions

Command	*Function*
Format	Formats the specific display of values or formula results in a cell or a range of cells
Label	Aligns text labels in their cells
Erase	Erases the contents of a cell or range of cells
Name	Assigns an alphabetical or alphanumeric name to a cell or range of cells
Justify	Fits text within a desired range by wrapping words to form complete paragraphs with lines of approximately the same length
Protect	Removes identification from an unprotected range when /**W**orksheet **G**lobal **P**rotection is enabled
Unprotect	Identifies (through increase in intensity or change of color) which cells' contents can be changed when /**W**orksheet **G**lobal **P**rotection is enabled
Input	Restricts cell-pointer movement to unprotected cells
Value	Converts formulas in a range to their values so that you can copy only the values to a new location
Transpose	Reorders columns of data into rows of data, or rows of data into columns of data

Ranges offer many advantages that make your work with 1-2-3 less tedious and more efficient. When you use ranges, you can launch actions that affect a large group of cells all at once instead of cell by cell. You will soon see that if you give a range a descriptive name, it will help you and others to recognize immediately the nature of a range's data. Once you have named a range, you can use that name with the GoTo (F5) command to move the cell pointer quickly to that range in the worksheet.

This range, which is one column in width, is specified by the first and last cells in the range, or G4..G9.

This range is made up of cells C4..E9.

This range is only one cell, A9.

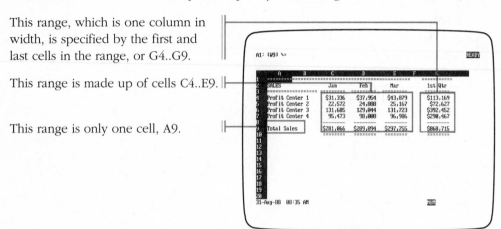

Entering a Range

When to use ranges in 1-2-3 depends to some degree on personal preference. In many cases, such as creating a formula or a macro, you decide whether to provide ranges. In other cases, however, 1-2-3 prompts you for ranges.

When you are using a 1-2-3 command and are asked to designate a range, you can do so in any one of three ways. You can enter the addresses of the cells in the range, use the cell pointer to point to the cells in the range, or simply enter a name you have assigned to the range.

After you designate a range, the cells of the range appear in inverse video. If you use the pointing method, the inverse-video rectangle expands or contracts *as* you use the arrow keys to define the range. Pointing is therefore an easy, visual way to designate ranges.

The *designation* of a range is a reference to the cell limits of a range. A range having more than one row or column is specified by diagonally opposite corners of the

Selecting
Commands from
Command Menus

**Using Ranges
in the
Worksheet**

Using
Worksheet
Commands

Moving the
Contents of
Cells

Copying the
Contents of
Cells

Summary

range—usually its upper left and lower right cells, as in A7..D10. The cells in the other set of corners—A10..D7—can identify the range just as well, however. Note that you can specify the far column first, as in D10..A7 or D7..A10. The order does not matter.

A range in just one column or one row is specified by the first and last cells of the range, as in B2..B10 (a 9-row range in one column) or B2..G2 (a 6-column range in one row). Again, the order does not matter. These two ranges could just as well be designated B10..B2 and G2..B2.

Naming Ranges

You can assign a name to a range of cells. Range names can be up to 15 characters long and should be descriptive. The reason is that a descriptive range name is easier to understand than cell addresses. For example, the phrase SALES_MODEL25 is a more understandable way of describing the sales for Model #25 than using the cell address A7..D10.

You create range names with the /**R**ange **N**ame **C**reate and /**R**ange **N**ame **L**abels commands. You use the former when you want to create a new range name, and the latter when you want to use as a range name a label already in the worksheet and adjacent to the range. You use /**R**ange **N**ame **C**reate to name any range. It can be just one cell or a large number of cells.

Using Range Names To Streamline Your Work

Using range names in commands and formulas reduces the amount of typing you must do and thus makes your work more efficient. Whenever you must designate a range, you can respond with a range name instead of entering cell addresses or pointing to cell locations. For example, suppose that you have assigned the range name SALES to the range A5..J5 in one of your worksheets. The simplest way to compute the sum of this range is to use the function @SUM(SALES).

Deleting Range Names

You can delete range names individually or all at once. The /**R**ange **N**ame **D**elete command is for deleting a single range name, and the /**R**ange **N**ame **R**eset command deletes all range names in one operation. If you delete a range name, 1-2-3 no longer uses that name and reverts to using the range's cell addresses. For example, @SUM(REVENUES) returns to @SUM(A5..J5).

Erasing Ranges

The **/R**ange **E**rase command erases sections of a worksheet. You can use this command on a range as small as a single cell or as large as the entire worksheet. When you issue the **/R**ange **E**rase command, 1-2-3 prompts you to specify the range to delete. You can specify it by pointing, entering the coordinates, or typing the range name. You can erase ranges more easily if you have already assigned names to them. If you can't remember the name of the range you want to erase, press the F3 (Names) key to produce in the control panel a list of the range names in the current worksheet. If you would like to see a full-screen display of the range names, press F3 again. After 1-2-3 displays the list, you can move the pointer to the name of the range you want to erase. After you press Enter, 1-2-3 erases the range immediately.

After you erase a range, you cannot recover it. If you want to restore the range, you will have to reenter all the data.

Going to a Range

You can use the Names key with the F5 (GoTo) key to select the name of a range to which you want to move the cell pointer. If you press F5 and then press F3, 1-2-3 displays in the control panel an alphabetical list of the worksheet's range names. If you would like to see instead a full-screen display of the range names, press F3 again. Select a range name and press Enter. The list disappears, and the cell pointer is positioned at the beginning of the selected range.

Formatting Cell Contents

1-2-3 expects you to enter data a certain way. If, for example, you try to enter **1,234**, the program beeps, switches to EDIT mode, and waits for you to remove the comma. You get the same result if you try to enter **10:08 AM**—the colon and AM are the offenders. If you try to enter **$9.23**, the program accepts the entry, but without the dollar sign.

1-2-3's usefulness would be limited if you could not change the way data is displayed on the screen, but you can control not only the display of commas, time, and currency but also a variety of other formats. You determine format with one of the **/R**ange **F**ormat or **/W**orksheet **G**lobal **F**ormat commands.

Table 13.2 proviods examples of the formats available in 1-2-3. These formats primarily affect the way numeric values are displayed in a worksheet.

An Overview of 1-2-3

Getting Started

1-2-3 Basics

Creating a Worksheet

Printing Reports

Creating and Printing Graphs

Managing Data

Table 13.2
1-2-3's Format Options

Format	Description	Value (or Formula) Entered	Value as Displayed (When Formatted with No Decimal Places)
Fixed	Controls the number of decimal places displayed.	15.56	16
Scientific	Displays large or small numbers, using scientific notation.	-21	-2E+01
Currency	Displays currency symbols and commas.	234567.75	$234,568
, (Comma)	Inserts commas to mark thousands and multiples of thousands.	234567	234,567
General	Displays values with up to 10 decimals or in scientific notation.	26.003	26.003
+/-	Creates horizontal bar graphs or time duration graphs of plus or minus signs on computers that cannot display graphs.	3 −3	+++ –––
Percent	Displays a decimal number as a whole number with a % sign.	0.25	25%
Date	Displays serial-date numbers. **/R**ange **F**ormat **D**ate **T**ime sets time formats.	@DATE(89,8,1) @NOW	01-Aug-89 07:48 AM
Text	Displays formulas as text, not the computed values that 1-2-3 normally displays.	+B5+B6 @SUM(C4..C8)	+B+B6 @SUM(C4..C8)
Hidden	Hides contents from the display and does not print them; hidden contents are still evaluated.	289	

All formats specified with **/R**ange **F**ormat display format indicators in the command line. You do not have to enter these indicators; 1-2-3 automatically provides them. The indicator for the default format of the worksheet, however, will not appear in the command line.

Although you will probably use the **/R**ange **F**ormat command frequently to format individual ranges in a worksheet, you can also change the default format for the whole worksheet. The **/W**orksheet **G**lobal **F**ormat command controls the format of all the cells in the worksheet, and the **/R**ange **F**ormat command controls specific ranges in the worksheet.

Generally, you use the **/W**orksheet **G**lobal **F**ormat command when you are just starting to enter data in a worksheet. You will want to choose a format that the majority of most cells will take. Once you have set all the cells to the format, you can use the **/R**ange **F**ormat command to override the global format setting for specific cell ranges.

Using Worksheet Commands

The first command option on the 1-2-3 main menu is the **W**orksheet command. When you select it, 1-2-3 offers the following group of subcommands:

Global **I**nsert **D**elete **C**olumn **E**rase **T**itles **W**indow **S**tatus **P**age

These **W**orksheet commands are similar to the **R**ange commands but affect the entire worksheet or preset segments of it. Table 13.3 lists each Worksheet command and describes briefly its function.

Table 13.3
The Worksheet Commands and Their Functions

Command	Function
Global	Affects the entire worksheet
Insert	Inserts columns and rows
Delete	Deletes columns and rows
Column	Sets column width and the display of columns
Erase	Clears the entire spreadsheet
Titles	Freezes the display of titles
Window	Splits the screen into two windows
Status	Checks the status of global settings
Page	Inserts a page break in a printed worksheet

Selecting
Commands from
Command Menus

Using Ranges
in the
Worksheet

**Using
Worksheet
Commands**

Moving the
Contents of
Cells

Copying the
Contents of
Cells

Summary

An
Overview of
1-2-3

Getting
Started

1-2-3 Basics

**Creating a
Worksheet**

Printing
Reports

Creating
and
Printing
Graphs

Managing
Data

Erasing the Worksheet

The /**W**orksheet **E**rase command clears the entire spreadsheet. This command not only erases all the contents of the worksheet but also restores all global settings to their default condition, destroys any range names or graph names in the worksheet, and clears any title lock or window split in the worksheet. You learn about locked titles and split windows later in this discussion of the **W**orksheet commands.

Be sure that you understand the difference between the /**W**orksheet **E**rase command and the /**R**ange **E**rase A1..IV8192 command. The /**R**ange **E**rase command will remove the contents of every cell in the worksheet, except those that are protected. The command will not, however, alter any of the global settings, including column widths or print settings. /**W**orksheet **E**rase, however, literally restores the 1-2-3 worksheet to its default configuration. After you issue the /**we** command, the worksheet is exactly as it was when loaded.

Setting Column Widths

You can control the width of columns in the worksheet to accommodate data entries that are too wide for the default column width of nine characters. You also can reduce column widths, perhaps to give the worksheet a better appearance when a column contains narrow entries. In 1-2-3, you can set the width of all the columns in the worksheet at once or separately control the width of each column.

The command for setting individual column widths is /**W**orksheet **C**olumn **S**et-Width. You can set one column width at a time either by entering a number or by using the left- and right-arrow keys followed by Enter. The advantage of the left- and right-arrow keys is that the column width expands and contracts each time you press a key. To get a good idea of what the width requirements are, experiment when you enter the command.

If you want, you can set the width of all the columns in the worksheet at once. To do this, you use the /**W**orksheet **G**lobal **C**olumn-Width command. It is one of the **G**lobal commands, which affect the entire worksheet.

Splitting the Screen

You can split the 1-2-3 screen into two windows, either horizontally or vertically. This feature helps you to overcome some of the inconvenience of not being able to see the entire spreadsheet at one time. By splitting the screen, you can make changes in one area and immediately see their effect in another area.

The command for splitting the screen is /**W**orksheet **W**indow. The **H**orizontal and **V**ertical menu choices split the screen in the manner indicated by their names. The F6 (Window) key lets you move the pointer between windows. To restore a full screen you use the **C**lear option on the /**W**orksheet **W**indow menu.

Freezing Titles on the Screen

The /**W**orksheet **T**itles command is similar to the /**W**orksheet **W**indow command. With both commands, you can see one area of a worksheet while you work on another area. The unique function of the /**W**orksheet **T**itles command, however, is that it freezes all the cells to the left or above (or both to the left and above) the cell pointer's current position so that those cells cannot move off the screen. With this command you can keep the column headings, for example, in view while you scroll the screen.

Inserting Columns and Rows

One of the techniques for improving a worksheet's appearance is to insert blank rows and columns in strategic places to highlight headings and other important items. The command for inserting rows and columns in 1-2-3 is /**W**orksheet **I**nsert. You can insert multiple rows and columns each time you invoke this command. After you select /**W**orksheet **I**nsert, you are asked for the method of insertion—**C**olumn or **R**ow. After you have selected one or the other, you are asked for an *insert range*. Depending on how you set up this range, one or more columns or rows will be inserted. Inserted columns appear to the left of the specified range, and inserted rows appear above the specified range.

Deleting Columns and Rows

Deleting rows and columns is the opposite of inserting them. With 1-2-3, you can delete multiple rows or columns at the same time with the /**W**orksheet **D**elete command. After you choose this command, you then choose **C**olumn or **R**ow from the submenu that appears on the screen. If you choose **R**ow, 1-2-3 asks you to specify a range of cells to be deleted. Just as for the /**W**orksheet **I**nsert command, the range you specify includes one cell from a given row.

Hiding Columns

With the /**W**orksheet **C**olumn **H**ide command, you can suppress the display of any column in the worksheet. When you select the /**W**orksheet **C**olumn **H**ide command,

An Overview of 1-2-3

Getting Started

1-2-3 Basics

Creating a Worksheet

Printing Reports

Creating and Printing Graphs

Managing Data

1-2-3 prompts you for the range of columns to hide. You must invoke the command once for each range of adjacent columns that you hide.

When you hide intervening columns, you can print on a single page a report of data from two or more separated columns. You can use this command also to fit noncontiguous columns on-screen, suppress the display of sensitive information, and hide the display of all cells having a numeric value of zero.

Although hidden columns are not evident on the screen, numbers and formulas in hidden columns are still present, and cell references to cells in hidden columns continue to work properly. You can tell which columns are missing only by noting the break in column letters at the top of the display. To redisplay hidden columns, use **/W**orksheet **C**olumn **D**isplay.

Suppressing the Display of Zeros

The **/W**orksheet **G**lobal **Z**ero command allows you to suppress the display of all the cells in the worksheet that have a numeric value of zero. This technique is often useful for preparing reports for presentation. You can enter formulas and values for all the items in the report, including the zero items, and then display the results with all the zeros removed. The **/W**orksheet **G**lobal **Z**ero command also has an option to reinstate the display of zero values. If you type **/wgz**, save the file, and then retrieve the file, the **/W**orksheet **G**lobal **Z**ero command will be disabled, and the display of zeros will no longer be suppressed.

Recalculating the Worksheet

One of the primary functions of a spreadsheet program is to recalculate all the cells in a worksheet when a value or a formula in one of the cells changes. When you select the **/W**orksheet **G**lobal **R**ecalculation command, 1-2-3 provides two basic recalculation methods: *automatic recalculation* and *manual recalculation.* In automatic recalculation, which is the default, 1-2-3 recalculates the worksheet whenever any cell in the worksheet changes. In manual recalculation, the worksheet is recalculated only when you request recalculation, either from the keyboard or by a macro.

1-2-3 also provides three orders of recalculation: *natural order* and two *linear orders*—either *columnwise* or *rowwise*. Natural order is the default, but you can choose any of the three orders. You use **C**olumnwise and **R**owwise recalculation for more specialized applications, but be extremely careful when you choose these orders of recalculation. If you use them improperly, they can cause forward and circular reference errors or may produce erroneous values on the worksheet.

1-2-3 offers a third method of recalculation—*iterative recalculation*—that lets you determine the number a times the spreadsheet is recalculated. Because of circular references, the spreadsheet may need to be recalculated several times when you request recalculation. A circular pattern is one in which each value in a set is dependent directly or indirectly on the other values of the set. You can specify that iterative recalculation be repeated up to 50 times to handle circular references.

If you are a beginning 1-2-3 user, you may not need to change the recalculation settings at all. 1-2-3's default settings are **A**utomatic recalculation in **N**atural order. To save processing time, however, you may want to switch to **M**anual recalculation so that 1-2-3 recalculates the worksheet only when you press F9 (Calc).

Checking the Status of Global Settings

Use the **/W**orksheet **S**tatus command to check the status of all the global settings for the worksheet. This command gives you an easy way to check the settings without having to experiment to find out what the settings are.

With the **/W**orksheet **S**tatus command, you can see all the global settings for the worksheet.

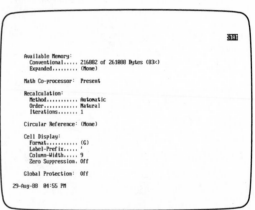

Entering a Page-Break Character

The **/W**orksheet **P**age command inserts a blank row and a page-break character (::) where the cell pointer is positioned. This command is similar to the **/W**orksheet **I**nsert **R**ow command, which inserts one or more rows at the location of the cell pointer. After **/W**orksheet **P**age inserts the new row at the pointer, the command places the page-break character in the cell directly above the pointer.

You use a page-break character when you want to print a range from the worksheet. The page break is effective only when it is positioned at the left edge of the range

An Overview of 1-2-3

Getting Started

1-2-3 Basics

Creating a Worksheet

Printing Reports

Creating and Printing Graphs

Managing Data

being printed. When the page break is in effect, the contents of the other cells in that row within the print range are not printed.

Moving the Contents of Cells

With the **/M**ove and **/C**opy commands, you can move and copy the contents of cells and ranges of cells from one part of the worksheet to another. The difference between moving and copying is that data *moved* from one cell to another disappears from the first cell; *copied* data appears in both cells.

In the following sequence of screens, you see how the contents of range C1..D3 is moved to the range E1..F3.

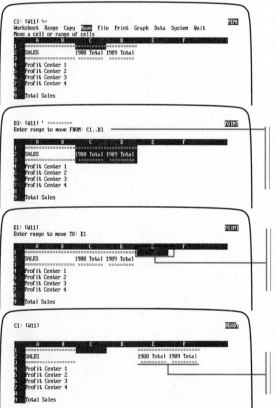

To move the range C1..D3 to E1..F3, you begin by selecting the **/M**ove command from the main menu.

At the `Enter range to move FROM:` prompt, specify the range of cells you want to move, and press `⏎Enter`.

At the `Enter range to move TO:` prompt, move the cell pointer to (or type the cell address of) the upper left cell of the new location.

When you press Enter, 1-2-3 moves the specified range to the new location.

Keep in mind that when you move a range of cells, the TO range is completely overwritten by the FROM range, and the previous contents of the cells in the TO range are lost forever. If the worksheet contains other cells whose formulas depend on the cell addresses of the lost cells, those other cells will be given the value ERR for error.

Copying the Contents of Cells

Many times you will want to copy cell contents to other locations in a worksheet. In this section, you look at four different ways to copy data in 1-2-3.

All copy operations have basically the same steps: first, issue the **/C**opy command; second, specify the FROM range; and third, specify the TO range. The only things that change are the size, shape, and locations of the FROM and TO ranges.

One way to copy is to copy cell contents *from one cell to another.* To do this, you issue the **/C**opy command. 1-2-3 then displays the Enter range to copy FROM prompt. If you want to copy from cell A1, you enter **A1** in response to this message. If the cell pointer is already on cell A1, you can simply press Enter. Next, 1-2-3 provides an Enter range to copy TO prompt. If you want to copy the contents of cell A1 to cell A2, you enter **A2** as the TO range.

Another way to copy is to copy cell contents *from one cell to a range of cells.* Suppose that you want to copy the contents of cell A1 into the range B2..H2. To do this, issue the **/C**opy command, specify **A1** as the FROM range, and then specify **B2..H2** as the TO range. Remember that you can either type the coordinates of the TO range from the keyboard or point to the range, using POINT mode.

A third way to copy is a little more complicated. You may want to copy *a range of cells to another range of equal size.* For example, suppose that you want to copy the range A1..H1 to the range A2..H2, as shown in the following screen. As always, issue the **/C**opy command and enter **A1..H1** as the FROM range. Then, when you enter the TO range, you can specify just **A2** rather than **A2..H2**. Although the short specification may seem illogical, it is not: 1-2-3 can deduce the rest of the destination range from the full specification of the FROM range.

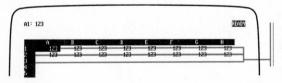

This screen shows the result of copying the range A1..H1 to A2..H2.

The fourth way to copy is to copy *a range of cells to a larger range of cells*. For example, suppose that you want to copy the range A1..H1 into the rectangular block A2..H20, as shown in the following screen. As before, you issue the /Copy command and define the FROM range as **A1..H1**. Then you can specify the TO range as **A2..A20**. 1-2-3 will know to copy the range A1..H1 downward 19 times.

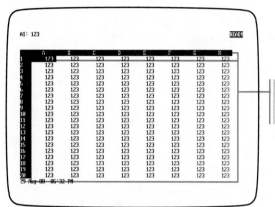

In this screen, the small range A1..H1 has been copied to the larger range A2..H20.

Addressing Cells

Although the connection may not be readily obvious, the way in which you address cells is tied closely to move and copy operations.

Two different methods of addressing cells can be used in replication: *relative* and *absolute*. These two methods of referencing cells are important for building formulas. In fact, talking about the two methods of addressing is difficult without treating both topics at once. The type of addressing you use when you reference cells in formulas can affect the results yielded by the formulas when you copy or move those formulas to different locations in the worksheet.

The following sections cover relative and absolute addressing as well as a combination of both methods known as *mixed addressing*.

Using Relative Addresses

1-2-3's default is relative addressing. A *relative address* is a cell address that is adjusted automatically to fit the new location when you copy or move a formula.

For example, suppose that you have summed contents of column C and now want to sum the contents of several columns of cells, but you don't want to enter the @SUM function over and over again. You can copy the @SUM function to the other cells by choosing **/C**opy, entering **C10** as the FROM range, and specifying **D10..G10** as the TO range. When you press Enter, 1-2-3 copies the @SUM function to all the cells in the specified TO range. The formula in the first line of the control panel contains the proper cell addresses for adding the cells in column D—not column C. 1-2-3 was smart enough to know that you meant the relative addresses of the cells in column D, not their absolute addresses.

Using Absolute and Mixed Addresses

In some cases, a formula has an important address that must not change as the formula is copied. In 1-2-3, you can create an *absolute address*—an address that will not change at all as the address is copied. You can create also a *mixed address*—an address that will change partially, depending on the direction of the /Copy command. In effect, *mixed cell-addressing* refers to a combination of relative and absolute addressing. Because a cell address has two components—a column and a row—you can fix (make absolute) either portion while leaving the other unfixed (relative).

If you plan to copy cells that have absolute addressing, you must prepare the cell by entering dollar signs in the appropriate column and row designations. This symbol tells 1-2-3 that the cell has been changed to an absolute address. If you forget to prepare the cell, you may get unfavorable results.

The formulas in G60, G62, G63, and G65 illustrate absolute addressing. All four formulas were created by copying the formula in G59 to G60, G62, G63, and G65.

An Overview of 1-2-3

Getting Started

1-2-3 Basics

Creating a Worksheet

Printing Reports

Creating and Printing Graphs

Managing Data

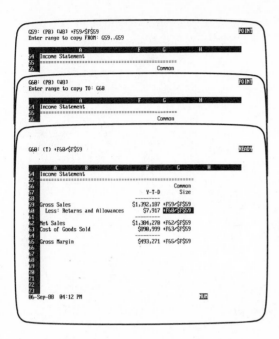

When you create the formula in G59, place a $ before the F and before 59 in the second part of the formula.

Copy the contents of G59 to G60, G62, G63, and G65.

Notice that the first address of each formula is adjusted to its new location, but the second address remains absolute as F59 in all four formulas.

There are two ways to enter dollar signs for absolute or mixed addresses in a formula. You can type the dollar signs as you create the formula, or you can later modify the formula by using the F4 (Abs) key to have 1-2-3 enter the dollar signs for you.

Use the F4 (Abs) key in POINT or EDIT mode to make a cell reference absolute, mixed, or relative. The F4 key is a four-way toggle. Simply press the F4 key repeatedly until you get the kind of cell reference you want.

Summary

This chapter showed you how to create worksheets by making use of many of the /**R**ange and /**W**orksheet commands and their subcommands. You learned how to use the /**R**ange commands to create and name ranges, delete range names and erase ranges, use range names to streamline your work and to move quickly to a named range and display existing range names in the control panel or on the full screen. You learned also how to format a cell or a range of cells to determine how values and formula results appear on-screen.

You saw that you can use the versatile /**W**orksheet commands to erase an entire worksheet, set column widths individually or globally, split the screen into horizontal or vertical windows, freeze titles for scrolling, insert and delete columns and rows, hide columns and suppress the display of zeroes, recalculate and protect the worksheet, check the status of the global settings, and insert page breaks in a printed report.

When you build a worksheet, you can use the /**M**ove command to relocate cells and cell ranges, and the /**C**opy command to replicate or multiply cells and cell ranges. By specifying relative, absolute, or mixed addressing, you can control cell references in your worksheets.

After you have created and used a worksheet, you will want to create and print a 1-2-3 report. Printing reports is the subject of the next chapter.

Review Questions

1. What are the two methods for accessing 1-2-3 commands?

2. What is a worksheet range? What are the advantages of using ranges in the worksheet?

3. What are the three methods for designating a range when you are prompted for a range when using a 1-2-3 command?

An
Overview of
1-2-3

Getting
Started

1-2-3 Basics

**Creating a
Worksheet**

Printing
Reports

Creating
and
Printing
Graphs

Managing
Data

4. What are the advantages to using range names rather than cell addresses?

5. Indicate which of the following operations are available through the /**W**orksheet command, /**R**ange command, or both; and indicate the command sequence for the specific operation.

Operation	/**W**orksheet?	/**R**ange?
Inserting a columns row	_____	_____
Splitting the screen	_____	_____
Formatting cells	_____	_____
Erasing data	_____	_____
Protecting cells	_____	_____

6. What function key enables you to move the cell pointer between windows when you split the screen?

7. What are the three orders of recalculation? Describe each one.

185

8. What command do you use to check such 1-2-3 settings as the type of recalculation, global format, and global column width?

9. Describe the three types of addressing: *Relative, Absolute,* and *Mixed.* Give an example of a formula for each.

14 *Printing Reports*

An Overview of 1-2-3

Getting Started

1-2-3 Basics

Creating a Worksheet

Printing Reports

Creating and Printing Graphs

Managing Data

1-2-3 is a powerful tool for developing information in column- and-row format. You can enter and edit your spreadsheet and database files on-screen, as well as store the input on disk. To make more use of your data, however, you can print it—for example, as a target production schedule, a summary report to your supervisor, or a detailed reorder list to central stores.

This chapter presents the basics of printing as these relate to 1-2-3's default, or standard, settings and printing on 8 1/2-by-11-inch paper. The chapter shows you also how to enhance printed reports by hiding columns and rows, adding headers and footers, and repeating column and row headings.

After completing this chapter, you will know how to do the following:

- Choose between **/P**rint **P**rinter and **/P**rint **F**ile
- Print a single page or multiple pages
- Add borders
- Exclude segments within a designated print range
- Control paper movement
- Add headers and footers
- Change page layout

▼

Key Terms in This Chapter

Print defaults   Preset, standard specifications for a 1-2-3 print job.

Border   A label that borders data and is repeated on subsequent pages.

Header   Information displayed at the top of a page. May include a date and a page number.

Footer   Information displayed at the bottom of a page. May include a date and a page number.

▲

Selecting /Print Printer or /Print File

You start any **/P**rint command sequence from 1-2-3's main menu. After initiating a **/P**rint command, you select one of the two options displayed: **P**rinter or **F**ile. To indicate that you want to use a printer on-line, choose **P**rinter. Select **F**ile if you want to create a file on disk. Later you can print the file from within 1-2-3 or incorporate the print file into a word processing file.

If you choose **F**ile, respond to the prompt for a print-file name by typing a name up to eight characters long. You do not need to add a file extension, because 1-2-3 will automatically assign a PRN (print file) extension.

You can incorporate the file back into a 1-2-3 spreadsheet by using the **/F**ile **I**mport command, but the file will not be the same as your original worksheet file. The reason is that imported PRN files are all long labels. You can also view a PRN file by using the DOS TYPE command, a word processor's print command, or a special printing routine.

After you select either **P**rinter or **F**ile, the second line of the control panel displays the main **P**rint menu. It presents the following choices:

> **R**ange **L**ine **P**age **O**ptions **C**lear **A**lign **G**o **Q**uit

The following list gives you an overview of the various options on the **/P**rint menu:

Menu Selection	Description
Range	Indicates what section of the worksheet is to be printed or saved to disk as a print file
Line	Adjusts the paper line-by-line in the printer
Page	Adjusts the paper page-by-page in the printer
Options	Provides options to change default settings and enhance the appearance of the printout
Clear	Erases settings previously entered
Align	Signals the beginning of each page in the printer
Go	Starts printing
Quit	Exits the **P**rint menu

Regardless of whether you select **P**rinter of **F**ile, you must specify a **R**ange to print, activate **G**o, and then select **Q**uit to return to the worksheet. All other selections are optional.

Selecting
/Print Printer
or /Print File

**Printing
Reports**

Controlling
Paper
Movement

Adding
Headers and
Footers

Changing Page
Layout: Margins
and Length

Summary

An
Overview of
1-2-3

Getting
Started

1-2-3 Basics

Creating a
Worksheet

**Printing
Reports**

Creating
and
Printing
Graphs

Managing
Data

Printing Reports

If you do not change any of the default print settings and have not entered other print settings during the current worksheet session, then printing a page or less involves only the following steps:

1. Choosing to print to the printer or file
2. Highlighting on the worksheet the area you want printed
3. Choosing the command to begin printing

You can easily print a report of a page or less by completing the following sequence of operations. First, make certain that your printer is on-line and that your paper is positioned where you want the data to print. Next choose **/P**rint **P**rinter. The main **P**rint menu will then appear.

To indicate what part of the worksheet you want to print, select **R**ange and highlight the area. You can use the PgUp, PgDn, and End keys to designate ranges when you print. If you want to designate a range that includes the entire active area of the spreadsheet, press the Home key to move the cursor to cell A1, type a period (.) to anchor the left corner of the print range, press the End key, and then press the Home key.

After you have highlighted the exact range you want to print, select **A**lign and **G**o. If you accidentally press Enter after you have already used the **G**o option, the file will print a second time—an act that can be particularly disconcerting. If this problem occurs, you can stop printing by pressing Ctrl-Break. The following illustrations show a highlighted range and the printed output.

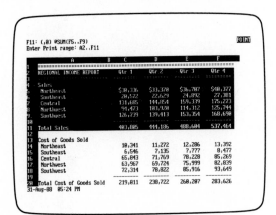

Designating a range to be printed.

Example of a draft-quality report of less than one page, printed with default settings.

```
REGIONAL INCOME REPORT          Qtr 1      Qtr 2      Qtr      Qtr 4
================================  =========  =========  ======  =========
Sales
  Northeast                      $30,336    $33,370    $36,707   $40,377
  Southeast                       20,572     22,629     24,892    27,381
  Central                        131,685    144,854    159,339   175,273
  Northwest                       94,473    103,920    114,312   125,744
  Southwest               /       126,739    139,413    153,354   168,690
                                 ---------  ---------  --------- ---------
  Total Sales                    403,805    444,186    488,604   537,464
```

If the area of your worksheet has more rows and columns than can be printed on one page, you can still use the basic steps for printing reports of a page or less. Be aware, however, that setting the print range so that a new page begins at the correct location may be a bit tricky. If you want to print a section of a large worksheet, you may need to use the **/P**rint **P**rinter **O**ptions **B**order command so that labels are repeated on each page.

Adding Borders

If you want information to be printed on pages correctly, you need to remember that 1-2-3 treats numeric and text data differently when splitting data from one page to the next. Numbers are printed complete because they can span only one cell. Text, on the other hand, such as long labels that lie across several cells, may be split in awkward places from one page to the next.

To make certain that 1-2-3 copies the labels correctly, choose the **/P**rint **P**rinter command. If you want the labels to print on both pages, you must use the **O**ptions **B**orders command on the main **P**rint menu.

When you select **O**ptions **B**orders, 1-2-3 asks whether the labels you want repeated are located down a column or across a row. Suppose that you want to print a report on two or more pages and repeat labels displayed down a column. To do so, you select **C**olumns after choosing **O**ptions **B**orders. (To print a report on two or more pages and repeat labels displayed across a row, you select **R**ows after choosing **O**ptions **B**orders.)

An Overview of 1-2-3

Getting Started

1-2-3 Basics

Creating a Worksheet

Printing Reports

Creating and Printing Graphs

Managing Data

After you choose Columns, the prompt Enter range for border columns: will appear. If your cell pointer is located in the column where the labels appear, press Enter; if not, move your cell pointer to the column and press Enter. To return to the main **P**rint menu, select **Q**uit.

The next step is to highlight the columns or rows of labels you wanted printed on each page. Once you have indicated the columns or rows of labels you want repeated on each page, you do not need to include those labels on your actual print range. 1-2-3 automatically places those labels in the first column or row on every page. When you specify the range to be printed, exclude the columns or rows you set with the **B**orders command.

When you select **A**lign and then **G**o from the **P**rint menu, the printer will print a multiple-page report with column and/or row borders represented on each page, as shown in the following examples. Choosing **A**lign ensures that printing will begin at the top of all succeeding pages after the first.

```
BALANCES IN WORKING CAPITAL ACCOUNTS    Jan        Feb        Mar
=====================================  =========  =========  =========

Assets
Cash                                   $31,643    $34,333    $36,657
Accounts Receivable                    510,780    533,597    551,287
Inventory                              169,209    176,671    189,246

Liabilities
Accounts Payable                       130,754    139,851    150,187
Line of Credit                               0          0          0

Net Working Capital                    580,878    604,750    627,003
                                       =========  =========  =========
```

The first page of a report printed on two pages.

```
BALANCES IN WORKING CAPITAL ACCOUNTS    Apr        May       Jun
=====================================  =========  =========  =========

Assets
Cash                                   $35,614    $29,146   $20,000
Accounts Receivable                    577,314    614,997   641,802
Inventory                              206,788    228,828   269,990

Liabilities
Accounts Payable                       163,732    180,351   203,669
Line of Credit                               0          0     1,834

Net Working Capital                    655,984    692,620   726,289
                                       =========  =========  =========
```

The second page of a report printed on two pages.

Although not discussed in this book, 1-2-3 lets you print a specialized report without labels that lists the contents of each cell in the worksheet. Keeping printouts of the cell contents helps safeguard your work, serves as a good backup, and can be a useful tool for "debugging" your worksheet. You produce this printed documentation of cell contents by selecting **O**ther from the **/P**rint **P**rinter **O**ptions menu, and then selecting either **A**s-Displayed or **C**ell-Formulas. Choosing **C**ell-Formulas produces a listing that shows the width of the cell (if the cell width is different from the default), the cell format, cell-protection status, and the contents of cells in the print range— one cell per line. By subsequently selecting **A**s-Displayed, you restore the default instructions to print the range as it appears on-screen.

Hiding Segments within the Designated Print Range

Because the **/P**rint commands require that you specify a range to print, you can print only rectangular blocks from the spreadsheet. Nevertheless, you can suppress the display of cell contents within the range. You can eliminate one or more rows, hide one or more columns, or remove from view a segment that spans only part of a row or a column. The following list shows you the commands used for each of these operations:

Rows	Marks the row to be hidden by entering two vertical bars (| |) in the leftmost cell
Columns	**/W**orksheet **C**olumn **H**ide
	/Print **P**rinter **O**ptions **O**ther **A**s-Displayed
Ranges	**/R**ange **F**ormat **H**idden

Controlling Paper Movement

Unless you stipulate otherwise, the top of a page is initially marked by the print head's position when you turn on the printer and load 1-2-3. If you print a range containing fewer lines than the default page length, the paper will not advance to the top of the next page; the next print operation will begin wherever the preceding operation ended. If you print a range containing more lines than the default page length, 1-2-3 will automatically insert page breaks in the document between pages, but the paper will not advance to the top of the next page after 1-2-3 has printed the last page.

If you don't want to accept 1-2-3's automatic paper-movement controls, you can change the controls from the keyboard. You can specify the "top" of a page in any

Selecting
/Print Printer   Printing
or /Print File   Reports

**Controlling
Paper
Movement**

Adding
Headers and
Footers

Changing Page
Layout: Margins
and Length   Summary

An
Overview of
1-2-3

Getting
Started

1-2-3 Basics

Creating a
Worksheet

**Printing
Reports**

Creating
and
Printing
Graphs

Managing
Data

paper position, advance the paper by line or by page, and insert page breaks exactly where you want them.

Using the Line, Page, and Align Options

If you are using continuous-feed paper, position the paper so that the print head is at the top of the page, and then turn on the printer. Do not advance the paper manually. Because 1-2-3 coordinates a line counter with the current page-length setting, any lines you advance manually are not counted, and page breaks will crop up in strange places.

If you want to advance the paper one line at a time (to separate several small printed ranges that fit on one page, for example), issue the **/P**rint **P**rinter **L**ine command. This command sequence causes the printer to skip a line.

If you want to advance to a new page after printing less than a full page, select **/P**rint **P**rinter **P**age. Whenever you issue this command, the printer skips to a new page. (The following section shows how you can embed a page-break symbol in the print range to instruct 1-2-3 to advance automatically.)

In many cases, a faster way to advance the paper is to take the printer off-line, adjust the paper manually, put the printer back on-line, and then issue the **/P**rint **P**rinter **A**lign command. Remember that whenever you begin a print job at the top of a page, you should select **A**lign before selecting **G**o.

To print an existing footer option on the last page, use the **P**age command at the end of the printing session. If you select the **Q**uit command from the **/P**rint menu without issuing the **P**age command, this final footer will not print. Although you can reissue the **/P**rint **P**rinter command, select **P**age, and the footer will still print.

Setting Page Breaks within the Spreadsheet

To enter a page break by using 1-2-3's commands, first move the cell pointer to the leftmost column of the range to be printed and then to the row that you want to begin on the new page. Then select the **/W**orksheet **P**age command, which automatically inserts a new blank row containing a page-break symbol (| ::). You could instead insert a blank row into your worksheet where you want a page break, and then type a page-break symbol into a blank cell in the leftmost column of the print range in that row. The contents of cells in any row marked by the page-break symbol will not print.

Move the cell pointer to column A and to the row where you want the page to break. Select **/W**orksheet **P**age. 1-2-3 then enters a page-break symbol (| ::) in the cell where the cell pointer is located.

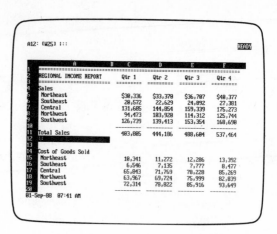

Adding Headers and Footers

1-2-3 reserves in a document three lines for a header and three for a footer. You can either retain the six lines (regardless of whether you use them) or eliminate all six by selecting **O**ther **U**nformatted (illustrated later in this chapter) from the **/P**rint **P**rinter **O**ptions menu.

Either the **H**eader or **F**ooter option lets you specify up to 240 characters of text within one line in each of three positions: left, right, and center. Actually, however, the overall header or footer line cannot exceed the number of characters printed per inch multiplied by the width of the paper in inches minus the right and left margins.

The header text, which is printed on the first line after any blank top margin lines, is followed by two blank header lines (for spacing). The footer text line is printed above the specified bottom-margin blank lines and below two blank footer lines (for spacing).

Although you can enter manually all features of the text, 1-2-3 provides special characters for controlling page numbers, the current date, and the positioning of text within a header or footer. The number sign (#) is used to print page numbers; the ampersand (@) prints the date; and the vertical bar (|) separates text and takes care of text alignment.

An Overview of 1-2-3

Getting Started

1-2-3 Basics

Creating a Worksheet

Printing Reports

Creating and Printing Graphs

Managing Data

To add a header, select **/P**rint **P**rinter, specify the **R**ange, and then choose **O**ptions **H**eader. At the `Enter Header Line:` prompt, type

> **@|YOUR FIRM NAME|#**

Then select **Q**uit from the **/P**rint **P**rinter **O**ptions menu; signal the top of the page to the printer, if necessary, by selecting **A**lign; and then select **G**o. The header will then appear on the report.

$$@ \; | \; \text{NATIONAL MICRO} \; | \; \#$$

| The @ sign places the date in the header. (Make sure that your computer is set to the correct date.) | The | character aligns the different items in this header line. | The # symbol tells 1-2-3 to print a page number. |

```
07-Sep-88                      NATIONAL MICRO                          1

REGIONAL INCOME REPORT      Qtr 1      Qtr 2      Qtr 3      Qtr 4
==========================  =========  =========  =========  =========
Sales
  Northeast                 $30,336    $33,370    $36,707    $40,377
  Southeast                  20,572     22,629     24,892     27,381
  Central                   131,685    144,854    159,339    175,273
  Northwest                  94,473    103,920    114,312    125,744
  Southwest                 126,739    139,413    153,354    168,690
                           ---------  ---------  ---------  ---------
  Total Sales              403,805    444,186    488,604    537,464
```

Whenever the print range output exceeds a single page, the header is reproduced on each succeeding page, and the page number increases by one. If you have used the special page-number character (#) and want to print your report a second time before you leave the **P**rint menu, you can reset the page counter and set the top of the form by selecting **A**lign before you choose **G**o.

If you have specified a header line, but the centered or right-justified text does not print, make sure that the right-margin setting is appropriate for the current pitch and paper width. To change the header, simply repeat the sequence to establish the text, press Esc to remove the display of the existing header from the control panel, and press Enter. (You can delete a header or footer without removing other specified options.)

Changing Page Layout: Margins and Page Length

Before you change the layout of a page, you should be aware of the default settings. 1-2-3's initial settings are for 8 1/2-by-11-inch paper, a printer output of 6 lines per inch, and a page length of 66 lines. 1-2-3 saves two lines at the top and bottom of each page for the top and bottom margins. 1-2-3 saves also three lines at the top and bottom for headers and footers. If you want to check the default settings, select /**W**orksheet **G**lobal **D**efault **S**tatus.

To change page layout temporarily, use the /**P**rint **P**rinter **O**ptions menu. To change the margins, select the **M**argins option and then select **L**eft, **R**ight, **T**op, or **B**ottom from the submenu. If you select **L**eft, you see the Enter Left Margin (0..240): prompt, which asks you to enter a value from 0 to 240. Similarly, to change the right margin, select **R**ight and enter a value from 0 to 240. For the top and bottom margins, you select **T**op or **B**ottom, respectively, and enter the margin specification from 0 to 32.

Be sure that you set left and right margins that are consistent with the width of your paper and the printer's established pitch (characters per inch). The right margin number must be higher than the left margin number. And make sure that settings for the top and bottom margins are consistent with the paper's length and the established number of lines per inch.

The specified page length must not be less than the top margin plus the header lines plus one line of data plus the footer lines plus the bottom margin, unless you use the /**P**rint **P**rinter **O**ptions **O**ther **U**nformatted command to suppress all formatting.

To maximize the output on every printed page of a large spreadsheet, you can combine the **U**nformatted option with setup strings that condense print and increase the number of lines per inch. The **U**nformatted option ignores margins, headers, and footers.

Summary

This chapter showed you how to print reports by selecting the /**P**rint command from 1-2-3's main menu. You can use the /**P**rint **P**rinter command to print a report on a printer, or the **P**rint **F**ile command to create a printer file that you or someone else can print later.

You learned how to print a document of one page or less, to add borders, and to hide worksheet segments for the print range. You learned also how to control paper movement; use line, page, and align options; and set page breaks within a spreadsheet.

The chapter indicated ways to enhance printouts. You can add headers and footers that can include the date and a number. You can also change the layout of a page, such as by adjusting the margins and the page length.

Now that you know how to create and print 1-2-3 ranges and whole worksheets, you are ready to learn how to create and print 1-2-3 graphs. These two tasks, which extend significantly the usefulness of your worksheets, are the subject of the next chapter.

Review Questions

1. What are the two main options on the **/P**rint menu? When would you choose either one?

2. What are the steps involved in printing a worksheet range?

3. What are the steps you follow to print repeating labels across a row or down a column for a multipage report?

4. If you wanted 1-2-3 to advance the paper to a new page after printing less than a full page, what command would you use?

5. How does the /**P**rint **P**rinter **A**lign command work?

6. How do you instruct 1-2-3 to enter page breaks when printing?

7. What command would you use to print a listing of all cell contents?

8. What characters do you use in a header or footer for aligning text and placing a page number and the date?

9. What are 1-2-3's default settings for a printed page? What command do you use to change margins?

15 *Creating and Printing Graphs*

An
Overview of
1-2-3

Getting
Started

1-2-3 Basics

Creating a
Worksheet

Printing
Reports

**Creating
and
Printing
Graphs**

Managing
Data

Lotus 1-2-3 can display important information graphically. The program offers five types of business graphs as well as limited options for enhancing the graphs' appearance. Although 1-2-3 is no match for many stand-alone graphics packages, its strength lies in its integration of graphics with the spreadsheet.

After reading this chapter, you will know how to do the following:

- Meet minimum requirements for constructing graphs
- Create a basic graph
- Select a graph type
- Enhance the appearance of a graph
- Preserve the graph on disk
- Access and Exit the PrintGraph program

▼

Key Terms in This Chapter

Graph type One of five types: line, bar, XY, stacked bar, and pie

Y-axis The vertical left edge of a graph

X-axis The horizontal bottom edge of a graph

Legend A description of the shading, color, or symbols assigned to data ranges in line or bar graphs, appearing across the bottom of those graphs

Tick marks On the y-axis of a graph, small marks that indicate the increments between the minimum and maximum graph values

▲

Before creating your first graph, you must determine whether your hardware can display and print graphs, 1-2-3 is correctly installed and loaded, and the spreadsheet contains on-screen the data you want to graph. You also should understand which type of graph is best suited for presenting specific numeric data in picture form.

Hardware Requirements

To view a graph on-screen, you need a graphics monitor or a monitor with a graphics-display adapter. Without such a monitor, you can construct and save a 1-2-3 graph, but you must print the graph to view it. If you have two graphics monitors installed, one monitor will display the spreadsheet while the other displays the graph. To print a graph, you need a separate set of PrintGraph instructions and a graphics printer supported by 1-2-3.

Creating a Graph

To create a 1-2-3 graph, you begin by selecting the /**G**raph command from the main menu while the worksheet containing the data you want to graph is displayed. Selecting /**G**raph from the main 1-2-3 menu produces the following menu:

Type **X A B C D E F R**eset **V**iew **S**ave **O**ptions **N**ame **Q**uit

These /**G**raph command options perform the following actions:

Type	Provides options for creating five types of graphs
X-F	Lets you enter the ranges of data you want to display in a graph
Reset	Clears the current graph settings
View	Displays a graph on the monitor screen
Save	Saves a graph in a special file format for printing the graph with 1-2-3's PrintGraph program
Options	Provides choices for labeling, enhancing, or customizing a graph
Name	Lets you name one or more graphs and store the graph settings for redisplaying the graph(s) whenever you retrieve the worksheet file
Quit	Quits the **G**raph menu and returns the worksheet to READY mode

You will use some of these commands whenever you create a graph. If you do not need to enhance, customize, or print a graph, then displaying only data points in a bar, stacked-bar, line, XY, or pie graph is easy. Just do these four steps:

Select **T**ype if the graph is not a line graph (the default type).

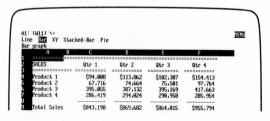

An
Overview of
1-2-3

Getting
Started

1-2-3 Basics

Creating a
Worksheet

Printing
Reports

**Creating
and
Printing
Graphs**

Managing
Data

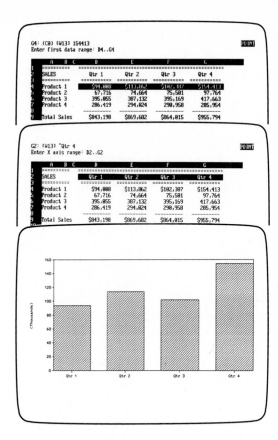

Use the **A-F** options from the **G**raph menu to indicate the ranges containing the data series you want to graph.

Select the **X** option from the **G**raph menu to indicate the data range for labeling the tick marks along the x-axis in a line, bar, or stacked-bar graph; for labeling each part of a pie graph; and for plotting the dependent variable in an XY graph.

Display the graph by selecting the **V**iew command from the **G**raph menu or pressing F10 (Graph).

Selecting a Graph Type

You can create five different graph types with 1-2-3. (See Chapter 10 for illustrations of the five types of 1-2-3 graphs.) The following list highlights the differences of each type.

Line: To show the trend of numeric data across time.

Bar: To show the trend of numeric data across time, often comparing two or more data items.

XY: To compare one numeric data series with another numeric data series across time, to determine whether one set of values appears to depend on the other.

Stacked-bar: To graph two or more data series that total 100 percent of a specific numeric category.

Pie: To graph only one data series, the components of which total 100 percent of a specific numeric category.

Selecting one of the five available graph types is easy. When you select **T**ype from the **G**raph menu, 1-2-3 displays the following options:

> **L**ine **B**ar **X**Y **S**tacked-Bar **P**ie

By selecting one of these options, you set that graph type, and automatically restore the **G**raph menu to the control panel.

To understand which type will best display specific numeric data, you must know something about plotting points on a graph, particularly, the two basic terms *x-axis* and *y-axis*. All graphs (except pie graphs) have two axes: the x-axis (the horizontal bottom edge) and the y-axis (the vertical left edge). 1-2-3 automatically provides tick marks for both axes. The program also scales the adjacent numbers on the y-axis, based on the minimum and maximum figures included in the plotted data range(s).

Every point plotted on a graph has a unique location (x,y): *x* represents the time period or the amount measured along the horizontal axis; *y* measures the corresponding amount along the vertical axis. The intersection of the x-axis and y-axis is called the *origin*. To minimize misinterpretation of graph results and to make graphs easier to compare, use a zero origin in your graphs. Later in this chapter, you will learn how to change manually the upper or lower limits of the scale initially set by 1-2-3.

Of the five 1-2-3 graph types, all but the pie graph display both x- and y-axes. Line, bar, and stacked-bar graphs display figures (centered on the tick marks) on the y-axis only. An XY graph displays figures on both axes.

Specifying a Data Series Range

To create a graph, you must specify data from the currently displayed spreadsheet as a data series in range form. To enter a data series from the main **G**raph menu, choose one of the options **X**, **A**, **B**, **C**, **D**, **E**, or **F**.

Notice that 1-2-3 does not permit you to type in data to be plotted on a graph. Plotting data points is not like typing descriptions, such as titles—a process illustrated later in this chapter.

An Overview of 1-2-3

Getting Started

1-2-3 Basics

Creating a Worksheet

Printing Reports

Creating and Printing Graphs

Managing Data

With line graphs, you can enter as many as six data series after you have accessed separately the **G**raph menu choices **A B C D E F**. You do not have to start with **A**.

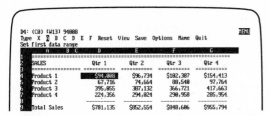

To enter a data series, choose one of the **X**, **A**, **B**, **C**, **D**, **E**, or **F** options.

With bar graphs, you can enter as many as six data series after you have accessed separately the **G**raph menu choices **A B C D E F**. Again, you do not have to start with **A**. Multiple data ranges appear on the graph from left to right in alphabetical order. Every data series displayed in black and white has unique shading. Every data series displayed in color is assigned one of three colors.

For XY graphs, to enter the data series being plotted as the independent variable, select **X** from the main **G**raph menu. Plot at least one dependent variable (usually, you would select **A**). 1-2-3 supplies symbols to mark the data points of each data series (**A-F**) used with **X**.

With stacked-bar graphs, follow the instructions for bar graphs. In a stacked-bar graph, multiple data ranges appear from bottom to top in alphabetical order.

For pie graphs, you enter only one data series by selecting **A** from the main **G**raph menu. (To shade and "explode" pieces of the pie, select also **B**.)

Remember that after you have selected a graph type and specified the range(s) containing the data series you want to graph, you display the graph by selecting the **V**iew command from the **G**raph menu or pressing F10 (Graph).

Enhancing the Appearance of a Graph

In addition to the four steps for creating and viewing a basic graph are options for enhancing and customizing a graph. To improve the appearance and final quality of your graphs, you can select one or more of the following choices from the / **G**raph **O**ptions menu:

Legend **F**ormat **T**itles **G**rid **S**cale **C**olor **B**&W **D**ata-Labels **Q**uit

These /**G**raph **O**ption commands perform the following actions:

/**G**raph **O**ptions **T**itles	Lets you enter titles you want displayed (and printed) at the top of a graph, below the x-axis, and to the left of the y-axis
/**G**raph **O**ptions **L**egend	Provides shadings and colors to identify data ranges in a line, bar, stacked-bar, or XY graph
/**G**raph **O**ptions **G**rid	Adds a horizontal and/or vertical grid to a graph
/**G**raph **O**ptions **F**ormat	Draws lines or symbols to present and connect data points in a line or XY graph
/**G**raph **O**ption **S**cale	Controls the scaling and formatting of values along the x-axis or y-axis
/**G**raph **O**ptions **C**olor	Changes the graph display from monochrome to color (if available)
/**G**raph **O**ptions **B**&W	Resets the graph display from color to monochrome
/**G**raph **O**ptions **D**ata-Labels	Adds labels for identifying different data points within the graph
/**G**raph **O**ptions **Q**uit	Returns to the **G**raph menu

As you add enhancements to your graphs, check the results frequently. If you have only one monitor, select **Q**uit to leave the **G**raph **O**ptions menu and return to the main **G**raph menu. Then select **V**iew to check the most recent version of the graph. Press any key to exit the graph display and restore the **G**raph menu to the screen.

To view the current graph from the worksheet's READY mode, press the F10 (Graph) key, which instantly redraws the graph with any updated information. Whenever the worksheet is not in MENU mode, you can use the F10 (Graph) key to "toggle" between the worksheet and the graph.

Adding Descriptive Labels and Numbers

To add descriptive information to a graph, you use the **L**egend, **T**itles, and **D**ata-Labels options from the **O**ptions menu, and the **X** option from the main **G**raph menu.

The data labels appear within the graph. Descriptions entered with the **X** option appear immediately below the x-axis. You can enter as many as four titles: two at the top, and one to describe each axis. Legends describing the shading, color, or symbols assigned to data ranges in line or bar graphs appear across the bottom of those graphs.

An
Overview of
1-2-3

Getting
Started

1-2-3 Basics

Creating a
Worksheet

Printing
Reports

**Creating
and
Printing
Graphs**

Managing
Data

Using the Titles Option

If you select **/G**raph **O**ptions **T**itles, the following options will be displayed in the control panel:

> **F**irst **S**econd **X**-Axis **Y**-Axis

You can enter one or two centered titles at the top of your graph. If you enter two titles, both will be the same size on-screen. If the graph is printed, however, the title you enter by selecting **F**irst will be twice the size of any other title specified.

The following illustrates titles added at the top, below the x-axis, and to the left of the y-axis.

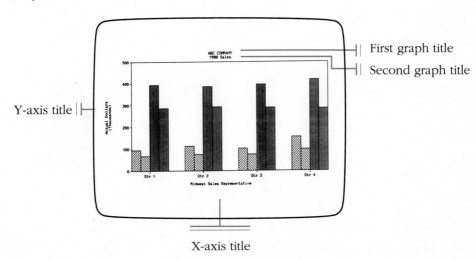

You enter titles by typing a new description, by specifying a range name, or by referencing the cell location of a label or a number already in the worksheet. The titles will appear on-screen in the same print style. When you print the graph, you can select one font (such as italic) for the top title, and another font for other titles and labels.

Note: **X**-Axis and **Y**-Axis titles have no significance when you construct a pie graph.

Entering Labels within a Graph

After you have graphed a data series, you can enter values or labels to explain each point plotted on the graph, as shown in the following illustration. First select **O**ptions **D**ata-Labels from the main **G**raph menu and then specify the data series (**A B C D E F**) to which the data labels apply. Instead of typing the labels (as you typed the titles), you must specify each data-label range by pointing to an existing range in the worksheet, providing cell coordinates, or specifying a previously determined range name.

Labels specifying the value for each point on a line graph.

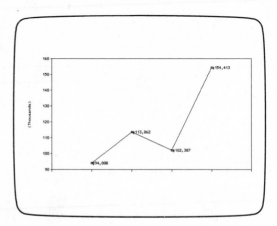

If you graph more than one data series, attach the data labels to the data series with the largest figures. Then select **A**bove to position the data labels above the data points plotted. To enter text or numbers as the plotted points, use the **C**enter option with line graphs that display **N**either lines nor symbols.

Entering Labels below the X-Axis

Instead of placing descriptive information within a graph, you may prefer to enter label information along the x-axis in bar, stacked-bar, and line graphs. For pie graphs, use the **X** option to label each slice, as in the following illustration. The main **G**raph menu's **X** option has two distinct functions. Use it to position labels below the x-axis in line, bar, and stacked-bar graphs, or to enter a data series in an XY graph. (XY graphs are discussed later in this chapter.)

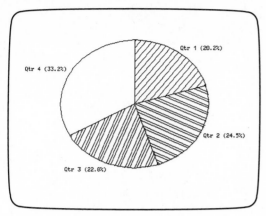

Pie graph with labelled slices.

If the x-axis labels or numbers are longer than 9 or 10 characters, parts of the extreme right or left descriptions may not be displayed.

Using the Legend Option

Whenever a graph contains more than one set of data, you need to be able to distinguish between those sets. If you are using a color monitor and select **C**olor from the main **G**raph menu, 1-2-3 differentiates data series with color. If the main **G**raph menu's default option **B**&**W** (black and white) is in effect, data series in line graphs will be marked with special symbols, as shown in the following illustrations.

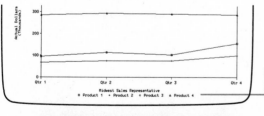

Data series marked with special symbols.

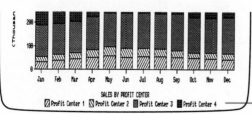

Data series in bar-type graphs are marked with unique patterns of crosshatches.

207

To provide explanatory text for the data represented by either symbols or shadings, use the /**G**raph **O**ptions **L**egend command to display legends below the x-axis.

Note: You cannot use the **L**egend option for a pie graph, which can have only one data series.

Specifying Connecting Lines or Symbols

You can change the way data points are displayed on line and XY graphs by specifying one of four display options: (1) Data points connected by lines, (2) Data points marked by symbols, (3) Data points marked by both lines and symbols, or (4) Data points marked by labels. With the /**G**raph **O**ptions **F**ormat option, you can specify one of these four types of ways to display line and XY graphs.

Setting a Background Grid

Ordinarily, you will use the default (clear) background for your graphs. Sometimes, however, you may want to impose a grid on a graph so that the data-point amounts are easier to read. Selecting /**G**raph **O**ptions **G**rid produces this menu:

> **H**orizontal **V**ertical **B**oth **C**lear

The first option creates a series of horizontal lines across the graph, spaced according to the tick marks on the y-axis. The second option creates a series of vertical lines across the graph, spaced according to the tick marks on the x-axis. The third option causes both horizontal and vertical lines to appear, and the fourth clears all grid lines from the graph.

Changing Axis Scale Settings

You can use /**G**raph **O**ptions **S**cale to alter three distinct default settings associated with the values displayed along a graph's x- and y-axes as described in the following screen.

An Overview of 1-2-3

Getting Started

1-2-3 Basics

Creating a Worksheet

Printing Reports

Creating and Printing Graphs

Managing Data

You can change the upper and lower scale values displayed on the y-axis of a line, XY, bar, or stacked-bar graph.

You can change the format of values displayed along the y-axis.

You can suppress the display of the magnitude indicator that appears along the y-axis.

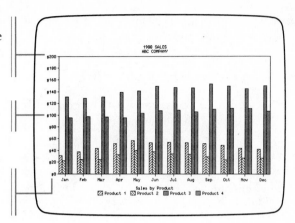

Spacing the Display of X-Axis Labels

You have seen how to use the first two options on the /Graph Options Scale menu to change three default scale settings. A third option—the Skip option—lets you make a fourth adjustment: to the *spacing* of displayed labels. The default setting of 1 causes every label to display. If you set the skip factor to 2, however, every other label will be displayed. Setting the skip factor to 2, for example, will change a bar graph displaying labels for every month to one displaying labels for every other month:

Changing the number of labels displayed along the x-axis.

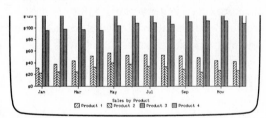

Preserving a Graph on Disk

Although using 1-2-3 to construct a graph from existing data in a spreadsheet is easy, having to rebuild the graph whenever you want to redisplay it on-screen or print it would be tedious.

To create a disk file (with the file extension PIC) that can be used only to print the graph, you use the /Graph Save command. To save the graph specifications along with the underlying worksheet, you first use the **/G**raph **N**ame **C**reate command to name the graph, and then you save the worksheet by using **/F**ile **S**ave.

Saving a PIC File for Printing

Suppose that you have constructed a graph that you want to store for subsequent printing through the PrintGraph program (discussed later in this chapter). After you verify that the chosen graph type is appropriate for your presentation needs, that the graph data ranges have been specified accurately, and that all desired enhancements have been added, choose **/G**raph **S**ave to create a PIC file on disk. 1-2-3 prompts you for a file name and displays (in menu form across the top of the screen) a list of the PIC files in the current directory.

Remember two points. First, **/G**raph **S**ave stores only an image of the current graph, locking in all data and enhancements for the sole purpose of printing it with the PrintGraph program. Therefore, when you are ready to print this print file, you cannot access it to make changes, such as adding a label or editing an underlying worksheet figure. Second, you cannot redisplay the graph on-screen unless you have named the graph and saved the worksheet (or unless the graph is the last active graph on the current worksheet).

To use **/G**raph **S**ave, first view your graph by choosing **/G**raph **V**iew or by pressing F10, to make sure that the graph is drawn as you want it. Second, select **/G**raph **S**ave, and then enter a name when the `Enter save file name:` prompt appears. 1-2-3 will add the PIC extension for you. After you have saved the graph settings for printing, you can print the graph with 1-2-3's PrintGraph program.

Creating Graph Specifications for Reuse

If you want to view on-screen a graph you created in an earlier graphing session, you must have given the graph a name when you originally constructed the graph (and you must have saved the worksheet, unless the same worksheet is still active). To name a graph, you issue the **/G**raph **N**ame command to access the following menu:

> **U**se **C**reate **D**elete **R**eset

Only one graph at a time can be the current graph. If you want to save a graph that you have just completed (for subsequent recall to the screen) as well as build a new graph, you must first issue a **/G**raph **N**ame **C**reate command, which instructs 1-2-3 to remember the specifications used to define the current graph. If you don't name a

An Overview of 1-2-3

Getting Started

1-2-3 Basics

Creating a Worksheet

Printing Reports

Creating and Printing Graphs

Managing Data

graph and subsequently either reset the graph or change the specifications, you cannot restore the original graph without having to rebuild it.

To save a graph with the underlying worksheet so that you can later access and change the graph, first use /Graph Name Create to name the graph.

To name a graph when 1-2-3 prompts you for a graph name, provide a name up to 15 characters long. To recall any named graphs from within the active spreadsheet, select /Graph Name Use.

To delete a single named graph, issue the /Graph Name Delete command. Again, 1-2-3 will list all the graph names stored in the current worksheet. You can select the graph you want to delete by either typing the appropriate name or pointing to the name on the list.

Note: If you want graph names to be stored with their worksheet, remember to save the worksheet file by using /File Save after creating the names.

Accessing and Exiting PrintGraph

The first part of this chapter showed you how to use 1-2-3 to create, display, and enhance graphs. Because the main 1-2-3 program cannot print graphics, you must use the PrintGraph program to print the graphs you saved as graph (PIC) files. You can use the PrintGraph program for quick and easy printouts of graphs. You can also choose from a variety of optional print settings for enhancing further the appearance of printed graphs.

You can use PrintGraph to perform these tasks:

- Access the PrintGraph program
- Use the status screen
- Print a graph by using PrintGraph default settings
- Change graph size, font, and color settings
- Select or alter hardware-related settings
- Use the keyboard to control paper movement
- Establish temporary PrintGraph settings

Accessing the PrintGraph Program

To access PrintGraph directly from DOS, type **pgraph** at the DOS prompt. (The PrintGraph program should reside in the current directory for a hard disk system; for a diskette system, the diskette containing the PrintGraph program should be in the active drive.) If you use a printer driver set other than the default 1-2-3 set, you must type also the name of that driver set (**pgraph hp**, for example) to reach the main PrintGraph menu.

However, you are more likely to use PrintGraph immediately after you have created a graph. If you originally accessed 1-2-3 by typing **lotus**, select **/Q**uit **Y**es to return to the Access menu. Then select **P**rintGraph instead of exiting to the DOS prompt. If you are using 1-2-3 on a diskette system, the program will prompt you to remove the 1-2-3 System diskette and insert the PrintGraph diskette, unless you use a IBM PS/2 computer. For the PS/2, the PrintGraph program resides on the System diskette.

Alternatively, if you have sufficient RAM, you can use PrintGraph after you have issued the **/S**ystem command. Then, instead of having to reload 1-2-3 after you leave PrintGraph, you can return directly to 1-2-3 by typing **exit** at the system prompt. Be careful, however. Before you use this technique, save your worksheet. In addition, because you must have at least 256K of remaining RAM to run PrintGraph and 1-2-3 simultaneously without overwriting your worksheet, use the **/W**orksheet **S**tatus report to check remaining internal memory (RAM) before you attempt to use **/S**ystem.

Exiting the PrintGraph Program

To leave the PrintGraph program, choose **E**xit from the main **P**rintGraph menu. The next screen to appear depends on the method you used to access PrintGraph. If you entered PrintGraph from the 1-2-3 Access System, the Access menu reappears. Select **E**xit to restore the DOS prompt, or select another Access menu option. If you entered PrintGraph by typing **pgraph** from the DOS prompt, the DOS prompt is restored.

If you want to enter 1-2-3 after you have exited PrintGraph and restored the DOS prompt, remember how you originally accessed the DOS prompt (before you typed **pgraph**). If you were using 1-2-3 and selected **/S**ystem to reach the DOS prompt, type **exit** and press Enter to return to the 1-2-3 worksheet. If you were not using 1-2-3 before the PrintGraph session, type **123** or **lotus** and then select **123** from the Access menu.

Summary

This chapter has shown you how to create and print graphs. You learned the four basic steps for creating a graph and how to select any one of 1-2-3's five types of graphs: line, bar, XY, stacked-bar, and pie.

An Overview of 1-2-3

Getting Started

1-2-3 Basics

Creating a Worksheet

Printing Reports

Creating and Printing Graphs

Managing Data

You learned, too, how to improve the appearance of graphs by creating titles, legends, grids, and numerical formats; altering the scaling of the x- and y-axes; assigning connecting lines and symbols; modifying colors; and adding data labels to data points.

So that you could preserve your work, the chapter told you how to save and name a graph as a special PIC file for printing later and how to access and exit 1-2-3's PrintGraph program.

Now that you have learned how to create 1-2-3 worksheets and related graphs, you are ready to tap 1-2-3's database capabilities in the next chapter.

Review Questions

1. What kinds of graphs can you produce with 1-2-3?

2. Describe the four main steps for creating and viewing graphs.

3. Describe the most appropriate use of the following graph types:
   Line

   Bar

   XY

   Stacked-bar

   Pie

4. How do you add titles to a graph?

5. How do you add legends to a graph?

6. How do you add labels to a graph?

7. Which function key enables you to view a graph?

8. What is the **/G**raph **O**ptions **F**ormat command used for?

9. What command aliows you to set a background grid on a graph? When might this feature be useful?

10. What's the difference between **/G**rave **S**ave and **/G**raph **N**ame **C**reate?

11. How do you access PrintGraph?

16 *Managing Data*

An Overview of 1-2-3

Getting Started

1-2-3 Basics

Creating a Worksheet

Printing Reports

Creating and Printing Graphs

Managing Data

In addition to financial spreadsheet and business graphics applications, 1-2-3 has a third type of application: database applications. A 1-2-3 database, like databases created with other software programs, is a collection of data organized so that you can list, sort, or search its contents. In 1-2-3 this data is organized in the 1-2-3 worksheet, and like creating a financial spreadsheet application, creating a 1-2-3 database involves entering text and values into the individual cells in the worksheet. 1-2-3's database feature is fast, easy to access, and easy to use.

The database's speed results from a reduction in the time required to transfer data to and from disks. Because the data in a 1-2-3 database is entered directly into the worksheet cells, the entire 1-2-3 database resides within main memory (RAM). By doing all the work inside the worksheet, 1-2-3 saves the time required for retrieving data from and storing data on a disk.

The 1-2-3 database is easily accessed because the entire database is visible within the worksheet. You can view the contents of the whole database by using worksheet windows and cursor-movement keys to scroll through the database.

The ease of use is a result of integrating data management with the program's spreadsheet and graphics functions. The commands for adding, modifying, and deleting items in a database are the same ones you have already seen for manipulating cells or groups of cells within a worksheet. And creating graphs from ranges in a database is as easy as creating them in a spreadsheet.

After completing this chapter, you will know

- The advantages and limitations of 1-2-3's database
- How to create, modify, and maintain data records
- How to carry out **S**ort and **Q**uery operations
- How to create data with other **/D**ata commands

▼

Key Terms in This Chapter

Database	A collection of data organized so that you can list, sort, or search its contents.
Record	A collection of associated fields. In 1-2-3, a record is a row of cells within a database.
Field	One information item, such as Address or Name. In 1-2-3, a field is a single cell.
Keys	The fields to which you attach the highest precedence when the database is sorted.
Input range	The range of the database on which data manipulation operations are performed.
Output range	The range to which data is copied when extracted from the database.
Criterion range	The range of the database in which you enter queries and criteria.

▲

What Is a Database?

As mentioned at the beginning of the chapter, a database is a collection of data organized so that you can list, sort, or search its contents. The list of data could contain any kind of information, from addresses to tax-deductible expenditures.

In 1-2-3, the word *database* means a range of cells that spans at least one column and more than one row. This definition, however, does not distinguish between a database and any other range of cells. Because a database is actually a list, its manner of organization sets it apart from ordinary cells. Just as a list must be organized to be useful, a database must be organized to permit access to the information it contains.

Remember nonetheless that in 1-2-3 a database is similar to any other group of cells. This knowledge will help you as you learn about the different **/D**ata commands that are covered in this chapter. In many instances, you can use these database commands in what you might consider "nondatabase" applications.

What Is a
Database?

Understanding
the /Data Menu

**Planning and
Building the
Database**

Sorting a
Database

Searching
for Records

Summary

An
Overview of
1-2-3

Getting
Started

1-2-3 Basics

Creating a
Worksheet

Printing
Reports

Creating
and
Printing
Graphs

**Managing
Data**

would for any other 1-2-3 application. The mechanics of entering database contents are simple; the most critical step in creating a useful database is choosing your fields accurately.

Determining Required Output

1-2-3's data-retrieval techniques rely on locating data by field names. Before you begin typing the kinds of data items you think you may need, write down the output you expect from the database. You'll also need to consider any source documents already in use that can provide input to the file.

When you are ready to set up the items in your database, you must specify for each information item a field name, the column width, and the type of entry. Before you set up the items, be sure to consider how you might look for data in that field. Will you search by date? By last name? Knowing how you will use your database before you design it will save you a great amount of time that could be lost in redesigning the database after the fact.

After you decide on the fields, you then need to choose the level of detail needed for each item of information, select the appropriate column width, and determine whether you will enter data as a number or as a label. For example, if you want to be able to sort by area code all records containing telephone numbers, you should enter telephone numbers as two separate fields: area code (XXX) and the main telephone number (XXX-XXXX). Because you will not want to perform math functions on telephone numbers, enter them as labels.

Be sure to plan your database carefully before you establish field names, set column widths and range formats, and enter data.

Entering Data

After you have planned your database, you can build it. The following paragraphs explain the steps involved in building a database.

Start with a blank worksheet. However, if you'd rather use a worksheet with data in it, select an area that is out of the way of the existing data. Selecting an area out of the way allows your database room to grow and won't affect other applications when you insert or delete rows in the database.

Enter the field names across a single row. The field names must be labels, even if they are numeric labels. Although you can use more than one row for the field names, 1-2-3 processes only the values that appear in the bottom row. For example, if you have the field name CONTRACT DATE assigned to column B with CONTRACT in row 3 and DATE in row 4, 1-2-3 will reference only DATE as a key field in sort or query operations. Also, keep in mind that all field names should be unique; any repetition of names confuses 1-2-3 when you search the database.

Set the cell display formats. Use 1-2-3's **F**ormat and **C**olumn **S**et-Width options to control the width of the cells and the way in which 1-2-3 displays the data. (For more information about these commands, see Chapter 13.)

Add records to the database. To enter the first record, move the cursor to the row directly below the field-name row and then enter the data across the row in the normal manner.

Sorting a Database

1-2-3's data management capability lets you change the order of records by sorting them according to the contents of the fields. Selecting **/D**ata **S**ort produces the following command menu:

Data-Range **P**rimary-Key **S**econdary-Key **R**eset **G**o **Q**uit

The following list describes the function of each command in the **/D**ata menu.

Data-Range	Specifies the range on which the sort operation will occur.
Primary-Key	First item on which the sort will be performed.
Secondary-Key	Second item on which the sort is performed.
Reset	Resets the sort options.
Go	Starts the search.
Quit	Leaves the **/D**ata **S**ort menu.

To sort the database, start by designating a **D**ata-Range. This range must be long enough to include all of the records to be sorted and wide enough to include all of the fields in each record. Remember not to include the field-name row in this range. (If you are unfamiliar with how to designate ranges or how to name them, see Chapter 13.)

The **D**ata-Range does not necessarily have to include the entire database. If part of the database already has the organization you want, or if you don't want to sort all

What Is a   Understanding   Planning and   Sorting a   Searching
Database?   the /Data Menu   Building the   Database   for Records   Summary
                                   Database

An
Overview of
1-2-3

Getting
Started

1-2-3 Basics

Creating a
Worksheet

Printing
Reports

Creating
and
Printing
Graphs

Managing
Data

the records, you can sort only a portion of the database. As the following figure illustrates, your **D**ata-Range should not include the field names in your **D**ata-Range and not include any blank rows.

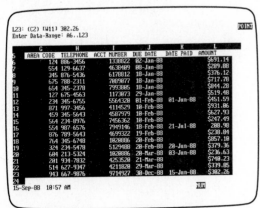

Specifying the **D**ata-Range.

After choosing the **D**ata-Range, you must specify the keys for the sort. Keys are the fields to which you attach the highest precedence when the database is sorted. The field with the highest precedence is the **P**rimary-Key, and the field with the next highest precedence is the **S**econdary-Key. You must set a **P**rimary-Key, but setting the **S**econdary-Key is optional.

After you have specified the range to sort, the key field(s) on which to base the reordering of the records, and whether the sort order, based on the key, is ascending or descending, select **G**o to execute the command. As a useful step for restoring the file to its original order, /**F**ile **S**ave the database to disk before you issue a **S**ort command. Then, if for some reason you want to restore the database to its original organization, you can retrieve the file with the database as it was before you issued the **S**ort command.

The One-Key Sort

One of the simplest examples of a database sorted according to a primary key (often called a single-key database) is the White Pages of the telephone book. All the records in the White Pages are sorted in ascending alphabetical order using the last name as the primary key.

To use 1-2-3's **S**ort capability to reorder records alphabetically on the LAST name field, select /**D**ata **S**ort **D**ata-Range, and specify the range you want to sort. The / **D**ata **S**ort menu then returns to the screen.

After choosing the **D**ata-Range, select **P**rimary-Key and then enter or point to the address of any entry (including blank or field- name cells) in the column containing the primary-key field. For example, if you want to sort the LASTNAME field in your database, and that field occupied column A, you could enter A1 as the address for the **P**rimary-Key. 1-2-3 then asks you to choose an ascending or descending sort order (**A** or **D**). If you choose ascending order, when you select **G**o, 1-2-3 sorts the database so that the last names are alphabetized from A to Z.

The Two-Key Sort

A double-key database has both a primary and secondary key. In the Yellow Pages, records are sorted first according to business type (the primary key) and then by business name (the secondary key). Another example of a double-key sort (first by one key and then by another key within the first sort order) could be to reorder an Addresses database first by state and then by city within state.

To perform a double-key sort on city and state, you first designate the range you want to sort as the **D**ata-Range. Select **P**rimary-Key from the **S**ort menu and specify the field location of the initial sort. (Remember that you can specify any cell in the field's column.) Enter **A** for ascending order for the sort by state. Select **S**econdary-Key, enter the column location of the second sort, and choose **A** for ascending sort order by city.

After you select **G**o, records are grouped first by state in alphabetical order (California, Indiana, Kentucky, etc.) and then by city within state (Bloomington, Indiana, before Indianapolis, Indiana). When you determine whether to use a primary or secondary key, be sure to request a reasonable sort. Remember to make the primary key field the first field on which you want your data range sorted.

Searching for Records

You have learned how to use the main **D**ata menu's **S**ort option to reorganize information from the database by sorting records according to key fields. In this section of the chapter, you will learn how to use **Q**uery, the menu's other data-retrieval command, to search for records and then edit, extract, or delete the records you find.

Looking for records that meet certain conditions is the simplest form of searching a 1-2-3 database. In an inventory database, for example, you could determine when to reorder items by using a search operation to find any records with an on-hand

An Overview of 1-2-3

Getting Started

1-2-3 Basics

Creating a Worksheet

Printing Reports

Creating and Printing Graphs

Managing Data

quantity of less than four units. Once you have located the information you want, you can extract the found records from the database to another section of the worksheet, separate from the database. For example, you can extract all records with a purchase order (P.O.) date, and print the newly extracted area as a record of pending purchases.

With 1-2-3's search operations, you also have the option of looking for only the first occurrence of a specified field value in order to develop a unique list of field entries. For example, you could search and extract a list of the different units of measure. Finally, you can delete all inventory records for which quantity on-hand equals zero (if you don't want to reorder these items).

Minimum Search Requirements

To initiate any search operation, you need to select the operation from the **/D**ata **Q**uery menu:

Input **C**riterion **O**utput **F**ind **E**xtract **U**nique **D**elete **R**eset **Q**uit

You can use the first three options to specify ranges applicable to the search operations. Choose **I**nput to specify the locations of the search area. Choose **C**riteria to specify the search conditions. Both the search area and search conditions must be specified in all **Q**uery operations. An output range, specified by using the **O**utput command, must be established only when you select a **Q**uery command that copies records or parts of records to an area outside the database.

The last two options signal the end of the current search operation. **R**eset removes all previous search-related ranges so that you can specify a different search location and conditions. **Q**uit restores the main **D**ata menu.

The four options in the middle of the **Q**uery menu perform the following search functions:

Find moves down through a database and positions the cursor on records that match given criteria. You can enter or change data in the records as you move the cursor through them. **E**xtract creates copies, in a specified area of the worksheet, of all or some of the fields in certain records that match given criteria. **U**nique is similar to **E**xtract, but recognizes that some of the field contents in the database may be duplicates of other cell entries in the same fields. **U**nique eliminates duplicates as entries are copied to output range. **D**elete deletes from a database all the records that match given criteria and shifts the remaining records to fill in the gaps that remain.

To perform a **Q**uery operation, you must specify both an input range and a criterion range and select one of the four search options. (Before issuing a **U**nique or **E**xtract command, you must also specify an output range.)

Listing All Specified Records

The **F**ind command has limited use, especially in a large database, because the command scrolls through the entire file so that you can view each record that meets the specified criterion. As an alternative to the **F**ind command, you can use the **E**xtract command to copy to a blank area of the worksheet only those records that meet specified conditions. (Before you issue the command, you must define the blank area of the worksheet as an output range.) You can view a list of all the extracted records, print the range of the newly extracted records, or even use the /**F**ile **X**tract command to copy only the extracted record range to a new file on disk.

Defining the Output Range

Choose a blank area in the worksheet as the output range to receive records copied in an extract operation. Designate the range to the right of, or below, the database. Designate the range to the right or below the database. In the following figure, for example, both the criterion range and the output range have been placed below the records in the database.

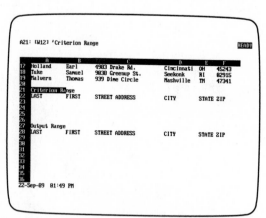

The criterion range and output range.

In the first row of the output range, copy the names of only those fields whose contents you want to extract. You do not have to copy these names in the same order as they appear in the database. (In the preceding illustration, the output-range

		Planning and			
What Is a	Understanding	Building the	Sorting a	**Searching**	
Database?	the /Data Menu	Database	Database	**for Records**	Summary

entry in cell A27 is for documentation purposes only, and all field names in row 28 have been reproduced in the existing order of the database.)

The field names in both the criterion and output ranges must match the corresponding field names in the input range. To avoid mismatch errors, use the /**C**opy command to copy the database field names in the criteria and output ranges.

Select /**D**ata **Q**uery **O**utput; then type, point to, or name the range location of the output area. You can create an open-ended extract area by entering only the field-name row as the range, or you can set the exact size of the extract area.

To limit the size of the extract area, enter the upper-left to lower-right cell coordinates of the entire output range. The first row in the specified range must contain the field names; the remaining rows must accommodate the maximum number of records you expect to receive from the extract operation. Use this method when you want to retain additional data that is located below the extract area. For example, as you can see in the preceding screen, naming A28..F36 as the output range limits records to eight (one row for field names and one row for each record). If you do not allow sufficient room in the fixed-length output area, the extract operation will abort and the message too many records will be displayed on-screen.

To create an open-ended extract area that does not limit the number of incoming records, specify as the output range only the row containing the output field names. For example, by naming A28..F28 as the output range in the preceding screen, you define the output area without limiting the number of records.

An extract operation first removes all existing data from the output range. If you use only the field-name row to specify the output area, all data below that row will be destroyed to make room for the unknown number of incoming extracted records.

Executing the Extract Command

To execute an **E**xtract command, you must type the search conditions in the worksheet; type the output field names in the worksheet; and set the input, criteria, and output ranges from the **D**ata **Q**uery menu.

Suppose that you had an address database similar to the one in the preceding illustration and wanted to create a list of all records with OH in the STATE field.

Assuming that rows 22 and 28 contain the field names, you would enter **OH** in cell E23. Select **/D**ata **Q**uery and specify the input (A1..F19), criteria (A22..F23), and output ranges (A28..F28). Then choose **E**xtract from the **Q**uery menu. The output range in the following screen contains three extracted records, each of which meets the condition of STATE = OH.

All records that meet the specified criteria in the criterion range are copied to the output area.

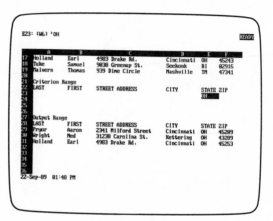

More Complicated Criterion Ranges

In addition to an "exact match" search on a single label field, 1-2-3 permits a wide variety of record searches: on exact matches to numeric fields; on partial matches of field contents; on fields that meet formula conditions; on fields that meet all of several conditions; and on fields that meet either one condition or another.

You can use 1-2-3's wild cards (?, *, and ~) for matching labels in database operations. In addition to using wild cards in the criteria used to search a 1-2-3 database, you can use formulas and setup multiple criteria as AND/OR conditions.

You can also set up multiple criteria as AND conditions (in which all the criteria must be met) or as OR conditions (in which any one criterion must be met). For example, if you wanted to search a database containing information on college students to extract those who are Accounting majors and male, you would specify the conditions on the criterion row immediately below the field names. After you issue an **E**xtract command, 1-2-3 extracts the records that meet both conditions, as shown in the following figure.

An Overview of 1-2-3

Getting Started

1-2-3 Basics

Creating a Worksheet

Printing Reports

Creating and Printing Graphs

Managing Data

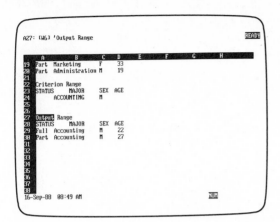

Using the AND operator to extract records.

Summary

Although used frequently for financial spreadsheet applications, 1-2-3 also is used for many types of database applications, some involving financial data but many involving numerical and text data not specifically related to financial applications. Because a 1-2-3 database is created within the column-row worksheet and uses the same cell pointer and cursor movement keys as used for other applications, 1-2-3's database feature is faster, easier to access, and easier to use than programs whose sole function is data management.

The **/D**ata command on 1-2-3's main menu leads to commands for performing common database applications such as sorting data, searching for records that meet a specific criteria, and extracting records from the main database. Although fast and easy to use, 1-2-3's sorting capabilities are limited to sorting data on one or two fields. When searching for and extracting records from a 1-2-3 database, you must indicate the exact range called an *Output Range*, where the data is located that you want to search. You must also create in the worksheet a range, called a *Criterion Range*, to specify the search conditions.

Search conditions in a 1-2-3 database can be text strings or numbers, but can also be much more complicated. More complicated conditions upon which to search a 1-2-3 database can include formulas or can include AND/OR conditions.

Now that you have learned the primary uses, screen features, special key functions, and commands for building and using worksheet applications, the next chapter introduces to the third type of application available in 1-2-3—graphics.

227

Review Questions

1. What is a *field* and *record* in a 1-2-3 database?

2. What command from the main 1-2-3 command menu lets you perform database operations?

3. What part of the database do you highlight when designating a data range before sorting the database?

4. Upon how many fields can you sort a 1-2-3 Release 2.01 database?

5. What sequence of commands would you select to sort according to the LASTNAME field a database containing customer information?

6. What are "Criterion" and "Input" ranges?

7. What is the difference between the **Ex**tract and **U**nique commands?

8. In addition to search a 1-2-3 database for an exact match, in what other ways can you search a database?

Part III

WordPerfect

WORDPERFECT   WORDPERFECT   WORDPERFECT

WordPerfect® 1

©WordPerfect Corporation

An Overview of WordPerfect
Editing and Working with Blocks
Formatting Lines, Paragraphs, and Pages
Proofreading and Printing
Managing Files
Creating Macros
Merging, Sorting, and Selecting
Using Columns
Referencing
Creating Graphics

17 *An Overview of WordPerfect*

WordPerfect is one of the most popular word processing software programs because it has all the "basic" features you would expect in a word processing package, plus a full complement of advanced features. The program is suited to your needs, whether they entail short memos or complex documents.

This chapter begins with the basics of WordPerfect: starting the program, looking at the editing screen, learning the keyboard, and using the Help feature. You learn some fundamental skills for using a word processor, including how to move around the editing screen, save a document, and exit WordPerfect. After you master these skills, you can begin to explore the program's many features.

After completing this chapter, you should have a basic understanding of the following:

- WordPerfect's basic and specialized features
- Starting WordPerfect on a hard disk system and on a dual floppy system
- The parts of the editing screen
- The use of the keyboard in WordPerfect
- Accessing the help feature and tutorial
- WordPerfect's built-in settings
- Typing text
- Moving the cursor
- Making a menu selection
- Saving, exiting, and clearing

Editing and
Working
with Blocks

Formatting
Lines,
Paragraphs,
and Pages

Proofreading
and
Printing

Managing
Files

Creating
Macros

Merging,
Sorting, and
Selecting

Using
Columns

Referencing

Creating
Graphics

Key Terms in This Chapter

Defaults   Standard WordPerfect settings that are automatically put into effect each time you start the program.

Status line	The bottom line on the WordPerfect editing screen. The status line indicates the disk drive and file name, and the position of the cursor.
Cursor	An on-screen marker that indicates where a character would appear if typed.
Word wrap	A WordPerfect feature that eliminates the need to press the Enter (Return) key each time you reach the right margin. With word wrap, you need to press Enter only when you come to the end of a paragraph, a short line, or a command.

An Overview of WordPerfect Features

WordPerfect offers a range of basic features for making your word processing tasks convenient and efficient. The program also offers more specialized features that allow you to create documents more quickly and to generate valuable reference materials.

Basic Features

One of the first features you notice when you start WordPerfect is the uncluttered editing screen. While many word processors display a number of indicators and codes on-screen while you edit, WordPerfect keeps these down to a minimum— freeing most of the screen for text. In addition, the screen display looks very much like your document will appear when printed.

WordPerfect's two document windows (areas on-screen in which you work) give you the flexibility to work on different parts of the same document at once, or on two different documents. You can shift between a full-screen view of each window, or you can split the screen to display both windows.

The block features in WordPerfect allow you to designate a specific portion of the document on which you want certain commands to have an effect. For example, you can use this feature to move and copy blocks of text, to display a certain portion of text in boldface, or to delete particular passages.

You can enhance the appearance of your text in WordPerfect with a multitude of formatting features. You can adjust margins, use boldface and italic typefaces, center text, justify text, change the line spacing and line height, instruct the printer to shift (left, right, up, or down) before printing, design headers and footers, choose page numbering positions, and control where pages break.

Some other features are useful in particular situations. The redline and strikeout features are excellent tools for marking suggested editing changes in a manuscript. The Compose and Overstrike features allow you to create special characters you might need for foreign languages or equations. The subscripts, superscripts, and half-line spacing options also are useful for typing equations.

WordPerfect's Styles feature is a powerful tool that lets you control the format of one document or a group of documents. You specify the formats you want in a particular style, and then you can apply that style to any future documents. You even can create a library of styles for use in a variety of document formats.

The built-in spell checker and thesaurus give you access to a 115,000-word dictionary and lists of alternative synonyms and antonyms you can access from the editing screen. Among the special printing features is View Document, which allows you to preview your document on-screen before you print.

File management is handled efficiently through the List Files screen. From that screen, you can manipulate files and directories from within WordPerfect to a much greater degree than most word processors allow. And with WordPerfect's Document Summary feature, you can easily keep track of your files' contents.

Specialized Features

A feature that can help you perform repetitive tasks more efficiently is WordPerfect's macro feature. The keystrokes and commands you want to include in a macro are recorded and then "played back" when you need them. You can keep macros for different tasks on-hand and call on them with as few as two keystrokes.

WordPerfect's Merge feature lets you merge text files and thereby increase office productivity. For example, you can merge data from an address list into a form letter, or piece together complicated reports. Other tools for handling data are WordPerfect's Sort and Select features. These allow you to sort phone lists, for example, or extract certain ZIP codes from a mailing list.

Two kinds of columns are available in WordPerfect: text columns and math columns. With text columns, you can prepare text in newspaper-style format (for magazine articles or newsletters) or in parallel-column format (for inventory lists or

Editing and Working with Blocks

Formatting Lines, Paragraphs, and Pages

Proofreading and Printing

Managing Files

Creating Macros

Merging, Sorting, and Selecting

Using Columns

Referencing

Creating Graphics

233

duty schedules). WordPerfect's math-columns feature, although limited in its utility, allows you to perform simple calculations.

WordPerfect's referencing features are quite broad in scope. You can supplement your documents with footnotes and endnotes, date and time codes, outlines, line numbers, document comments, indexes, tables of authorities, lists, and automatic cross-references. You also can piece together a large project by creating a master document to keep track of all the subdocument files that make up the project. You can use WordPerfect's document comparison feature to compare a new version of a document with a previous one.

With WordPerfect's graphics capabilities, you can import graphic images, create text boxes, enhance your document with borders, rules, shading, and many other features. These options are ideal for creating newsletters, brochures, and fliers.

Although WordPerfect comes with built-in settings for formatting, screen display, and file locations, you can customize the program with the Setup menu. After you become familiar with WordPerfect's standard settings, you may change a number of these options for all your future documents.

Hardware Requirements

You can run WordPerfect 5 on an IBM PC or compatible computer with a hard disk drive or dual floppy disk drives. WordPerfect requires DOS 2.0 or later and at least 384K of memory. At least 512K of random-access memory (RAM) is recommended.

Because WordPerfect comes on approximately twelve 5 1/4-inch floppy disks or seven 3 1/2-inch microfloppy disks, you frequently must swap disks in and out of your drives if you have a dual floppy system. To run WordPerfect with fewer interruptions, you probably should invest in a hard disk. Although WordPerfect is already a speedy program, it runs faster and performs better on a hard disk system.

WordPerfect runs on a wide variety of printers, from dot-matrix to laser. To take full advantage of WordPerfect's graphics capabilities, you need a graphics card, such as a Hercules Graphics Card or an InColor card.

Starting WordPerfect

This section tells you how to start WordPerfect on a hard disk system and on a dual floppy disk system. Before you start the program, you must install it.

An Overview of
WordPerfect
Features

Starting
WordPerfect

**Learning
WordPerfect
Basics**

Saving,
Exiting, and
Clearing

Summary

Starting WordPerfect on a Hard Disk System

To start WordPerfect on a hard disk system, first check to be sure that the floppy drive(s) is empty. Then turn on your computer. If necessary, respond to the prompts for date and time. When the C> prompt appears, type **cd \wp50** and press Enter. Type **wp** and press Enter. You should see the opening screen for just a moment, and then the editing screen is displayed.

Starting WordPerfect on a Dual Floppy System

To start WordPerfect on a dual floppy disk system, first insert the working copy of your WordPerfect 1 disk into drive A and insert a formatted data disk into drive B. Then turn on your computer. If necessary, respond to the prompts for date and time. When the A> prompt appears, type **b:** and press Enter. Drive B is now the default drive, which means that any data you save to disk is saved to the disk in drive B. Type **a:wp** and press Enter. WordPerfect's opening screen appears. This screen contains WordPerfect copyright information, the version number of your copy, and an indication of the default directory that the system will use. Remove the WordPerfect 1 disk from drive A and insert the WordPerfect 2 disk into drive A. Press any key.

Learning WordPerfect Basics

Before you begin to use WordPerfect, you should take a few minutes to become familiar with WordPerfect's screen display and keyboard. You also should know that WordPerfect has an on-line Help feature that you can access while working on WordPerfect documents, as well as a tutorial that can help you get started learning the program. Among other basics you will need as you start using WordPerfect is knowing about WordPerfect's built-in settings that help you begin to create documents easily. You also will need to learn how to enter text, move around the screen, save your work, and exit the program.

Understanding the Editing Screen

WordPerfect displays your document almost exactly as it will appear when it is printed. What you see on-screen is approximately one-half of a standard typed page. The main portion of the screen displays the document.

Editing and
Working
with Blocks

Formatting
Lines,
Paragraphs,
and Pages

Proofreading
and
Printing

Managing
Files

Creating
Macros

Merging,
Sorting, and
Selecting

Using
Columns

Referencing

Creating
Graphics

235

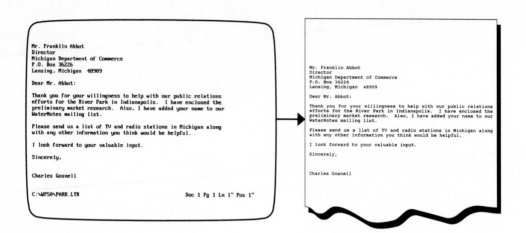

The line of information that appears at the bottom of the screen is called the *status line*, because that information describes the cursor's status. The left side of the status line shows the current document's name. From time to time, the document name is replaced temporarily by system messages and prompts.

The next item in the status line (Doc 1 or Doc 2) indicates which of two available documents is currently displayed on-screen. WordPerfect is capable of holding two documents in memory simultaneously.

Pg identifies the number of the page on which the cursor currently rests.

Ln indicates the cursor's vertical position, in inches, centimeters, points, or lines on your document page.

Pos is called the *position indicator*. This part of the status line tells you the cursor's horizontal position on the document page.

Note: Through the Setup menu, you can customize many aspects of WordPerfect's screen display. For example, you can change the appearance and color of normal text (if you have a color monitor), specify whether the current file name is displayed on the status line, and change the way menu letter options are displayed on-screen.

Learning the Keyboard

WordPerfect uses the following three main areas of the keyboard:

- The function keys, labeled F1 to F12 at the top of the IBM Enhanced Keyboard (or F1 to F10 at the left of the PC keyboard).

An Overview of
WordPerfect
Features

Starting
WordPerfect

**Learning
WordPerfect
Basics**

Saving,
Exiting, and
Clearing

Summary

**An
Overview of
WordPerfect**

Editing and
Working
with Blocks

Formatting
Lines,
Paragraphs,
and Pages

Proofreading
and
Printing

Managing
Files

Creating
Macros

Merging,
Sorting, and
Selecting

Using
Columns

Referencing

Creating
Graphics

- The alphanumeric or "typing" keys, located in the center of the keyboard. (These keys are most familiar to you from your experience with typewriter keyboards.)
- The numeric and cursor keys, found at the right end of the keyboard.

Function Keys

As the WordPerfect function key template illustrates, each function key can carry out four tasks when used by itself or in combination with another key. You routinely use the function keys to give your computer instructions called *commands*. To issue a WordPerfect command, you press a function key alone or in combination with the Ctrl, Shift, or Alt key.

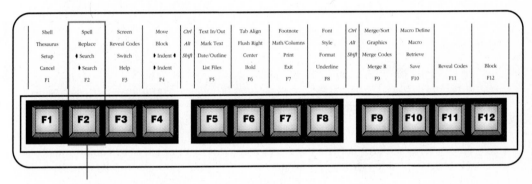

To issue the Spell command, for example, you press and hold the Ctrl key while you press the F2 key. Or to issue the Forward Search command, you press the F2 key alone.

The commands assigned to the functions keys when you first start WordPerfect are the default definitions for those keys. WordPerfect also gives you the option of switching to other keyboard definitions so that the keys on your keyboard—the function keys as well as other special keys—perform other commands or functions. The program also allows you to customize your keyboard by assigning alternate definitions to specified keys. To access WordPerfect's feature for alternate keyboard definitions, you use the Keyboard Layout option on the Setup menu.

Alphanumeric Keys

The alphanumeric keys work similar to those on a typewriter. Keep in mind one critical but easily overlooked difference between composing with a typewriter and

237

composing with WordPerfect: When you type normal text, you do not need to end lines at the right margin by pressing the Enter key. When you type text in Word-Perfect and reach the end of a line, the text "wraps" automatically to the next line.

The Enter key can be used as a carriage return. You also press Enter to insert blank lines in your text, such as the lines that separate paragraphs.

The Shift, Alt, and Ctrl (Control) keys are part of the alphanumeric keyboard. The Shift key creates uppercase letters and other special characters, just as it does on a typewriter keyboard. Shift is used also with the function keys to carry out certain operations in WordPerfect. The Alt and Ctrl keys are used in combination with other keys to provide WordPerfect capabilities that a single key can't provide. The Alt and Ctrl keys don't do anything by themselves, but work with the function keys, number keys, or letter keys to operate various commands in WordPerfect.

Cursor-Movement Keys

The cursor is the blinking underline character that marks the location on the screen where the next character you type will appear. The cursor also marks the location in your text where codes (such as those used to create new margin settings) will be entered.

You use the keys marked with arrows at the far right of the keyboard to control cursor movement. When you press an arrow key, the cursor moves in the direction indicated by the arrow on that key. You will learn more about cursor movement later in this chapter.

When the Num Lock key is activated, the cursor-movement keys become the numeric keys used to perform math functions.

Note: WordPerfect offers an option for changing the rate of speed at which the cursor moves. The Cursor Speed option is available through the Setup menu.

Accessing the WordPerfect Help Feature and Tutorial

WordPerfect provides two tools for helping you learn the program: the Help feature and the tutorial. The screens in the Help system, which you can access while you are working in a document, can help you learn more about WordPerfect commands and keys. The Help system also provides an alphabetical listing of all WordPerfect features and an on-screen function key template. From within a document, press the

An Overview of
WordPerfect
Features

Starting
WordPerfect

**Learning
WordPerfect
Basics**

Saving,
Exiting, and
Clearing

Summary

**An
Overview of
WordPerfect**

Editing and
Working
with Blocks

Formatting
Lines,
Paragraphs,
and Pages

Proofreading
and
Printing

Managing
Files

Creating
Macros

Merging,
Sorting, and
Selecting

Using
Columns

Referencing

Creating
Graphics

F3 (Help) function key to access the Help system. Then press the key about which you want to know more.

WordPerfect's self-paced tutorial, WordPerfect Tutor, includes a series of lessons in which you gain experience with the program's features. Most of the lessons range from 12 to 20 minutes for a total of about 2 1/2 hours.

Typing Text

With a word processor, you can get words on-screen as fast as you can type them. In a short time, you will realize that putting words on-screen can be far easier than putting them on paper. WordPerfect doesn't think or plan for you, of course, but it certainly simplifies self-expression.

At any stage of the writing process, you easily can revise your words on-screen. With a word processor, you can alter what you write with great freedom; you easily can insert new words, delete ones you don't want, or move up and down through a document to see what you've written. Because altering text can be accomplished so effortlessly, you can focus on first getting words on-screen. Then, you can wait until later to edit, revise, and spell-check the text. If you're a poor typist, you can leave spelling errors for WordPerfect's Speller to catch.

WordPerfect's Built-In Settings

Before you even put fingers to keys and begin typing, WordPerfect has been at work for you. You will recall from your experience with a typewriter that you must set margins, line spacing, and tabs, for example, before you begin composing. With WordPerfect, you don't need to make any formatting decisions before you begin unless the preset values do not suit you.

WordPerfect comes with a number of default settings—for margins, page numbers, tab settings, base font (basic character style), line spacing, and other features. You should be familiar with the basic default settings before you begin writing. Subsequent chapters, especially those devoted to formatting and printing, explore the many ways you can alter the look of a document.

Note: Through the Initial Settings option on the Setup menu, you can change a number of WordPerfect's built-in settings. For example, you can change the formatting specifications for all future documents, change the date format, and turn off the feature that sounds a "beep" when you've made an error.

239

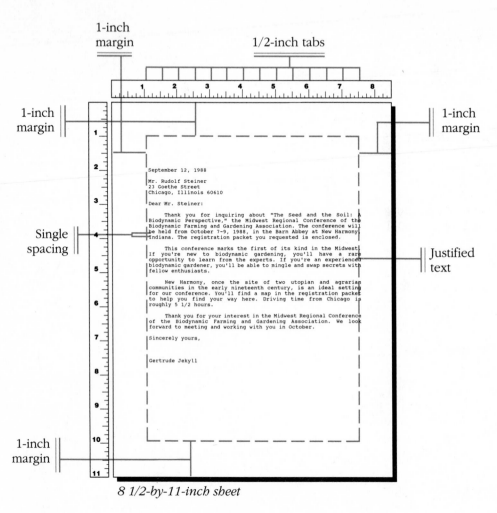

1-inch margin

1/2-inch tabs

1-inch margin

1-inch margin

Single spacing

Justified text

September 12, 1988

Mr. Rudolf Steiner
23 Goethe Street
Chicago, Illinois 60610

Dear Mr. Steiner:

 Thank you for inquiring about "The Seed and the Soil: A Biodynamic Perspective," the Midwest Regional Conference of the Biodynamic Farming and Gardening Association. The conference will be held from October 7-9, 1988, in the Barn Abbey at New Harmony, Indiana. The registration packet you requested is enclosed.

 This conference marks the first of its kind in the Midwest. If you're new to biodynamic gardening, you'll have a rare opportunity to learn from the experts. If you're an experienced biodynamic gardener, you'll be able to mingle and swap secrets with fellow enthusiasts.

 New Harmony, once the site of two utopian and agrarian communities in the early nineteenth century, is an ideal setting for our conference. You'll find a map in the registration packet to help you find your way here. Driving time from Chicago is roughly 5 1/2 hours.

 Thank you for your interest in the Midwest Regional Conference of the Biodynamic Farming and Gardening Association. We look forward to meeting and working with you in October.

Sincerely yours,

Gertrude Jekyll

1-inch margin

8 1/2-by-11-inch sheet

Entering Text

As you type in WordPerfect, characters appear at the position of the cursor, just as they do when you use a typewriter. After you type a few words, look at the Pos indicator on the status line. This value increases as you type and as the cursor moves horizontally across the line to the right. Unlike a typewriter, WordPerfect doesn't require you to press Enter to end a line. Word wrap inserts what is known as a soft return at the end of each line and "wraps" the text to the beginning of the next line.

An Overview of
WordPerfect
Features

Starting
WordPerfect

**Learning
WordPerfect
Basics**

Saving,
Exiting, and
Clearing

Summary

Moving the Cursor

Move the cursor through text in WordPerfect with the cursor-movement keys: the up, down, left, and right arrow keys; the PgUp, PgDn, Screen Up, and Screen Down keys; the GoTo (Ctrl-Home) key combination; or the Repeat key (Esc). When you press an arrow key, the cursor moves in the direction indicated by the arrow on that key. Keep in mind that WordPerfect does not permit the cursor to move where nothing exists. The cursor moves only through text, spaces, or codes.

↑ moves the cursor up one line.

↓ moves the cursor down one line; this key also reformats existing text when you move the cursor through it with the down arrow.

← moves the cursor one position to the left.

→ moves the cursor one position to the right.

Ctrl → moves the cursor one word to the right.

Ctrl ← moves the cursor one word to the left.

Home → or End moves the cursor to the right end of the line.

Home ← moves the cursor to the left edge of the screen.

PgUp PgUp **and** PgDn **PgDn**

PgUp moves the cursor to the top of the preceding page.

PgDn moves the cursor to the top of the next page.

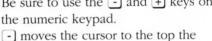 **Screen Up and + Screen Down**

Be sure to use the [-] and [+] keys on the numeric keypad.

[-] moves the cursor to the top the screen or to the preceding screen.
[+] moves the cursor to the bottom of the screen or to the next screen.

Ctrl Home **GoTo**

To move to a specific page in your document, press Ctrl Home, the page number, and ↵Enter.
To move to a specific character in your document, press Ctrl Home and the character (nonnumeric).
To move to the top of the page, press Ctrl Home ↑.
To move to the bottom of the page, press Ctrl Home ↓.
To return to the cursor's original position, press Ctrl Home.

Esc **Repeat Key**

To repeat an operation *n* number ot times, press Esc, enter the number of repetitions (*n*), and press the key you want to repeat..

Making a Menu Selection

WordPerfect uses two types of menus. Many times when you press a function key combination, a one-line menu appears at the bottom of the screen. Other commands in WordPerfect display full-screen menus.

Select an option from either type of menu in either of two ways:

- Press the number next to the menu selection.
- Press the highlighted letter in the name of the menu option.

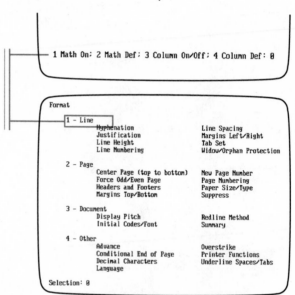

```
1 Math On; 2 Math Def; 3 Column On/Off; 4 Column Def: 0
```

```
Format
 1 - Line
           Hyphenation              Line Spacing
           Justification            Margins Left/Right
           Line Height              Tab Set
           Line Numbering           Widow/Orphan Protection

 2 - Page
           Center Page (top to bottom)   New Page Number
           Force Odd/Even Page           Page Numbering
           Headers and Footers           Paper Size/Type
           Margins Top/Bottom            Suppress

 3 - Document
           Display Pitch            Redline Method
           Initial Codes/Font       Summary

 4 - Other
           Advance                  Overstrike
           Conditional End of Page  Printer Functions
           Decimal Characters       Underline Spaces/Tabs
           Language

Selection: 0
```

When you press the Math/Columns key (Alt-F7), for instance, a one-line menu appears at the bottom of the screen. To turn on Math, press 1 or M for Math On.

When you press the Format key (Shift-F8), the Format menu appears on-screen. If you want to change the margins, for example, you press 1 or L for Line to choose that option. Another menu is then displayed, from which you can choose other options to adjust the margin settings.

Using the Cancel Key

The Cancel key (the F1 "oops" key) allows you to back out of a menu without making a selection, or to restore deleted text either to its original location or to another location.

When used to back out of a menu, F1 (Cancel) cancels the most recent command and returns you either to the preceding menu or to your document. When used to restore text, Cancel (F1) retrieves one of the last three items you've deleted. An *item* in this case means the characters (numbers, letters, or punctuation) deleted before moving the cursor. Cancel (F1) always acts as an "undelete" key when a menu is not visible. You will learn more about how to use the Cancel key to restore text in Chapter 18, "Editing and Working with Blocks."

Saving, Exiting, and Clearing

What you see on-screen is a *temporary* display; only the documents you transfer to disk storage are secured for future use. Usually you keep copies on disk of the documents you create. As a rule, you should save your work every 10 or 15 minutes. Use either of two methods to save a document to disk. Save the document with Save (F10) and remain in WordPerfect, or save the document with Exit (F7) and exit WordPerfect. Keep in mind that before you can work on a new document or before you can retrieve a document, you must clear the current document from the screen.

Note: WordPerfect offers two automatic backup features through the Setup menu: Timed Backup and Original Backup. With the Timed Backup option, at specified intervals, WordPerfect automatically saves to disk the document displayed on-screen. With the Original Backup option, WordPerfect saves both the original file and the edited version.

Saving a Document To Disk and Remaining in WordPerfect

The first time you save a document, WordPerfect prompts you for a file name. Suppose that you've created a document, and you now want to save the file. With your document on-screen, you press Save (F10). The prompt Document to be saved: appears on the status line. Next, you type a file name for the document and press Enter. When you name a file, you must observe your operating system's (MS-DOS or PC DOS) guidelines for naming files. After you name and save a file, the file name is displayed on the status line in the left corner of the screen. The document remains on-screen, and you can continue working.

WordPerfect responds a bit differently when you want to save a file you've saved before. When you press Save (F10), WordPerfect asks whether you want to replace the file on disk. You can press Y to replace the previous version of the file with the new version. Or, you can press N, rename the file, and save it under a different name.

Saving a Document To Disk and Exiting WordPerfect

The other method for saving a document to disk is to use Exit (F7). The prompt
`Save document? (Y/N) Yes` is displayed. To begin the Save process, press Y.
When WordPerfect prompts you to enter the name of the document to be saved, type
the file name and press Enter.

If the document already exists, WordPerfect prompts `Replace (file name)?`
`(Y/N) No`. Press Y to save the document with the old name; or press N, type the file
name, and press Enter. Your document is stored to disk under the name you select.
The message, `Exit WP? (Y/N) No` appears on-screen. Press Y to exit WordPerfect
and return to DOS.

Clearing the Screen

You must clear the current document from the screen before you start work on a
new document—or before you retrieve a document. You can use Exit (F7) to clear
the screen without saving the document. If you do not clear the current document
before starting a new document, or before retrieving a document from memory, the
old and the new documents will merge with one another.

If you don't want to save the document you've created, or if you've saved the
document previously but you want to clear your screen, press Exit (F7). In response
to the `Save Document? (Y/N) Yes` prompt, press N.

The prompt `Exit WP? (Y/N) No` appears on-screen. In response to the prompt,
press N or Enter to clear the screen and stay in WordPerfect. If you press Cancel (F1),
you will return to the document displayed on-screen.

Summary

This chapter has introduced you to the range of word processing features available in
WordPerfect. The program's basic features are convenient and efficient for creating,
editing, formatting, and printing documents. WordPerfect's specialized features give
you a full range of tools for further supplementing your documents with elements
such as graphics, footnotes, and lists. You have learned about the hardware
requirements for using WordPerfect. You also learned how to start the program on a
hard disk and on a dual floppy system.

An Overview of
WordPerfect
Features

Starting
WordPerfect

Learning
WordPerfect
Basics

Saving,
Exiting, and
Clearing

Summary

The chapter introduced the editing screen, from which you perform most of your work in WordPerfect, and explained how to use the keyboard, access the help feature and tutorial, type text, move the cursor, and make a menu selection. You also learned about WordPerfect's built-in settings that help you begin to create documents quickly. Finally, you learned to save your work, and exit the document and the program. In the next chapter, you will learn about WordPerfect's features for editing a document. You also will learn how to manipulate blocks of text.

Review Questions

1. What kinds of supplemental reference material can you create with WordPerfect?

2. Describe the kind of file and status information that WordPerfect displays constantly on the editing screen.

3. How are the function keys used in WordPerfect?

4. Which key can you use to access on-screen help, and what kind of help is provided?

5. Describe WordPerfect's word-wrap feature.

6. What is a program *default* setting?

7. Which keys do you use to move the cursor in WordPerfect?

8. What are the two types of menus that appear in WordPerfect, and how do you make menu selections?

9. Which key do you use to cancel a menu selection or restore deleted text?

10. What are the two ways you can save a document to disk in WordPerfect, and how do these methods differ?

18 *Editing and Working with Blocks*

Revising a draft is an important part of creating any polished document. Revision can consist of changing, adding to, or deleting material; correcting grammar and punctuation; and making any other changes to your document. WordPerfect lets you revise text easily by using a number of built-in editing tools.

The most powerful and flexible command for editing and enhancing your documents in WordPerfect is the Block command (Alt-F4, or F12 on the Enhanced Keyboard). You use this command with other WordPerfect features to block (identify) specific segments of text so that only the blocked text is affected by the selected feature.

After completing this chapter, you should be able to perform the following tasks:

- Retrieve files
- Insert, delete, and restore deleted text
- Display and delete Reveal Codes

- Use both document windows
- Define a block of text
- Move, copy, delete, and save any size block

Key Terms in This Chapter

Insert mode   When you type in Insert mode (WordPerfect's default), new characters are inserted and existing text moves forward.

Typeover mode   When you type in Typeover mode, the characters you type replace the original text.

Reveal Codes   The hidden codes inserted in the text when you press certain keys. Hidden codes tell WordPerfect when to execute tabs, margin settings, hard returns, and so on.

Document window	An area in which to work. In WordPerfect, you can open two document windows, Doc 1 and Doc 2.
Block	A segment of text marked (identified) as a unit so that only that segment is affected by a selected WordPerfect function.

▲

Retrieving Files

You can retrieve documents stored on disk in two ways: select Retrieve (Shift-F10) or select List Files (F5) to use the List Files screen. When you use the Retrieve command, you must know the exact name of the file you want. The List Files screen displays a two-column alphabetized list of your files from which you can choose the file you want to retrieve; the screen also displays the file size and the date and time each file was last saved. Before you retrieve a file using either method, be sure to clear the screen using Exit (F7).

Using the Retrieve Command

To retrieve a file using the Retrieve command, select Retrieve (Shift-F10). At the prompt for a file name, type the exact name of the document and press Enter. If the message ERROR: File Not Found is displayed, either you have typed the name incorrectly or the file doesn't exist in the directory. Type the name again. If you cannot remember the name of the document you want to retrieve, use List Files.

Using the List Files Screen

To retrieve a document with List Files, select List Files (F5). WordPerfect displays a file specification similar to the following in the lower left corner of the screen:

```
Dir C:\WP50\*.*
```

To view the documents stored on the named drive, press Enter. Or, to view files on a drive other than the one designated, type the letter of the disk drive, a colon, and the path name (**c:\letters**, for example). Then press Enter.

An Overview of WordPerfect

Editing and Working with Blocks

Formatting Lines, Paragraphs, and Pages

Proofreading and Printing

Managing Files

Creating Macros

Merging, Sorting, and Selecting

Using Columns

Referencing

Creating Graphics

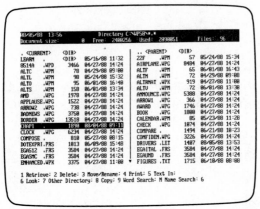

Use the arrow keys to move the highlight bar to the file you want to retrieve. Then select the Retrieve (1) option.

Editing Text

After you enter the text of a document, you can use a variety of WordPerfect features to edit the text. You can insert and delete various amounts of text, restore deleted text to the same or a different location, and insert spaces and blank lines.

Inserting Text

You can improve what you have written by inserting additional text using Insert mode or by typing over and replacing the existing text with new text using Typeover mode. The basic difference between Typeover mode and Insert mode is that Typeover mode replaces your original text; Insert mode adds new text to existing text.

WordPerfect normally operates in Insert mode. Insert mode means that as you type, the new characters are inserted, and existing text moves forward and is automatically formatted. As you type, sentences may push beyond the right margin and may not immediately wrap to the next line. Don't worry. The lines adjust as you continue to type. Or, you can press the down-arrow key to reformat the text. To add text by using Insert mode, place the cursor where you want to insert new text. Then type the new text.

You generally use Typeover mode if you have typed text incorrectly. For example, you probably would select Typeover mode to replace text if you mistakenly had typed the name *Jane* instead of *Dane*. To add text by typing over existing text, place the cursor where you want the new text to begin. Then press Ins to turn off Insert mode and turn on Typeover mode. The `Typeover` mode indicator appears at the lower left of your screen. Next, type the new text, and then press Ins again to return to Insert mode.

In Insert or Typeover mode, you can add blank character spaces by pressing the space bar. You can insert blank lines by pressing the Enter key once for each blank line you want to insert. Inserting blank lines causes existing lines of text to move down on the page.

Deleting Text

With WordPerfect, you can delete unwanted text of various lengths. To delete a single character, press Del if the cursor is under the character, or Backspace if the cursor is to the right of the character. To delete a word, press Ctrl-Backspace if the cursor is within the word or in the blank space to the right of it, or press Home-Del if the cursor is on the first character of the word. To delete a single line, press Ctrl-End; or to delete several lines, press Esc, type the number of lines you want to delete, and press Ctrl-End. To delete a page, press Ctrl-PgDn. And to delete a blank line, move the cursor to the left margin and press Del.

Restoring Deleted Text

Press Cancel (F1) to restore deleted text either to its original location or to another location. Remember, however, that WordPerfect stores only the last three deletions. When you make a fourth deletion, the oldest of the three preceding deletions is erased from memory.

Using Reveal Codes

Many times when you press a key in WordPerfect, a hidden code is inserted into the text. The term *hidden* is used because you cannot see the code on-screen. By hiding the codes, WordPerfect keeps the document editing screen uncluttered. These hidden codes, called *Reveal Codes*, tell WordPerfect when to execute tabs, margin settings, hard returns, indents, and so on. Some codes—such as the codes for math and columns—turn those features on and off. Other codes—such as the codes for bold, underline, and italic—work as a pair. The first code in a pair acts as a toggle switch to turn on the feature; the second code serves to turn off the feature. You can view the hidden codes in your document.

Retrieving
Files

Editing
Text

**Using
Reveal
Codes**

Using Both
Document
Windows

Working
with Blocks

Summary

Displaying Hidden Codes

```
August 18, 1988

Dear Dane,

There's been a change in the location for this year's drivers
school for the Windy City Chapter, and I know you'll love this one!
Instead of going to Blackhawk Farms, we'll be going up to Road
America in beautiful Elkhart Lake, Wisconsin.

The dates will remain the same, September 12 and 13. Lodging, as
always, will be available at Siebkens and Barefoot Bay in Elkhart
                                        Doc 1 Pg 1 Ln 1" Pos 1"
[▲         ▲    ▲   ▲  ▲    ▲   ▲  ▲   ▲   ▲     ]  ▲
[Center Pg]August 18, 1988[HRt]
[HRt]
Dear Dane,[HRt]
[HRt]
There's been a change in the location for this year's drivers[SRt]
school for the Windy City Chapter, and I know you'll love this one![SRt]
Instead of going to Blackhawk Farms, we'll be going up to Road[SRt]
America in beautiful Elkhart Lake, Wisconsin.[HRt]
[HRt]
The dates will remain the same, September 12 and 13. Lodging, as[SRt]

Press Reveal Codes to restore screen
```

To see the hidden codes, press Reveal Codes (Alt-F3, or F11 on the Enhanced Keyboard). The screen splits in half. The same text is displayed in both windows, but the text in the bottom half includes the hidden codes.

The bar between screens—the *tab ruler*—displays the tab and margin settings for the line on which the cursor rests. The curly braces, { and }, mark the left and right margins. Instead of braces, you may see brackets, [and]. The braces indicate margins and tabs at the same position; the brackets indicate margins alone. The triangles mark the tab stops.

In the Reveal Codes screen, codes are highlighted and appear in brackets. Press Reveal Codes (Alt-F3, or F11) again to restore the normal screen.

Editing in Reveal Codes

Editing in Reveal Codes is a little different than editing in the document editing screen. The cursor in the upper window looks the same, but the cursor in the lower window is displayed as a highlight bar. When the cursor comes upon a hidden code (in the lower window), the cursor expands to cover the entire code.

Deleting Hidden Codes

You can delete hidden codes in the normal typing screen or in the Reveal Codes screen. Because you can see the codes in the Reveal Codes screen, deleting them with Reveal Codes is easier. To delete codes, first move the cursor to the place in your document where the code is likely to be located. Then press Reveal Codes (Alt-F3, or F11). Use the arrow keys to position the cursor on the hidden code. Then press Del to delete the hidden code. To return to the normal typing screen, press Reveal Codes (Alt-F3, or F11) again.

Using Both Document Windows

WordPerfect gives you two "sheets of paper" to work on at once if you choose to do so. The two document windows you can open are called Doc 1 and Doc 2. The status line tells you which window is the "active" work space. The cursor's position determines whether the window is active. You can type in both windows and switch back and forth between them with ease. Initially, each window is the entire size of the screen. You can split the screen to look at two documents or at different parts of the same document at once.

Switching between Windows

To switch between document windows, press Switch (Shift-F3). The status line displays Doc 2, and the second document window is displayed in a full screen. Although any text in the first window is not visible now, the text is not lost. To display the Doc 1 window, press Switch (Shift-F3) again.

Splitting the Screen

You can split the screen so that WordPerfect's 24-line display is split between two windows. When you display two documents at once, WordPerfect reserves 2 lines for its own use.

To split the screen, press Screen (Ctrl-F3). From the displayed menu, select Window (1). In response to the prompt for the number of lines in the window, type the number of lines you want in the first window and press Enter.

For example, to split the screen in half, type **11**. The screen is split in half, with WordPerfect's tab ruler line displayed across the middle.

```
Mr. Franklin Abbot
Director
Michigan Department of Commerce
PO Box 36226
Lansing, Michigan 48909

Dear Mr. Abbot:

Thank you for your willingness to help with our public relations
efforts for the River Park in Indianapolis. I have enclosed the
                                          Doc 1 Pg 1 Ln 1.83" Pos 1"
[  ▲    ▲   ▲    ▲   ▲    ▲   ▲    ▲   ▲    ▲   ▲    ▲   ]  ▲  1"
Notes from letter to F. Abbot (8/08/88)

1.  Follow up in two weeks with phone call if we haven't received
    the list of TV and radio stations.

2.  Send him zoo's preliminary market research (get Elizabeth
    Ferguson's OK to send him this data).

3.  Put him on mailing list for WaterNotes.


                                          Doc 2 Pg 1 Ln 1" Pos 1"
```

To resize the window to a full-screen display, press Screen (Ctrl-F3). From the menu, select Window (1). At the prompt, type **24** and press Enter.

Working with Blocks

With WordPerfect's Block command, you can select, or *highlight*, an area of text. Highlighting text is the first step in many timesaving WordPerfect functions, such as moving and copying text. The Block command, used in combination with other commands, gives you powerful editing capabilities. A block of text can be as short as a single letter or as long as several pages. Flexibility is the Block command's strength. You define the size and shape of the block, and then you specify what to do with that selected text.

Before you do anything to a block of text, you must tell WordPerfect exactly what portion of the text you want affected. To do so, you first use the Block (Alt-F4, or F12) command to define the block of text. Then you can perform any number of operations on the defined block.

Defining a Block

To define a block of text, first move the cursor to the character that begins the block of text you want to define. Then press Block (Alt-F4, or F12). The `Block on` message flashes in the lower left corner of your screen. Move the cursor until the last character in the block of text is highlighted.

Performing a Block Operation

After a block is highlighted, you press the key that invokes the feature you plan to use on the highlighted block of text. The feature you select executes only on the highlighted block of text. If the feature you've selected will not work with the Block command, WordPerfect signals you with a beep. (Although the Block function is flexible, it can't be used with all WordPerfect features.)

Moving and Copying a Block

Moving a block of text is a "cut-and-paste" operation—except that you don't fuss with scissors, paper, paste, and tape. Using WordPerfect, you simply define the block, cut it from its current location, and paste it to a new location in your document. The block is erased from its previous location and appears in the new location. The new location can even be in another document. When you copy a block of text, WordPerfect places into memory a duplicate of the block you've defined. You then can retrieve this block from memory and insert the block at another location in your document or in another document.

Moving a Block

When you move a block, the text is deleted from the original location and appears at the new location you specify.

```
When you brainstorm a writing assignment on-screen, you record your
ideas in list form as they occur to you. When you brainstorm, you
don't worry about typos, spelling, or style. You turn off the
inclination to hone each sentence before you move on to the next
one. You can handle those matters later. Your goal is, rather, to
generate as many ideas as possible about the topic, the purpose,
or the audience.

When you have trouble determining a sharp focus for a document--
when you are uncertain what you want to say--consider trying a
semistructured writing exercise known as "brainstorming."
```

Copying a Block

When you copy a block, the text appears both in the original location and in the new location you specify.

```
When you have trouble determining a sharp focus for a document--
when you are uncertain what you want to say--consider trying a
semistructured writing exercise known as "brainstorming."

When you brainstorm a writing assignment on-screen, you record your
ideas in list form as they occur to you. When you brainstorm, you
don't worry about typos, spelling, or style. You turn off the
inclination to hone each sentence before you move on to the next
one. You can handle those matters later. Your goal is, rather, to
generate as many ideas as possible about the topic, the purpose,
or the audience.

When you have trouble determining a sharp focus for a document--
when you are uncertain what you want to say--consider trying a
semistructured writing exercise known as "brainstorming."
```

To either move or copy a block of text, first press Block (Alt-F4 or F12), and then press Ctrl-F4 (Move). From the Move menu, select Move (1) or Copy (2), depending on the operation you want to perform. Next move the cursor to the location in your document where you want the block to appear. Finally, press Enter to insert the block at the new location.

If the block you want to move or copy is a sentence, paragraph, or page, WordPerfect highlights the block for you. Instead of using the Block command,

An
Overview of
WordPerfect

**Editing and
Working
with Blocks**

Formatting
Lines,
Paragraphs,
and Pages

Proofreading
and
Printing

Managing
Files

Creating
Macros

Merging,
Sorting, and
Selecting

Using
Columns

Referencing

Creating
Graphics

press Move (Ctrl-F4); select Sentence (1), Paragraph (2), or Page (3); select Move (1) or Copy (2); move the cursor to the new position; and press Enter.

Deleting a Block

In a few keystrokes, you can delete a sentence or three full pages of text. To delete a block of text, first use Block (Alt-F4, or F12) to define the block to be deleted. Then press the Del key or the Backspace key. When you are prompted to confirm the deletion, you press Y. (If you press N, you are returned to the highlighted text.) The block is deleted from your document. You can delete as many as three blocks and restore all of them using the Cancel (F1) feature.

Saving a Block

When you must type the same block of text in one document several times, WordPerfect's Block Save function helps reduce the amount of work. With Block Save, you define the block of text you plan to use frequently, and then you save the block to a separate file. Block Save enables you to build a timesaving library of frequently used blocks of text. You can even build an entire document from these files.

To save a block of text, first use Block (Alt-F4, or F12) to define the block you want to save. Then press Save (F10). When WordPerfect prompts you to enter a block name, type the name of the file in which you want to save the block and press Enter.

Summary

This chapter introduced WordPerfect's numerous editing tools for revising a document. You learned to retrieve files you have saved to disk, and to insert, delete, and restore deleted text in those files. You also learned to display and delete WordPerfect's hidden codes. WordPerfect's capability to display two document windows at once was explored, and you learned to switch between windows as well as to split the screen into two windows.

Knowing how to use WordPerfect's block feature gives you great versatility for performing your editing tasks. This chapter illustrated that after a block is defined, you can move or copy it, delete it, or save it, as well as perform other functions to the defined unit of text.

The next chapter, "Formatting Lines, Paragraphs, and Pages," shows you many ways you can enhance your text. You will learn to change WordPerfect's built-in settings to suit your particular needs.

Review Questions

1. Describe the two methods you can use to retrieve a file from disk in WordPerfect.

2. How does inserting text differ when you are in Insert mode and when you are in Typeover mode?

3. What are Reveal Codes and how do you display them?

4. When two windows are displayed on-screen, how do you determine which one is "active"?

5. What is the first step in any block operation?

6. How do the results of a move operation and a copy operation differ?

7. After a block is highlighted, what keys can you use to delete it?

8. What are some possible uses for the Block Save command?

19 *Formatting Lines, Paragraphs, and Pages*

An
Overview of
WordPerfect

Editing and
Working
with Blocks

**Formatting
Lines,
Paragraphs,
and Pages**

Proofreading
and
Printing

Managing
Files

Creating
Macros

Merging,
Sorting, and
Selecting

Using
Columns

Referencing

Creating
Graphics

WordPerfect presets all initial or default settings for margins, tabs, and other basic features. If these settings do not fit your needs, you either can change the settings temporarily for the document on which you are working, or you can change the settings permanently with the Setup (Shift-F1) menu. This chapter tells you primarily how to change the settings temporarily for the current document only.

Designing a document means making formatting choices at several levels. You can format lines and paragraphs. You also can make formatting choices for a page, a group of pages, or an entire document.

In this chapter, you should have a basic understanding of the following formatting tasks:

- Changing the units of measurement
- Changing the left and right margins
- Enhancing text by boldfacing it, underlining it, and changing the font attributes or base font
- Setting tab stops, indenting text, and aligning text on a particular character
- Making text flush right, centering a line of text, and justifying text
- Using hyphenation
- Changing the line height and line spacing, changing the top and bottom margins, and centering pages top to bottom
- Designing headers and footers
- Numbering pages and controlling page breaks

▼

Key Terms in This Chapter

Initial font The font in which text is normally printed, also called default *base* font or *current* font. Other font sizes and appearances are usually variations of the initial font.

Header	Information that prints automatically at the top margin of the page.
Footer	Information that prints automatically at the bottom margin of the page.
Soft page break	A page break that occurs automatically. Soft page breaks appear on-screen as a dashed line.
Hard page break	A page break you insert to force a break at a certain spot. On-screen a hard page break appears as a line of equal signs.

Formatting Lines and Paragraphs

If you have been using a typewriter, you will enjoy how WordPerfect handles the mundane chores of setting margins and tabs; centering, justifying, underlining, and boldfacing text; indenting text; and hyphenating words. Most formatting choices in WordPerfect begin at the Format menu and are accomplished simply and logically. WordPerfect even lets you choose the unit of measurement for your settings.

Changing the Unit of Measure

The default unit of measurement in WordPerfect is inches. If you prefer, you can change this measurement to centimeters, points, or units (lines and columns).

To change the default unit of measurement, press Setup (Shift-F1). From the Setup menu, choose Units of Measure (8).

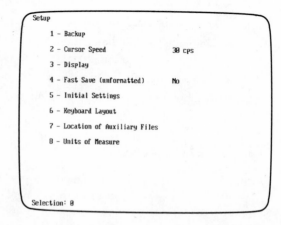

```
Setup

    1 - Backup

    2 - Cursor Speed             30 cps

    3 - Display

    4 - Fast Save (unformatted)  No

    5 - Initial Settings

    6 - Keyboard Layout

    7 - Location of Auxiliary Files

    8 - Units of Measure



Selection: 8
```

An
Overview of
WordPerfect

Editing and
Working
with Blocks

**Formatting
Lines,
Paragraphs,
and Pages**

Proofreading
and
Printing

Managing
Files

Creating
Macros

Merging,
Sorting, and
Selecting

Using
Columns

Referencing

Creating
Graphics

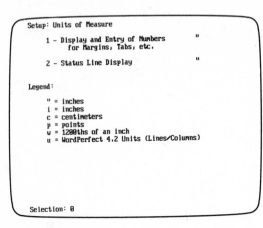

```
Setup: Units of Measure

    1 - Display and Entry of Numbers          "
        for Margins, Tabs, etc.

    2 - Status Line Display                   "


    Legend:

        " = inches
        i = inches
        c = centimeters
        p = points
        w = 1200ths of an inch
        u = WordPerfect 4.2 Units (Lines/Columns)




    Selection: 0
```

Choose Display and Entry of Numbers for Margins, Tabs, etc. (1) and select a new unit to use for menu selections. Choose Status Line Display (2) and select a new unit to use in the status line.

Changing Left and Right Margins

WordPerfect's default margins are 1 inch for the left and 1 inch for the right—appropriate margins for 8 1/2-by-11-inch paper. You can change the margins temporarily (for the current document only) or permanently (for all future documents).

Changing Margins Temporarily

```
Format

    1 - Line
            Hyphenation                    Line Spacing
            Justification                  Margins Left/Right
            Line Height                    Tab Set
            Line Numbering                 Widow/Orphan Protection

    2 - Page
            Center Page (top to bottom)    New Page Number
            Force Odd/Even Page            Page Numbering
            Headers and Footers            Paper Size/Type
            Margins Top/Bottom             Suppress

    3 - Document
            Display Pitch                  Redline Method
            Initial Codes/Font             Summary

    4 - Other
            Advance                        Overstrike
            Conditional End of Page        Printer Functions
            Decimal Characters             Underline Spaces/Tabs
            Language

Selection: 0
```

To change the settings for left and right margins temporarily for the current document only, first place the cursor at the left margin of the line where you want the new margin setting to begin. Then press Shift-F8 to display the Format menu.

Many of WordPerfect's formatting tasks begin at this Format menu.

From the Format menu, select Line (1) to display the Format: Line menu. At that menu, press 7 to select Margins (Right/Left). Type a value for the right margin and press Enter; and then type a value for the left margin and press Enter.

The margins in this example have been changed to 3/4-inch (0.75").

```
Format: Line

   1 - Hyphenation                        Auto
   2 - Hyphenation Zone - Left            10%
                         Right            4%
   3 - Justification                      Yes
   4 - Line Height                        Auto
   5 - Line Numbering                     No
   6 - Line Spacing                       1
   7 - Margins - Left                     0.75"
                 Right                    0.75"
   8 - Tab Set                            0", every 0.5"
   9 - Widow/Orphan Protection            No


Selection: 0
```

Changing Margins Permanently

If you only occasionally produce a document with margins different from WordPerfect's default settings, you can change the settings for individual documents. You may, however, always use different settings—3/4-inch margins, for example. In this case, you can change the margins permanently with Setup (Shift-F1).

To change your margins permanently for all future documents, press Setup (Shift-F1) to display the Setup menu. Choose Initial Settings (5), select Initial Codes (4), and press Format (Shift-F8). From this point, follow the same steps you followed to change the margins temporarily: select Line (1), select Margins (7), and type new left and right margins.

Enhancing Text

You can enhance your document by changing the size and appearance of your text. You accomplish some formatting tasks as you enter text simply by pressing the appropriate key, typing the text, and pressing the key again. For instance, from anywhere within your document, you can make text bold or underlined as you type. You apply other text enhancements by selecting them from the Font menu. For example, to make text italic, you choose the type style from the menu.

Enhancing Text from within the Document

A common text enhancement you make from within the document is to boldface or underline a portion of text. You can add a text enhancement either to text you are about to type or to existing text.

An
Overview of
WordPerfect

Editing and
Working
with Blocks

**Formatting
Lines,
Paragraphs,
and Pages**

Proofreading
and
Printing

Managing
Files

Creating
Macros

Merging,
Sorting, and
Selecting

Using
Columns

Referencing

Creating
Graphics

Suppose that you want to enhance text you are about to type. To boldface a portion of text, for example, first press Bold (F6). Then type the text. The text you type after pressing Bold (F6) appears brighter (or a different color) on-screen. The Pos indicator in the status line also changes in brightness or color. Press Bold (F6) again to turn off the Bold feature. To underline text you are about to type, first press Underline (F8). Then type the text. Press Underline (F8) again to turn off the Underline feature. Both the Bold (F6) and Underline (F8) keys work as on/off toggle switches. You press the key once to turn on the feature; you press the key again to turn off the feature.

To enhance text you've already typed, use the Block command, as described in the preceding chapter. Press Alt-F4 or F12 and highlight the block of text you want to boldface or underline. Then press either F6 for Bold or F8 for Underline.

Enhancing Text from the Font Menu

WordPerfect's Font feature lets you choose among the fonts (typefaces) available for use with your printer. The feature also controls size, color, and certain other variations of printed text, such as outline and shadow printing, subscripts, and superscripts.

When you installed your printer, you selected an *initial* font, also called the default *base* font or the *current* font. The *base* font is the font in which text is normally printed. Other font size and appearance options are usually variations of the base font. If 10-point Helvetica is the base font, for example, boldface text will be printed in 10-point Helvetica Bold; italic text will be printed in 10-point Helvetica Italic.

Changing Font Attributes

Font *attributes* refer to the variations in a font's size and appearance that are available with your printer for a given base font: italic, boldface, shadow printing, outline, small caps, and so on. How the variations appear depends on your printer.

You change the appearance of a base font by changing the font attributes. Press Font (Ctrl-F8) to display the Font menu:

1 Size; **2 A**ppearance; **3 T**emporary Font; **4 B**ase Font; **5 P**rint Color; **6 N**ormal: **0**

Press 1 to choose Size or press 2 to choose Appearance.

If you choose Size (1), WordPerfect displays the following attribute menu:

1 Suprscpt; **2** Subscpt; **3** Fine; **4** Small; **5** Large; **6** Vry Large; **7** Ext Large: **0**

If you choose Appearance (2), WordPerfect displays a different attribute menu:

1 Bold **2** Undrln **3** Dbl Und **4** Italc **5** Outln **6** Shadw **7** Sm Cap **8** Redln **9** Stkout: **0**

Press the number associated with the attribute of your choice.

When you select options such as Fine, Large, Vry Large, and Ext Large from the Size menu, WordPerfect automatically chooses the correct line spacing (so that a large font won't overprint the preceding line, and fine print doesn't print with too much line spacing).

Changing the Base Font

In addition to changing font attributes, you can change the base font the printer uses. You can change the base font permanently or temporarily. You can change the base font permanently when you install WordPerfect or from the Print menu.

To change the base font temporarily for the current document only, you use the Font menu. First move the cursor to the point in your document where you want to change the base font. Next, press Font (Ctrl-F8) to display the Font menu. From the Font menu, select Base Font (4).

WordPerfect displays a list of the fonts available for use with your printer. The fonts listed are the printer's built-in fonts, plus any fonts you've selected with the Cartridges and Fonts feature. Use the cursor keys to highlight the font you want. Then choose Select (1) or press Enter to return to your document. The screen display adjusts to reflect the number of characters that can be printed in a line with the new base font in the current margin settings.

Setting Tab Stops

WordPerfect comes with tab stops predefined at one-half-inch intervals. Four basic kinds of tabs are available: left, center, right, and decimal. In addition, each type of tab can have a *dot leader* (a series of dots before the tab). You can change tab

An
Overview of
WordPerfect

Editing and
Working
with Blocks

**Formatting
Lines,
Paragraphs,
and Pages**

Proofreading
and
Printing

Managing
Files

Creating
Macros

Merging,
Sorting, and
Selecting

Using
Columns

Referencing

Creating
Graphics

settings for the current document only or for all future documents. When you change the settings for your current document only, the settings affect only the text from the point at which you make the change forward. To change the setting for all future documents, you need to use the Initial Codes option through the Setup (Shift-F1) menu.

To change tab stops for the current document only, press Format (Shift-F8), select Line (1), and choose Tab Set (8) to display the tab ruler.

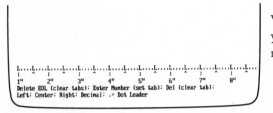

When the tab ruler is displayed, you can delete or add single or multiple tab stops.

Indenting Text

Although WordPerfect's Tab and Indent features are similar, they each have specific uses.

The Tab Key

Use the Tab key to indent only the first line of the paragraph from the left margin. Each time you press Tab in WordPerfect, the cursor moves across the screen to the next tab stop.

Indent

Use Indent (F4) to indent the entire paragraph from the left margin. Move the cursor to the left margin. Press F4, the Indent key. The cursor moves to the next tab setting. Type your text and press Enter to end indenting.

Left-Right Indent

Use Left-Right Indent (Shift-F4) to indent the entire paragraph from both the left and right margins. Press Shift-F4, the Left-Right Indent key. Type your text. Press Enter to end indenting and return to the original margin settings.

The first line of text indented with
the Tab key

An entire paragraph indented from
the left margin with Indent (F4)

An entire paragraph indented from
both the left and right margins with
Left-Right Indent (Shift-F4)

Using Tab Align

Use Tab Align (Ctrl-F6) to align text at the right on a specific character. For example,
you might want to use this feature to align numbers within columns, or names and
addresses.

Numbers aligned on a decimal point

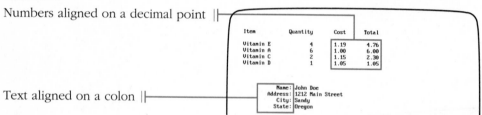

Text aligned on a colon

To align text on an alignment character, press Tab Align (Ctrl-F6). Type your text, and
then type the alignment character (the default is a period). Type any additional text, if
necessary. Then press Ctrl-F6 to tab to the next column or press Enter to end the line.

The alignment character can be changed either permanently (through the Setup
menu) or temporarily (through the Format: Other menu) to any character you want.
The default, a period, works well with numbers. To align names and addresses, use a
colon (:). To align numbers in an equation, an equal sign (=) is best. To align
monetary amounts, use a dollar sign ($).

Using Flush Right

Use Flush Right (Alt-F6) to align text with the right margin. This command aligns the
right edge of all headings, columns, and lines of text even (flush) with the right
margin. You can make text align flush right either before or after you type the text.

To create flush right text as you type, select Flush Right (Alt-F6) to move the cursor to
the right margin. Type your text. As you type, the cursor stays at the right margin,
and the text moves to the left. Press Enter to end Flush Right.

To align existing text with the right margin, place the cursor at the left margin. Select Flush Right (Alt-F6) to move the cursor and text to the right margin. If some of the text disappears past the right edge of the screen, press the down-arrow key to adjust the screen display.

Centering a Line

WordPerfect lets you center text instantly, without laboriously counting characters. You can center a line of text between the right and left margins as you type it or after you type it.

To center text you are about to type, first move the cursor to the left margin of the line. Then select Center (Shift-F6), type your text, and press Enter. To center an existing line of text, press Alt-F3 or F11 to turn on Reveal Codes, and then check to be sure that the line of text you want to center ends with a Hard Return code ([HRt]). Press Alt-F3 or F11 to turn off Reveal Codes. Then place the cursor at the left margin of the line of text you want to center. Select Center (Shift-F6), and then press the down-arrow key.

Using Right-Justification

WordPerfect's right-justification feature inserts space between words and letters so that the text aligns flush with the right margin. Text that is not justified has a ragged right margin. You cannot see right-justification on the regular editing screen. When you print your document, the text prints even with the right margin. The default setting for right-justification is on.

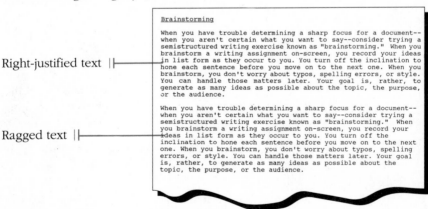

Right-justified text

Ragged text

An
Overview of
WordPerfect

Editing and
Working
with Blocks

**Formatting
Lines,
Paragraphs,
and Pages**

Proofreading
and
Printing

Managing
Files

Creating
Macros

Merging,
Sorting, and
Selecting

Using
Columns

Referencing

Creating
Graphics

To turn off justification temporarily for the current document only, first move the cursor to the beginning of the document, and then press Format (Shift-F8) to display the Format menu. Select Line (1), choose Justification (3), and then press N to turn off justification.

Using Hyphenation

When a line of text becomes too long to fit within the margins, the last word wraps to the next line. With short words, wrapping doesn't present much of a problem. With long words, two problems can occur: (1) If justification is off, large gaps can appear at the right margin, producing a document with very ragged text; (2) If justification is on, large spaces between words become visually distracting. Hyphenating the word at the end of the line solves these formatting problems. When you use WordPerfect's hyphenation feature, the program fits as much of the word as possible on the line, hyphenates the word, and wraps the rest of the word to the next line.

To control hyphenation, use one of three possible settings: off, manual, or automatic. When you use Manual hyphenation, WordPerfect prompts you to position the hyphen in a word that needs to be broken. If you set hyphenation to Auto, WordPerfect uses an internal set of rules to hyphenate common words. Because many words are not covered by these rules, WordPerfect prompts you for the proper hyphenation of these words just as if you had selected Manual hyphenation.

To turn on hyphenation, press Format (Shift-F8), choose Line (1), and select Hyphenation (1) to display the Hyphenation menu. Next, select the type of hyphenation you want: Manual (2) or Auto (3). To turn off hyphenation, repeat the procedure, but select Off (1) from the Hyphenation menu.

Changing Line Height and Line Spacing

To format your text, you can change both the line height and the line spacing. *Line height* is the vertical distance between the base of a line of text and the base of the line of text above or below. *Line spacing* controls the blank lines between lines of text; for example, double-spacing leaves one blank line between the lines of text.

WordPerfect automatically controls line height. Sometimes, however, you may want to adjust the line height manually, for example, to fit an extra line or two on a page. To change line height temporarily, first move the cursor to the location in your document where you want to change the line height. Next, choose Format (Shift-F8), select Line (1), and select Line Height (4). Then select Fixed (2), type the line

An
Overview of
WordPerfect

Editing and
Working
with Blocks

**Formatting
Lines,
Paragraphs,
and Pages**

Proofreading
and
Printing

Managing
Files

Creating
Macros

Merging,
Sorting, and
Selecting

Using
Columns

Referencing

Creating
Graphics

measurement you want (with up to two decimal places), and press Enter. To switch back to WordPerfect's automatic line height settings, repeat this procedure, but select Auto (1) instead of Fixed (2).

WordPerfect's line spacing default is single-spacing. To double-space or triple-space a document, you can change the line spacing default rather than enter hard returns as you type. You won't see changes in line spacing on-screen except when you select an increment such as single (1) or double (2) line spacing.

To change line spacing temporarily, first move the cursor to the location in your document where you want to change the line spacing. Next, select Format (Shift-F8), choose Line (2), and select Line Spacing (6). Type the amount of line spacing you want and press Enter. For instance, to double-space, type **2**.

Formatting Pages

Formatting a page or a group of pages involves making decisions about how the pages in your document should look. What are the top and bottom margin settings? Is text centered, top to bottom, on the page? Are there headers and footers? Are there automatic page numbers, and if so, where on the page should they appear? Must certain pages end at a particular point in the text? WordPerfect conveniently includes most formatting choices in the Format menu.

WordPerfect is preset for 8 1/2-by-11-inch paper. In this chapter, the discussions about formatting options that deal with an entire page or pages assume that you are using 8 1/2-by-11-inch paper. If you want to use a different size paper, change the default settings from the Print menu, as explained in Chapter 20.

Changing Top and Bottom Margins

WordPerfect's built-in settings leave 1-inch margins at the top and bottom of the page. The top margin is the distance between the top edge of the paper and the first line of text. The bottom margin is calculated from the bottom edge of the paper to the last line of text. Page numbers, headers, footers, and footnotes must fit within the allotted text area.

To change the top and bottom margins, first move the cursor to the position in your document where you want to set margins—usually at the beginning of the document. Then press Format (Shift-F8) to display the Format menu. Next, select Page (2) to display the Format: Page menu.

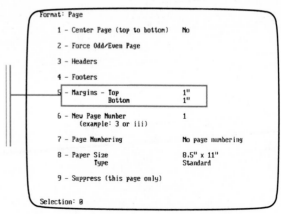

From the Format: Page menu, select Margins (Top/Bottom) (5). Type a new top margin and press Enter; then type a new bottom margin and press Enter.

```
Format: Page

    1 - Center Page (top to bottom)    No

    2 - Force Odd/Even Page

    3 - Headers

    4 - Footers

    5 - Margins - Top                  1"
                 Bottom                1"

    6 - New Page Number                1
          (example: 3 or iii)

    7 - Page Numbering                 No page numbering

    8 - Paper Size                     8.5" x 11"
           Type                        Standard

    9 - Suppress (this page only)

Selection: 0
```

Centering Pages Top to Bottom

When you center a page top to bottom, the setting applies to just one page—the page where you make the setting. You may, for example, want to center the title page of a sales report. The end of a centered page can be defined by either a soft page break or a hard page break. Ending the centered page with a hard page break ensures that the page never accidentally merges with the next page.

Before you center a page, be sure that the cursor rests at the beginning of the page, before any other formatting codes and text. You can press Reveal Codes (Alt-F3, or F11) to verify the cursor position. Then press Format (Shift-F8), select Page (2), and choose Center Page (1). Although the page doesn't appear centered on-screen, it will be centered when you print your document.

Designing Headers and Footers

A *header* is information (text, numbers, or graphics) that prints automatically at the top margin of each page. A *footer* is information that prints automatically at the bottom margin of each page. Typical header and footer information may include chapter titles and page numbers, or revision numbers and dates.

You cannot see headers or footers on-screen. You can use either View Document (Shift-F7, 6) or Reveal Codes (Alt-F3, or F11) to view header and footer text.

Creating a Header or Footer

To create a header or footer, press Format (Shift-F8), select Page (2), and choose either Headers (3) or Footers (4). You can create two headers (A and B) and two

An
Overview of
WordPerfect

Editing and
Working
with Blocks

**Formatting
Lines,
Paragraphs,
and Pages**

Proofreading
and
Printing

Managing
Files

Creating
Macros

Merging,
Sorting, and
Selecting

Using
Columns

Referencing

Creating
Graphics

footers (A and B). From the menu that appears, select the header or footer you
want to create.

From the next menu that appears, select one of the following specifications: select
Every Page (2) if you want the header (or footer) to appear on every page;
select Odd Pages (3) if you want the header (or footer) to appear on odd pages
only; or select Even Pages (4) if you want the header (or footer) to appear on even
pages only. Next, type the header (or footer) text, using any of WordPerfect's
formatting features.

Including Page Numbers in a Header or Footer

In addition to including and formatting text, you can add automatic page
numbering by including ^B (Ctrl-B) in the header or footer. For example, you can
specify the footer to read *Page 1*, with pages numbered consecutively. To include
automatic page numbering in headers and footers, first type any text that will
precede the page number, such as *Page*. Then press Ctrl-B.

Numbering Pages Automatically

Numbering pages automatically, not as part of a header or footer, is easy as telling
WordPerfect how and where you want the numbers to appear on the page.
Numbering begins with whatever number you select. Place the cursor at the beg-
inning of your document if you want page numbering to begin on the first page.

To select a page number position, press Shift-F8 to display the Format menu. Then
select Page (2) to display the Format: Page menu.

To select a page number position,
select Page Numbering (7) and
type the number that corresponds
to the position where you want
page numbers to appear.

To turn off page numbering,
select Page Numbering (7) at the
Format: Page menu. Then select
No Page Numbers (9).

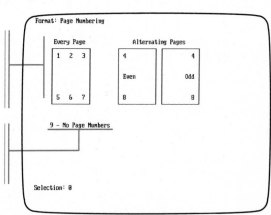

To change the starting page number, select New Page Number (6) at the Format: Page menu. Then type the new page number and press Enter.

To suppress page numbering, press 9 for Suppress (this page only) at the Format: Page menu. Then choose Suppress Page Numbering (4), and press Y.

Controlling Page Breaks

WordPerfect offers a number of options to control where one page ends and the next begins. The options include WordPerfect's automatic page breaks, hard page breaks, the Block Protect command, the Conditional End of Page function, and the Widow/Orphan Protection feature. This text describes only the first two options.

WordPerfect's automatic page breaks are based on an 8 1/2-by-11-inch page with 1-inch top and bottom margins.

WordPerfect inserts a dashed line in your document on-screen wherever an automatic page break occurs.

```
  This conference marks the first of its kind in the Midwest.
If you're new to biodynamic gardening, you'll have a rare
opportunity to learn from the experts. If you're an experienced
biodynamic gardener, you'll be able to mingle and swap secrets with
fellow enthusiasts.
----------------------------------------------------------------
  New Harmony, once the site of two utopian and agrarian
communities in the early nineteenth century, is an ideal setting
for our conference. You'll find a map in the registration packet
to help you find your way here. Driving time from Chicago is
roughly 5 1/2 hours.




                                           Doc 1 Pg 2 Ln 3.83" Pos 1"
```

This *soft page break* produces a hidden [SPg] code. When you add or delete text from a page, soft page breaks are recalculated automatically.

To force a page break at a certain spot—for example, at the beginning of a new section in a report—enter a *hard page break*. The page always ends at that point. On-screen a hard page break appears as a line of equal signs and produces a [HPg] code.

To insert a hard page break, first move the cursor to the point where you want the page break to occur. Then press Ctrl-Enter to insert a [HPg] code. To delete a hard page break, press Reveal Codes (Alt-F3, or F11). Then delete the [HPg] code. Finally, press Reveal Codes (Alt-F3, or F11) again.

Summary

This chapter showed you how to select from among WordPerfect's numerous formatting options to determine the format for the lines, paragraphs, and pages of your document. You learned that you can change the unit of measurement used in the formatting options. And you learned to change the settings for the left and right margins and to enhance your text by boldfacing it, underlining it, and changing the font attributes or base font. You also learned how to indent text, align text, and use hyphenation.

In addition to these formatting options, which affect primarily lines and paragraphs, you learned about formatting options for a page or group of pages. The text showed you how to change the top and bottom margins, center pages top to bottom, design headers and footers, number pages automatically, and control page breaks. You also read about WordPerfect's Styles feature for establishing formats you can use repeatedly to create particular kinds of documents.

The next chapter, "Proofreading and Printing," introduces some of WordPerfect's utilities for checking your work and for previewing and printing your documents.

Review Questions

1. What units of measurement are available for setting formatting options, and through which WordPerfect menu do you choose an alternate unite of measurement?

2. Through which WordPerfect menu are most formatting decisions made?

3. What are WordPerfect's default settings for the left and right margins? For the top and bottom margins?

4. In what ways can you enhance the appearance of text from within the document?

5. Describe the three kinds of indents you can create with WordPerfect and tell what commands you use to create them.

6. What are headers and footers, and what kind of information might they include?

7. How does WordPerfect indicate an automatic page break on-screen?

20 *Proofreading and Printing*

This chapter discusses two important topics for preparing any document: proofreading and printing. You learn first how to give your document some final checks, and then how to use WordPerfect's various printing options.

WordPerfect makes two powerful tools available to you every time you begin your editing tasks—Search and Replace. If you've ever experienced the frustration of searching, sentence-by-sentence, for a mistake you know you've made, you will welcome these time-savers. In addition to these capabilities, you can use the Speller and Thesaurus to check and fine-tune your work.

You can print all or part of the document that currently appears on-screen directly from the screen, or you can print all or part of a document you have previously stored to disk. You can specify a paper size other than the default 8 1/2 by 11 inches. And before you print, you can use WordPerfect's View Document feature to preview how the printed document will look and to avoid wasting time and paper.

In this chapter, you learn to perform the following tasks:

- Use the Search feature to search for a string—a single character, word, phrase, sentence, code, or combination of these
- Use the Replace feature to replace a string with another string
- Check the spelling of a word, a page, or an entire document
- Find synonyms and antonyms with the Thesaurus feature
- Print from the screen
- Print from disk
- Select an alternate paper size
- Preview a document before printing

Key Terms in This Chapter

String   A set of characters, including text, codes, and spaces, that WordPerfect uses in Search and Replace operations.

Wild-card   A character that can represent any other character(s).

Synonym   A word with the same or similar meaning as another word.

Antonym   A word with the opposite or nearly opposite meaning as another word.

Headword   The word you look up using the Thesaurus. This word has a body of similar words attached to it.

Proofreading

This section shows you how to use WordPerfect's features for checking your document. You will learn to use the Search feature to search for particular text or a code, and to use the Replace feature to replace that text or code with something else that you specify. Then you will learn how to use WordPerfect's spelling and thesaurus features.

Using Search

The Search feature enables you to search for a single character, word, phrase, sentence, or code in either a forward or reverse direction from the location of your cursor. The group of characters, words, or codes you want to locate is called a *string*.

Suppose that you want to find where a particular topic, word, or phrase appears in a long document. Searching the document manually is time-consuming. But with WordPerfect's Search feature, you can find character strings, even codes, easily.

Launching a Search

Press Forward Search (F2) to search from the cursor position forward to the end of the document. Or press Backward Search (Shift-F2) to search from the cursor to the beginning of the document. If you select Forward Search, the →Srch: prompt

An
Overview of
WordPerfect

Editing and
Working
with Blocks

Formatting
Lines,
Paragraphs,
and Pages

**Proofreading
and
Printing**

Managing
Files

Creating
Macros

Merging,
Sorting, and
Selecting

Using
Columns

Referencing

Creating
Graphics

appears at the lower left corner of the screen. If you select Backward Search, the
←Srch: prompt appears.

At either prompt, type the text string or codes you want to find. You can type as
many as 60 characters in your text string. Then press Forward Search (F2) or Esc to
begin the search. At this point, pressing Forward Search (F2) works for both
Forward and Backward Search. When WordPerfect finds the first occurrence of the
search target, the search stops.

If you want to continue the search, press Forward Search (F2). You don't need to
retype your text string or code because WordPerfect remembers your last search
request. Press Forward Search (F2) or Esc again to find the next occurrence of the
text string or code. If WordPerfect can't find the search text, a * Not Found *
message is displayed. To return the cursor to its location before the search, press
GoTo (Ctrl-Home) twice.

Guidelines for Defining a Search String

To use the Search feature effectively, you need to know how WordPerfect
interprets a string. Here are some of the rules WordPerfect follows:

- If you type a string in lowercase, WordPerfect looks for *either* upper- or
  lowercase characters. For example, if you ask the program to find *search*,
  WordPerfect stops at *search*, *Search*, and *SEARCH*. But if you ask the
  program to find *Search*, it stops at *Search* and *SEARCH*.
- Be careful how you enter a search string. If you enter the string **the**, for
  example, WordPerfect matches your string to every occurrence of the word
  the as well as to words that contain the string, such as *anes**the**sia*. To
  locate only the word *the*, enter a space before and after the word.
- If you are searching for text that includes an element that changes from
  one occurrence to the next—for example, (1), (2), (3)—or if you are
  uncertain about the correct spelling of a word, use the matching character
  ^X (press Ctrl-V and then Ctrl-X). This *wild-card* character matches any
  single character within a character string. Enter (**^X**) at the →Srch:
  prompt, and the cursor stops at (1), (2), (3), (4), and so on. When you are
  uncertain about the spelling, enter **c^Xt**, for example, at the →Srch:
  prompt; the cursor stops at *cat, CAT, Cat, cot, cattle, cutting,* and so on.
- If you need to find a hidden code, such as a margin setting, use the normal
  search procedure, but when the Srch: prompt appears, press the function
  key that creates the hidden code. When the search finds the hidden code,
  press Reveal Codes (Alt-F3, or F11) to view the code and edit it.

Using Replace

WordPerfect's Replace feature automatically finds every occurrence of a string or code and replaces it with another string or code. You also can use Replace to remove a string or code completely. For instance, if you complete a long sales report and then need to remove all boldface type, you can use Replace to find all occurrences of the code and replace them with nothing. Or you might use Replace to enter a string of text that occurs frequently in a document. For example, enter a backslash (\) wherever you want *methyl ethyl chloride* to appear. When you finish typing, replace the backslash with the chemical term.

To replace a string, first press Replace (Alt-F2). WordPerfect displays the following w/Confirm? (Y/N) No. Press Y if you want to approve each replacement separately. Or press N or Enter if you want all occurrences replaced without confirming them.

At the →Srch: prompt, type your search string. Then press Forward Search (F2) or Esc. At the Replace with: prompt, type the replacement string and press Enter. If you want the search string deleted and not replaced with anything, don't enter anything in response to the second prompt. Finally, press Forward Search (F2) or Esc to start the search.

If you press N at the w/Confirm? (Y/N) No prompt, WordPerfect replaces all occurrences automatically. If you press Y at the prompt, the cursor stops at each occurrence of the search string and WordPerfect prompts: Confirm? (Y/N) No. You can press Y to replace the string or N if you don't want to replace the string.

If you want to cancel the Replace operation, press Cancel (F1). Otherwise, WordPerfect continues searching the document. When all the occurrences have been found, the cursor stops. To return the cursor to its location before the Replace operation, press GoTo (Ctrl-Home) twice.

Using the Speller

WordPerfect's Speller contains a dictionary with more than 115,000 words. You can use the Speller to search for spelling mistakes and common typing errors such as transposed, missing, extra, or wrong letters—even typing errors such as double words (*the the*). You also can use the Speller when you know what a word sounds like but you're unsure of its spelling. WordPerfect's Speller will check a single word, a page, a block of text, or an entire document. The Speller compares each word in your document with the words in its dictionary. Words found in the dictionary are considered correct.

You can check a word, page, or entire document. To check a word or page, first position the cursor anywhere in the word or page. When you check an entire document, the position of the cursor doesn't matter. Next, press Spell (Ctrl-F2) to display the Spell menu:

Check: 1 Word; **2 P**age; **3 D**ocument; **4 N**ew Sup. Dictionary; **5 L**ook Up; **6 C**ount: **0**

Press the number or letter that identifies your menu selection. Choose from these options:

- **Word (1):** WordPerfect checks its dictionaries for the word.
- **Page (2):** WordPerfect looks up every word on the page.
- **Document (3):** WordPerfect looks up every word in your document.
- **New Sup. Dictionary (4):** Type the name of the supplemental dictionary, and press Enter.
- **Look Up (5):** In response to the Word or Word Pattern prompt, type your "rough guess" of the word's spelling and press Enter. WordPerfect offers a list of words that fit the pattern.
- **Count (6):** WordPerfect counts the number of words.

```
┌──────────────────────────────────────────────────────────────────┐
│                      Writing Guideline                             │
│ ================================================================== │
│                                                                    │
│ Brainstorming                                                      │
│                                                                    │
│ When ███ have troubel determining a sharp focus for a document--   │
│ when you are uncertain what you want to say--consider trying a     │
│ semistructured writing exercise known as "brainstorming."          │
│                                                                    │
│ When you brainstorm a writing assignment on-screen, you record your│
│ ideas in list form as they occur to you. When you brainstorm, you  │
│ ================================================================== │
│                                                                    │
│   A. yo              B. you             C. a                        │
│   D. aa              E. aaa             F. au                       │
│   G. away            H. awe             I. aweigh                   │
│   J. aye             K. e               L. ewe                      │
│   M. eye             N. i               O. ia                       │
│   P. ie              Q. ii              R. iii                      │
│   S. iou             T. iowa            U. iwo                      │
│   V. o               W. oui             X. ov                       │
│ Press Enter for more words                                         │
│                                                                    │
│ Not Found: 1 Skip Once; 2 Skip; 3 Add Word; 4 Edit; 5 Look Up; 0   │
└──────────────────────────────────────────────────────────────────┘
```

When the Speller comes across a word that is not in any of the dictionaries, the Speller stops, highlights the word, provides a list of alternative spellings, and displays the Not Found menu.

You have a number of options for correcting the highlighted word. If you do not see the correct spelling and WordPerfect prompts you to Press Enter for More Words, do so. When the correct spelling appears, type the letter next to the alternative you want to select. After you correct the word, the Speller continues checking the rest of your document.

Many correctly spelled words do not appear in WordPerfect's dictionary. If the correct spelling is not displayed, you can choose from the options on the Not Found menu at the bottom of the screen:

Not Found: 1 Skip Once; **2** Skip; **3** Add Word; **4** Edit; **5** Look Up: **0**

Here is a description of the each of the options:

- **Skip Once (1):** Skip the word once, but stop at every occurrence of the word thereafter.
- **Skip (2):** Skip the word throughout the document.
- **Add Word (3):** Add the word to the dictionary.
- **Edit (4):** The cursor moves to the word. Make the corrections using the → and ← keys. You can move only in the line containing the word to be corrected. Press F7. The Speller rechecks the word you've corrected. If the corrected version is not in the dictionary, the Speller stops.
- **Look Up (5):** Look up a word you type.

In addition to finding misspellings, the program also stops on double words and displays a slightly different Not Found menu.

Using the Thesaurus

The Thesaurus is similar to the Speller, except that the Thesaurus lists alternative word choices instead of alternative spellings. The Thesaurus displays *synonyms*—words with the same or similar meanings—and *antonyms*—words with the opposite or nearly opposite meanings of the selected word.

Displaying Synonyms and Antonyms

To use the Thesaurus, place the cursor anywhere in the word you want to look up and press Thesaurus (Alt-F1). The word is highlighted, and the screen is split, with the document text in the top half and the Thesaurus menu and word list in columns in the bottom half.

An
Overview of
WordPerfect

Editing and
Working
with Blocks

Formatting
Lines,
Paragraphs,
and Pages

**Proofreading
and
Printing**

Managing
Files

Creating
Macros

Merging,
Sorting, and
Selecting

Using
Columns

Referencing

Creating
Graphics

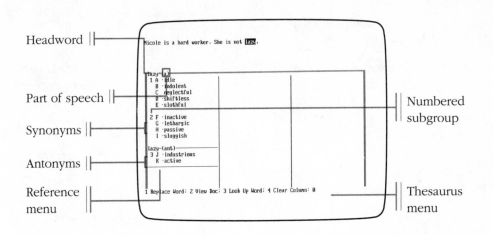

The word you look up is called the *headword* because it has a body of similar words attached to it. The headword appears at the top of the column. Synonyms and antonyms for your headword are also noted. Words are divided into numbered groups and parts of speech. The column of letters to the left of the words is called the Reference menu. Remember that words marked with a bullet also are headwords; you can look up any of these words.

With the Thesaurus menu displayed at the bottom of the screen, you can select among the following options:

- **Replace Word (1):** Type the letter that corresponds to the replacement word. Use → or ← to move the letter choices to other columns.
- **View Doc (2):** Display more of your document.
- **Look Up Word (3):** Type the word you want to look up and press Enter.
- **Clear Column (4):** Clear the column.

If you don't see a word that is exactly right or you want to try other words, you can expand the word list. Display more alternatives for any headword—a word with a bullet next to it—by pressing the letter associated with the word.

Printing

This chapter gives you the basics you need for printing from either the screen or from a disk file, for changing to an alternate paper size, and for previewing a document before printing. Note that WordPerfect gives you a great deal of flexibility for controlling your print jobs.

Many more printing options that are not reviewed in this chapter also are available in WordPerfect. For example, you can install many printers at once and choose the one you want at print time. You can keep track of multiple print jobs and print them in the order you specify. And if you suddenly have a rush job, you can interrupt the printing and bump the job to first place in the printing queue. Other options allow you to select the binding width, number of copies, and graphics and text quality.

Printing from the Screen

Printing a document from the screen is quicker than printing a document from disk— especially if your document is short. From the screen, you can print the entire document, a single page, or a block of text.

To print the entire document from the screen, first display the document and place the cursor anywhere in it. Then press Print (Shift-F7) to display the Print menu. From this menu, choose Full Document (1).

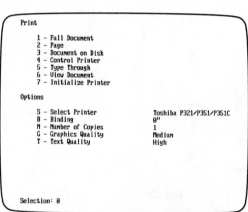

```
Print

    1 - Full Document
    2 - Page
    3 - Document on Disk
    4 - Control Printer
    5 - Type Through
    6 - View Document
    7 - Initialize Printer

Options

    S - Select Printer        Toshiba P321/P351/P351C
    B - Binding               8"
    N - Number of Copies      1
    G - Graphics Quality      Medium
    T - Text Quality          High




Selection: 0
```

To print a single page from the displayed document, place the cursor anywhere in the page you want to print. Then press Print (Shift-F7) and select Page (2).

Printing from Disk

With WordPerfect, you can print a document from disk without displaying it on-screen. You can print from either the Print menu or the List Files menu. With both methods, you can specify which pages to print.

Printing from the Print Menu

When you print from the Print menu, you must know the complete file name before starting the operation. You cannot use List Files to look up the file after you've pressed Print (Shift-F7).

To use the Print menu to print a document from disk, first press Print (Shift-F7). Then select Document on Disk (3), type the file name, and press Enter. To print the entire document, press Enter. To print only particular pages, type the pages you want to print and then press Enter. WordPerfect reads the file from disk, creates a print job, and adds the document to the print queue.

Printing from List Files

Printing from the List Files screen has two advantages: you don't need to remember the name of the file you want to print, and you can mark any number of files to print. The files are printed in the order they appear on the List Files screen.

To use the List Files screen to print a document from disk, first press List Files (F5). If the file resides in the current drive and directory, press Enter. If the file is in a different directory, type the drive, path, and directory name, and then press Enter.

Next, highlight the name of the file you want to print. Then select Print (4). In response to the Pages: (All) message, press Enter to print the entire document, or type the pages you want to print and press Enter.

Changing Paper and Form Sizes

WordPerfect is preset for 8 1/2-by-11-inch paper. If you use that size paper, you don't need to change the default settings. If you want to use a different size paper, you can change the settings. You can choose any of nine predefined paper sizes, or you can define your own size.

Specifying paper size is a two-part process: you must define the form size and type for the printer, and you must specify the paper size and type in the document. You define the form size and type for the printer through the Select Printer menu. You identify the paper size and type through the Format: Page menu. The paper and form always must match. If you use the Format: Page menu to specify in the document that the paper type is an envelope, for example, a corresponding envelope form must be listed in the Select Printer menu.

Defining a Form for the Printer

To define a form for your printer, first press Print (Shift-F7). Then choose Select
Printer (S) and use the cursor keys to highlight the name of the printer you want to
edit. (The current printer is already highlighted.) Next, choose Edit (3). From the
Select Printer: Edit screen, select Forms (4) to display a list of form definitions in the
Select Printer: Forms menu. From this menu, select Add (1) to add a form or Edit (2)
to edit a form.

WordPerfect displays the Select Printer: Form Type menu, from which you choose a
form type. After you choose a form type, WordPerfect displays the Select Printer:
Forms menu. From this menu, choose an option and enter the new information.

When you define or edit a form type, you can specify not only the paper size, but
also such other options as the orientation (whether text should be printed vertically
or sideways on the page) and whether the paper is continuous or hand-fed.

Specifying Paper Size and Type in a Document

After you define the form, you must specify the paper size and type in the document,
if you are using a size and type other than the default. To change the paper size and
type from the default paper, first press Format (Shift-F8), select Page (2), and choose
Paper Size/Type (8). From this menu, select the paper size you want—for example,
legal, label, or letterhead.

After you choose a paper size, WordPerfect displays the Format: Paper Type menu.
Select a paper type from the predefined types listed. If you select Other (0) at the
Paper Size menu, WordPerfect prompts for width and length measurements. Use this
option to define your own paper size and type so that you can print on nonstandard-
size paper.

Using View Document

Use the View Document feature to preview your document before printing it. You
save costly printer paper and time by first previewing your document, making
changes if needed, and then printing the document when you're certain that it's
perfect. Document pages appear on-screen as they will appear when printed on
paper, including graphics (if your system can display graphics), footnotes, page
numbers, line numbers, headers, footers, and justification.

To view a document, first display the document you want to preview in either the Doc 1 or Doc 2 window. Then position the cursor anywhere on the page you want to view. Next, press Print (Shift-F7) and select View Document (6). At this point, you have a number of options: Select 100% (1) to view the document at its actual size; select 200% (2) to view the document at twice its actual size; select Full Page (3) to view the entire page; or select Facing Pages (4) to view the current page and its facing page (odd-numbered pages are displayed on the right side of the screen, even-numbered pages on the left).

An Overview of Printing

One of WordPerfect's great flex
ways of printing documents. The
printing the document you are c
called printing from the screen
way, you have the option of pri
document, a specific page, or a

1 100% 2 200% 3 Full Page 4 Facing Pages: 2   Doc 1 Pg 13

A document viewed on-screen at twice its actual size.

You can press PgUp, PgDn, or GoTo (Ctrl-Home) to view other pages of the document. Note that you cannot edit this preview version of your document.

Summary

This chapter introduced you to WordPerfect's features for checking a document, as well as to the printing features. You learned how to use the Search feature to search for a string—a single character, word, phrase, sentence, code, or combination of these. You also learned how to use the Replace feature to replace a string with another string. You next explored the many options available through WordPerfect's Speller and Thesaurus features.

You studied some of WordPerfect's many printing features, examining first how to print from the screen and then how to print from disk. You reviewed the basic process for selecting an alternate paper size, and you learned how to preview a document before printing. In the next chapter, you will learn how to manage your files through the List Files screen. You also will learn how to create document summaries to keep track of your documents' contents.

Review Questions

1. For what kinds of elements can you search a document in WordPerfect?

2. When you are using the Speller, what options does the program offer when encountering a word that isn't in the WordPerfect dictionary?

3. Describe the type of information displayed when you look up a word with WordPerfect's Thesaurus.

4. Describe some of the basic printing options WordPerfect offers.

5. Which WordPerfect menus do you use to specify an alternate paper size and type for your document?

6. What are some advantages of previewing a document on-screen before you print?

21 *Managing Files*

In this chapter, you learn how WordPerfect can help you deal with DOS and manage your computer system. With WordPerfect's List Files feature, you can manipulate files and directories to a much greater degree than most word processing programs allow. You also learn to use another WordPerfect feature, Document Summary, to keep track of your files' contents.

In this chapter, you learn to perform the following tasks:

- Use all parts of the List Files screen: the heading, the file listing, and the menu options
- Create document summaries

Key Terms in This Chapter

Directory	A disk area in which information about files is stored. Displayed on-screen, a directory is a list of files.
File specification	The drive and path name you enter for a file listing.

Using the List Files Screen

With List Files, you can accomplish—from within WordPerfect—much of the file and directory management you ordinarily perform from DOS. To get to the List Files screen, first press List Files (F5). WordPerfect displays DIR in the lower left corner, followed by a file specification for all files in the current directory, such as

```
Dir C:\WP50\*.*
```

This message says that WordPerfect is ready to list all files in the current directory. If this is the directory you want, press Enter. If it is not the directory you want, edit the specification, and then press Enter to display the List Files screen. The three areas on this screen are the heading, the file listing, and the menu.

Heading

File listing

Menu

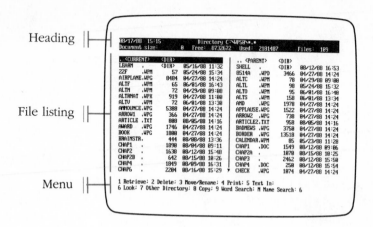

The Heading

The first line of the two-line heading displays the date, the time (given as 24-hour time), and the directory being listed. The second line shows the size of the document being edited, the amount of free space left on the disk, the amount of disk space taken up by files in the current file listing, and the number of files in the listing.

The File Listing

The two-column file listing displays file names and directories alphabetically across the screen. The listing shows the complete file name, file size, and date and time the file was created or last modified.

<DIR> indicates that the item is a directory. The entry labeled <CURRENT> refers to the currently listed directory. The entry labeled <PARENT> refers to the parent directory of the listed directory. A highlight bar appears on the top left name. You can use the cursor keys to move this bar to highlight any name in the listing.

Note: With the Location of Auxiliary Files option on the Setup menu, you can specify that certain types of files are stored automatically in separate directories. For example, you can designate separate directories for backup files and macros.

The List Files Menu

From the List Files menu, you can select from 10 command choices. Each choice acts on the highlighted file or directory.

An Overview of WordPerfect

Editing and Working with Blocks

Formatting Lines, Paragraphs, and Pages

Proofreading and Printing

Managing Files

Creating Macros

Merging, Sorting, and Selecting

Using Columns

Referencing

Creating Graphics

Name Search

Select Name Search (N) to move the highlight bar to a file name as you type the name. Type the first letter of the file name for which you want to search. If you want to find the file BUSINESS.LTR, for example, type **B**. Then type the second letter of the name. For example, type **U**. When the correct file is highlighted, press Enter, F1, or an arrow key to end Name Search.

Retrieve

Select Retrieve (1) to bring a file into WordPerfect for editing. This option works like Retrieve (Shift-F10) from the editing screen.

Delete

Select Delete (2) to delete either files or directories. If the highlight bar is on a file, that file is deleted. If the bar is on a directory, the directory is deleted *as long as the directory does not contain any files*. Press Y in response to the prompt asking you to confirm the deletion.

Move/Rename

Select Move/Rename (3) to move the file to a different directory or disk drive, or to rename the file. To move or rename a file, first highlight the name of the file, and then press Move/Rename (3). If you are moving the file, type the directory or drive where you want to move the file and press Enter. *Moving* a file means transferring it to a different directory or disk drive. If you are renaming the file, type the new name (the displayed name disappears) and press Enter.

Print

Choose Print (4) to print the highlighted file on the currently selected printer. Unlike many programs, WordPerfect can print while you continue to edit another document.

Text In

Choose Text In (5) to retrieve a *text* file (sometimes called an ASCII file), not a WordPerfect format file. This option is the same as retrieving a DOS text file into the editing screen with Text In/Out (Ctrl-F5) and the Dos Text (1) option.

Look

Choose Look (6) to display the highlighted file without retrieving it into the editing screen. Use Look to examine files quickly. You may, for example, want to look at several files if you've forgotten which file you need to edit. The file name and size are displayed at the top of the screen. You can move the cursor through the file with the usual WordPerfect cursor-movement commands, but you cannot edit the file.

You also can use Look to display other directories. Place the highlight bar on a directory entry (other than <CURRENT>) in the file listing, and then press Enter. WordPerfect displays a Dir message followed by the file specification. Press Enter again, and WordPerfect displays the file listing of this highlighted directory.

Other Directory

Select Other Directory (7) to change the current directory or create a new one. Use the cursor keys to move the highlight bar to any directory name other than <CURRENT>. Press 7 to select Other Directory. WordPerfect displays in the lower left corner of the screen the message New directory = followed by the name of the highlighted directory. Press Enter, and WordPerfect displays the file specification for all the files in the highlighted directory. Finally, press Enter to change to the new directory and display its listing.

Create a new directory by selecting Other Directory (7) and entering a unique name. For example, if you enter **book**, WordPerfect prompts Create c:\book? (Y/N) No. Answer Y to create a new subdirectory called BOOK.

Copy

You use the Copy (8) option to make a duplicate of a file. This option copies the file just as the DOS COPY command does. To copy a file, highlight the name of the file you want to copy and select Copy (8). WordPerfect displays the message Copy this file to:. You can copy the file to another disk or directory by typing the drive or directory, or you can make a copy of the file in the current directory by entering a new file name.

Word Search

Select Word Search (9) to search one or more files in the file listing for a word or phrase without retrieving the files into WordPerfect. For example, determine which documents are about a subject by searching for a word related to that subject.

An
Overview of
WordPerfect

Editing and
Working
with Blocks

Formatting
Lines,
Paragraphs,
and Pages

Proofreading
and
Printing

**Managing
Files**

Creating
Macros

Merging,
Sorting, and
Selecting

Using
Columns

Referencing

Creating
Graphics

Marking Files

On the List Files screen, you can mark particular files and then perform certain List Files operations on only those files, such as printing, copying, deleting, or moving. Move the highlight bar to each file you want to mark and press the asterisk key (*).

Using Document Summaries

With WordPerfect, you can place a document summary box at the beginning of your file before you save the document to disk. Use this feature to display the file name, the date the document was created, the author's name, the typist's name, and any other informative comments that may help you identify the document and its contents. You can view document summaries on-screen, but they are not printed.

Entering Document Summary Information

You can create and edit a document summary from anywhere in your document. To create a document summary, first display your document, and then press Format (Shift-F8), select Document (3), and choose Summary (5). A screen for creating the summary is displayed.

If you have previously saved the file, WordPerfect automatically enters your file name and the date the file was created. If you have not saved the file, a (Not named yet) message appears, and the file name is added when you save the document.

```
Document Summary

        System Filename        C:\WP50\CHAP1

        Date of Creation       August 17, 1988

    1 - Descriptive Filename   Opening Chapter for Writing Guidelines

    2 - Subject/Account        Writing Guidelines

    3 - Author

    4 - Typist

    5 - Comments
        ┌─────────────────────────────────────────────────────────────┐
        │ Think of a place you can either visit or remember quite clearly, a place │
        │ to which you have strong reactions. It could be a room, a forest, an │
        │ interesting building, King Tut's tomb anything that interests you.  Write │
        │ a personal description of it, attempting to re create for your reader the │
        │ experience of seeing or entering the place you've chosen to write about. │
        └─────────────────────────────────────────────────────────────┘

Selection: 0
```

Next, you need to select each of the options, in turn, and enter the requested information.

Enter a description of the document, the subject, the name of the author, the name of the typist, and any comments. Each entry (except for the comments) can be up to 40 characters long; comments can be as many as 780 characters long.

To look at a document summary, press List Files (F5) and display the directory that contains the file you want to view. Then move the highlight bar to that document and select Look (6).

Summary

This chapter showed you how to manipulate files and directories with WordPerfect's List Files feature. You learned what types of information are displayed on the List Files screen, and how to use the List Files menu options to perform operations such as retrieving a file, deleting a file, and moving or renaming a file. You also learned to use WordPerfect's Document Summary feature to keep track of your files' contents. In the next chapter, you will learn the basics of creating a macro, a series of prerecorded keystrokes that can save you time in performing repetitive tasks.

Review Questions

1. What information does the heading on the List Files screen provide?

2. How do you display a different directory with List Files?

3. What kind of information can you store in a document summary?

4. How do you display a document summary?

22 *Creating Macros*

If you perform any task repeatedly, you can do it more quickly with a macro. Macros can perform operations that include both text and WordPerfect commands. You can use a macro to automate a simple task such as deleting a line, or a slightly more complex task, such as entering the headings for a memo. After you create a macro, you press only one or two keystrokes to do almost instantly what would otherwise require many keystrokes.

In this chapter, you learn to perform the following tasks:

- Create a macro
- Run a macro
- Stop a macro
- Edit a macro

Key Terms in This Chapter

Macro A series of prerecorded keystrokes assigned to a single key or key combination. Macros greatly relieve the tedium of repetitive typing.

Interactive macro A macro that pauses and waits for input from the keyboard.

Macro editor A utility that allows you to modify a macro by using some of the same commands you use in the normal editing screen.

Creating a Macro

You can create macros that have two different kinds of names: Alt-letter names and descriptive names. Alt-letter names consist of the Alt key plus a letter from A to Z—for example, Alt-K. Descriptive names have one to eight characters—for example, MARGIN5.

The macros that are simplest to create and use are the ones with Alt-letter names. Therefore, choose Alt-letter names for the macros you will use most often. Be sure to use macro names that will remind you of what your macros do; for example, you might use the name Alt-C for a macro that centers text.

Macros are saved to disk in a file with the macro name you've specified and the extension .WPM—for example, ALTA.WPM or LTRHEAD.WPM. You don't have to provide the .WPM extension for macros with either type of name.

When you create a macro, you enter into your current document the keystrokes and commands you want the macro to "play back" when you run the macro. When you create a macro to change your tab settings, for example, you also change your tab settings at the cursor position in your current document. So that these macro keystrokes and commands do not interfere with any of your permanent files, you should save any document you are working on and clear your screen before you practice with macros. If you need some text for the macro to work on, you can type a few lines.

To create a macro, you first press Macro Define (Ctrl-F10). The screen displays the prompt `Define macro:`. You type the name of the macro. For an Alt-letter macro, you press the Alt key and a letter from A to Z. For a descriptive macro, you type one to eight characters (letters or numbers) and press Enter.

The screen displays the prompt `Description:`. You type a short description of what the macro does and press Enter. You can use any description, up to 39 characters, that will help remind you of the macro's commands.

`Macro Def` blinks at the bottom of the screen. This blinking message reminds you that the program is recording your keystrokes.

You next type the keystrokes you want to record for this macro. You type them in the exact order you want them played back when you run the macro. When you finish recording the keystrokes for the macro, press Macro Define (Ctrl-F10) again.

Suppose that you want to create a macro that creates standard memo headings. The macro will be interactive—that is, when you run the macro, it will pause and wait for entries from the keyboard. Follow these steps to create the macro:

1. Press Macro Define (Ctrl-F10).
2. Type the name of the macro. Either press Alt-M for memo to give the macro an Alt-letter name, or type **MEMO** and press Enter to give the macro a descriptive name.

3. Type a short description (up to 39 characters) of what the macro does, and then press Enter. For the example, type **Enter memo headings** and press Enter.
4. Press Center (Shift-F6).
5. Press Bold (F6).
6. Type **MEMORANDUM**.
7. Press Bold (F6) again to end boldface for the title.
8. Press Enter four times to put enough blank lines between the title and the first heading.
9. Type **TO:** and press Tab twice.
10. To enter a pause in the macro, press Ctrl-PgUp, 1, and Enter.
11. Press Enter twice to insert a blank line between the first and second headings.
12. Type **FROM:** and press Tab once.
13. Repeat Step 10 to insert a macro pause.
14. Press Enter twice to insert a blank line between the second and third headings.
15. Type **DATE:** and press Tab once.
16. Press Date (Shift-F5) and 2 to insert today's date.
17. Press Enter twice to insert a blank line between the third and fourth headings.
18. Type **SUBJECT:** and press Tab once.
19. Repeat Step 10 to insert the final macro pause.
20. Press Enter four times to insert several blank lines between the headings and the body of the memo.
21. Press Macro Define (Ctrl-F10) to end macro definition.

The memo headings macro being created.

An Overview of WordPerfect

Editing and Working with Blocks

Formatting Lines, Paragraphs, and Pages

Proofreading and Printing

Managing Files

Creating Macros

Merging, Sorting, and Selecting

Using Columns

Referencing

Creating Graphics

When you invoke this macro, at the first pause, type the recipient's name and press Enter. At the next pause, type your name and press Enter. At the final macro pause, type the subject of the memo and press Enter.

Running a Macro

When you run (play back) a permanent macro, the steps vary depending on whether you are running an Alt-letter macro or a descriptive macro.

To run an Alt-letter macro you have created, press the Alt-letter combination. If you have created an Alt-M macro to enter memo headings, for example, invoke the macro by holding down the Alt key while you next press the letter M.

To run a descriptive macro you have created, press Macro (Alt-F10), type the name of the macro (one to eight characters), and then press Enter. For example, you might type **memo** and press Enter to run the memo headings macro.

Stopping a Macro

You use the Cancel key (F1) in many situations to "back out" of a process you started. You can use this key also to back out of a definition you are creating for a macro or to stop a macro in progress.

Backing Out of a Macro Definition

Before you name a macro, you can back out of a macro definition. If you start to create a macro using Macro Define (Ctrl-F10) and have not yet named it, pressing Cancel (F1) cancels the macro definition and returns you to your document.

After you name a macro, you cannot cancel it, but you can end macro definition by pressing Macro Define (Ctrl-F10). Although the macro still is created with the name you assigned it, you then can delete, rename, replace, or edit the macro.

Stopping a Macro in Progress

You can stop a macro while it is running by pressing Cancel (F1). For example, if the macro is not doing what you expected, you can press Cancel (F1).

An
Overview of
WordPerfect

Editing and
Working
with Blocks

Formatting
Lines,
Paragraphs,
and Pages

Proofreading
and
Printing

Managing
Files

Creating
Macros

Merging,
Sorting, and
Selecting

Using
Columns

Referencing

Creating
Graphics

After you cancel a macro, press Reveal Codes (Alt-F3, or F11) to check your document for any unwanted codes. An incomplete macro can create codes in your document that you don't want.

Editing a Macro

Imperfect macros, fortunately, are replaced easily. You may want to replace a macro you created for any of several reasons:

- You get an error message when you run the macro.
- The macro finishes but does not do what you want.
- You change your mind about exactly what you want the macro to do.

You can change what a macro does in either of two ways. The first way is to replace the macro. To do this, first press Macro Define (Ctrl-F10) and enter the same name as the previous version of the macro. When the program asks whether you want to Replace (1) or Edit (2) the named macro, choose Replace (1). At this point, continue as if you are creating a new macro.

The second way to change a macro is to edit it with the macro editor. To edit a macro, press Macro Define (Ctrl-F10), enter the same name as the previous version, and choose Edit (2).

```
Macro: Edit

     File          MEMO.WPM
  1 - Description   Enter memo headings
  2 - Action

    {Center}{Bold}MEMORANDUM{Bold}{Enter}
    {Enter}
    {Enter}
    {Enter}
    TO:{Tab}{Tab}{PAUSE}{Enter}
    {Enter}
    FROM:{Tab}{PAUSE}{Enter}
    {Enter}
    DATE:{Tab}{Date/Outline}1{Enter}
    {Enter}
    SUBJECT:{Tab}{PAUSE}{Enter}
    {Enter}
    {Enter}

Selection: 0
```

The memo headings macro displayed in the macro editor.

Although the use of the macro editor is beyond the scope of this book, keep in mind that this feature is available as you become more experienced with WordPerfect.

Summary

In this chapter you learned the basics of creating a macro. You practiced the procedure by creating an interactive macro for entering memo headings. You learned to name macros, run them, and stop them while they are running. You also took a look at the example macro as it appears in the macro editor. In the next chapter, you will learn about WordPerfect's merging, sorting, and selecting features.

Review Questions

1. What are the two kinds of names you can assign to a macro, and what file name extension does WordPerfect automatically add to macro files?

2. What are the two ways to run a macro?

3. How do you stop a macro in progress?

23 *Merging, Sorting, and Selecting*

An
Overview of
WordPerfect

Editing and
Working
with Blocks

Formatting
Lines,
Paragraphs,
and Pages

Proofreading
and
Printing

Managing
Files

Creating
Macros

**Merging,
Sorting, and
Selecting**

Using
Columns

Referencing

Creating
Graphics

The Merge feature, frequently referred to as mail merge, is one of WordPerfect's most versatile tools for increasing office productivity. You use Merge anytime you need to insert variable data into a fixed format. For example, you can use Merge to create personalized form letters from an address list, produce phone lists, print labels, piece together complicated reports, or fill in forms.

Although WordPerfect's Sort feature cannot compete with specialized database management programs in all areas, it has enough power and versatility to handle many record-keeping tasks. Examples of two simple applications of the Sort command are sorting lines to create alphabetical phone lists or rosters and sorting mailing lists by ZIP code to conform with postal service rules for large mailings.

The Select option of WordPerfect's Sort menu lets you select particular data from a database. By specifying criteria, you can make your selection precise. The Select option is useful for extracting particular records from a large database.

In this chapter, you learn to perform the following tasks:

- Create primary and secondary merge files
- Merge two files to the screen or to the printer
- Sort by line, paragraph, or secondary merge file
- Select particular data

▼

Key Terms in This Chapter

Merge	To assemble a document by inserting variable data into a fixed format.
Primary file	A skeleton document into which pieces of data are merged.
Secondary merge file	A file that contains the data (or variable information) that is merged into the primary file. Information in the secondary merge file is organized like information on filing cards.
Fields	The units of information that make up a record. Each field should contain the same type of information: for example, a person's name; a street address; and a city, state, and ZIP code.

Record   A collection of fields with related information in a file: a line of data, a paragraph, or a name and address in a secondary merge file.

Keys   The characters or numbers in a specific file location that WordPerfect uses to sort and select.

Merging Documents

A Merge operation requires a primary file, often in combination with a secondary merge file. A *primary file* is a skeleton document into which pieces of data are merged. The *secondary merge file* contains data (or variable information that is organized like information on filing cards). The information on one filing card (or one secondary merge file entry) is known as a *record*. Each record is divided into *fields*.

The primary file contains two items: fixed text and merge codes. You plant merge codes where you want to insert variable items into fixed text. When a merge is completed, the codes are replaced with entries from the keyboard or from a secondary merge file. The document is completed with a minimum of effort.

The most typical and timesaving merge requires a secondary merge file that contains related variable data, such as an address list. All the information related to one person is a record. The separate items within each record, such as name, street, and ZIP code, are fields. WordPerfect inserts these items into the primary file by matching the codes in the primary and secondary merge files.

Secondary Merge File

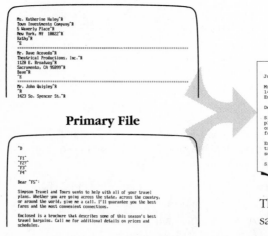

Primary File

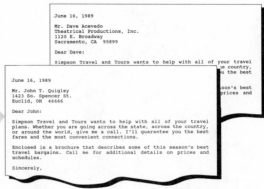

These letters resulted from merging the sample secondary merge file and primary file.

Fields, records, and other items are controlled by merge codes. You must place these codes in the right places and in the right order for a merge to be successful.

A text file merge combines two existing files—a primary and a secondary merge file. Before you can execute such a merge, you must create these files. Create the secondary merge file first so that you know the field layout before you build the primary file.

Creating a Secondary Merge File

A secondary merge file consists of records, which have a number of fields. The structure must be uniform; otherwise, the merge won't work properly. Every data record must have the same number of fields, and the fields must be in the same order in all records.

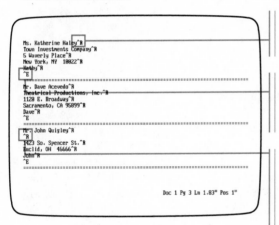

Use ^R to indicate the end of a field and to enter a hard return code. To enter ^R, press Merge R (F9).

Use ^E to indicate the end of a record and to enter a hard page code. To enter ^E, press Merge Codes (Shift-F9) and then press E.

When a field is blank, you must acknowledge the blank field's presence by inserting a ^R code. For instance, Mr. Quigley's record contains no company name.

When you finish entering data into your secondary merge file, save the file with a name that indicates the file's purpose. For example, you might call your address file ADDRESS.SMF.

Creating a Primary File

A primary file contains fixed text and certain merge codes. The codes tell WordPerfect to insert certain items from the secondary merge file where the codes are implanted.

```
^D
 ^F1^
 ^F2?^ ─────
 ^F3^
 ^F4^

 Dear ^F5^:

 Simpson Travel and Tours wants to help with all of your travel
 plans. Whether you are going across the state, across the country
 or around the world, give me a call. I'll guarantee you the best
```

Use ^F*n*^ codes to tell WordPerfect where to insert certain items from the secondary merge file. For example, when you specify ^F3^, you instruct WordPerfect to enter at that particular location the information found in field number 3. To enter ^F*n*^, press Merge Codes (Shift-F9), press F, enter a field number, and press Enter.

Use ^F*n*?^ codes to prevent blank lines from appearing where empty fields exist in the secondary merge file. For example, you might change the code for the ^F2^ field to ^F2?^ in your primary file.

When you finish creating the primary file, save the file with a name that indicates the file's purpose. For example, you might call the file TRAVEL.PMF.

Note: When you merge text files, you need to use both a secondary merge file and a primary file. If you merge from the keyboard, however, you need only a primary file that contains ^C codes where appropriate. When you merge from the keyboard, WordPerfect pauses whenever it encounters a ^C code and waits for input from the keyboard. Merging from the keyboard is handy, for example, for creating a memo in which the time, date, and subject of a monthly meeting change regularly.

Running a Merge

After you create the primary and secondary merge files, you are ready to start the merge. If you have a small secondary merge file, you can merge the files to the screen. If you have a large secondary merge file, merge directly to the printer.

If you merge files to the screen, you can view the results before you print. Merging to the screen is a good way to check for errors in the merge. To merge the text files to the screen, first press Merge/Sort (Ctrl-F9) to display the Merge/Sort menu:

```
1 Merge; 2 Sort; 3 Sort Order: 0
```

Merging
Documents

**Sorting
Data**

Selecting
Data

Summary

An
Overview of
WordPerfect

Editing and
Working
with Blocks

Formatting
Lines,
Paragraphs,
and Pages

Proofreading
and
Printing

Managing
Files

Creating
Macros

**Merging,
Sorting, and
Selecting**

Using
Columns

Referencing

Creating
Graphics

From this menu, select Merge (1). When WordPerfect prompts for the name of your primary file, type the name and press Enter. When WordPerfect prompts for the name of your secondary merge file, type the name and press Enter.

When you are creating a large number of form letters, all the merged letters may not fit in memory. WordPerfect therefore won't be able to complete the merge and display the letters on-screen. To solve this problem, you can send the results of a merge operation directly to the printer.

Before you can merge to the printer, you need to enter the merge codes ^T^N^P^P at the end of the primary file. To enter each merge code, position the cursor at the spot where you want the code entered, press Merge Codes (Shift-F9), and then press the letter of the code. After you add the ending merge codes, save the letter, turn on your printer, and merge the text files with the same procedure you used to merge to the screen. WordPerfect then prints your letters.

Sorting Data

You can sort files displayed on-screen or files stored on disk, and you can return the sorted results to the screen or to a new file on disk. Sort works with three kinds of data: line, paragraph, or a secondary merge file. You must use a different type of sort for each kind of database. Use line sort when records are lines (a name or an item, for example); use paragraph sort when records are paragraphs (as in a standard legal clause or a glossary); use merge sort when records are in a secondary merge file (a list of names and addresses, for instance).

Understanding the Sort Screen

To display the Sort screen, first press Merge/Sort (Ctrl-F9). When WordPerfect displays the Merge/Sort menu, select Sort (2). At the prompt for an input file, press Enter if you want to sort the file already displayed on-screen, or type the input file name if you want to sort a file stored on disk. At the prompt for the output file, press Enter if you want the sorted results to replace the screen display, or type the output file name if you want the sorted results saved to disk in a new file. The Sort screen is then displayed.

The heading
displays the
current Sort type.
The default is
Sort by Line.

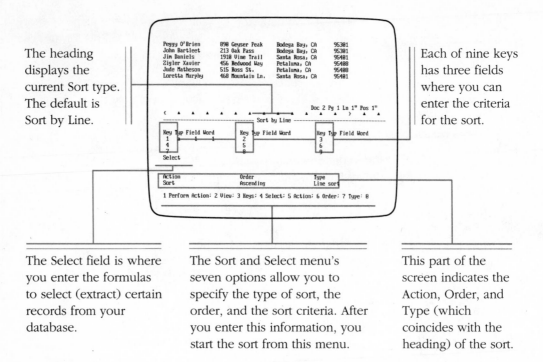

Each of nine keys
has three fields
where you can
enter the criteria
for the sort.

The Select field is where
you enter the formulas
to select (extract) certain
records from your
database.

The Sort and Select menu's
seven options allow you to
specify the type of sort, the
order, and the sort criteria. After
you enter this information, you
start the sort from this menu.

This part of the
screen indicates the
Action, Order, and
Type (which
coincides with the
heading) of the sort.

Sorting Lines and Paragraphs

WordPerfect can sort the lines in any standard text file, as long as the file is formatted
correctly. A line record must end with a hard or soft return, and records must be
formatted with one tab per field with no unused tabs between fields. A paragraph
record must end with two hard returns.

Sorting Lines

Suppose that you want to sort the lines by ZIP code. You also want to sort the last
names within each ZIP code.

An
Overview of
WordPerfect

Editing and
Working
with Blocks

Formatting
Lines,
Paragraphs,
and Pages

Proofreading
and
Printing

Managing
Files

Creating
Macros

**Merging,
Sorting, and
Selecting**

Using
Columns

Referencing

Creating
Graphics

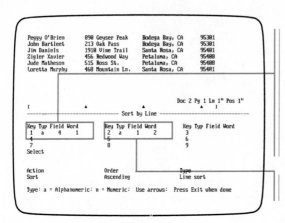

The ZIP code is specified by Key1 as the first word in field number 4. Notice that the type is a (alphanumeric) for all the keys, including ZIP codes, because ZIP codes that begin with a zero (such as 01772) won't sort properly if you choose the numeric type.

The last name is specified by Key2 as the second word in the first field.

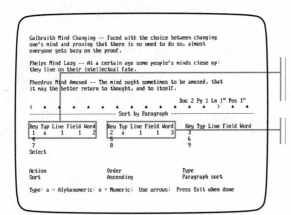

The lines are sorted by ZIP code. Within each ZIP code, the last names are listed alphanumerically.

Sorting Paragraphs

Each paragraph in the following example is a field. The first three words in each paragraph, however, are an index for each quotation: speaker, main topic, and subtopic. Suppose that you want the paragraphs sorted by main topic and then by subtopic.

The main topic is the second word in the first tab on the first line.

The subtopic is the third word in the first tab on the first line.

The paragraphs are sorted alphanumerically by the main topic (second word); within the main topic, they are sorted by the subtopic (third word).

```
Phaedrus Mind Amused -- The mind ought sometimes to be amused, that
it may the better return to thought, and to itself.

Galbraith Mind Changing -- Faced with the choice between changing
one's mind and proving that there is no need to do so, almost
everyone gets busy on the proof.

Phelps Mind Lazy -- At a certain age some people's minds close up:
they live on their intellectual fate.
```

Sorting Secondary Merge Files

A secondary merge file is nothing more than a database with merge codes. WordPerfect can sort your secondary merge files so that the form letters, mailing lists, or labels you have previously typed will print in any order you choose. Before you perform a sort, you must be sure that your data file is set up properly. Each field in the secondary merge file must end with a ^R merge code, and each record must end with a ^E merge code.

Suppose that you want to sort a secondary merge file by state. Within each state, you also want to sort entries by last name and then by first name. For all three keys, select alphanumeric sorting.

Key1 is the state abbreviation (first word from the right in the third field).

Key2 is the last name (first word from the right in the first field).

Key3 is the first name (first word in the first field).

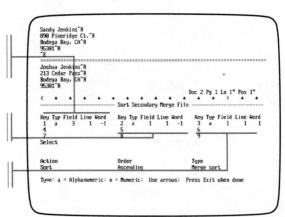

The records are sorted by state. Within each state, entries are sorted by last name and then by first name.

Selecting Data

When you are working with a large database, you often need to select only particular data, and you need to be precise about your selection. Using the Select feature (included in WordPerfect's Sort menu), you can choose only those paragraphs, lines, or secondary merge records that contain a specific combination of data—for example, the names of customers who live in Texas. The steps in selecting are the same as those used in sorting, but you must include *selection criteria*—a statement that describes the records you want to select.

You enter selection criteria after you specify the key locations. To return to the Sort and Select menu after you have specified the key locations, press Exit (F7). Then choose Select (4). WordPerfect moves the cursor under the word `Select` and displays a list of Select codes at the bottom of the screen.

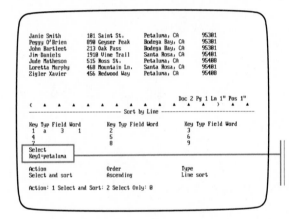

Under `Select`, the statement `Key1=petaluma` is specified as the criteria.

Per the criteria statement, only those records in which the city is *petaluma* or *Petaluma* are selected.

Press Exit (F7) to return to the Sort and Select menu. Then choose Action (5). From the displayed menu, choose Select and Sort (1) if you want to sort and select the records, or choose Select Only (2) if you want to select records without sorting them. After either selection, WordPerfect returns you to the Sort and Select menu.

An
Overview of
WordPerfect

Editing and
Working
with Blocks

Formatting
Lines,
Paragraphs,
and Pages

Proofreading
and
Printing

Managing
Files

Creating
Macros

**Merging,
Sorting, and
Selecting**

Using
Columns

Referencing

Creating
Graphics

Choose Perform Action (1), and WordPerfect sends the selected records either to the screen or to a disk file (as you requested).

Summary

This chapter introduced three of WordPerfect's powerful data management features: Merge, Sort, and Select. You learned how you can use the Merge feature to increase office productivity by combining primary and secondary merge files. The text showed you how to merge these files to either the screen or to the printer. And you learned how to use WordPerfect's Sort feature to handle record-keeping tasks. You explored WordPerfect's capabilities to sort by line, paragraph, or secondary merge file. Finally, you learned how to extract particular data from a large database by specifying selection criteria and using the Select feature. In the next chapter, you will learn about two types of text columns.

Review Questions

1. Describe the type of information stored in a secondary merge file.

2. Describe the type of information stored in a primary file.

3. What are the three kinds of data you can sort in WordPerfect?

4. Give an example of a selection criteria statement and describe what it does.

24 *Using Columns*

WordPerfect offers you a powerful feature that lets you display your text in one of two types of columns: newspaper style or parallel. Text in newspaper-style columns wraps from the bottom of one column to the top of the next column and then wraps back to the first column on the left of the next page. Newspaper columns are read from top to bottom. Parallel columns are read from left to right; therefore, text entries are arranged across the page. Newspaper-style columns are used for magazine articles, newsletters, lists, and indexes. Parallel columns are handy for inventory lists, personnel rosters, and duty schedules.

In this chapter, you learn to perform the following tasks:

- Define newspaper-style columns
- Define parallel columns
- Enter text into columns

Newspaper Style

Johannes Gutenberg, the fifteenth-century inventor of movable type, brought the written word to the public, and thus is responsible for publishing as it has been known for five hundred years. In the last quarter century, Gutenberg's metal type has been replaced by electronic typesetting--faster, more flexible, but still very expensive, and still only part of the complex process or publishing. Today, personal computers bring a new generation of publishing to the individual. The technology is called "desktop publishing," and it represents a whole new approach to a very old art.

Desktop publishing starts with a personal computer. Your high-powered computer, along with the right software, gives you all the tools you need to design and publish a variety of printed material at your own desk. Write a press release or create a simple letterhead with a word processing program like WordPerfect.

Newspaper-style columns are read from top to bottom. The text flows from the bottom of one column to the top of the next. You can define newspaper-style columns either before or after you type the text. Keep in mind that you can use the normal editing commands to modify text within a newspaper-style column.

An Overview of WordPerfect

Editing and Working with Blocks

Formatting Lines, Paragraphs, and Pages

Proofreading and Printing

Managing Files

Creating Macros

Merging, Sorting, and Selecting

Using Columns

Referencing

Creating Graphics

To define newspaper-style columns before you type the text, first move the cursor to the position where you want the columns to begin. Then press Math/Columns (Alt-F7) to display the Math/Columns menu:

1 Math On; **2 M**ath D**e**f; **3 C**olumn On/Off; **4 C**olumn Def: **0**

From this menu, select Column Def (4) to display the Text Column Definition screen.

At the Text Column Definition menu, you do not need to select Type (1) because Newspaper is WordPerfect's default setting. Choose Number of Columns (2) from the menu, enter the number of columns you want on your page (up to 24), and press Enter.

```
Text Column Definition

  1 - Type                              Newspaper

  2 - Number of Columns                 3

  3 - Distance Between Columns          0.5"

  4 - Margins

  Column  Left    Right    Column   Left    Right
    1:    1"      2.83"      13:
    2:    3.33"   5.16"      14:
    3:    5.66"   7.5"       15:
    4:                       16:
    5:                       17:
    6:                       18:
    7:                       19:
    8:                       20:
    9:                       21:
   10:                       22:
   11:                       23:
   12:                       24:

  Selection: 0
```

Next, select Distance Between Columns (3). WordPerfect automatically calculates the margin settings, with 0.5" (one-half inch) between columns, but you can space your columns as close together or as far apart as you want. In most cases, you will accept the default margin settings. To accept the default settings, press Enter. If you plan to use columns of different widths, however, you must type the margin specifications.

After you enter your column specifications on the Text Column Definition screen, press Exit (F7) to return to the Math/Columns menu. From this menu, select Column On/Off (3) to turn on the Column feature. Then begin typing. Text wraps within the column until you reach the bottom of the page, and then text wraps to the top of the next column. To turn off the Column feature, press Math/Columns (Alt-F7), and then choose Column On/Off (3).

To create newspaper-style columns from existing text, first place the cursor at the beginning of the text you want to change to column format. Then press Math/Columns (Alt-F7), define the columns according to the procedure described in the preceding text, and press Exit (F7). From the Math/Columns menu, next select Column On/Off (3) to turn on the Column feature. Then press the down-arrow key, and WordPerfect automatically reformats your text into columns.

An
Overview of
WordPerfect

Editing and
Working
with Blocks

Formatting
Lines,
Paragraphs,
and Pages

Proofreading
and
Printing

Managing
Files

Creating
Macros

Merging,
Sorting, and
Selecting

**Using
Columns**

Referencing

Creating
Graphics

Parallel

Parallel columns are read from left to right across the page. You might, for example, use parallel columns in a script in which names or brief instructions are typed in the first column and the words to be spoken are typed in the second column. You first define the columns you need, and then you enter the headings and text. You can use the normal editing commands to modify text within a parallel column.

```
   Date        Hotel      Location    Sightseeing       Remarks

Oct. 24     Luxembourg   Hotel       Tour of the     The Kasematten are
                         Aerogolf    Kasematten      an ancient
                                     and if time     fortification; the
                                     permits, a      Luxembourg Swiss
                                     short visit     area is one of the
                                     to the Lux-     most picturesque
                                     embourg         areas of the
                                     Swiss area.     country.

Oct. 25     Trier        Dorint      Porta Nigra;    Supposedly founded
                         Hotel       Cathedral       in 2000 B.C.
                                     and Imperial
                                     Baths
```

To define parallel columns, first press Math/Columns (Alt-F7). Then choose Column Def (4). Next, select Type (1) to display the Column Type menu:

Column Type: 1 Newspaper; **2 P**arallel; **3 P**arallel with **B**lock Protect: **0**

At this point, you can choose either Parallel (2) or Parallel with Block Protect (3). The Parallel with Block Protect option prevents a horizontal block of columnar text from being split between pages. If a column reaches the bottom margin and is too long to fit on the page, the entire block of columns is moved to the next page.

Next, select Number of Columns (2), type the desired number of columns, and press Enter. Then select Distance Between Columns (3) and press Enter to accept the default (0.5"). If you want to specify a distance between columns or margins that differ from the default, enter new specifications. To return to the Math/Columns menu, press Exit (F7). Then select Column On/Off (3) to turn on the Column feature.

Above each of your parallel columns, you can enter a centered column heading. To do so, first press Center (Shift-F6). Then type the first column heading. Next, press Hard Page (Ctrl-Enter) to move to the next column. With the cursor in that column, again press Center (Shift-F6) and type the column heading. Repeat this procedure until all the column headings have been entered. After you type the last column heading, press Hard Page (Ctrl-Enter). WordPerfect inserts a blank line and positions the cursor at the first column location at the left of your page.

You type text into parallel columns by moving from column to column across the page. After typing the text in the first column, press Hard Page (Ctrl-Enter) to move the cursor to the next column location. When you press Hard Page in the far right column, the cursor returns to the first column on the left, where you can begin typing the next group of column entries. WordPerfect automatically inserts one blank line to separate the groups of text. To create an empty column, press Hard Page (Ctrl-Enter) twice.

Summary

This chapter described WordPerfect's feature for creating two types of text columns: newspaper-style and parallel. You learned to create newspaper-style columns both as you type the text and from existing text. In the next chapter, you will learn about WordPerfect's numerous referencing features.

Review Questions

1. Describe some types of documents in which you would use newspaper columns.

2. Describe some types of documents in which you would use parallel columns.

3. What options do you specify on the Text Column Definition screen?

25 *Referencing*

An
Overview of
WordPerfect

Editing and
Working
with Blocks

Formatting
Lines,
Paragraphs,
and Pages

Proofreading
and
Printing

Managing
Files

Creating
Macros

Merging,
Sorting, and
Selecting

Using
Columns

Referencing

Creating
Graphics

When you create a formal document, you often need to develop the manuscript through a number of drafts. Moreover, the document may need to include elements beyond the main text, such as footnotes and a table of contents. WordPerfect has a number of referencing tools to help you both develop the main manuscript and create the related elements.

As you develop a manuscript, you will find WordPerfect's outline, paragraph numbering, and line numbering features valuable for getting your project organized, and you also will find those features convenient when conferring with others about particular passages. In addition, you can use the document comment feature to make notes to yourself about items that need further research or development.

In this chapter, you learn to perform the following tasks:

- Create footnotes and endnotes
- Create outlines and numbered paragraphs
- Number lines automatically
- Insert document comments

In addition, you are introduced to some of WordPerfect's more advanced referencing features. Although the specifics of using these features are beyond the scope of this book, you will be acquainted with WordPerfect's referencing tools for creating a list, an index, and a table of contents. You also will learn about WordPerfect's features for creating automatic references, producing a master document, and comparing documents.

▼

Key Terms in This Chapter

Document comments   Notes and reminders you can type into a WordPerfect file. The comments appear on-screen but are not printed.

311

Master document   A document, such as a dissertation, compiled from a number of subdocuments, such as a title page, table of contents, and list of tables.

▲

Creating Footnotes and Endnotes

Footnotes and endnotes provide a simple, standard way of referencing sources as well as offering the reader additional parenthetical information. Footnotes appear at the bottom or foot of the page; endnotes are grouped at the end of your document. (Some authors group endnotes at the end of each chapter or section.) Both types of notes are marked in the text either by a number or by a character you specify. If you don't like the format WordPerfect has chosen for footnotes and endnotes, you can change it by selecting different options.

To create a footnote or an endnote, move the cursor to the position where you want to insert a note number. Then press Footnote (Ctrl-F7) to display the Footnote/ Endnote menu.

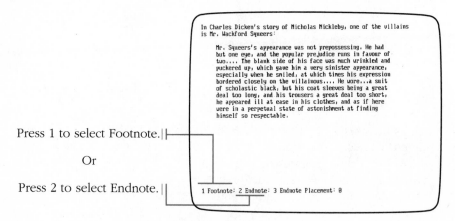

Press 1 to select Footnote.

Or

Press 2 to select Endnote.

WordPerfect then displays the following menu:

Footnote: 1 Create; **2 E**dit; **3 N**ew Number; **4 O**ptions: **0**

Note: The menu for endnotes is the same, but the first word is `Endnote`.

Select Create (1), and an editing screen appears with the cursor to the immediate right of the current footnote or endnote number.

An
Overview of
WordPerfect

Editing and
Working
with Blocks

Formatting
Lines,
Paragraphs,
and Pages

Proofreading
and
Printing

Managing
Files

Creating
Macros

Merging,
Sorting, and
Selecting

Using
Columns

Referencing

Creating
Graphics

> 1Charles Dickens, The Life and Adventures of Nicholas Nickleby
> (Philadelphia: University of Pennsylvania Press, 1982), vol. 1, p.
> 24.

As you enter text, you can use all the normal editing and function keys.

WordPerfect inserts a code that includes the first 50 characters of the note. You can view the code and partial text with Reveal Codes (Alt-F3, or F11). To see how the notes will appear when printed, use View Document (Shift-F7, 6).

Unlike footnotes, which are printed at the bottom of the page on which you create them, endnotes are placed together at the end of the document (unless you enter a code that specifies a different placement). To generate endnotes, press Mark Text (Alt-F5), choose Generate (6), and select Generate Tables, Indexes, Automatic References, etc. (5). At the prompt, press Y. To print endnotes on a separate page, press Ctrl-Enter to insert a Hard Page code before the Endnote Placement code.

Outlining

With WordPerfect's outline feature, you can create an outline and generate paragraph numbers automatically. If you prefer to enter paragraph numbers manually, you can use WordPerfect's paragraph numbering feature instead. The paragraph numbering feature is convenient when you have few numbers and a large amount of text.

Creating an Outline

If you want to title your outline, first press Center (Shift-F6), type the title, and press Enter. Then, to create the outline, move the cursor to the position where you want the outline to begin and press Date/Outline (Shift-F5) to display the following menu:

1 Date Text; **2 D**ate Code; **3 D**ate Format; **4 O**utline; **5 P**ara Num; **6 D**efine: **0**

Next, select Outline (4); the Outline indicator appears at the bottom left corner of the screen. While Outline appears on-screen, the Enter and Tab keys perform special functions. Each time you press Enter, you create a new paragraph number. Within the line, each time you press Tab, you create a different level number.

Press Enter to insert the first paragraph number in the outline ("I." in Outline style). The default numbering style is Outline: uppercase Roman numerals for level one, uppercase letters for level two, Arabic numbers for level three, and so on.

Press Indent (F4) to establish the level number and position the cursor, and then type the text for the first entry. Consecutive lines of text wrap underneath the indent. When you press Enter, WordPerfect moves the cursor to the next line and automatically enters the next number. If you want, you can press Enter again to insert a blank line and move the number down.

Press Tab to move in one level. The number follows and changes to the next level number ("A." in Outline style). Press Indent (F4), type the text for the entry, and press Enter.

```
                              Water Supply

        I.   Water Supply Requirements
             A.   Population Trends
             B.   Per Capita Consumption
             C.   Design Flows
             D.   Summary of Projected Water-Supply Requirements

        II.  The Present Water System and Recommended Improvements
             A.   The Raw Water Collection System
                  1.   The Present System
                  2.   Recommended Improvements
             B.   The Pumping Station
                  1.   The Present Pumping Station
                  2.   Recommended Improvements
                       a.   Pump Number 1
                       b.   Pump Number 2
                       c.   Pump Number 3
                       d.   Pump Number 4




        1 Date Text: 2 Date Code: 3 Date Format: 4 Outline: 5 Para Num: 6 Define: 0
```

Use the Enter, Tab, and Indent (F4) keys to complete the outline.

If you press Tab too many times, you can move back one level by pressing Margin Release (Shift-Tab). To turn off the Outline feature, press Date/Outline (Shift-F5) and choose Outline (4).

Numbering Paragraphs Manually

Paragraph numbering differs from outlining because you must insert numbers manually. Also, unlike the outline feature, the paragraph numbering feature lets you choose the level number, regardless of the cursor position. You can edit numbered paragraphs using the same techniques you use to edit an outline. When you add or delete a paragraph number, WordPerfect automatically renumbers the remaining sections.

To number paragraphs, position the cursor where you want to begin the paragraph. Then press Date/Outline (Shift-F5) and choose Para Num (5). At the prompt, press

Creating
Footnotes and
Endnotes   Outlining

**Numbering
Lines**

Using
Document
Comments

Using Other
Referencing
Features   Summary

Enter to have WordPerfect insert the number that corresponds to the level at the cursor position, or type the level number you want to assign and press Enter. Finally, press Indent (F4) and type the paragraph.

Numbering Lines

In addition to numbering paragraphs, WordPerfect can number the lines in your document. With line numbering, you easily can refer to a particular clause in a legal document or to a specific passage in a manuscript. For instance, you can cite a passage by referring to page 11, line 26.

When you number lines in WordPerfect, the body text as well as the footnotes and endnotes are numbered; headers and footers are not numbered. Numbers are not displayed on-screen; they appear when you print the document (as shown here) or when you use View Document (Shift-F7, 6).

```
 1    Brainstorming
 2
 3    When you have trouble determining a sharp focus for a document--
 4    when you are uncertain what you want to say--consider trying a
 5    seminstructured writing exercise knwon as "brainstorming."
 6
 7    When you brainstorm a writing assignment on-screen, you register
 8    your ideas in list form as they occur to you. When you brainstorm,
 9    you don't worry about typos, spelling, or style. You turn off the
10    inclination to hone each sentence before you move on to the next
11    one. You can handle those matters later. Your goal is, rather, to
12    generate as many ideas as possible about the topic, the purpose,
13    or the audience.
14
15    Keeping an Idea File
16
17    An idea file is an extension of a brainstorming file. You can save
18    an idea file and retrieve it when you want to add more ideas later.
19
20    Using a Prewriting Template
21
22    Prewriting is everything you do up to the actual step of writing
23    that first draft. It is very much a part of the planning stage.
```

To number lines automatically, first move the cursor to the position where you want line numbering to begin (usually at the beginning of your document). Then press Format (Shift-F8), select Line (1), and choose Line Numbering (5). Press Y to turn on line numbering and display the Format: Line Numbering menu.

If you want to accept the default line numbering settings, press Enter. Otherwise, select the option (such as counting blank lines, numbering every *n* lines, or restarting the numbering every page) you want to change and enter the desired modification. Press Exit (F7) to return to the editing screen.

An
Overview of
WordPerfect

Editing and
Working
with Blocks

Formatting
Lines,
Paragraphs,
and Pages

Proofreading
and
Printing

Managing
Files

Creating
Macros

Merging,
Sorting, and
Selecting

Using
Columns

Referencing

Creating
Graphics

To turn off automatic line numbering, press Format (Shift-F8), select Line (1), and choose Line Numbering (5). Then press N. Press Exit (F7) to return to your document.

Using Document Comments

You can insert notes and reminders called comments in your document. Document comments are useful for reminding you what you had in mind during a particular writing session. The comments are displayed only on-screen; they are not printed. If you want to print the comments, however, you can do so by first converting them to text.

To create a document comment, first press Text In/Out (Ctrl-F5) to display the following menu:

> **1 D**OS **T**ext; **2 P**assword; **3 S**ave **G**eneric; **4 S**ave **W**P 4.2; **5 C**omment: **0**

Then select Comment (5) to display the Comment menu:

> **Comment: 1 C**reate; **2 E**dit; **3 C**onvert to **T**ext: **0**

From this menu, choose Create (1). WordPerfect places the cursor in the Document Comment editing box. In this box, type the text of your comment. You must keep your text within the lines of the box—approximately seven lines of text. You can use bold or underline to emphasize text within the box. Press Exit (F7) to return to your document.

The document comment appears on-screen in the middle of your text as a double-ruled box.

Creating
Footnotes and
Endnotes   Outlining

Numbering
Lines

Using
Document
Comments

**Using Other
Referencing
Features**   Summary

An
Overview of
WordPerfect

Editing and
Working
with Blocks

Formatting
Lines,
Paragraphs,
and Pages

Proofreading
and
Printing

Managing
Files

Creating
Macros

Merging,
Sorting, and
Selecting

Using
Columns

Referencing

Creating
Graphics

Using Other Referencing Features

When you create a professional document, especially a lengthy one, you often need to include supplementary reference material. For example, when you create a book, manual, or research report, you might include lists of figures and tables, a table of contents, and an index. WordPerfect has built-in features to make the preparation of these materials easier. In addition, WordPerfect offers three other features that are handy when preparing reference materials: automatic referencing, master document, and document comparison. Although the specifics of these reference features are beyond the scope of this book, this section introduces you to the kinds of reference documents you can create with WordPerfect.

You use WordPerfect's Mark Text (Alt-F5) key to control the creation of reference materials. You use the options offered to identify those items you want to incorporate into a list, table of contents, index, or table of authorities (for a legal document). You also use the options to specify the format and style of these special sections of your document and to generate the references where they need to be included.

Whether you are creating a list, table of contents, or index, you follow the same basic procedure. First use Block (Alt-F4, or F12) to highlight the entry. Then press Mark Text (Alt-F5) to display the following menu:

Mark for: 1 ToC; **2** List; **3** Index; **4** ToA: **0**

To mark the text, choose the appropriate option from this menu. You can mark text as you create your document, or you can go back later and do so.

Next, press Mark Text (Alt-F5) to display the following menu:

1 Auto **R**ef; **2 S**ubdoc; **3 I**ndex; **4** To**A** Short Form; **5 D**efine; **6 G**enerate: **0**

From this menu, select Define (5) to display the Mark Text: Define menu. From that menu, select the item you want to define; from the definition menu, choose the format and specify how you want the reference material to look on the page. Finally, press Mark Text (Alt-F5), select Generate (6), and then press 5 to generate the reference material at the appropriate place in the document.

Table of Contents

When you create a table of contents, you generally use text taken directly from the document—chapter headings, for example. A table of contents is included as part of a document's front matter.

Index

WordPerfect's indexing feature creates an alphabetized list of index headings and subheadings (called entries) for a document. You can generate an index only at the end of a document.

List

If your document contains figures, illustrations, tables, maps, and other illustrations, you can list these resources in a reference table. Usually a list appears on a page by itself following the table of contents. You can create up to nine lists per document.

Automatic References

Use WordPerfect's automatic reference feature to reference page numbers, footnote numbers, section numbers, endnote numbers, and graphics box numbers. If you make changes, the references are renumbered automatically.

```
                      Writing Guidelines
=========================================================

                      Table of Contents

Brainstorming. . . . . . . . . . . . . . . . . . . . .   3

Keeping an Idea File . . . . . . . . . . . . . . . . .   7

Freewriting. . . . . . . . . . . . . . . . . . . . . .   9

Using a Prewriting Template. . . . . . . . . . . . . .  11

Planning Documents . . . . . . . . . . . . . . . . . .  13
```

```
Exercises
     brainstorming  3
     idea file  7
     prewriting template  11

Freewriting   5
```

```
                    List of Exhibits

          Page numbers record first mention of each
               exhibit in this affidavit.

Exhibit A. . . . . . . . . . . . . . . . . . . . . . .1
Exhibit B. . . . . . . . . . . . . . . . . . . . . . .2
Exhibit C. . . . . . . . . . . . . . . . . . . . . . .2
Exhibit D. . . . . . . . . . . . . . . . . . . . . . .3
Exhibit E. . . . . . . . . . . . . . . . . . . . . . .3
```

```
Brainstorming

When you have trouble determining a sharp focus for a document--
when you are uncertain what you want to say--consider trying a
semistructured writing exercise known as "brainstorming."

When you brainstorm a writing assignment on-screen, you register
your ideas in list form as they occur to you. When you brainstorm,
you don't worry about typos, spelling, or style. You turn off the
inclination to to hone each sentence before you move on to the next
one. You can handle those matters later. Your goal is, rather, to
generate as many ideas as possible about the topic, the purpose,
or the audience. See the discussion of planning documents on
page 9.

Keeping an Idea File

An idea file is an extension of a brainstorming file. You can save
an idea file and retrieve it when you want to add more ideas later.

                                    Doc 1 Pg 3 Ln 3" Pos 1"
```

Creating
Footnotes and
Endnotes
Outlining
Numbering
Lines
Using
Document
Comments
Using Other
Referencing
Features
Summary

An
Overview of
WordPerfect

Editing and
Working
with Blocks

Formatting
Lines,
Paragraphs,
and Pages

Proofreading
and
Printing

Managing
Files

Creating
Macros

Merging,
Sorting, and
Selecting

Using
Columns

Referencing

Creating
Graphics

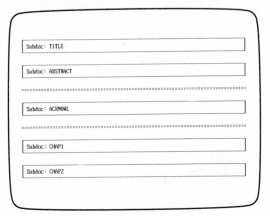

Master Document

A master document consists of a master document file and subdocument files. The master document file contains codes that reference the subdocument files. Each subdocument contains the text for a particular section of the total document.

Document Comparison

Use WordPerfect to compare the new version of a document with an old version. Sections of the on-screen document that don't exist in the disk file are redlined. Text that exists in the disk file but not in the on-screen document is copied to the on-screen document and marked with strikeout.

Summary

This chapter introduced many of WordPerfect's referencing tools for developing a manuscript through a number of drafts and creating supporting elements for a formal document. You explored WordPerfect's features for creating footnotes and endnotes, generating outlines and paragraph numbers, numbering lines, and inserting document comments. The text also gave you an overview of other WordPerfect referencing features, including tables of contents, indexes, lists, automatic references, master documents, and document comparison. In the next chapter, you will learn about WordPerfect's graphics capabilities.

Review Questions

1. What WordPerfect commands must you use to view footnotes or endnotes on-screen?

2. What is the difference between WordPerfect's Outline and Paragraph Numbering features?

3. Give an example of when using WordPerfect's line numbering feature might be useful.

4. What advanced referencing features can you access from WordPerfect's Mark Text (Alt-F5) key?

5. What kinds of lists might you create with WordPerfect to supplement a formal document?

26 *Creating Graphics*

An
Overview of
WordPerfect

Editing and
Working
with Blocks

Formatting
Lines,
Paragraphs,
and Pages

Proofreading
and
Printing

Managing
Files

Creating
Macros

Merging,
Sorting, and
Selecting

Using
Columns

Referencing

**Creating
Graphics**

With WordPerfect's Graphics feature, you can enhance the appearance of your document with graphics boxes and lines. You can use four types of boxes: figure, table, text box, and user-defined box.

In the boxes, you can insert text; graphics from the Fonts/Graphics disk; or graphics, charts, and graphs created with external programs such as 1-2-3. You can insert the text or graphics at the time you create the box; or you can create an empty box and enter text or graphics later. Graphics boxes can be placed in the body of a document as well as in headers, footers, and endnotes.

Here is an example of a publication created with WordPerfect. Notice the variety of graphics features used in this page.

Horizontal line

Graphics box with imported clip-art image

Caption

Border

Shaded box

Vertical line

Text wrapped around a box

Text box

Although WordPerfect offers many advanced graphics capabilities, not all computers are equipped to match WordPerfect's power. If you have a graphics card, such as a Hercules Graphics or InColor card, then graphics appear correctly on the regular editing screen. If you don't have a graphics card, you will have to use the View Document feature to see lines, boxes, shades, and imported graphics.

In this chapter, you learn to perform the following tasks:

- Create figures, tables, text boxes, and user-defined boxes
- Select the options for each type of box—for example, the borders of the box, the caption style, and the spacing
- Import graphics into boxes
- Edit a graphics image, making it smaller or larger, rotating it, or inverting it
- Draw lines

Key Terms in This Chapter

Offset	A short distance established as a boundary to avoid the collision of two elements, such as a graphics image and a box.
Graphics box	An empty box defined to hold a figure, table, text, or user-defined elements, and to have certain characteristics such as border type, caption style, and spacing.
Graphics image	The contents of a box, such as an imported clip-art figure, statistical data, text, or a photograph.

Defining Graphics Boxes

Each box type has a default definition. The definition includes the border of the box, the inside and outside border space, the caption numbering method and style, the minimum offset, and the shading. You can use the default box styles, or you can define your own. Defining boxes gives you a consistent set of boxes to use in your documents. For instance, you can place clip art in figure boxes, statistical data in table boxes, text in text boxes, and photographs (which you paste in later) in user-defined boxes.

Defining
Graphics
Boxes

**Creating
Graphics
Boxes**

Editing
Boxes and
Images

Creating
Graphics
Lines

Summary

To change the default box definition, first press Graphics (Alt-F9) to display the following menu:

1 Figure; **2 T**able; **3** Text **B**ox; **4** User-defined Box; **5 L**ine: **0**

Figure 1: BOOK.WPG

Figure

Table

1: Text Box

Text Box

1. THINKER.WPG

User-defined Box

From the menu, select a box type: figure, table, text box, or user-defined box. Then choose Options (4) to display a screen in which you can specify graphics features.

```
Options:    Figure

  1 - Border Style
       Left                        Single
       Right                       Single
       Top                         Single
       Bottom                      Single
  2 - Outside Border Space
       Left                        0.16"
       Right                       0.16"
       Top                         0.16"
       Bottom                      0.16"
  3 - Inside Border Space
       Left                        0"
       Right                       0"
       Top                         0"
       Bottom                      0"
  4 - First Level Numbering Method   Numbers
  5 - Second Level Numbering Method  Off
  6 - Caption Number Style           [BOLD]Figure 1[bold]
  7 - Position of Caption            Below box, Outside borders
  8 - Minimum Offset from Paragraph  0"
  9 - Gray Shading (% of black)      60%

Selection: 0
```

Among the options you can specify for a graphics box are the border style for each side of the box (such as double, dashed, dotted, thick); the space between the border of the box and the text; the space between the border and the contents of the box; the text and numbering style for the caption (such as numbers, letters, or Roman numerals); the position of the caption; the minimum paragraph offset; and the percentage of shading.

Creating Graphics Boxes

When you create a box for a figure, table, text, or a user-defined element, you specify its contents, caption, type, placement on the page, and size. To create a graphics box, first move the cursor to the position where you want the box to appear. Then press Graphics (Alt-F9) and select a box type. Choose Create (1) to display the Definition menu.

Among the box options you specify on the Definition menu when you create a box are the name of the file, the text for the caption, the type of text to which the box is anchored (paragraph, page, or character); the vertical alignment of the box; the horizontal position of the box; the width, height, or both; text that automatically wraps around the box; and text to be inserted in the box.

```
Definition: Figure

    1 - Filename              PENCIL.WPG (Graphic)

    2 - Caption               Figure 2

    3 - Type                  Paragraph

    4 - Vertical Position     8"

    5 - Horizontal Position   Right

    6 - Size                  1.54" wide x 2.89" (high)

    7 - Wrap Text Around Box  Yes

    8 - Edit


Selection: 8
```

To import a file (text file or graphics file, for instance), select the Filename (1) option, type the name of the file (such as **pencil.wpg**), and press Enter. WordPerfect inserts the file in the box. WordPerfect's Fonts/Graphics disk contains clip-art files (with a .WPG extension) you can import.

To create a caption for the pencil, select Caption (2), edit the displayed default caption, and press Exit (F7) to return to your document. Move the cursor past the box to display an outline of the image.

To view the document as it will appear when printed, use View Document (Shift-F7, 6).

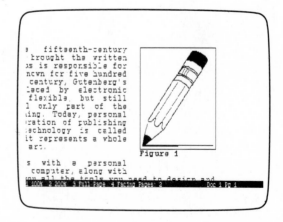

Defining
Graphics
Boxes

Creating
Graphics
Boxes

Editing
Boxes and
Images

**Creating
Graphics
Lines**

Summary

An
Overview of
WordPerfect

Editing and
Working
with Blocks

Formatting
Lines,
Paragraphs,
and Pages

Proofreading
and
Printing

Managing
Files

Creating
Macros

Merging,
Sorting, and
Selecting

Using
Columns

Referencing

**Creating
Graphics**

Editing Boxes and Images

You can edit both the box and the image within it. You can edit the box, for instance, by changing the numbering or type of box. If you import a graphics file into a box, you can edit the image by moving, scaling, rotating, mirroring, or inverting it.

To edit a graphics box, first press Graphics (Alt-F9) and select the type of box you want to edit. Then choose Edit (2), type the number of the box, and press Enter. Next, choose an option and make the desired changes. You can renumber boxes, for example, to begin a new chapter (stored in its own disk file) with the proper numbering. Or you might want to change the box type.

To edit an imported graphics image, first press Graphics (Alt-F9) and choose the type of box you want to edit. Then select Edit (2). Type the number of the figure, table, text box, or user-defined box, and then press Enter. Next, select Edit (8) from the Definition menu. The graphic appears on-screen. The bottom of the screen shows the editing changes you can make: you can move, scale, rotate, or invert (mirror) the image. The top of the screen shows shortcuts to make those changes. With shortcuts, the image is changed by the amount shown in the bottom of the screen. Change this amount by pressing Ins until the amount you want appears: 1%, 5%, 10%, or 25%.

Creating Graphics Lines

With WordPerfect, you can create vertical and horizontal lines on the printed page. For example, you might want to include vertical lines between the columns of a newsletter or a horizontal line under the masthead. The lines can be shaded or black.

To create graphics lines, first position the cursor and press Graphics (Alt-F9). Then select Line (5). Next, choose Horizontal Line (1) or Vertical Line (2). WordPerfect displays the Horizontal Line menu or the Vertical Line menu, respectively. You can accept the defaults for the line, or you can choose from this menu an option and enter the appropriate information. With these menu options, you can specify the horizontal position of the line, the vertical position of the line (for vertical lines only), the length of the line, the width of the line, and the percentage of shading (or black). To see how a line will print, use View Document (Shift-F7, 6).

325

Summary

In this chapter, you learned to define four types of graphic boxes, and to import images into those boxes. You explored some of the options for each type of box, such as the border style, the caption style, and the spacing. You learned that you can edit a graphic image in WordPerfect by changing its size or rotating it. And you learned about WordPerfect's capabilities for drawing horizontal and vertical lines to enhance your documents. This chapter completes your introduction to WordPerfect.

Review Questions

1. Name the four types of graphics boxes you can create with WordPerfect, and give examples of what might be displayed in each type.

2. Describe some of the options you can specify when you define a box.

3. How do you import a graphics image into a box?

4. In what ways can you edit a graphics image you have imported into a box?

Part IV

dBASE

dBASE III

SYSTEM DISK #1

Format: IBM PC, PC/XT, PCAT, 3270 PC and 100% compatibles

©Ashton Tate 1986 All rights reserved.

ASHTON·TATE®

An Overview of dBASE
Getting Started
Designing and Creating a Database
Organizing and Searching Data
Viewing and Editing Data
Designing Reports and Labels
Programming in dBASE

SORT ON fieldnam TO newfilename

SORT ON

* | INDEX ON fieldname TO indexname
   | SET INDEX TO index name.

SNOOPY . DBF

SNOOPY . NDX

Sort something

TRY . DBF
LAST . NDX
FIRST . NDX
AGE . NDX
CITY . NDX   } Belong to this
             database file
             called Try.

27 *An Overview of dBASE*

Businesses collect, hold, and process data in a variety of ways. They may, for example, generate follow-up letters to customers using a word processor such as WordPerfect 5 or prepare budgets using the row-and-column format of a 1-2-3 spreadsheet. When data items are related, businesses often use a database management system (DBMS).

dBASE III Plus, published by Ashton-Tate, is one of the most popular and powerful database management system programs in use. (Although Ashton-Tate released an upgrade, dBASE IV, in early 1989, this text focuses primarily on dBASE III Plus.) Merchandising firms use a DBMS, such as dBASE III Plus, to maintain accurate data concerning the quantity of goods on hand and the lead times for reordering, as well as to schedule workers according to required skill levels. Organizations providing services use a DBMS to monitor constraints on resources, such as the beds available in a hospital. And most firms receive payments from customers and generate payroll checks—tasks that can be handled with a DBMS.

Before you start using dBASE, you need to know what a database is and how it is used. This chapter begins with an explanation of a database management system and then contrasts "manual" and "electronic" databases. The text next shows you the wide range of capabilities offered by dBASE and helps you understand how dBASE is useful for many business applications.

After completing this chapter, you should have a general understanding of the following topics:

- The advantages of a computerized database over a manual one
- The characteristics of relational and multiple-interface databases
- The capabilities of dBASE

▼

Key Terms in This Chapter

Data   Basic elements of information, such as numbers, letters, words, or facts. For example, data includes phone numbers, dollar amounts, dates, descriptions, opinions, and assumptions.

329

Database   A collection of related data. An automobile dealership, for example, collects in a database the same data about each vehicle sold, such as customer name, vehicle identification number, price paid, and delivery date.

DBMS   Database management system; a systematic approach to storing, updating, reporting on, and deleting related data. For example, a DBMS can update the database for the current week's sales and print a list of vehicle sales for the month just ending, subtotaled by salesperson.

Field   A specific data item within a database record.

Record   A collection of related fields in a database.

▲

What Is a Database Management System?

The systematic approach to storing, updating, reporting on, and deleting related data is called a database management system. A DBMS can be manual or automated. This section discusses the limitations of a manual database system and the advantages of an automated system.

Limitations of Manual Database Systems

You can store data in a manual database in your mind or on paper. If you store data only in your mind, you may not remember everything, and only you can access the data. The larger the database, the more important it is to store data in an organized manner and in a physical form accessible to others.

In a manual system of tracking vehicle sales data, the salesperson keeps records on paper about each sale, places the paper in a folder marked with the customer's name, and stores the folder in a file cabinet in alphabetical order by customer name. Periodically, clerical staff members remove folders to prepare required reports.

In database terminology, each data item in the folder—such as customer name, date of sale, and salesperson—is a *field*. The collection of related data items about one sale is a *record* (in this case, the folder). All the sales folders (records) in the file cabinet make up the sales *database*.

The Manual System

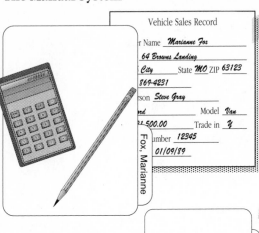

Sales File

The clerical staff prepares the weekly sales report from the only copy of each record.

Colonial Imports		
SALES REPORT		
Week of 8-26-89		
Model	Package	Sales $
327A	Yes	26,800
327B	No	32,400
316A	Yes	14,300
115C	Yes	22,340
332A	No	33,120
221E	Yes	12,330
337A	No	9,230
Total		150,520

The preparation takes days. To complete the job takes one sales clerk, one warranty clerk, and one accounting clerk.

331

The manual process has several limitations. If you know the customer's name, you can easily find data in the file cabinet—the manual database. However, what if you want to know both the total sales for the month of January and the total sales made by a particular salesperson? Using this manual database, you must physically look at every record, remove the ones meeting your search conditions, manually calculate the required totals, and refile the records in their original order.

Report generation is often a time-consuming task; and during the activity, the removed folders are not readily available to other staff members. In addition, few firms make duplicate copies of their paper files and therefore place themselves at risk should fire or theft result in loss of data.

Advantages of Automated Database Systems

In an automated system of tracking vehicle sales data, the salesperson enters from the keyboard data about each sale and saves on disk the update to the vehicle sales database. With just a few keystrokes, a single clerical staff member can generate reports and labels, and create a backup of the database on disk.

In addition to the potential to reduce staff requirements, an automated DBMS has several other advantages over a manual one. Entering and editing data with a computer keyboard and monitor is faster and easier than manipulating data by hand. The computer performs the necessary calculations. Records can be organized on any field instead of being physically arranged by a single field such as last name.

Report generation is no longer a time-consuming task that prevents other staff members from accessing the database records. Using a computer database, you can copy data quickly to inexpensive disks or tapes and store these backup files in a separate, and safe, location.

How Do Automated Systems Vary?

Database management systems are classified according to two main criteria: the data storage method and the type of user interface. dBASE uses a relational storage method and a multiple-interface.

dBASE: A Relational DBMS

The file storage methods commonly used with IBM-compatible personal computer database management systems are *flat-file* and *relational*. Other types of file storage

What Is a Database
Management
System?

**How Do
Automated
Systems Vary?**

Why Is dBASE
a Powerful
System?

What
Hardware Do
You Need?

Summary

**An
Overview of
dBASE**

The Automated System

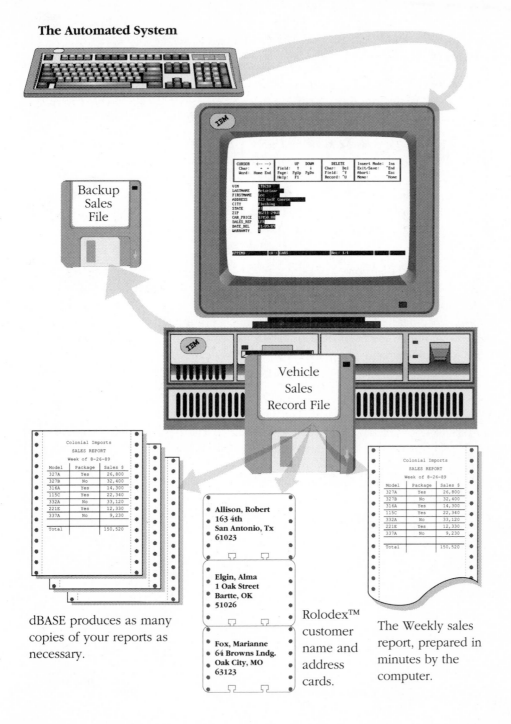

Getting
Started

Designing
and Creating
a Database

Viewing,
Organizing,
and Updating
Data

Searching
the
Database

Designing
Reports and
Labels

Programming
in dBASE

dBASE produces as many
copies of your reports as
necessary.

Rolodex™
customer
name and
address
cards.

The Weekly sales
report, prepared in
minutes by the
computer.

methods, which are more often associated with mainframes or with personal computers that are not IBM-compatible, are not included in this discussion.

A flat-file storage DBMS views each database as a unit independent of other database management systems. In other words, no two databases created under a flat-file DBMS can be connected or related to each other to produce a larger view of data.

For example, if you develop a database using 1-2-3 Release 2.01 (as described in Chapter 16), you create a flat-file database. To access data in two 1-2-3 spreadsheets at the same time, you must use a /File Combine command sequence to copy one flat-file into another. In some cases, a flat-file storage feature may be adequate for your needs. For instance, if your database needs are fairly basic and relate to a simple list, such as names and addresses or records of investments, you can use a flat-file DBMS to define and maintain a database with ease.

Suppose, however, that you have certain fields which are repeated in different records. A car dealership, for example, maintains a vehicle sales database as well as a database for related warranty records, and both databases contain fields for a complete customer address. In this case, you may end up with redundant data in the databases. Although inefficient space utilization isn't a problem in small databases, it becomes a problem for a personal computer DBMS when databases grow to thousands of records.

Selecting a relational DBMS, such as dBASE, can significantly reduce this redundancy. The word *relational* indicates that the database management system provides a means to relate or link files using a common field defined in more than one database. For example, customer name and address fields are included in the vehicle sales database but not the warranty records database. By linking the databases on the common field VIN (vehicle identification number), you can produce a warranty work report that contains name and address data.

With a relational DBMS, you can easily change database relationships as the need arises. Internal tables used in a relational DBMS define the relationships between fields in a record and link fields between databases. The internal tables, established when the database structure is entered into the DBMS, make a relational DBMS efficient to use and the process of relating databases relatively easy and dynamic.

Multiple Databases

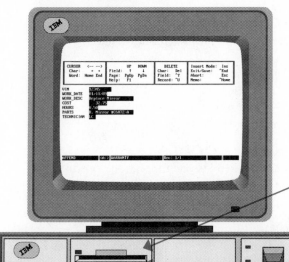

Vehicle Sales Record File — Customer Name, Address, City, State, ZIP, Phone Number, Sales Person, MFG, Model, Price, Trade in, VIN, Date

▲
Vehicle ID Number
▼

Customer Warranty Records File — VIN, Work Order Date, Labor Description, Cost, Hours, Materials, Supplies, Parts, Technician

Two database files are created to provide information about different aspects of dealership operations. The two databases are linked by a common field—in this case, the VIN (vehicle identification number).

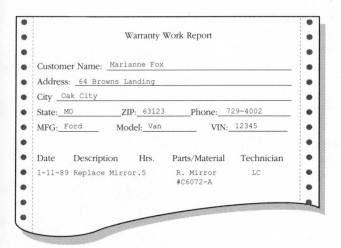

Warranty Work Report

Customer Name: Marianne Fox

Address: 64 Browns Landing

City: Oak City

State: MO   ZIP: 63123   Phone: 729-4002

MFG: Ford   Model: Van   VIN: 12345

Date	Description	Hrs.	Parts/Material	Technician
1-11-89	Replace Mirror	.5	R. Mirror #C6072-A	LC

dBASE: A Multiple-Interface DBMS

The link between the visual and keyboard work that people do in a DBMS environment is called the *user interface*. You can use four basic user interfaces to access DBMS services: a system of menus, commands issued on a command line, operation of a program that issues DBMS requests internally, or some combination of these. Using the menu approach, you select from menu options that are displayed on-screen. The command-line approach requires you to type the appropriate directions from the keyboard. If you use a program approach, you activate a series of instructions that are stored on disk.

A *menu-driven* DBMS, such as Paradox or R:BASE, guides you through the process of using a database by providing menus you must learn to navigate. One menu may lead to another and yet another. By knowing the menu structure and selecting individual menu items, you learn how to extract the needed information. Menu systems are easy to learn because they are tutorial by nature. Each possible action is available as a menu item.

A *command-driven* system performs basically the same tasks as a menu-driven system, but requires you to type commands instead of selecting menu items. Command-driven systems are usually more flexible than menu-driven but require that you learn many commands. Most DBMS users find that learning a command-driven DBMS is initially more difficult than using a menu-driven system. After learning the commands, however, users find that the command-driven approach is faster, more flexible, and more specific than a menu-driven system.

Program-driven user interfaces can be viewed at two levels. At one level you simply operate a program (a series of instructions) that someone else has written. At the other level, you actually write programs to request DBMS services. The common feature of both levels is that a program must exist in order to use the DBMS resource.

If you operate a program that someone has written, you use the features provided by the program. Although using a prewritten program is convenient, it is by nature limiting. You cannot access information in a way other than the way provided by the program. On the other hand, DBMS programs that limit access to information are quite appropriate for activities involving routine data entry and report generation. For some users, the program is desirable because it makes using the DBMS less complicated. For users who want to create their own databases and update or query them in an *ad hoc* fashion, the preprogrammed DBMS is not an appropriate information tool.

An Overview of dBASE

Getting Started

Designing and Creating a Database

Viewing, Organizing, and Updating Data

Searching the Database

Designing Reports and Labels

Programming in dBASE

An alternative to using prewritten programs with a program-driven DBMS is writing your own programs. This requires you to know a particular programming language, such as Oracle, in order to enter, retrieve, and otherwise manipulate data. Although by writing programs, you can then perform sophisticated DBMS work, programming languages are beyond most people's expertise.

Most of the popular DBMS systems offer a *combination* of the three interfaces. dBASE offers a menu-driven interface, a command line, and a complete programming language. Paradox gives a choice of a menu-driven system, a programming language, but no command-driven feature. With the three user interfaces available, a user can select the interface that best suits the activity at hand.

Why Is dBASE a Powerful System?

dBASE III Plus and dBASE IV are relational DBMS products. (Both versions of dBASE share common characteristics; for this overview discussion, you can think of the two collectively as dBASE.) dBASE includes all the features representative of the DBMS discipline of personal computer productivity. In addition, dBASE enjoys a larger user base than any other relational DBMS. The dBASE features allow you to complete common DBMS activities that include designing and creating a database; viewing, organizing, and updating data; searching the database; generating reports and labels; and writing programs.

Designing and Creating a Database

Before you start to implement a new DBMS, you should specify the database objectives, analyze the current system for flaws and potential enhancements, determine desired outputs, and then select appropriate inputs. These actions constitute *designing* the database.

To *create* a database, you must define its structure and enter records. The structure defines the characteristics of the fields you want your database to contain. A DBMS allows you to create, display, modify, and copy the database structure. After you establish the structure, you can add records. Chapter 29 discusses designing a database, creating a database structure, and adding records.

Viewing, Organizing, and Updating Data

All database management systems, including dBASE, offer commands for viewing data after it has been entered. In this context, the word *view* means to look at data on-screen or produce printed output. dBASE allows you to view complete records or limit the output to only selected fields in a record. As an added dBASE feature, you can create new information to view by performing calculations on the contents of existing fields. dBASE also allows you to organize records in a database on the field(s) of your choice.

dBASE provides options for updating a database—to revise or delete existing records, as well as to add records. The program provides an Edit mode to revise one record on the screen and a Browse mode to edit multiple records. dBASE also allows you to replace contents of records and recall deleted records. You explore viewing, organizing (reordering), and updating databases in Chapter 30.

Searching the Database

Searching for records in your database may be the most important function you perform. Using the term *search* in a broad sense, a search tells a DBMS which records to access. dBASE allows you to limit the number of records you view by specifying a scope. You also can find only those records meeting simple or complex search conditions.

Generating Reports and Labels

Printing custom reports is a common feature of database management systems. A simple listing of selected database contents might suffice for some tasks, such as documenting the current day's sales. But a multiple-page listing of an entire month's sales activities warrants some enhanced features. You can, for example, add headings, page numbers, subtotals, and totals to create a custom report. The dBASE III Plus report generator creates columnar reports. Using dBASE IV you can produce a wide variety of report formats. With both versions of the program, you also can create and print custom labels. Chapter 32 shows you how dBASE makes designing reports and labels easy.

Writing Programs

dBASE offers a complete programming language that has become a standard in microcomputers. If you know the language, you can write programming code to control a multitude of database activities. For example, a program to manage vehicle sales data might verify data entry (for example, reject inaccurate salespersons' initials) and offer the user a selection of custom reports. The power of dBASE programming is the focus of Chapter 33.

What Hardware Do You Need?

You can run dBASE on an IBM personal computer or compatible with DOS 2.0 or later and at least 256K of RAM for dBASE III Plus or 360K for dBASE IV. To run dBASE III Plus, the system should have either two 360K double-sided floppy disk drives or one 360K floppy drive and a hard disk drive. For larger databases and faster processing, a hard disk is highly recommended. To run dBASE IV, you must have a hard disk, as well as a 5 1/4-inch, 360K disk drive or a 3 1/2-inch, 720K disk drive. Other hardware requirements include a printer with a capacity of at least 80 columns.

Summary

Businesses process and store large amounts of data by developing database management systems. The systems can be manual or automated. Automated systems vary according to the type of file storage and user interface.

Three terms describe the components of a database: each data item is a *field*; the collection of related data items is a *record*; the records make up the *database*. The larger the database, the more important it is to store data in an organized manner, to make data accessible to a variety of users, and to provide backup copies of the data. You can achieve these results using database management system software such as dBASE III Plus or dBASE IV.

In this chapter you learned that dBASE embodies the best features of a database management system: designing and creating a database; viewing, organizing, and updating data; searching the database; generating reports and labels; and writing programs. The power of dBASE is best realized in actually using the program. The next chapter shows you how to get started.

Getting Started

Designing and Creating a Database

Viewing, Organizing, and Updating Data

Searching the Database

Designing Reports and Labels

Programming in dBASE

Review Questions

1. How would you differentiate the terms *database* and *database management system?*

2. Is a relational database always preferred over a flat-file database?

3. Is dBASE a relational database or a flat-file database?

4. Why might a DBMS user prefer a command-driven interface over a menu-driven interface?

5. Which user interfaces does dBASE support?

An
Overview of
dBASE

Getting
Started

Designing
and Creating
a Database

Viewing,
Organizing,
and Updating
Data

Searching
the
Database

Designing
Reports and
Labels

Programming
in dBASE

28 *Getting Started*

For just for a moment, compare using dBASE to driving your car. It sounds like a simple task to start the car, drive to your destination, and then stop the car. But driving safely and reaching your stopping point in a reasonable amount of time requires knowing more than simply how to turn the steering wheel and insert the ignition key.

You must know the layout and operation of your car's features, such as the horn and windshield wipers. You must be able to interpret dashboard displays, such as the fuel gauge and speedometer. You should plan the route and know how to call for help if needed. In addition, you must understand such requirements and constraints as carrying your driver's license and securing your seatbelt. And, you must know these items before you turn the ignition switch!

If you take the time to acquire some general knowledge about dBASE, then starting the program, completing your desired activity, and exiting the program can be relatively easy tasks. The purpose of this chapter is to introduce the dBASE environment. You learn the types of dBASE III Plus files and some of the technical limitations of the program. You learn how to enter and leave dBASE. You explore the layout of the menu structure, called the Assistant, and learn to access dot prompt mode. You become acquainted with cursor-movement, function, and control keys. You are introduced to the operation of the Help feature. And, finally, you learn about the dBASE IV environment.

After completing this chapter, you should be able to do the following:

- Understand the basic file types and limitations of dBASE III Plus
- Start and exit dBASE III Plus
- Use the dBASE III Plus menu-driven interface
- Access the dBASE command-driven interface
- Know how to use the keyboard with dBASE III Plus
- Access the dBASE III Plus help system
- Understand the dBASE IV environment

▼

Key Terms in This Chapter

Assistant A screen that indicates you are using the menu-driven interface of dBASE III Plus.

Dot prompt A period (.) that indicates you are using the command-driven interface of dBASE.

Menu bar A horizontal menu that appears on the top row of the Assistant screen.

Message line The line at the bottom of the Assistant screen, which displays instructions to complete the current task.

Navigation line The line near the bottom of the Assistant screen, which displays the keys you use to move the cursor for the current task.

Pull-down menu A menu on which the options are listed one after another in a single column.

▲

Understanding File Types and Limitations

Before you acquire and use any application software, you should understand how the software organizes its files and whether or not the software places limits on the file sizes. For example, 1-2-3 Release 2.01 uses a single .WK1 extension file to manage a database, and the program's spreadsheet format limits you to 256 fields (columns) and 8,191 records (rows). dBASE III Plus, in contrast, generates up to 13 types of files for managing a database and allows 128 fields and 1 billion records per database. This section reviews the file types and program limitations of dBASE III Plus that will affect the work you do in subsequent chapters.

Types of Files

Recall from the DOS chapters that a file can have a two-part identification: a *file name* up to eight characters and an *extension* up to three characters. 1-2-3 automatically assigns one of three extensions: .WK1 (worksheet file), .PRN (print file), or .PIC (picture file). In contrast, WordPerfect lets the user specify the extension in a document file name. Because different types of information are used in a dBASE application, different kinds of data structures are defined in separate disk files that relate to a single database.

dBASE assigns the extensions to help you understand the uses of the separate files. For example, in later chapters, you will create files such as a database file (.DBF extension) in Chapter 29, an index file (.NDX extension) in Chapter 30, and a report form file (.FRM extension) in Chapter 32. Once you understand the types of files that a program generates, you should ascertain whether the program limits your use of those files.

Program Limitations

To use any software application, you should understand the capabilities and constraints of the package. The type of processor used in the microcomputer and the amount of available memory are considerations that provide a *hardware* limit to the size of a database. The available storage space on the disk determines the number of files that can be stored. Program specifications provide a *software* limit to the size of a database. For example, dBASE III Plus limits your use of the package to 10 database (.DBF) files being active at one time and 7 index (.NDX) files associated with each database file.

A database (.DBF) file can contain as many as 2 billion characters of information or a maximum of 1 billion data records. Each data record can hold up to 4,000 characters and can be divided into as many as 128 data fields.

The numbers rightfully suggest that dBASE is a very powerful DBMS. The remaining sections of this chapter show you that it is also quite easy to use the program.

Starting and Exiting dBASE III Plus

Software programs arrive from the manufacturer on disks. After you properly configure and install the disk contents according to the documentation that accompanies the disks, you can access the program with just a few keystrokes. This section tells you how to start dBASE III Plus on a two floppy system, how to start it on a hard disk system, and how to exit the program.

Starting dBASE on a Two Floppy System

To start the dBASE III Plus program on a two floppy drive system, follow this procedure:

1. Access the A> disk operating system prompt on your computer system.
2. Insert the dBASE III Plus System Disk #1 into drive A.
3. Type **dbase** and press Enter.
4. After a copyright message appears, press Enter to assent to the License Agreement.
5. When the message `Insert System Disk 2 and press Enter, or press Ctrl-C to abort` appears at the bottom of the screen, remove System Disk #1 from drive A, insert System Disk #2 into drive A, and press Enter.

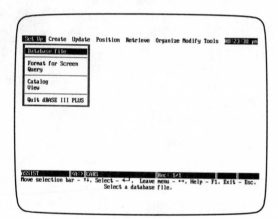

The dBASE III Plus Assistant screen is displayed.

Starting dBASE on a Hard Disk System

When you turn on your computer, if a menu of program names appears (such as a word-processing program, a spreadsheet program, and dBASE III Plus), you need only select the number of the dBASE III Plus option to access the dBASE program. However, if you see an operating system prompt such as C> or D> when you turn on your computer, you must set the current directory to the location of your dBASE program.

The following instructions assume that your dBASE III Plus program is located in the directory DBASE on drive C. Change the name of the directory or the letter of the drive if you have a different setup on your computer.

Follow these steps to start dBASE III Plus on a hard disk system:

1. Access the C> disk operating system prompt on your computer system.
2. Type **cd \dbase** and press Enter.

3. Type **dbase** and press Enter.

4. After a copyright message appears, press Enter to assent to the License Agreement.

The dBASE III Plus Assistant screen appears, as shown earlier.

Exiting dBASE III Plus

When you initially access the Assistant screen, a highlight bar rests on Set Up, the first menu choice. When you have finished using dBASE III Plus, you can exit the program by choosing Quit dBASE III PLUS from the list of options that appears when Set Up is highlighted.

When you are working in dot prompt mode (described in the next section), you bypass the dBASE menus and issue commands from the dot prompt. In dot prompt mode, you can type **quit** and press Enter to leave dBASE.

Exiting dBASE properly is absolutely essential. You must select the Quit dBASE III PLUS option on the Assistant screen or type **quit** at the dot prompt to exit. Otherwise, information in your database files may be lost.

Using Menu-Driven and Command-Driven Modes

If you access a software feature by selecting from menu options, you are working in menu-driven mode. The menu system in dBASE III Plus is called the *Assistant*. If you access a software feature by typing the instructions from the keyboard without benefit of menus, you are working in command-driven mode. When you bypass the dBASE menu system and type your own command line, you are working from the *dot prompt*. Both menu-driven mode and command-driven mode actively involve the user. Each is considered to be an example of interactive processing.

The Assistant Screen

The basic components of the Assistant screen, the menu-driven system that appears after you access the dBASE III Plus program, are the menu bar, the current time window, the submenu and user entry area, the command line, the status bar, the navigation line, and the message line. The Assistant screen in the example shows a command being selected, which will list only those database records that contain a yet-to-be-specified entry in the INTEREST field.

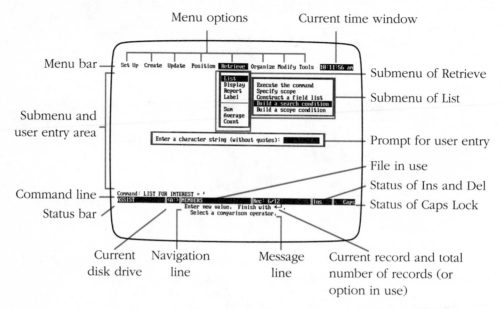

The *menu bar* across the top of the Assistant screen displays the major categories of dBASE operations. To select a horizontal menu bar option, press the right- or left-arrow key until your choice is highlighted. Do *not* press Enter to select an option.

The *current time window* appears in the upper right corner of the Assistant screen. The time, continuously updated, appears in this window.

The *submenu and user entry area* occupies the portion of the Assistant screen below the menu bar and above the command line. Submenus, referred to as *pull-down menus*, appear in columns. To select an option from a pull-down submenu, press the down- or up-arrow key to highlight your choice, and then press Enter. Some actions selected from submenus require additional user input. If that is the case, windows appear above the command line, prompting the user to enter the required input. To cancel the current submenu operation, press the Esc key.

The *command line* displays the current dBASE III Plus command being generated by the selections from the Assistant menus and any additional input from the user.

The *status bar* displays at the far left the mode indicator, which reflects the current operation. The next item on the status bar tells you which disk drive is active and

Understanding
File Types and
Limitations

Starting and
Exiting dBASE
III Plus

**Using Menu-Driven
and Command-
Driven Modes**

Learning
the
Keyboard

Accessing the
dBASE Help
Feature

An Overview of
the dBASE IV
Environment

Summary

which file is in use. The subsequent portion either indicates the current record and the total number of records, or displays information about the option in use. The remaining portions of the status bar indicate the status of toggle keys such as Ins and Caps Lock.

The *navigation* and *message* lines appear at the bottom of the screen. Generally the navigation line shows you how to move between menu or submenu options, and the message line indicates actions to complete the current menu option. Both lines may contain additional instructions to the user.

The Dot Prompt

For beginning users of a software package, menu-driven mode seems an easy, natural way of manipulating information. However, to use menu-driven mode, you often need to make several selections and respond to one or more screen prompts. In contrast, using command-driven mode—operating dBASE from the dot prompt—is a quick, efficient way to manipulate data *if* you know how to type the command.

A simple dBASE III Plus example illustrates the difference between using command-driven as opposed to menu-driven mode. Suppose, for example, that the current database contains an INTEREST field, and that the allowable entries in that field are Genealogy, Medical, History, and Military. Further assume that you want to list on-screen only those records for which the entry in the INTEREST field is *Genealogy*. Eight menu selections and one response to a screen prompt are required to complete the task using the Assistant screen.

If you bypass the menu system, you can type the dBASE command at the dot prompt and produce the desired results.

The single dot in the lower left corner of the screen prompts the user for the next command.

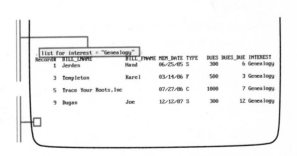

To access the dot prompt from the Assistant screen, press Esc until the screen clears except for a dot at the lower left corner. To restore the Assistant screen from the dot prompt, type **assist** and press Enter, or press the Assist (F2) function key.

Getting
Started

Designing
and Creating
a Database

Viewing,
Organizing,
and Updating
Data

Searching
the
Database

Designing
Reports and
Labels

Programming
in dBASE

347

(You learn about function keys in the next section.) Most dBASE illustrations in this book have the beginner in mind, and therefore focus on using the Assistant screen rather than the dot prompt.

Learning the Keyboard

You use many keys and key combinations to move around menus and execute dBASE III Plus commands. This section discusses some commonly used groups of keys: function keys and the keystrokes for processing and screen editing.

Function Keys

Function keys appear on all keyboards. Each software package, such as 1-2-3 or WordPerfect, assigns tasks to the function keys. dBASE III Plus has been programmed by the manufacturer to perform the following actions when you press the function key indicated.

F1 **Help**
Accesses the help feature.

F2 **Assist**
Restores the Assistant screen when pressed from the dot prompt.

F3 **List**
Displays the current database records without pausing.

F4 **Dir(ectory)**
Lists database file names along with the number of records, the date of the last update, and the size of each file.

F5 **Display Structure**
Shows the data structure of an active database file.

F6 **Display Status**
Shows the current processing situation, including the names of active files.

F7 **Display Memory**
Shows the contents of active memory variables.

F8 **Display**
Shows the contents of the data records, pausing after each screen.

F9 **Append**
Adds a data record to the end of the active database file.

F10 **Edit**
Displays the current record for editing.

An Overview of dBASE

Getting Started

Designing and Creating a Database

Viewing, Organizing, and Updating Data

Searching the Database

Designing Reports and Labels

Programming in dBASE

Keystrokes for Processing and Screen Editing

A few key combinations relate to processing activities. For example, pressing Ctrl-P toggles the printer on and off. (You press and hold down the Ctrl key, press the letter P, and then release both keys.) Pressing Ctrl-X erases the command line during interactive processing.

Numerous keys and key combinations allow you to perform screen editing tasks. For example, pressing the up-arrow key moves the cursor up one line or data field. Pressing Ctrl-T erases one word to the right of the cursor.

You don't need to memorize the key combinations. dBASE III Plus provides a box of reminders at the top of the screen.

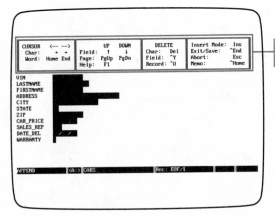

Keystrokes active when you add a record to an existing database.

For example, pressing Ctrl-U (shown as ^U on-screen) deletes the contents of the current record. The display of keystrokes varies depending on the current dBASE operation.

If the routine assistance you get through keystroke explanations, navigation lines, and message lines is insufficient, dBASE also provides a help facility to explain command options.

Accessing the dBASE Help Feature

As part of a trend toward easy-to-use software, most developers include an on-screen help facility accessed by pressing a function key. You reach the dBASE III

Plus help facility by pressing F1 (Help). Help is generally *context sensitive*, which means that Help messages and screens refer to the task or command you are performing when you request Help.

When you highlight Browse on the Update pull-down menu and then press F1 (Help), dBASE provides this on-screen assistance.

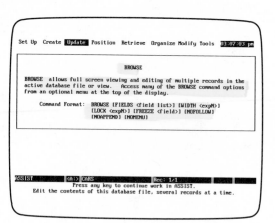

To exit the help screen, follow the instruction that appears in the navigation line: `Press any key to continue work in ASSIST.`

An Overview of the dBASE IV Environment

The latest version of dBASE—dBASE IV—makes major changes to the dBASE environment. This version of the program must be run on a hard disk system, and available file types and program limitations have been upgraded. For example, this version expands the list of types of files, allowing you to create such files as a master index file (.MDX extension) that relates all the index fields in one database. dBASE IV also increases the maximum number of fields per record to 255, as opposed to 128 in dBASE III Plus.

All function keys except Help (F1) have been reassigned. In addition, 10 more actions have been automated and assigned to the Shift and function key combinations.

Although you continue to start the program by typing **dbase**, you access a different interface screen. The Assistant has been replaced by a more sophisticated menu-driven interface called the *Control Center*.

An
Overview of
dBASE

**Getting
Started**

Designing
and Creating
a Database

Viewing,
Organizing,
and Updating
Data

Searching
the
Database

Designing
Reports and
Labels

Programming
in dBASE

```
 Catalog  Tools  Exit                                    3:23:56 pm
                        dBASE IV CONTROL CENTER
                        CATALOG: A:\UNTITLED.CAT

      Data      Queries     Forms     Reports    Labels   Applications
   <create>   <create>   <create>   <create>   <create>   <create>
   CUSTOMER




   File:        New file
   Description: Press ENTER on <create> to create a new file

   Help:F1  Use:←┘  Data:F2  Design:Shift-F2  Quick Report:Shift-F9  Menus:F10
```

The dBASE IV Control Center

Summary

In this chapter you explored the dBASE environment. You learned that dBASE III Plus is a powerful DBMS that can manage up to a billion records if sufficient memory exists. A menu-driven interface called the Assistant allows a beginner to tap the power of dBASE with little instruction. A command-driven interface, the dot prompt, provides a quick, efficient way to manipulate data once you know how to type the commands.

The chapter introduced you to the features of the Assistant screen: the menu bar, the current time window, the submenu and user entry area, the command line, the status bar, the navigation line, and the message line. Finally, the chapter acquainted you with the Help (F1) feature and summarized the changes in dBASE IV as compared to dBASE III Plus. Now that you have become familiar with the dBASE environment, you are ready to begin using dBASE III Plus by designing and creating a database, as described in the next chapter.

Review Questions

1. Describe some of the types of files you can create with dBASE III Plus.

351

2. Assuming that sufficient memory exists, what is the maximum number of records in a dBASE III Plus database?

3. What is the name of the screen you see when you access dBASE III Plus? Name the parts of the screen.

4. Contrast the layout of menu bar options with the layout of pull-down menu options. Include a description of how to select options from both types of menus.

5. What prompt is associated with the command-driven interface, and how do you access it from the menu-driven interface?

6. Differentiate the types of on-screen help available while using dBASE III Plus: Navigation line

   Message line

   Help box at the top of the screen

   Help (F1) function key

29 *Designing and Creating a Database*

An
Overview of
dBASE

Getting
Started

**Designing
and Creating
a Database**

Viewing,
Organizing,
and Updating
Data

Searching
the
Database

Designing
Reports and
Labels

Programming
in dBASE

You work with a database all the time—your own mind! Your mind stores an amazing amount of data (facts or assumptions). You, however, don't have to organize input to your mind in fixed categories, such as names, numbers, dates, places, and events. Somehow, if Columbus comes to mind, you know whether you mean Columbus, the capital city of Ohio, or Columbus, who discovered America. You know automatically whether 26450 is your ZIP code or the price you just paid for your new van. You don't have to plan input of data or retrieval of information. But when you need to share a vast amount of information with many others or to project the information from the shortcomings of the human memory—the electronic database management system becomes a very useful tool.

You can maintain a powerful database in computer memory. Keep in mind, however, that the computer is only a machine—it cannot work for you without structure and rules. The rules vary from one program to another. For example, if you type the phone number 123–4567 in a WordPerfect 5 document, the number appears just as you type it. If you type the same number into a 1-2-3 spreadsheet, however, the program displays the negative number –4444. A spreadsheet interprets the hyphen as a minus sign and subtracts the last four digits from the first three digits. You must take the time to learn the rules for data in each program you use.

The first step in the life cycle of any database is to design the structure of the data. Based on the design, you then create the structure and add records. A good DBMS, such as dBASE III Plus, also allows you to modify the structure and to change the contents of records.

After completing this chapter, you should know how to do the following:

- State the database objective
- Determine database inputs based on required outputs
- Select field names and field types
- Create a data dictionary
- Create and modify a database structure

353

- Add records to a database
- Understand how database creation differs in dBASE IV

Key Terms in This Chapter

Data dictionary   A listing of each database field and its characteristics.

Field type   The classification of data stored in the field, such as character, numeric, date, logical, or memo.

Append   Add a record to a database.

Designing a Database

Resist the urge to sit down at the keyboard and begin creating the database structure before you plan carefully what you expect the database to do. That is, what information is the database expected to provide? For example, suppose that you plan to create a name and address database and you select the following fields: name, address, city, state, ZIP code, and phone number. If you enter a name in a single *name* field (first name, then last name) you will not be able to produce an alphabetical listing of database records according to last name. However, if you create two name fields, *first name* and *last name*, you can produce the required listing.

Some simple planning techniques can help you design your DBMS. These techniques include stating the database objectives, analyzing the current system, determining inputs from outputs, and creating a data dictionary.

Stating the Database Objectives

To state the database objectives, write a clear and concise paragraph that describes how you plan to use the database. The statement should be brief (it should not include specific data, databases, or output reports) and should list who will use the data, what information needs must be met, and how timely the data must be collected and available. Refer to this statement as you design the database structure.

An Overview of dBASE

Getting Started

Designing and Creating a Database

Viewing, Organizing, and Updating Data

Searching the Database

Designing Reports and Labels

Programming in dBASE

Vehicle Sales Database

Statement of Objectives:

sales person:

Develop an information system that will provide management with new car sales information specific to each customer. Provide contact information and follow-up contact list; provide the service department with a record of warranty work performed on new cars that includes customer contact information. Information is collected by sales persons at the time of sale or the service writer at the time of service. Information is available in the information system within 48 hours.

24

A sample objectives statement for a vehicle sales database.

Analyzing the Current System

If you already use a paper or computer database system, you can use it as a starting point in designing a new database application. A system already in place can indicate what information, expected outputs, and data fields you must have in your database.

In the unlikely event that the current system is providing all required information, your task may be as simple as automating the manual system with dBASE III Plus or converting from other computer software to dBASE. Be sure to interview users of the current system to learn about the existing flaws and desired enhancements.

Determining Inputs from Outputs

The *outputs* from a database include reports, lists, and labels. If you first determine the desired outputs from your database, you then can select appropriate input fields. Unless your database needs are minimal, you should put this design phase in writing. First, create a list of the reports you want to receive from the database and write a brief objective statement about each report. Next, design the layout of each report, list, and label so that you can visualize your data fields.

A proposed
output listing
for a vehicle
sales
database.

Vehicle Sales Database

1. Sales Recap Report	*List of all new car sales for the month, organized by salesperson and date of delivery. Subtotal by salesperson and grand total at end of report. Include vehicle identification number, date of delivery, price paid, trade-in yes/no, first-time buyer yes/no, and warranty yes/no for each car sold.*
2. Customer List	*List of all customers, arranged alphabetically by last then first name. Include customer last name, first name, address, city, state, ZIP code, and phone number.*
3. Index Card Labels	*List of all customers, arranged by salesperson, by customer's last name and first name. Include Customer's last name, first name, address, city, state, ZIP code, phone number, and any comments.*

Several suggested layouts.

Sales Recap - month

Vehicle ID No.	Date of Delivery	Price Paid	Trade In	First Time	Warranty

Sales Rep: xxx

| xxxxxxx | mm/dd/yy | | | | |

Customer List - as of mm/dd/yy

Last Name, First Name *Address* *City, State ZIP* *Phone Number*	*Last Name, First Name* *Address*
Last Name, First Name *Address* *City, State Zip* *Phone Number*	

Customer Labels for index cards

Last Name, First Name *Address* *City, State ZIP* *Phone* *Sales Rep* *Comments*
Last Name, First Name *Address* *City, State ZIP* *Phone* *Sales Rep* *Comments*

As you design the layouts, determine in what order the information should appear, what totals and subtotals are necessary, and which database records you need. After you assemble the output-related information, you can establish a listing (often called a data dictionary) of up to 128 input fields necessary to produce the desired outputs.

An Overview of dBASE

Getting Started

Designing and Creating a Database

Viewing, Organizing, and Updating Data

Searching the Database

Designing Reports and Labels

Programming in dBASE

Creating a Data Dictionary

A *data dictionary* is a listing of each database field and its characteristics. A dBASE listing should include a description of each data item, the field name, the field type, size of the field, and number of decimal places.

	Vehicle Sales Data Dictionary				
Num	*Description*	*Field Name*	*Field Type*	*Width*	*Dec*
1	Vehicle ID Number	Vin	Char	10	
2	Customer Last Name	LastName	Char	12	
3	Customer First Name	FirstName	Char	10	
4	Customer Street Address	Address	Char	22	
5	Customer City	City	Char	15	
6	Customer State Code	State	Char	2	
7	Customer ZIP Code (10 digits)	ZIP	Char	10	
8	Price of Car	Car_Price	Num	8	2
9	Sales Rep Initials	Sales_Rep	Char	3	
10	Delivery Date	Date_Del	Date	8	
11	Warranty Purchased	Warranty	Log	1	
12	Trade-in Allowed	Trade_In	Log	1	
13	First-Time Buyer	First_Buy	Log	1	
14	Sales Rep Comments	Comments	Memo	10	
15	Phone	Phone	Char	14	

A sample data dictionary for a vehicle sales database.

The description column shown in the data dictionary does not become part of the database file. However, each field's name, type, and size becomes part of the actual database structure.

One final word of warning as you create the data dictionary: although you do not want to omit an important field, resist the "everything-but-the-kitchen-sink" approach of building in more data than you need. Any extra data takes up space, makes the system run slower, and costs money to maintain. Keep in mind that dBASE allows you to add, delete, and change data fields whenever necessary and with little effort.

Choosing a Field Name

Every DBMS requires you to choose a name for each data item (field) in your database. Field names in dBASE can be from 1 to 10 characters long and contain letters, numbers, and the underscore character. The first character must be a letter. Although N, for example, is a valid name for a field, the single-character name makes remembering what data the field contains difficult. Try to choose a field name that describes the data in the field. As an added suggestion, insert the underscore to improve readability. For example, you might name a last name field LAST_NAME instead of LNAME. Do not include any blank spaces in field names.

Selecting a Field Type

The field type tells a DBMS the classification of data stored in the field. Using dBASE, you may select one of five data types: character, numeric, date, logical, and memo. Select *Character* as the field type if one of the other categories, described in the following text, is not appropriate.

Numeric. Use the numeric data type for all fields containing values to be used in calculations. Caution: If data looks numeric but is not used in calculations (such as a phone number, ZIP code, or Social Security number), select the character data type.

Date. Use the date data type for all fields containing dates.

Logical. Use the logical data type for fields that contain a value representing true or false. You can type the value as upper- or lowercase T (True), F (False), Y (Yes), or N (No), as appropriate. For example, you might maintain a trade-in (yes or no) field in a vehicle sales database.

Memo. Use the memo data type to attach lengthy narrative about the current record. As a rule of thumb, use a character field in place of a memo field if you do not expect the memo to exceed 254 characters.

Specifying a Field Width

Use the field width specification to indicate the maximum number of characters or digits a field can hold. You must specify widths for two types of fields (character and numeric); dBASE supplies the widths for the three other types (date, logical, and memo).

Character. The field width can be as narrow as 1 or as wide as 254.

Designing a
Database

**Creating the
Database
Structure**

Adding
Records to
the Database

An Overview of
dBASE IV
Database Creation

Summary

An
Overview of
dBASE

Getting
Started

**Designing
and Creating
a Database**

Viewing,
Organizing,
and Updating
Data

Searching
the
Database

Designing
Reports and
Labels

Programming
in dBASE

Numeric. Enter a field width between 1 and 20, and a number of decimal places (Dec) that is at least two less than the specified width of the field. For example, if the largest unit price in your inventory record is 8 digits (6 digits and 2 decimal places), set the width at 10 to reserve space for a period (.) and a sign (–).

Date. dBASE automatically assigns a date field width of 8. Dates appear in the format dd/mm/yy (day/month/year), such as 01/09/44.

Logical. dBASE automatically assigns a logical field width of 1.

Memo. dBASE automatically assigns a memo field width of 10. The field in the record displays only the word memo; dBASE stores the memo contents at a location outside the database (.DBF) file.

The designing phase—deciding what fields to include—is the hard part of setting up a database. Creating the actual database structure is primarily a matter of typing, using the data dictionary as a reference.

Creating the Database Structure

To create a database structure using dBASE III Plus, you must first access a screen that prompts you to enter the field characteristics. To reach this screen, highlight Create on the Assistant menu bar, select Database file from the Create pull-down menu, specify the disk drive on which to store the database, and enter the name of the file.

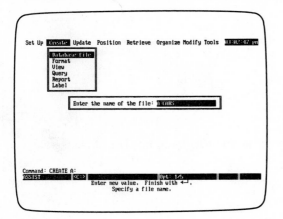

The menus and user prompt you see when you start to create a database named CARS on drive A.

As soon as you press Enter, you can begin to specify field characteristics. To complete the operation, you need to save the structure, list it, and make any necessary modifications.

Specifying Field Characteristics

After you press Enter to accept the file name you assigned to the new database, you access the screen for creating the database structure. The cursor rests in the Field Name column next to the number 1. You are ready to type the first field name in your database structure.

Type the first field name and press Enter. Character automatically appears in the Type column. If you want the field to be a character field, press Enter. Otherwise, select the field type by pressing the space bar until the appropriate data type (Numeric, Date, Logical, or Memo) appears, and then press Enter. Depending on the field type you specify, you may be required to enter information about the width and decimal places.

As you enter fields, use the keystrokes listed in the four boxes at the top of the screen. For example, use the left- and right-arrow keys to move the cursor within a field. Use the up- or down-arrow key to move up or down one field description, respectively. Make corrections using the Ins and Del keys. And use Ctrl-N to insert a field at the cursor location or Ctrl-U to delete the current field.

Continue to type field characteristics until you have defined all the data fields. Review the entries in your structure and correct any errors you find.

The field specifications for the vehicle sales database.

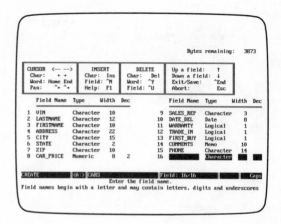

Designing a
Database

**Creating the
Database
Structure**

Adding
Records to
the Database

An Overview of
dBASE IV
Database Creation

Summary

An
Overview of
dBASE

Getting
Started

**Designing
and Creating
a Database**

Viewing,
Organizing,
and Updating
Data

Searching
the
Database

Designing
Reports and
Labels

Programming
in dBASE

Saving the Database Structure

After entering the field characteristics, you must save the newly created database structure. To save the structure, press Ctrl-End (^End), as indicated in the rightmost box at the top of the screen; this command saves the structure and exits to the Assistant screen. The navigation line displays prompts to confirm the current structure and to begin adding records. (To leave a dBASE III Plus screen without saving your work, press Esc to abort the process.)

Listing and Modifying the Database Structure

You should check the accuracy of the DBMS database structure by comparing it to the contents of the data dictionary.

To list a dBASE III Plus database structure, highlight Tools on the Assistant screen, and then select the List structure option from the pull-down menu.

A prompt appears for the user to direct the structure display to the screen or to a printer.

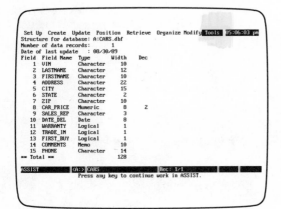

A screen display of the vehicle sales database structure.

To edit the database structure (alter a field width, insert a field, or select a different field type), highlight Modify on the Assistant screen and select Database file. Using the keystrokes listed in the boxes across the top of the screen, make the necessary changes and save the revised structure. When you are satisfied that the database structure reflects your database design, you can begin to add records.

Adding Records to the Database

After you design a database, create its structure, and collect data, you can begin entering records. Before you can add records, check the status line to make sure that the database to which you want to add records is active. If the name of the database you want does not appear, highlight the Set Up option on the Assistant screen menu bar, select Database file from the pull-down menu, and specify a disk drive and file name.

To add records to the active database, first highlight the Update option on the menu bar and select Append from the pull-down menu.

As soon as you press Enter, you can begin entering field contents. To complete the operation, you need to save the new records.   ∧ END

Using the Append Option

After you select Append, the cursor rests in the first field of an empty record. You then can begin to enter data, one field after another, down a column. After each completed record, the cursor rests on the first field of a new record.

Designing a
Database

Creating the
Database
Structure

**Adding
Records to
the Database**

An Overview of
dBASE IV
Database Creation

Summary

An
Overview of
dBASE

Getting
Started

**Designing
and Creating
a Database**

Viewing,
Organizing,
and Updating
Data

Searching
the
Database

Designing
Reports and
Labels

Programming
in dBASE

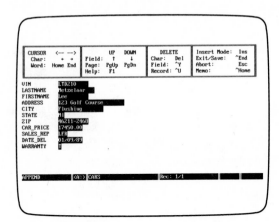

The first fields of a record being added to the vehicle sales database.

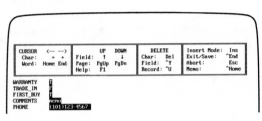

The rest of the fields for the same record being added to the database.

To enter data, position the cursor in the appropriate data field and type. Keep in mind the following guidelines as you enter data:

- To move automatically to the next field, you must fill the field. Typing a month-day-year combination in a date field or a Y (Yes) or N (No) in a logical field fills the field. A beep sounds when the field is filled, and then the cursor moves to the next field.

- To move to the next field if you have not filled the field, you must press Enter. For example, if you type a 12-character city name in a field defined as 18 characters wide, you have not filled the field.

- To move the cursor within a field, use the left- or right-arrow keys. If the cursor is at the beginning of a field when you press the left arrow, the cursor moves to the previous field; if the cursor is at the end of a field when you press the right arrow, the cursor moves to the next field.

- Do not enter slashes in a date field (dBASE does it for you); or any punctuation (a dollar sign or comma, for example) in a numeric field except a decimal point.

Saving Records

When you finish entering records, remember to save your work. Do not turn off the computer without first exiting your current dBASE operation, or you risk loss of data.

dBASE III Plus consistently applies two exit procedures throughout the program: press Esc to leave the current screen without saving your work; or press Ctrl-End to leave the current screen and save your work. Each time you complete the data fields in one record and position the cursor on the first field of a blank record, the previous record is saved to the database. You then can press Esc to stop adding records without saving the blank record. If, however, the cursor rests at the end of a completed record, press Ctrl-End to save and exit to the Assistant screen.

When you exit to the Assistant screen, the database is still open. To complete the saving process, you must close the database and exit dBASE by highlighting Set Up on the Assistant menu bar and selecting Quit dBASE III PLUS. When you are adding a large number of records, you should exit and save the database periodically and then reenter Append mode to continue adding records. Periodic saving reduces the likelihood of losing work during a power failure.

An Overview of dBASE IV Database Creation

When you design a dBASE IV database, as opposed to a dBASE III Plus database, you can include up to 255 fields instead of 128. In addition, you can select a sixth field type—*float*. You can use the float data type for scientific applications, which use very large or small numbers that are frequently multiplied. For example, select float as the field type when the entries will contain 5 or more digits or decimal places, such as pi or the speed of light.

Recall that a more sophisticated menu-driven interface in dBASE IV (the Control Center) replaces the Assistant in dBASE III Plus. Among the many menu enhancements in dBASE IV is the option "Save this database file structure." You can select this menu option to save a database structure instead of pressing the Ctrl-End key combination.

dBASE IV also provides two screen displays for adding records. Edit mode in dBASE IV resembles the Append screen in dBASE III Plus. The screen is blank except for one record in which fields are listed one to a row.

Designing a
Database

Creating the
Database
Structure

Adding
Records to
the Database

An Overview of
dBASE IV
Database Creation

Summary

An
Overview of
dBASE

Getting
Started

**Designing
and Creating
a Database**

Viewing,
Organizing,
and Updating
Data

Searching
the
Database

Designing
Reports and
Labels

Programming
in dBASE

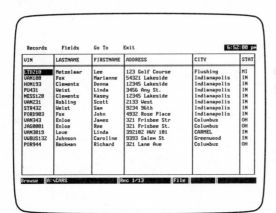

Records	Fields	Go To	Exit		6:52:00 pm	
VIN	LASTNAME	FIRSTNAME	ADDRESS		CITY	STAT
LTD210	Metzelaar	Lee	123 Golf Course		Flushing	MI
VAN100	Fox	Marianne	54321 Lakeside		Indianapolis	IN
HON193	Clements	Donna	12345 Lakeside		Indianapolis	IN
PU431	Weist	Linda	3456 Any St.		Indianapolis	IN
MESS128	Clements	Kasey	12345 Lakeside		Indianapolis	IN
VAN231	Robling	Scott	2133 West		Indianapolis	IN
STR432	Weist	Sam	9234 96th		Indianapolis	IN
FORD903	Fox	John	4932 Rose Place		Indianapolis	IN
VAN343	Enloe	James	321 Frisbee Str		Columbus	OH
JAG0001	Enloe	Ree	321 Frisbee St.		Columbus	OH
VAN3019	Love	Linda	392102 HWY 101		CARMEL	IN
VVBUS132	Johnson	Caroline	9393 Salem St		Greenwood	IN
POR944	Beckman	Richard	321 Lane Ave		Columbus	OH

| Browse | A:\CARS | | | Rec 1/13 | | File | | |

Browse mode in dBASE IV allows a number of records to be displayed on-screen at one time. Fields within a record occupy columns across the screen, and a record occupies each row.

Summary

In this chapter you learned that the most important part of developing a DBMS is the database design phase, which should include stating the database objectives, analyzing the current system, determining inputs from outputs, and creating a data dictionary. The data dictionary defines the field specifications. You learned that rules for data vary among programs and that dBASE III Plus places restrictions on field names, types, and sizes.

The chapter also illustrated how you use the Assistant screen to create and save a database structure, modify its structure, and add (append) records. Adding records is only one part of maintaining and using a database. In the next two chapters, you learn a variety of techniques for viewing, organizing, updating, and searching data.

Review Questions

1. What is the role of database objective statements in designing a DBMS?

2. Describe the components of a dBASE III Plus data dictionary and discuss its role in designing a DBMS.

3. Which of the following are not acceptable dBASE field names? State your reason(s).

   a. INV-NUM

   b. MF123DATA

   c. MF_123

   d. 123MF

   e. MF_123_DATA

4. What are the field types provided by dBASE III Plus?

5. Describe the process you use to access the dBASE III Plus screen for creating a database structure, creating the structure, and saving the structure.

6. Describe the layout of the dBASE III Plus screen for adding records and comment on the process for saving a newly entered record.

7. Contrast the features of dBASE III Plus and dBASE IV concerning field types and record entry screens.

An
Overview of
dBASE

Getting
Started

Designing
and Creating
a Database

**Viewing,
Organizing,
and Updating
Data**

Searching
the
Database

Designing
Reports and
Labels

Programming
in dBASE

30 *Viewing, Organizing, and Updating Data*

To make the information in your database accessible, you first need to learn the features of your DBMS software, design the database, create the database structure, and add records to the database. After these tasks are accomplished, the next step is to learn how to view the data in a meaningful form and with the assurance that you can rely on the accuracy of what you see.

The purpose of this chapter is to introduce the dBASE commands that update the database and control the display of record contents. dBASE provides commands to show the contents of one or more records on-screen or send the data as output to a printer. Furthermore, you can change the order in which the records appear. With the Assistant, you easily can keep the database contents current by editing and deleting records; making the required changes promptly is up to you!

After completing this chapter, you should know how to do the following:

- Position the record pointer
- List one or all records to the screen
- Sequence records on the field of your choice
- Revise records in Edit or Browse mode
- Replace field contents
- Delete records from the database

Key Terms in This Chapter

Browse mode	A screen displaying multiple records with fields organized horizontally across the screen.
Edit mode	A screen displaying one record with fields organized vertically down the screen.

Index	The process of organizing each record by pointing to a tag for every record in the database. Tags (sometimes called index records) contain only the record key and instructions about the location of the complete record. Records are not physically rearranged when organized by an index.
Record key	A field on which to organize records. For example, use the LASTNAME field in a vehicle sales database as the *record key* to organize records by customers' last names.
Record pointer	An internal dBASE index file, separate from the database, which stores the sequence of numbers that point to where the records are stored in the database.
Sort	The process of physically organizing each database record on disk according to the contents of a select field (record key).

▲

Positioning the Record Pointer

When viewing or manipulating data, you often need to know which record is the current one. When you create a database file, the records are assigned numbers reflecting the order in which the records were entered. The record pointer stores the number of the current record, and the number is constantly updated to reflect the record being processed.

To position the record pointer, highlight Position on the Assistant menu bar and select Goto Record from the pull-down menu. You then can choose to go to the top record in the database, the bottom record in the database, or specify a record by its record number.

This sequence of menu selections moves the record pointer to record #4.

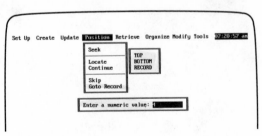

Viewing Data

To view data records that have been stored in an existing database file, highlight the Retrieve option on the Assistant menu bar, and then select either List or Display. One, some, or all of the data fields in the current record, in all existing records, or in selected records will appear on the screen or be sent as output to a printer.

Using the List and Display Commands

After you select List or Display from the Retrieve pull-down menu, dBASE III Plus displays a window to the right of the pull-down menu.

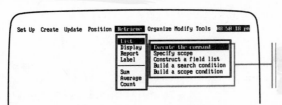

Five options appear in the window after you select either List or Display.

The first selection in the window is "Execute the command." When you select List and then "Execute the command," dBASE prompts you to indicate whether the output should be sent to the printer or to the screen. All fields in all records are then sent to the printer or displayed on-screen.

Record numbers

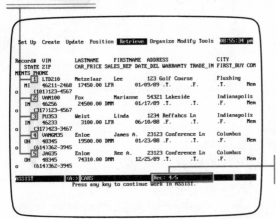

This screen display was produced by executing a List command when the vehicle sales database containing five records was in use. Every field in each record lists to the screen, even though the status bar indicates that the current record is #4 out of 5.

The current record is #4 of 5 records.

An
Overview of
dBASE

Getting
Started

Designing
and Creating
a Database

**Viewing,
Organizing,
and Updating
Data**

Searching
the
Database

Designing
Reports and
Labels

Programming
in dBASE

If a record contains more than 80 characters of information, its contents wrap around to the next display line, filling as many rows as necessary. The resulting display is often difficult to read.

If you choose Display instead of List, and then select "Execute the command," only the current record appears on-screen—record #4 in the example vehicle sales database.

Of the remaining four selections in the List or Display window, one option (Construct a field list) allows you to limit the *fields* that appear within displayed records. The other three options allow you to limit your view of *records* by setting scope and search conditions; these options are discussed in the next chapter on searching data.

Constructing a Field List

Periodically, a listing should be made of the complete contents of every record in the database. The listing can be used to verify the accuracy of data entry and to reenter data should equipment failure destroy the electronic database. You seldom, however, need to display the information in every field when you use the database on a day-to-day basis. You can select only those fields to provide information for a specific task.

From the Retrieve pull-down menu, choose List and then select "Construct a field list" to limit the display of fields in the vehicle sales records. Fields are limited to last name, first name, phone number, sales representative, and date delivered.

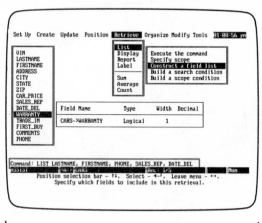

Reading a display of limited fields is much easier than reading all the fields in a record.

An Overview of dBASE

Getting Started

Designing and Creating a Database

Viewing, Organizing, and Updating Data

Searching the Database

Designing Reports and Labels

Programming in dBASE

Organizing Data

If you maintain your database electronically, you can rearrange records according to the contents of any field you choose. For example, you can order records in a vehicle sales database by delivery date, customer last name, price paid, or salesperson. In database terminology, the field that your database records are organized around is the *record key*.

Record keys indicate *what* to organize. In terms of *how* to organize, dBASE offers two choices: sorting and indexing. Both methods result in an arrangement of database records in a sequence that makes sense to you; but each method works differently. Initially, records are stored on disk by dBASE in the order you enter them. If you choose to reorder records by indexing, you do not physically rearrange the original records sorted on disk. The indexed records only appear in a different arrangement on-screen or in printed output. If, however, you choose to reorder records by sorting, you create a second database on disk in which the records are physically rearranged.

Using Record Keys

Before you decide how to organize your records, you must select useful record keys. All files have one or more data items suitable for a record key. For example, suppose that you keep a birthday database that holds just four fields: last name, first name, birth month, and birth date. You enter names and dates as your family and friends come to mind—that is, in no particular sequence—knowing that dBASE can later arrange the records in an order you specify.

To pick the record key(s) for these birthday records, first decide how you could use a rearranged set of records. You could rearrange the records alphabetically on the last name if you want to look up a specific person's birthday. Your record key would be the LASTNAME field. If you want to see at a glance how many birthday cards to buy for February, you could rearrange the original order by birth month. The BIRTHMONTH field can be another record key. Anytime you use your database, you can select any field to be a record key.

Indexing Records

Indexing records is generally preferred over sorting. Database records organized with an index are not physically sorted. The original database remains intact, and dBASE creates a user-specified index (called a *master index*) in a separate file with an .NDX extension. Each separate index contains only the record key—just a small part of the whole record—and instructions (pointers) to locate each whole record.

One advantage of an index is the speed with which records are rearranged. An index reorders records quickly because the contents of the index are very small records. Unlike a sort operation, an index operation does not need to read each large record into dBASE. Instead, dBASE reads each shorter record key in the index, rearranges the record keys, and displays or prints the records in the order of the record number in the index.

To create an index, highlight the Organize option on the Assistant menu bar and select Index from the pull-down menu. After you respond to the prompt to enter the index (record) key expression, provide a disk drive and file name for storing the index.

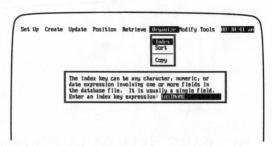

After reordering the records in a vehicle sales database on the LASTNAME field and issuing the List command, dBASE displays this screen. The records no longer appear in order by record number, but instead are listed in alphabetical order by last name.

Revised order of record numbers |⊢

Records in order by last name |⊢

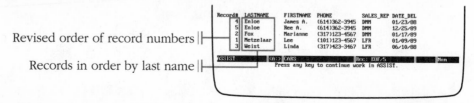

You can put an index in use at the time you open a database by highlighting Set Up on the Assistant menu bar, selecting Database file, and responding Y (Yes) to the prompt Is the file indexed? [Y/N]. Select the name of the desired index from a window displaying the available index files.

Sorting Records

Sorting involves physically arranging each record according to a selected record key. You might, for instance, sort on the date of a car sale in descending order (most recent date first) and the last name of the car buyer in ascending order. Mixing the Date field type and Character field type is fairly easy in a sort operation. (The same

An Overview of dBASE

Getting Started

Designing and Creating a Database

Viewing, Organizing, and Updating Data

Searching the Database

Designing Reports and Labels

Programming in dBASE

combination in an index operation would require converting a Date field to a Character field prior to rearranging records.)

Sorting a file is more time-consuming than indexing it because entire records must be moved, often several times, before the sort is complete. The results of a sort are placed in a separate file, thereby requiring much more disk space than an index. One advantage to a sort is that you can specify several keys, mixing data types as well as ascending and descending options for each sort key. If you master dBASE's powerful index features, however, there are few occasions when you need a sort.

To create a separate database of sorted records based on the contents of the current dBASE III Plus database, highlight the Organize option on the Assistant menu bar and select Sort from the pull-down menu. After you select the sort (record) key, you must provide a disk drive and a unique file name for storing the sorted database.

Revising Record Contents

A database is useful only if you update its contents on a regular basis. Some databases require considerable editing. In a patient records database, for example, the addresses, insurance providers, and places of employment change frequently. Other databases require less maintenance. For example, the field contents concerning vehicle identification number and car sales price won't change in a vehicle sales database (unless there was an error in the original entry). If the vehicle sales database is to be used for future contact with previous buyers, however, then any changes in a customer's phone number and address should be incorporated.

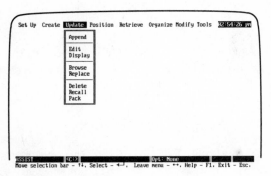

To revise database records, use the Update options on the dBASE III Plus Assistant menu.

Select Append to add records and Display to view the current record. Select Edit or Browse to view existing records and make changes. If you select Edit mode, you see one record at a time on-screen. If instead you access Browse mode, you see multiple records per screen, one record per line. The remaining options allow you to replace field contents and remove unwanted records.

Editing in Edit Mode

Edit mode displays one record at a time, in the same layout you see when you select Append. Data is displayed one field per line using as many screens as necessary to display the record. A dBASE III Plus record structure can have as many as 128 fields. As you scroll down (or up) the screen, fields move off the top (or bottom) of the screen and others move onto the screen. Scrolling the record structure gives you much the same effect as looking through a movie camera as it pans a view of a tall building.

Key assignments in Edit mode

To edit a specific record, position the record pointer on the appropriate record number, highlight Update on the Assistant menu bar, and then select Edit. The current record appears on-screen.

The instructions in the help boxes at the top of the screen remind you how to position the cursor. For example, while you are in Edit mode, you can press PgUp or PgDn to access records prior to and following the initial record, respectively. After you make the required changes, press Ctrl-End to save the revisions and restore the Update pull-down menu.

Editing in Browse Mode

Use Browse mode when you want to see and edit more than one record on-screen at one time. The Browse screen is organized into rows (records) and columns (fields).

An Overview of dBASE

Getting Started

Designing and Creating a Database

Viewing, Organizing, and Updating Data

Searching the Database

Designing Reports and Labels

Programming in dBASE

Fields appear from left to right across the screen in the order each was defined in the database structure. Most records are too long to fit on-screen from left to right; furthermore, most databases have too many records to fit on a single screen, top to bottom. In Browse mode, your screen becomes a window, panning left and right or up and down the database.

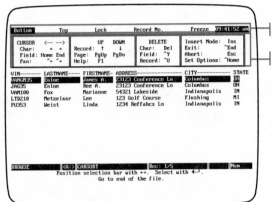

Browse menu bar

Key assignments in Browse mode

To access Browse mode, highlight Update on the Assistant menu bar, and then select Browse. Multiple records appear on-screen.

The instructions in the help boxes at the top of the screen are nearly identical to those found in Edit mode except for the addition of Pan and Set Options. Press the Pan keys—Ctrl-left arrow or Ctrl-right arrow—to scroll through the fields (columns) in the database records. Press the Set Options key combination—Ctrl-Home—to display the Browse menu bar at the top of the screen.

Three options on the Browse menu bar relate to positioning the cursor: Bottom (last record in the database), Top (first record in the database), and Record No. (your choice of record number). Select Lock from the menu bar to keep a specified number of columns (fields) on-screen. For example, consider locking in the name-related fields in the vehicle sales database so that you can see the car sales associated with each field of data in a record that extends beyond the edge of the screen. Use Freeze to limit the cursor's movement to one field—for example, when you have many changes to make to just one field in the database.

You make most changes to a database one record at a time, as described in the preceding text. dBASE does, however, provide the means to replace a field's contents in some or all records with a single command, as described in the text that follows.

Replacing Field Contents

Many DBMS software packages, including dBASE, allow you to replace field contents on a global level or on a selective basis. For example, suppose that a sales representative in a vehicle sales database makes a name change. Formerly the salesperson's initials were DMM; now the initials are DMR. You don't need to revise each record individually.

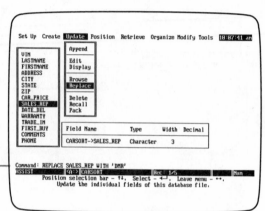

To replace all the occurrences of the old initials with the new initials in a single command sequence, first select the Replace option from the Update menu, and then highlight the SALES_REP field name.

A partially completed command line to replace the contents of a field.

To complete the command sequence, you indicate that the replacement initials must be applied to only one salesperson, not all salespersons. You can limit the replacement operation by specifying a search condition in which the contents of the SALES_REP field must be "DMM" in order for the initials to be replaced by "DMR." You learn more about search conditions in the next chapter.

Deleting Records

Part of the updating process includes removing unwanted records from your database. Some databases require more records to be deleted than other databases. For example, a historical database such as CARS, which contains a history of past sales, requires few if any deletions. A database of patient records may require frequent deletions as patients are no longer active. In many DBMS software packages, including dBASE III Plus, deleting records is a two-part process. Records first are marked for deletion, and then they are physically removed.

In dBASE III Plus, when a record is marked for deletion, it remains in the database with the other records. The records marked for deletion can either appear with

An Overview of dBASE

Getting Started

Designing and Creating a Database

Viewing, Organizing, and Updating Data

Searching the Database

Designing Reports and Labels

Programming in dBASE

asterisks along with other records in the database, or the records can be hidden from view—as if they were not in the database. In the patient record example, leaving deleted records in the database for a short period of time may be desirable in case a patient returns. A record marked for deletion can be "undeleted" (recalled). If, after a longer period of time, a patient has not returned, the marked record can be physically removed from the database.

Marking Records for Deletion

In many DBMS software packages, including dBASE III Plus, an extra character is added to the length of the record so that the program can store a code indicating whether the record is to be deleted or not. You can mark records individually, or you can mark an entire group of records. While you are in Edit mode, pressing Ctrl-U marks the current record for deletion.

Sometimes you may need to delete an entire group of records. For example, suppose that you want to remove all the records in the CARS database for sales representative LFR. You can highlight Update on the Assistant menu bar, select the Delete option, and choose "Build a search condition" to find all records with LFR in the SALES_REP field. Executing the command causes all records that meet the search condition to be marked for deletion.

If you list all records in the database, you see an asterisk (*) in the first position of those marked for deletion.

Records marked for deletion can be unmarked in dBASE III Plus using the Recall option on the Update menu.

Using the Pack Command

To physically remove all records in the database that are marked for deletion, highlight Update on the Assistant menu bar and select Pack. The Pack command copies the database, omitting all records marked for deletion. dBASE III Plus packs the database without displaying any warning message asking you to confirm the command. After the database is packed, the deleted records cannot be recovered.

Before removing records, an excellent practice is to make a backup copy of the database. Then, if you eliminate records accidentally, you can restore the old database and try again.

An Overview of dBASE IV Enhancements

A number of improvements in the way records are viewed, organized, and updated have been included in dBASE IV. A Quick Report option, available by pressing Shift-F9, replaces the dBASE III Plus List command.

Quick Report produces a more formal-looking list with a date, page numbers, and column headings.

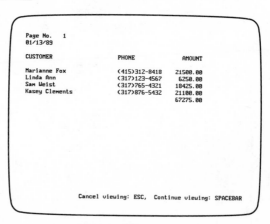

dBASE IV uses a master index concept where up to 49 indexes are stored as one large table with the same name as the database. All indexes are updated anytime data in the database changes. You can create an index at the time you create the database structure or through the Data panel on the Control Center.

More menu options for editing are available in dBASE IV. For example, you can change the size of a data field for viewing without changing the actual size of the

Positioning
the Record   Viewing   Organizing
Pointer   Data   Data

Revising
Record   Deleting
Contents   Records

An Overview
of dBASE IV
Enhancements   **Summary**

field in the database. While in Edit mode, you can search the database backward and forward or search the database using index keys.

Summary

In this chapter you learned to view records using the List and Display commands. Using the "Construct a field list" option, you can limit the display of fields and arrange them in any order you specify.

Records are originally arranged in the database in the order you added them. You learned to organize the database using data from fields in each record. Sorting a database means to create a second database with the records arranged according to the data in one or more fields. Indexing a database means to create a special file, called an index. While indexed records appear rearranged, they are not physically sorted.

You also learned to revise records in both Edit mode (one record per screen) and Browse mode (multiple records per screen). Another form of edit, Replace, allows you to make the same change to many records in the database at one time. You also can update a database by marking and deleting records.

Once you master viewing and maintaining the database, you can put the database to use—executing the searches discussed in the next chapter.

Review Questions

1. What is the function of the record pointer?

2. Differentiate the purpose of the List and Display commands.

3. What does it mean to construct a field list?

4. Explain how an indexed database is different than a sorted database.

5. Briefly discuss the differences between Edit and Browse mode.

6. How is the Replace command used to update records?

7. Describe the process of deleting records from a database.

31 *Searching the Database*

An
Overview of
dBASE

Getting
Started

Designing
and Creating
a Database

Viewing,
Organizing,
and Updating
Data

**Searching
the
Database**

Designing
Reports and
Labels

Programming
in dBASE

If your database is small and your information needs are simple, viewing records in either Browse or Edit mode (as described in the last chapter) may meet your database search requirements. However, as databases increase in size--in both number of fields and number of records--search criteria can become complex, increasing the search time dramatically. For example, in a medical-center database of several thousand patients, each record may contain 50 fields (name fields, complete-address fields, physical-description fields, prior-medical-history fields, and so on). Instead of searching records by a single string (such as the name of the referring doctor), you might want to find the names and phone numbers of all patients over 45 years of age, with a family history of heart disease, and who have not had an electrocardiogram within the last 2 years.

Searching for records in your database may be the most important function you perform. To edit large numbers of records or print reports and labels, you must be able to tell your DBMS what records you want to access. dBASE III Plus offers several commands and techniques for searching a database. For example, all the commands on the Assistant's Retrieve menu allow you to build a search condition that controls access to multiple records. Another command simply searches for the first record that meets a search condition. Still another technique allows you to establish a filter so that you can access only the records in which you are interested. dBASE III Plus search techniques can be divided into three categories: those that interactively perform a sequential search, those that interactively search an indexed database, and those that establish search conditions in files stored on disk.

After completing this chapter, you should know how to do the following:

- Establish search conditions
- Limit the scope of a search
- Differentiate the Locate and Seek commands
- Set a database filter
- Create a Query (.QRY) file

Key Terms in This Chapter

Filter

A search process for hiding database records that do not match specified search conditions.

Interactive search

A query in which all the steps to establish a search condition(s) and execute a search-related command must be entered from the keyboard.

Query

A synonym for *search*.

Relational operator

A symbol used in a search to select a record based on a variety of data matches or numeric conditions. An operator shows the relationship between data and search criteria.

Search string

A user-specified search condition for accessing selected records in a database.

Understanding Relational Operators

Using operators, you can state complex search conditions. dBASE allows you to select the following relational operators through the Assistant:

=	Equal to
<=	Less than or equal to
<	Less than
>	Greater than
>=	Greater than or equal to
<>	Not equal to

By looking at a few examples of relational operators used in search conditions, you will understand how all the operators can be applied to Character, Numeric, and Date fields. Select the Equal to (=) operator to enter exact match search criteria. For example, you can create a search condition in a vehicle sales database that finds all records in which the salesperson's initials are LFR.

Use the Greater than (>) operator to find all records where the field content exceeds the stated amount. For example, you can create a search condition that finds all customers who paid more than $15,000 dollars for a car. On the other hand, you can

An Overview of dBASE

Getting Started

Designing and Creating a Database

Viewing, Organizing, and Updating Data

Searching the Database

Designing Reports and Labels

Programming in dBASE

find all persons who paid less than $15,000 by using the Less than (<) operator. You also can use the Greater than or Less than operators to locate character-field contents that fall after (>) or before (<) a certain letter or letter combination. For example, to find the records of all car buyers whose last names start with M or a subsequent letter of the alphabet, you can specify **>"L"** as the search condition. Imagine the searches you can perform by applying basic operators to dates. If you use the search condition **<01/15/90**, for example, you can find all records dated before January 15, 1990.

A good DBMS allows you to establish more than one search condition for a query. For example, using dBASE, you can search for all records in which the salesperson's initials are LFR AND the car price exceeds $15,000. You also can search for all records in which the last name is Enloe OR Fox. You use relational operators in several dBASE searches.

Executing a Sequential Search

Searching a file sequentially is perhaps the easiest method to understand. This type of search checks every record against the search condition(s), and therefore the process is relatively slow. This method of searching generally is efficient only when most of the records in the database meet the search condition(s). You must search a database sequentially if you do not establish an index for the field being searched (see "Indexing Records" in Chapter 30).

Using dBASE III Plus, you can search sequentially after specifying a search condition by selecting the List, Locate, and Continue options. You also can set a filter for the database.

Building a Search Condition

When you establish a search condition, you specify that the contents of one or more fields in a record must bear a specified relationship to the stated field contents in order for a record to be selected. All the options on the Assistant's Retrieve pull-down menu allow you to build a search condition.

To build an exact-match search condition for finding records in a vehicle sales database in which the sales representative's initials are LFR, first highlight Retrieve on the Assistant menu bar, select List on the pull-down menu, and select "Build a search condition." From the list of field names that appears in a window on the left side of the screen, choose the field to be searched--SALES_REP in this example.

383

The list of available fields

The command line

After you select a field name, a menu of relational operators appears in a window on the right side of the screen. Select the relational operator = Equal To.

Relational operators

The command being expanded

Enter the character string **LFR** for an exact-match search condition.

The command being expanded

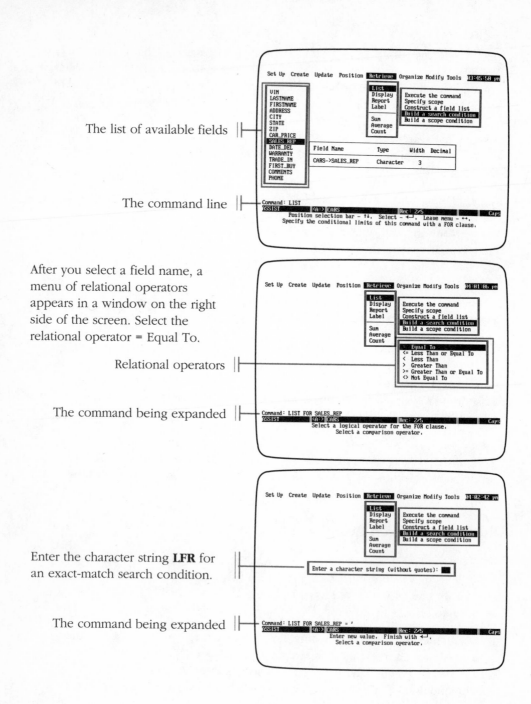

An Overview of dBASE

Getting Started

Designing and Creating a Database

Viewing, Organizing, and Updating Data

Searching the Database

Designing Reports and Labels

Programming in dBASE

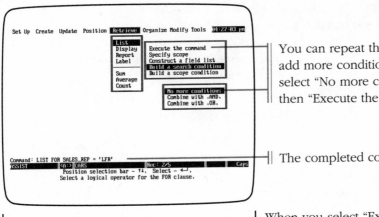

You can repeat the process and add more conditions, or you can select "No more conditions" and then "Execute the command."

The completed command

When you select "Execute the command," dBASE searches every record in the current database. In this case, the search lists those records in which the content of the field SALES_REP equals LFR. Only two records meet the search condition.

Searching with Locate and Continue

If you want to edit each record that dBASE III Plus finds in a search, select the Locate option on the Position pull-down menu to initiate the search. When you execute the command, the first record that meets the search criteria becomes the current record. You then can select the Edit command from the Update pull-down menu to access the record and make the required changes.

After you change the first record meeting the search criteria, select the Continue option on the Position pull-down menu. dBASE remembers the search criteria specified in the last Locate command and looks for the next record that meets the criteria. Keep selecting Continue and editing records until the message End of LOCATE scope appears on-screen.

Searching an Indexed Database

Searching an indexed database has two advantages over searching a database in which all records are arranged in the order in which they were entered. First, when records are organized on the field to be searched, all the records meeting the search criteria already are grouped together in the database. In addition, you can apply the Seek command to an indexed database to find the first occurrence of a record meeting the search criteria. You thereby can find the desired records in seconds, no matter how many records are in the database.

Searching an Indexed Database Sequentially

You can search an indexed database sequentially. The advantage of sequentially searching an indexed file is that the records are accessed and displayed in the order of the controlling index. For example, a vehicle sales database might be indexed on the customer's last name field.

When you list the file using the search condition **SALES_REP = "DMM"**, only the records for the designated salesperson appear, and those records are already sequenced by the customer's last name. The salesperson now has a phone list in alphabetical order.

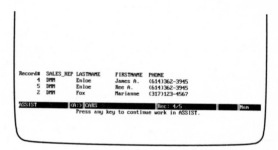

Searching with Seek

If you use the Locate command to find records meeting specified criteria in a large database, every record must be accessed because the command searches a database sequentially. You can greatly reduce search time by using the Seek command. Keep in mind, however, that you can apply Seek only to an indexed database.

The Seek command searches the current index, finds the first occurrence of a record meeting the search criteria based on the current index, and sets the record pointer to that record. After the record pointer is positioned, select "Build a scope condition" from the Retrieve menu to list any subsequent records in which the contents of the indexed field match the search criteria.

Suppose, for example, that you open a vehicle sales database and set an index to SALES_REP (sales representative). By setting this index, you are specifying that all records for salesperson LFR should be grouped together.

An Overview of dBASE

Getting Started

Designing and Creating a Database

Viewing, Organizing, and Updating Data

Searching the Database

Designing Reports and Labels

Programming in dBASE

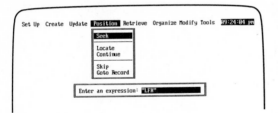

Highlight Position on the Assistant menu bar, select Seek, and enter the expression **"LFR"** when prompted for the search condition.

When you press the right or left arrow to restore the Assistant menu, the record pointer is pointing at the first record for sales representative LFR.

Now that the record pointer marks the first occurrence of LFR in the SALES_REP field and all the LFR records are grouped together because of the current index, select an option from the Retrieve pull-down menu. For example, select List, and then select the "Build a scope condition" option. The menus for the scope condition are identical to the menus for building a search condition. If you specify the scope condition **SALES_REP = "LFR"**, the command line at the bottom of the screen reads LIST WHILE SALES_REP = "LFR". dBASE lists every record, beginning with the current record, until reaching the first record whose SALES_REP field does not contain LFR. If your database is very large, using the Seek command is the best way to create a list of records in an acceptable amount of time.

Using a Query File

The dBASE III Plus search commands that use sequential and indexed files have one thing in common. These commands are interactive. Each time you want to use them, you must enter all parts of the commands from the keyboard. If you want to repeat the same search or have someone else perform the job for you, the commands must be typed again; this typing is tedious work and may lead to errors in entering specifications. You can, however, create a Query file using dBASE III Plus and store the search criteria on disk.

A Query file stores search specifications that determine which database records are accessed. The process for creating a Query file, which is similar to that used for building a search condition, involves making menu selections and responding to prompts. You can connect up to seven logical statements to be used to filter unwanted records from the database. All records that do not meet a condition established in the Query file are filtered out of the database. The filtered records are not physically removed, but you cannot access them until you remove the filter(s) by selecting another database or exiting dBASE.

Suppose that you want to access only those records in a vehicle sales database in which the contents of the CAR_PRICE field equal or exceed $20,000. Highlight Create on the Assistant menu and select Query. After you indicate a disk drive, you must provide a file name, such as CAR20000.

dBASE displays the Query file screen, with the Query Definition menu bar at the top.

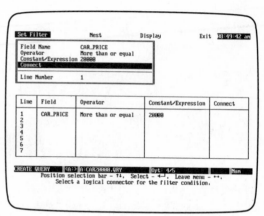

Highlight Set Filter and enter **CAR_PRICE** next to the Field Name option. (To enter the field name, press F10 to access a menu of field names, and then select the desired field name from the menu.) Proceed to select the Operator option and choose "More than or equal." To complete the Line 1 filter specifications, select the Constant/Expression option and enter the number **20000**. After you enter up to 7 filter statements, exit Create Query mode and save the file.

When you want to access your database using the filtering conditions stored in the Query file, highlight Set Up on the Assistant menu bar, select Query, and choose the name of the Query file—in this case, CAR20000. Then highlight Retrieve, select List, and immediately choose "Execute the command."

Only database records with a CAR_PRICE that equals or exceeds $20,000 are displayed.

Understanding
Relational
Operators

Executing a
Sequential
Search

Searching
an Indexed
Database

Using a
Query File

An Overview of
dBASE IV Searching
Enhancements

Summary

An Overview of dBASE IV Searching Enhancements

dBASE IV offers a greatly expanded search capability. For example, a new feature, Soundex, lets you find field contents based on a "sounds like" search condition.

The Queries panel on the Control Center in dBASE IV performs the same function as Create Query does in dBASE III Plus. The panel provides a means of creating and storing a query that can be used repeatedly and updated as necessary. The Queries panel is more powerful and easier to use than the query feature in dBASE III Plus.

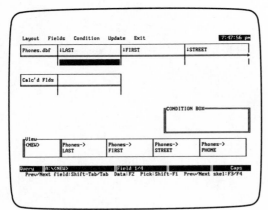

Starting from the Queries panel, you can access a screen on which to specify both query and view conditions on the same screen.

dBASE IV relies on the Queries panel for search activities and has removed access to most of the commands on the dBASE III Plus Position and Retrieve menus. In dBASE IV, these menu selections are part of the Data, Form, Reports, and Labels menu functions.

Summary

In this chapter, you learned that search conditions can be specified in conjunction with many dBASE commands. These search conditions also can be placed in a Query file and stored on disk for subsequent use without entering specifications from the keyboard. Queries act as filters that limit which records you can list; the queries deny access to the unwanted records as if they were not in the file.

Databases can be searched using sequential methods that cause each record to be examined for a match to the specified search criteria. Because all records are searched, this process is slow, particularly when accessing large databases. If a database is indexed, the index can be searched in seconds no matter how many records are in the database.

Search conditions include relational operators applied to Character, Numeric, Logical, and Date fields. In many cases, a simple listing of records that meet the search criteria is sufficient to fit your current output needs. If you need more polished output, you can create custom reports and labels, as described in the next chapter.

Review Questions

1. Of what importance are relational operators in searching a database?

2. Differentiate the steps you would take to search sequentially an indexed database as opposed to a nonindexed database.

3. Describe the purpose of the Locate and Continue command combination.

4. What kind of situation might require using the Locate and Continue commands as opposed to a Seek command?

5. Discuss the idea of filtering records in a database as a form of searching for records.

6. Briefly comment on a primary advantage and a primary disadvantage of using a Query file.

7. Describe the process for creating a Query file.

An
Overview of
dBASE

Getting
Started

Designing
and Creating
a Database

Viewing,
Organizing,
and Updating
Data

Searching
the
Database

**Designing
Reports and
Labels**

Programming
in dBASE

32 *Designing Reports and Labels*

In the preceding chapter, you saw the usefulness of being able to conduct simple searches for records in your database and to display those records on-screen. Suppose, however, that you would like to use the vehicle sales database presented earlier to create a multiple-page report—such as a sales report that begins with a title; lists items including vehicle identification number, date of delivery, and car price; and subtotals the sales according to the salesperson. Or suppose that you would like to send out many letters at once to new car buyers and print mailing labels. dBASE III Plus provides you with more flexible and powerful ways of displaying your data through custom reports and labels.

With the dBASE report feature, you create a custom report form that can be saved in a report form file (with an .FRM extension). The report form specifies the details of the report's headings, the appearance of data, and the calculation of subtotals and totals.

The dBASE custom label generator lets you easily create labels for file folders, mailing labels, inventory tags, Rolodex address files, and many other uses. The feature guides creation of a custom label form, which can be saved in a label form file (with an .LBL extension). The label form specifies the details of data placement and the number of labels printed across a page.

After completing this chapter, you should be familiar with the following:

- The elements of custom reports and labels
- The options on the report form and label form menus
- How to create, save, and print custom reports and labels

▼

Key Terms in This Chapter

Report form file   A file (.FRM) that contains specifications about the format of a custom report.

Control break field   A field in a record on which a calculation is based or which triggers a subtotal to be printed.

Label form file   A file (.LBL) that contains specifications about the format of a custom label.

▲

Understanding Common Report Features

Before you begin entering specifications for a report, you must decide what data you want in your report, what subtotals should be calculated, and how the data should appear. Ideally, report designs are readily available, having been developed during the database design phase of implementing a DBMS (discussed in Chapter 29).

This report was created from the vehicle sales database. The labeled portions of the figure illustrate components that are common to all reports.

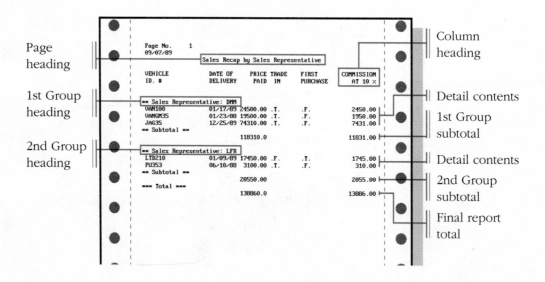

Most dBASE custom reports that contain calculations include three headings. The *page heading*, a centered title, appears at the top of every page. A descriptive *column heading* precedes each column of data. A *group heading* appears at the beginning of a set of related records. In the sample report, the records are grouped by sales representative.

An Overview of dBASE

Getting Started

Designing and Creating a Database

Viewing, Organizing, and Updating Data

Searching the Database

Designing Reports and Labels

Programming in dBASE

Detail contents, the related records, appear below each associated group heading. The contents may be from fields in the database or may be calculated as part of the report. In the sample report, the field COMMISSIONS AT 10% is created at the time the report is printed by multiplying the contents of each car price field by 10 percent. After the last record of a group is printed, specified numeric fields in the group records are totaled on the *group subtotal* line.

The group heading, detail contents, and group subtotal repeat for each sales representative in the database. After all records are printed, a *final report total* appears. Keep this report layout in mind as you go on to create the custom report form.

Creating a Custom Report

dBASE III Plus provides a menu bar with selections for creating and storing a custom report. These options allow you to control the page layout (such as margins and headings), select fields (columns) to include in the report, and choose groups on which to subtotal data. After these decisions have been made, you can save the report form to disk, and then print the report.

Accessing the Create Report Feature

Before you create a custom report, you need to put an existing database in use. Recall that you can use the Assistant to open a database by highlighting Set Up, selecting Database file from the pull-down menu, and providing the appropriate disk drive and database file name.

To access the report feature from the Assistant, highlight Create and select Report from the pull-down menu. Then specify on which disk drive the new report form is to be stored and give the file a name.

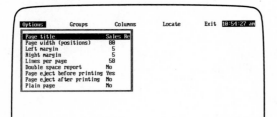

The Create Report menu bar appears, from which you can select Options, Groups, Columns, Locate, or Exit.

Specifying Report Options

You make selections from the Options pull-down menu to specify important information about the report format and to control the printer. Select Page title to specify up to four lines of text for display at the top of each report page. In the sample report, for example, a single title appears—Sales Recap by Sales Representative. You can accept the default page width, margins, and lines per page that appear on the pull-down menu, or you can enter your own specifications.

Additional menu selections allow you to specify double or single spacing for the report. For some print jobs, you want to tell the printer to "Page eject before printing" or "Page eject after printing." Ejecting a page after printing avoids the annoying problem of having part of the last page of the report left in the printer. On the other hand, if you have a preprinted form aligned in the printer, you want to tell the printer not to eject before printing.

dBASE automatically displays the page number and current system date in the upper left corner of a report. You can, however, set Plain page to Yes to suppress that feature. Suppressing the display might be necessary if you are printing on preprinted forms.

Defining Group Control Breaks

Access the Groups selection on the Create Report menu bar to tell dBASE III Plus which data field(s) should be used to group and subgroup records within the report and to specify whether the report should include detail contents or only summary information.

The options on the Groups pull-down menu are set for producing the "Sales Recap by Sales Representative" report.

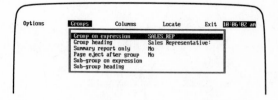

Selecting "Group on expression" allows you to specify the *control break field*—a field in a record on which a calculation is based or which triggers a subtotal to be printed. In the example, SALES_REP is the control break field; each time a different set of initials is encountered in the SALES_REP field, records are subtotaled. Before you print the report, you must organize the database records in an order based on the control break field—in this case, by sales representative (see "Indexing Records" in Chapter 30).

An Overview of dBASE

Getting Started

Designing and Creating a Database

Viewing, Organizing, and Updating Data

Searching the Database

Designing Reports and Labels

Programming in dBASE

Because the field names in a database are limited to 10 characters, you may have assigned an abbreviated name to the control break field, such as SALES_REP. You can, however, select Group heading to improve the appearance of the subheading that precedes each record grouping in your report. In the example, the user-specified group heading is `Sales Representative:`. dBASE prints the subheading preceded by two asterisks and fills in the appropriate salesperson's initials for each new grouping.

Use the "Summary report only" option to direct dBASE to print only the group subtotal and final report total lines, suppressing the detail contents lines. This option is useful when the report is to be sent to managers who do not need to see the detail information. Set "Page eject after group" to Yes if for distribution or filing purposes you would like each salesperson's subtotal to be printed on a separate page from the others.

The example does not show user specifications for the "Sub-group on expression" and "Sub-group heading" options on the Groups pull-down menu. Use these two options to set another control break field within a control break field. For example, an annual vehicle sales summary report might show records grouped according to salesperson; within each salesperson's records, the detail contents may be organized by month of sale.

Creating Data Columns

To finish creating the report form, define the detail contents using the Columns option on the Create Report menu bar.

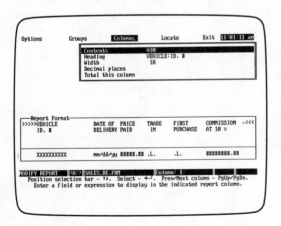

The options on the Columns pull-down menu are set to produce the six columns of data shown in the "Sales Recap by Sales Representative" report.

While you are selecting fields to appear in the report columns, dBASE uses the bottom half of the Columns screen to display the report format. The example shows a completed format in which the first column of data is the vehicle identification number. Select Contents to specify a field name—such as VIN—for inclusion in the report. Select Heading to specify the field description to appear in the report. For example, you can enter **VEHICLE;ID. #** to describe the VIN field. The text following a semicolon in the heading description appears on a second line.

dBASE automatically assigns the Width, selecting either the width of the field in the database or the width of the column heading, whichever is larger. You can, however, override the automatic width and establish an even wider setting for your own spacing requirements.

As soon as the heading and width information is complete, you see the heading appear in the Report Format box along with a pattern of characters that simulates how data will appear. Xs indicate that the data is the character type, mm/dd/yy indicates a date, ######.## represents a number with two decimal places, and .L. stands for a logical field (true/false). After you finish entering a column's specifications, press the PgDn key to access another blank Columns pull-down menu. Repeat the process of entering column specifications until each field on the report is defined.

Saving and Printing a Custom Report

A report form is complete when you select all report options, set a control break field(s), and specify the fields (columns) to include in the report. To save the report, highlight Exit on the Create Report menu bar and select Save from the Exit pull-down menu. The report form is saved to disk under the file name you selected when you first accessed the Create Report feature.

To print the report, highlight Retrieve on the Assistant menu, select Report from the Retrieve pull-down menu, and choose "Execute the command." dBASE displays the prompt Direct the output to the printer? (Y/N). Respond Yes to print the report or No to display the report on-screen.

Modifying a Custom Report

dBASE makes it easy to revise a report form. For example, you may want to change the Page or Column titles, add or delete a field, or change the report to "Summary report only." To make changes, highlight Modify on the Assistant menu bar, select

Report from the Modify pull-down menu, and specify the appropriate disk drive and report form name. A Modify Report menu bar appears, containing the same choices as the Create Report menu bar.

You already know how to enter specifications using the Options, Groups, and Columns choices. Follow the same procedures to revise specifications. You also can highlight Locate and immediately access the specifications of the column you select. To save the changes, highlight Exit and select Save.

You can create as many reports for each database as you like, as long as you specify a different name for each report form file. In addition, you may want to generate labels based on the contents of a database.

Understanding Common Label Features

Before you begin entering your label specifications, you must decide what data you want to include in your labels and how the data should appear. Ideally, label designs are readily available, having been developed during the database design phase of implementing a DBMS (discussed in Chapter 29).

An Overview of dBASE

Getting Started

Designing and Creating a Database

Viewing, Organizing, and Updating Data

Searching the Database

Designing Reports and Labels

Programming in dBASE

```
Fox Marianne
54321 Lakeside
Indianapolis, IN 46256
(317)123-4567
DMM
01/17/89
VAN100 24500.00

Enloe James A.
23123 Conference Ln
Columbus, OH 48345
(614)362-3945
DMM
01/23/88
VANGM35 19500.00

Enloe Ree A.
23123 Conference Ln
Columbus, OH 48345
(614)362-3945
DMM
12/25/89
JAG35 74310.00

Metzelaar Lee
123 Golf Course
Flushing, MI 46211-2468
(101)123-4567
LFR
01/09/89
LTD210 17450.00

Weist Linda
1234 Reffahcs Ln
Indianapolis, IN 46233
(317)423-3467
LFR
06/10/88
PU3533100.00
```

These custom labels were printed using a label form file called CUSTOMER. The sample labels reflect vehicle sales data and include customer and vehicle purchase information.

The labels in the example are printed in two columns. dBASE allows one to five labels to be printed across a page. With the label format in mind, you are ready to create the label form file.

Creating Custom Labels

The process for creating a label form file is similar to that of creating a report form file. You use the Assistant to access the Create Label menu bar, and then select options from pull-down menus to design or modify the label layout and save the specifications to a file with an .LBL extension. You can print labels repeatedly by retrieving the label form file and directing the output to a printer.

Accessing the Create Label Feature

Before you create a custom label, you need to put an existing database in use. Recall that you can use the Assistant to open a database by highlighting Set Up, selecting Database file from the pull-down menu, and providing the appropriate disk drive and database file name.

To access the label feature from the Assistant, highlight Create and select Label from the pull-down menu. Then specify on which disk drive the new label form should be stored and give the file a name.

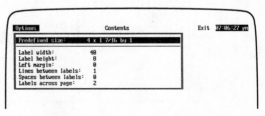

The Create Label menu bar appears, from which you can select Options, Contents, or Exit.

Specifying Label Options

Use the Options pull-down menu on the Create Label menu bar to specify the label format. You can specify Label width, Label height, Left margin (the number of blank characters from the left edge of the label), Lines between labels, Spaces between labels, and Labels across page. Each of these specifications can be entered individually. However, dBASE III Plus offers five predefined sizes that represent common label sizes. Select one of the automatic sizes by highlighting the menu option "Predefined size" and pressing Enter until the size label you want appears on the menu. After you complete the Options specifications, you are ready to enter the contents of the label.

An Overview of dBASE

Getting Started

Designing and Creating a Database

Viewing, Organizing, and Updating Data

Searching the Database

Designing Reports and Labels

Programming in dBASE

Defining Label Contents

Highlight Contents on the Create Label menu bar to enter the names of data fields (from the database structure) that you want to appear on each label.

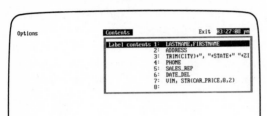

The field specifications shown in the Contents pull-down menu were used to produce the sample labels related to vehicle sales.

The sample Label contents box contains eight lines. dBASE automatically displays the number of lines available according to the label dimensions specified through the Options menu. Line 1 contains instructions to print the LASTNAME field followed by the FIRSTNAME field. Entering ADDRESS in line 2 will produce the customer's street address on the second line of each label.

As you continue to enter the label fields, you may need to know certain dBASE rules for joining fields. For example, all the fields in a label must be Character fields, and certain techniques apply to entering multiple fields on a single line.

The city, state, and ZIP code fields in the preceding example are set up to print on line 3. The dBASE function TRIM, spaces, and symbols are used to create this line. (A *function* is a built-in dBASE command to perform a specific task or calculation.) TRIM(CITY) tells dBASE to trim all blank characters from the end of the field contents in order to print the state immediately following the city regardless of the CITY field length. The +", "+STATE portion causes the city to be followed by a comma, a space, and the state abbreviation. This information then prints in the traditional format that follows:

Carmel, IN 46032

The specification prevents the information from being printed as follows:

Carmel   IN 46032

Line 7 displays the vehicle identification number and sale price of the car. Because all data displayed on a label must be Character data, CAR_PRICE must be converted from Numeric to Character using a dBASE function called STR. (This conversion applies to the printing process but does not actually change the field type in the database.)

Saving, Printing, and Modifying Custom Labels

After you complete the Label contents box, you are ready to save the label form and print labels. Follow the same procedures for saving, printing, and modifying labels as were described for the report form. Prior to printing labels, you may want to organize the database so that the labels print in a specified order. For example, the sample vehicle sales-related labels appear in sequence by sales representative. They could have been organized by customer name within each sales representative's records; in this way, if you attach the labels to Rolodex cards, the cards are easier to file. Mailing labels are usually sequenced by ZIP code to take advantage of presorted bulk mail rates.

An Overview of dBASE IV Custom Reports and Labels

dBASE IV improves the process for designing custom reports and labels by providing design work surfaces with expanded menu bars. For example, the menu bars for both reports and labels contain a Fields option through which you can highlight fields to include and copy the field names to the work surfaces. Both menu bars also offer a Words option that provides a variety of word processing features including selection of text styles such as bold, underline, and italic.

The Reports-design work surface

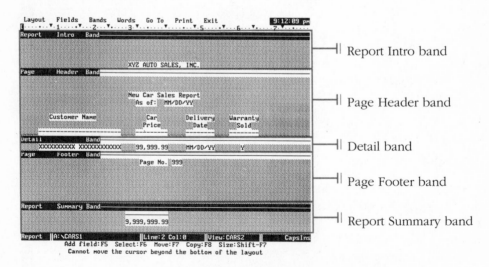

An Overview of dBASE

Getting Started

Designing and Creating a Database

Viewing, Organizing, and Updating Data

Searching the Database

Designing Reports and Labels

Programming in dBASE

The Dimensions option on the Labels-design work surface expands the available predefined label sizes to nine, including two Rolodex and two envelope sizes. dBASE IV also offers a Quick Layout option with three selections: Column layout (the only dBASE III Plus report format), Form layout, and Mailmerge layout.

Summary

In this chapter, you learned to print custom reports and labels by creating, storing, and retrieving report and label forms. Through the Assistant, you can access Create Report and Create Label menu bars to guide the creation process through menu selections. You can create as many reports or label forms as you like for each database, and dBASE makes it easy to modify existing forms. The next chapter introduces you to programming in dBASE.

Review Questions

1. Describe the basic parts of a dBASE III Plus report: page heading, column headings, group headings, detail contents, group subtotals, and final report total.

2. What is a report form (.FRM extension) file?

3. What is the function of a control break field?

4. Why is it necessary to index a database on a control break field prior to printing a report containing the control break?

5. Describe the report specifications you set using the Options choice on the Create Report menu bar.

6. Compare the report specifications you set using the Groups choice on the Create Report menu bar with those you set using the Columns choice.

7. Describe the process for modifying an existing report form.

8. What is a label form (.LBL extension) file?

9. Compare the label specifications you set using the Options choice on the Create Label menu bar with those you set using the Contents choice.

10. Briefly describe dBASE IV enhancements for the creation of custom reports and labels.

33 *Programming in dBASE*

An
Overview of
dBASE

Getting
Started

Designing
and Creating
a Database

Viewing,
Organizing,
and Updating
Data

Searching
the
Database

Designing
Reports and
Labels

Programming
in dBASE

In the previous chapter, you learned how to generate a custom report and custom labels using the Assistant feature. The Assistant allows you to create report form (.FRM extension) and label (.LBL extension) files that can be stored on disk for repeated use. The report and label files are programs created by dBASE. You generated the programs through menu selections, but you did not write those programs.

Stated in very broad terms, a program is a group of computer instructions. A dBASE program is a set of dBASE commands designed to perform a particular task. Although you can execute many commands using the Assistant, there are times when the Assistant does not let you use all the features of a command. For example, you cannot use the Assistant to organize records based on only part of the contents of a field. You can, however, exit the Assistant and write your own command—in this case, a command to sort on partial field contents.

If you write a collection of commands, you are programming. By writing and storing instructions on disk, you can repeatedly execute the program without retyping the commands. Showing you how to write your own programs is beyond the scope of this book. However, a few simple examples demonstrate the process and let you glimpse the power of dBASE as a programming language.

After completing this chapter, you should have a general understanding of the following:

- The advantages of using dBASE III as a programming language.
- Writing dBASE III commands from the dot prompt.
- The dBASE III command structure.
- The difference between interactive and stored programs.

405

▼

Key Terms in This Chapter

Command   A computer instruction that is typed according to specific rules of syntax.

Program   A group of computer instructions.

Programming   The process of writing and storing computer instructions.

Text editor   The dBASE word processor used to write and edit dBASE programs stored on disk.

▲

Writing dBASE Commands

dBASE III Plus provides three means to invoke commands: the Assistant, the dot prompt, and stored programs. The first two alternatives require repeated actions on the part of the user, and are therefore considered to be examples of interactive processing. The third alternative—stored programs—typifies batch processing. Batch processing involves executing a series of commands with a single instruction. The collection of commands constitutes a program, and the program is stored on disk.

If you choose to write your own commands, you do so using interactive mode or batch-processing mode. Whichever mode you select for the current task, you must understand the required command structure (syntax).

Interactive Versus Batch-Processing Mode

You can let the Assistant "write" a command by selecting among the Assistant menu options and responding to the associated screen prompts. The Assistant-generated command appears in the command line near the bottom of the screen, just above the status bar. You can also press Esc to exit the Assistant screen and type the command yourself from the dot prompt (Chapter 28 introduces the dot prompt). Whether you use the Assistant or enter commands at the dot prompt, you are working in interactive mode. But either interactive mode—Assistant or dot prompt—can be tedious, time-consuming, and inefficient for a repetitive task.

Many database management tasks are repetitive in nature. For example, a manager of a dBASE vehicle sales database might print the same summary reports month after month. Other tasks require considerable knowledge of the DBMS by the user. For

An Overview of dBASE

Getting Started

Designing and Creating a Database

Viewing, Organizing, and Updating Data

Searching the Database

Designing Reports and Labels

Programming in dBASE

example, a data entry operator must know the valid entries in a dBASE logical field, such as "T," "F," "Y," or "N". Using batch processing (executing stored collections of commands) can automate repetitive tasks and reduce staff training time.

The commands are typed using a word processor (dBASE includes a simple word processor called the text editor), and stored on disk for subsequent execution. The commands, however, must be typed according to a specific format.

Understanding the dBASE Command Structure

In general, a complete dBASE command consists of up to three parts: the command verb, the condition, and the expression. Commands require one or more parts.

The dBASE command verb specifies the action to take. For example, typing the command **LIST** from the dot prompt tells dBASE III Plus to call to the screen all records in the database currently in use. If the size and number of the fields exceeds the width of the screen, the record contents wrap to subsequent lines as shown for a vehicle sales database in the following figure. Displaying all records in a database may be difficult to see, and provide more information than is necessary.

```
                          NumCaps
. list
Record# VIN      LASTNAME   FIRSTNAME ADDRESS           CITY
        STATE ZIP        CAR_PRICE SALES_REP DATE_DEL WARRANTY TRADE_IN FIRST_BUY COM
MENTS PHONE
       1 LTD210    Metzelaar   Lee       123 Golf Course   Flushing
    MI   46211-2468 17450.00 LFR      01/09/89 .T.      .F.      .T.        Mem
o     (101)123-4567
       2 VAN100    Fox       Marianne  54321 Lakeside    Indianapolis
    IN   46256     24500.00 LAW      01/17/89 .T.      .T.      .F.        Mem
o     (317)123-4567
       3 HON999    Clements  Donna     12345 Lakeside    Indianapolis
    IN   46256     23700.00 DMM      02/13/89 .T.      .F.      .F.        Mem
o     (317)123-2345
       4 PU353     Weist     Linda     1234 Reffahcs Ln  Indianapolis
    IN   46233      3100.00 LFR      06/10/88 .F.      .T.      .F.        Mem
o     (317)423-3467
       5 VANGM35   Enloe     James A.  23123 Conference Ln Columbus
    OH   48345     19500.00 DMM      01/23/88 .F.      .T.      .F.        Mem
o     (614)362-3945
       6 JAG35     Enloe     Ree A.    23123 Conference Ln Columbus
    OH   48345     74310.00 DMM      12/25/89 .T.      .T.      .F.        Mem
o     (614)362-3945
```

Results of typing a LIST command.

The second part of a dBASE command may involve a condition. For example, adding a FOR condition to a LIST command limits which records appear on the screen. Applying the following command to a vehicle sales database causes only records that contain the letters LFR in the field SALES_REP to be displayed:

LIST FOR SALES_REP = "LFR"

The display of a limited number of records is easier to read than the display of all records, as shown in the following figure. However, there is seldom a need to view an entire record, and the display remains difficult to read.

Results of including a condition in a LIST command.

```
. LIST FOR SALES_REP = "LFR"
Record#  VIN        LASTNAME    FIRSTNAME  ADDRESS              CITY
         STATE ZIP             CAR_PRICE SALES_REP DATE_DEL WARRANTY TRADE_IN FIRST_BUY COM
MENTS PHONE
       1 LTD210     Metzelaar   Lee        123 Golf Course      Flushing
   MI    46211-2468  17450.00 LFR    01/09/89 .T.      .F.      .T.       Mem
o      (101)123-4567
       4 PU353      Weist       Linda      1234 Reffahcs Ln     Indianapolis
   IN    46233       3100.00 LFR    06/10/88 .F.      .T.      .F.       Mem
o      (317)423-3467
```

dBASE commands may contain a condition, an expression, or a combination of the two. An expression statement can limit fields, determine the order in which fields appear, create new fields using data from existing, and produce many other data manipulations. Consider, for example, the following command:

LIST DATE_DEL, FIRSTNAME, LASTNAME, CAR_PRICE,
CAR_PRICE*.1 FOR SALES_REP = "LFR"

This command adds the expression list DATE_DEL, FIRSTNAME, LASTNAME, CAR_PRICE, CAR_PRICE*.1 to the previous example. The total command lists only records in which LFR appears in the SALES_REP field and it limits the fields in those records to date delivered (DATE_DEL), customer first and last names (FIRSTNAME, LASTNAME) and the price of the car (CAR_PRICE). It also computes and displays a 10 percent sales commission (CAR_PRICE*.1). Comparing the results of the three LIST command variations gives you some idea how command verbs, conditions, and expressions can be part of a dBASE command.

Results of including a condition and an expression in a LIST command.

```
. LIST DATE_DEL, FIRSTNAME, LASTNAME, CAR_PRICE, CAR_PRICE=.1 FOR SALES_REP = "L
FR"
Record#  DATE_DEL FIRSTNAME  LASTNAME      CAR_PRICE  CAR_PRICE=.1
       1 01/09/89 Lee        Metzelaar      17450.00      1745.000
       4 06/10/88 Linda      Weist           3100.00       310.000
```

A single command—typed from the dot prompt or assembled from Assistant screen menu options and prompts—does not constitute a dBASE program. You can, however, program by writing a collection of commands to perform a specific task and storing the instructions on disk as a command or program file (.PRG extension).

Writing
dBASE
Commands

**Writing
dBASE
Programs**

An Overview
of dBASE IV
Programming   Summary

An
Overview of
dBASE

Getting
Started

Designing
and Creating
a Database

Viewing,
Organizing,
and Updating
Data

Searching
the
Database

Designing
Reports and
Labels

**Programming
in dBASE**

Writing dBASE Programs

Executing commands interactively from the keyboard is quick and efficient for many tasks. However, if you find yourself typing the same commands frequently, or want someone else to do the task for you, the commands can be stored in a "command file" on disk. Each command stored in the file will be executed one at a time, as if the commands were being entered from the keyboard.

dBASE III Plus provides a limited word processor—called the text editor—to assist you in typing program commands. Once you store a completed program, you should test the program and make revisions and enhancements as necessary.

In the sections that follow, you see how to access the text editor and create, execute, and revise a sample program.

Accessing the Text Editor

To invoke the text editor, press Esc at the Assistant screen to access the dot prompt. Type **MODIFY COMMAND** *filename*, substituting your file name choice in place of the word *filename*. For example, to create a program called CARS, access, the dot prompt and type **MODIFY COMMAND CARS** (this example assumes that a CARS command file does not exist yet). dBASE creates a file and automatically invokes the text editor, which presents a blank screen. If a file exists, dBASE accesses that file and presents the commands stored in the file on the screen. Because the text editor is a word processor, you can add and delete commands (lines) and change existing lines.

Writing a Sample Program

Recall that a group (batch) of commands forms a program or command file. Suppose that you wanted to use the text editor to create a program named CARS consisting of the previous set of commands for the vehicle sales database. The CARS program would appear as follows in the text editor.

Text editor displaying the CARS program.

The following steps cover writing and storing a program to put a CARS database in use, executing a limited LIST command, and closing the database.

1. At the dot prompt, type **MODIFY COMMAND CARS** and press Enter to access the dBASE III Plus text editor.

2. On line 1, enter **USE CARS**. (This command tells dBASE which file to use.)

3. On line 2, enter **LIST DATE_DEL, FIRSTNAME, LASTNAME, CAR_PRICE, CAR_PRICE*.1 FOR SALES_REP = "LFR"**. (This command tells dBASE to display limited records and limited fields on the screen.)

4. On line 3, enter **CLOSE DATABASE**. (This command tells dBASE that you no longer need the database open.)

5. Press the key combination Ctrl-End. (This command saves the text as the file CARS.PRG, exits the text editor, and restores the dot prompt.)

Executing a Program

You can execute (run) a stored dBASE III Plus program with a single instruction. After accessing the dot prompt, type **DO** *filename* and press Enter. (Substitute the name of the stored program in place of the word *filename*.) For example, to execute the commands stored in the CARS.PRG file one at a time, access the dot prompt and enter **DO CARS**.

You can also execute a dBASE program at the time you start dBASE. Recall that to access dBASE from the operating system prompt you type **dBASE**. If you type **dBASE CARS**, you access the dBASE software and automatically run the program called CARS.

Revising the Sample Program

dBASE III Plus is a full-featured programming language. You can create programs whose complexity is limited only by your knowledge of the language and your ingenuity. For example, the sample program CARS limits displayed information to one SALES_REP "LFR". You can make the program more versatile by changing the program to include clearing the screen, prompting the user for the initials of any SALES_REP, and displaying the records of the user-specified salesperson.

The following screen shows the revised command file in the text editor.

Writing
dBASE
Commands

**Writing
dBASE
Programs**

An Overview
of dBASE IV
Programming

Summary

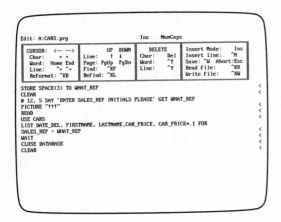

Text Editor displaying the
modified CARS program.

An
Overview of
dBASE

Getting
Started

Designing
and Creating
a Database

Viewing,
Organizing,
and Updating
Data

Searching
the
Database

Designing
Reports and
Labels

**Programming
in dBASE**

The following steps cover revising the sample program:

1. At the dot prompt, type **MODIFY COMMAND CARS** and press Enter. The current version of the program appears on the text editor screen.

2. Move to line 1 and press Enter. (This command inserts a blank line.)

3. At line 1, enter **STORE SPACE(3) TO WHAT_REP.** (This command creates a blank three character field in memory to store the initials of the user-specified SALES_REP.)

4. At line 2, enter **CLEAR**. (This command clears the screen.)

5. At line 3, enter **@ 12,5 SAY 'ENTER SALES_REP INITIALS PLEASE' GET WHAT_REP PICTURE "!!!".** (This command displays a prompt on row 12, position 5 of the screen, creates an input area where the user enters three characters, and converts the three characters to uppercase.)

6. On the line following the @SAY/GET command, enter **READ**. (This command causes dBASE to accept the user's entry of saleperson's initials.)

7. Change the LIST statement to read: LIST DATE_DEL, FIRSTNAME, LASTNAME, CAR_PRICE, CAR_PRICE*.1 FOR SALES_REP = WHAT_REP.

8. Immediately following the LIST statement, enter **WAIT**. (This command causes dBASE to pause after the last screen of data to allow the user viewing time.)

9. On the next-to-last line, enter **CLOSE DATABASE.** (This command tells dBASE to close the database.)

10. On the last line, enter **CLEAR**. (Tells dBASE clear the screen.)

11. Press the key combination Ctrl-End to exit the text editor and save the revised CARS.PRG file.

When you execute the revised program, the prompt SALES_REP INITIALS PLEASE appears. Once the user enters the appropriate initials, dBASE immediately searches for and displays any records that match the search condition, as shown in the following figure.

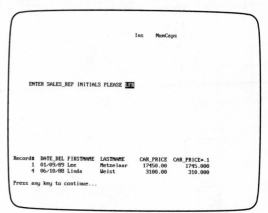

Output results of the modified CARS program.

As you can see from the complexity of the revised commands, programming requires extensive knowledge of the language. Fortunately, dBASE allows you to select an appropriate user interface to meet your needs: menu-driven (the Assistant), command-driven (the dot prompt), and programming-driven.

An Overview of dBASE IV Programming

dBASE IV improvements include additional programming commands, a text editor that can create programs up to 65,000 characters long (as opposed to 5,000 characters in dBASE III Plus), improved word processing features, and a "debug" mode for detecting problems in programming code.

More importantly, with dBASE IV you do not need to write all programming code from scratch. You can use dBASE IV's Applications Generator to guide you through the process of setting up your own system of related menus and programs. Setting up an application with dBASE IV involves creating data-entry screens, reports, and queries, then using the Applications Generator to create a menu-driven application. The programs created by the Applications Generator are compiled into a special language the computer understands called an *object* program; in fact, programming with dBASE IV can be characterized as *object-oriented* programming. dBASE IV object programs run many times faster than programs in dBASE III Plus.

Writing   Writing   An Overview
dBASE   dBASE   of dBASE IV
Commands Programs   Programming   **Summary**

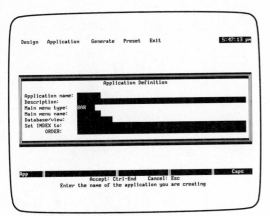

You use dBASE IV's Application
Generator to create applications.

Summary

In this chapter you learned that the dBASE III Plus Assistant may not provide all the options you need to perform database management tasks. As an alternative, you can enter a command from the dot prompt. Both methods typify interactive processing.

Commands can contain three general parts: the required command verb that tells dBASE what to do, the condition which limits what records are accessed, and the expression which determines which database fields and calculated fields are acted upon.

To save retyping frequently used sets of commands, you can enter commands once in the dBASE word processor (the text editor) and store the commands as a program or command file on disk. A program is a collection of two or more commands arranged in sequence to accomplish a task. To execute the program, type the command DO and provide the name of the program. Using a program to execute a series of commands typifies batch processing.

dBASE IV provides a number of programming enhancements compared to dBASE III Plus, including increased speed of execution, a debug feature, a more powerful text editor, and an applications generator on the Control Panel.

Review Questions

1. Differentiate the two interactive processing modes available in dBASE III Plus.

413

2. Discuss the purpose of the three parts of a dBASE command (the command verb, the condition, and the expression).

① *assistant* – ⎫ *interactive*   *assist menu & respond to screen prompts*
② *Dot Prompt* – ⎭ *processing*   *ESC to leave assist & type command at the dot prompt.*

③ *Stored Commands – batch processing*

3. Discuss the difference between using dBASE commands interactively and in a stored program.

4. Describe the function of the dBASE text editor.

5. Explain how to save and execute a dBASE program.

6. If the dot prompt gives you access to the complete power of all dBASE commands, discuss the advantages and disadvantages of having an Assistant feature.

7. Discuss the improvements in dBASE IV as these relate to programming in dBASE.

Index

— X —

Using 1-2-3 Release 3

Developed by Que Corporation

Only the spreadsheet experts at Que can bring you this comprehensive guide to the commands, functions, and operations of new 1-2-3 Release 3. Includes a comprehensive Command Reference, a useful Troubleshooting section, and easy-to-follow instructions for Release 3 worksheets, graphics, databases, and macros.

$24.95 USA
Order #971
0-88022-440-1
862 pp.

Using 1-2-3 Release 2.2, Special Edition

Developed by Que Corporation

Learn professional spreadsheet techniques from the world's leading publisher of 1-2-3 books! This comprehensive text leads you from worksheet basics to advanced 1-2-3 operations. Includes Allways coverage, a Troubleshooting section, a Command Reference, and a tear-out 1-2-3 Menu Map. The most complete resource available for Release 2.01 and Release 2.2!

$24.95 USA
Order #1040
0-88022-501-7
850 pp.

Using WordPerfect 5

by Charles O. Stewart III, et al.

The #1 best-selling word processing book! Introduces WordPerfect basics and helps readers learn to use macros, styles, and other advanced features. Also includes **Quick Start** tutorials, a tear-out command reference card, and an introduction to WordPerfect 5 for 4.2 users.

Order #843
$24.95 USA
0-88022-351-0, 867 pp.

Using WordPerfect, 3rd Edition

by Deborah Beacham and Walter Beacham

The perfect tutorial and reference for WordPerfect 4.2! **Quick Start** modules and a tear-out command chart make it easy.

Order #98
$21.95 USA
0-88022-295-6, 437 pp.

Using DOS

Developed by Que Corporation

The most helpful DOS book available! Que's *Using DOS* teaches the essential commands and functions of DOS Versions 3 and 4—in an easy-to-understand format that helps users manage and organize their files effectively. Includes a handy **Command Reference**.

Order #1035
$22.95 USA
0-88022-497-5, 550 pp.

Using PC DOS, 3rd Edition

by Chris DeVoney

This classic text offers a complete overview of the new commands and user interface of DOS 4.0 and a useful **Command Reference** section.

Order #961
$23.95 USA
0-88022-419-3, 850 pp.

dBASE III Plus Handbook, 2nd Edition

by George T. Chou, Ph.D

A complete, easy-to-understand text! Progresses from basic dBASE III Plus concepts to advanced command-file programming.

Order #68
$22.95 USA
0-88022-269-7, 517 pp.

dBASE IV Handbook, 3rd Edition

by George T. Chou, Ph.D.

A complete introduction to dBASE IV functions! Beginning users will progress systematically from basic database concepts to advanced dBASE features, and experienced dBASE users will appreciate the information on the new features of dBASE IV. Includes Quick Start tutorials.

$23.95 USA
Order #852
0-88022-380-4
785 pp.

Upgrading and Repairing PCs

by Scott Mueller

The ultimate resource for personal computer upgrade, repair, maintenance, and troubleshooting! This comprehensive text covers all types of IBM computers and compatibles—from the original PC to the new PS/2 models. Defines your system components and provides solutions to common PC problems.

$27.95 USA
Order #882
0-88022-395-2
750 pp.

Using Computers in Business

by Joel Shore

This text covers all aspects of business computerization, including a thorough analysis of benefits, costs, alternatives, and common problems. Also discusses how to budget for computerization, how to shop for the right hardware and software, and how to allow for expansions and upgrades.

Order #1020
$24.95 USA
0-88022-470-3, 450 pp.

Inside AutoCAD, 5th Edition

by Don Raker and Harbert Rice

Control AutoCAD Release 10 with *Inside AutoCAD*, 5th Edition. This easy-to-understand book serves as both a tutorial and a lasting reference and includes information on AutoShade, AutoLISP, and Release 10's new 3-D graphics features.

Order #915
$29.95 USA
0-934035-49-0, 750 pp.

Inside AutoLISP

by Joe Smith and Rusty Gesner

The most comprehensive book available on AutoLISP for Auto-CAD Release 10! Presents essential AutoLISP commands and functions and shows you how to customize AutoLISP.

Order #918
$29.95 USA
0-934035-47-4, 672 pp.

1-2-3 Release 2.2 QuickStart

Developed by Que Corporation

Que's award-winning graphics approach makes it easy for you to get up and running with 1-2-3 Release 2.2! More than 200 pages of illustrations explaining the program's worksheets, reports, graphs, databases, and macros. Also covers Release 2.01.

Order #1041
$19.95 USA
0-88022-502-5, 450 pp.

dBASE IV QuickStart

Developed by Que Corporation

The fast way to teach yourself dBASE IV! Follows Que's award-winning, visual approach to learning. Two-page illustrations show you how to create common dBASE applications, including address lists and mailing labels.

Order #873
$19.95 USA
0-88022-389-8, 400 pp.

MS-DOS QuickStart

Developed by Que Corporation

The visual approach to learning MS-DOS! Illustrations help readers become familiar with their operating systems. Perfect for all beginning users of DOS—through Version 4.0!

Order #872
$21.95 USA
0-88022-388-X, 350 pp.

WordPerfect QuickStart

Developed by Que Corporation

WordPerfect QuickStart **shows** how to produce common documents and leads users step-by-step through the most essential features of WordPerfect 5.

Order #871
$21.95 USA
0-88022-387-1, 350 pp.

Free Catalog!

Mail us this registration form today, and we'll send you a free catalog featuring Que's complete line of best-selling books.

Name of Book _____

Name _____

Title _____

Phone (___) _____

Company _____

Address _____

City _____

State _____ ZIP _____

Please check the appropriate answers:

1. Where did you buy your Que book?
   - ☐ Bookstore (name: _____)
   - ☐ Computer store (name: _____)
   - ☐ Catalog (name: _____)
   - ☐ Direct from Que
   - ☐ Other: _____

2. How many computer books do you buy a year?
   - ☐ 1 or less
   - ☐ 2-5
   - ☐ 6-10
   - ☐ More than 10

3. How many Que books do you own?
   - ☐ 1
   - ☐ 2-5
   - ☐ 6-10
   - ☐ More than 10

4. How long have you been using this software?
   - ☐ Less than 6 months
   - ☐ 6 months to 1 year
   - ☐ 1-3 years
   - ☐ More than 3 years

5. What influenced your purchase of this Que book?
   - ☐ Personal recommendation
   - ☐ Advertisement
   - ☐ In-store display
   - ☐ Price
   - ☐ Que catalog
   - ☐ Que mailing
   - ☐ Que's reputation
   - ☐ Other: _____

6. How would you rate the overall content of the book?
   - ☐ Very good
   - ☐ Good
   - ☐ Satisfactory
   - ☐ Poor

7. What do you like *best* about this Que book?

   _____
   _____

8. What do you like *least* about this Que book?

   _____
   _____

9. Did you buy this book with your personal funds?
   - ☐ Yes   ☐ No

10. Please feel free to list any other comments you may have about this Que book.

   _____
   _____
   _____

que

Order Your Que Books Today!

Name _____

Title _____

Company _____

City _____

State _____ ZIP _____

Phone No. (___) _____

Method of Payment:

Check ☐ (Please enclose in envelope.)

Charge My: VISA ☐   MasterCard ☐

American Express ☐

Charge # _____

Expiration Date _____

Order No.	Title	Qty.	Price	Total

You can **FAX** your order to **1-317-573-2583**. Or call **1-800-428-5331, ext. ORDR** to order direct.
Please add $2.50 per title for shipping and handling.

Subtotal	
Shipping & Handling	
Total	

que

BUSINESS REPLY MAIL
First Class Permit No. 9918   Indianapolis, IN

Postage will be paid by addressee

11711 N. College
Carmel, IN 46032

BUSINESS REPLY MAIL
First Class Permit No. 9918   Indianapolis, IN

Postage will be paid by addressee

11711 N. College
Carmel, IN 46032